AF560149

UNITED PROVINCES' POLITICS, 1939: THE END OF THE FIRST CONGRESS MINISTRY

Governors' Fortnightly Reports and other Key Documents

United Provinces' Politics, 1939: The End of the First Congress Ministry

Governors' Fortnightly Reports and other Key Documents

compiled and edited by

LIONEL CARTER

Former Librarian, Centre of South Asian Studies, University of Cambridge

MANOHAR

2010

First published 2010

ISBN 978-81-7304-868-5

Published by
Ajay Kumar Jain *for*
Manohar Publishers & Distributors
4753/23 Ansari Road, Daryaganj
New Delhi 110 002

Printed at
Salasar Imaging Systems
Delhi 110 035

Contents

Editor's Introduction

This is the third volume in a series which prints in full the fortnightly confidential reports which the Governors of the United Provinces sent the Viceroy.[1] Other important communications which the Governors or their Secretaries sent to the Viceroys or their Private Secretaries are also included. Enclosures to the documents are, however, only reproduced when they are of importance. Space does not allow the Viceroys' replies to be included but footnotes are provided when they are needed for an understanding of references in the Governors' correspondence. The origins of the system of Governors' Reports in the late raj are explained in the Editor's Introduction to the first volume in this series. The present volume covers the last ten months of the first Congress Ministry in the United Provinces and also the last eleven months of Sir Harry Haig's tenure as Governor.

1939 was the most difficult period which the first U.P. Congress Ministry faced. The communal situation was deteriorating even in January and February. (Nos. 1 and 11.) By late March Haig was reporting that feeling between Hindus and Muslims was more acute than he had ever known it. (No. 26.) The Muslim League was growing in importance and difficulties were increased by the continuing dispute and violence between Sunnis and Shias in Lucknow. In the third quarter of the year a potentially violent Muslim volunteer army of Khaksars entered the U.P. from the Punjab and elsewhere, allegedly to intervene in the Lucknow dispute. (See particularly Nos. 26, 31, 38, 40, 44, 52, 57 and 98 for the Lucknow dispute and Nos. 55, 57, Enclosures to Nos. 70, 74, 76 and 80 for the Khaksar invasion.) In addition to these communal problems, the Ministry itself lacked stability in the early part of the year and at one point it seemed possible that the Premier, Pandit G.B. Pant, might be displaced. (No. 11.) Mahatma Gandhi's epic Rajkot fast, begun at the start of March, added a further worrying note as it was clear that the Ministry would not survive the death of the Mahatma while fasting. (No. 21.)

The main reason for the instability of the Ministry was the increase in the strength of the left wing both within and, more particularly, outside the government. This was a time when the militant and sectarian Hindu Mahasabha was gaining in strength while left wing movements in Congress and ideological organisations such as the Youth League were commanding great influence. In late January the famous Bengali left winger, Subhas Chandra Bose, was re-elected as President of Congress against the wishes of the right-wing. According to Haig (No. 11), the powerful U.P. Muslim Minister of Revenue, Rafi Ahmad Kidwai, had played a significant part in Bose's surprise re-election.

The upshot of these happenings was that Pant was to be at the forefront of moves to control or unseat Bose. At the Tripuri session of Congress in March, Pant introduced a resolution (subsequently passed) which called on Bose 'to appoint the Working Committee in accordance with the wishes of Gandhiji'. This Bose found it impossible to do and at the end of April he resigned. The right-winger, Dr Rajendra Prasad, was thereupon elected President for the remainder of 1939. Pant's manoeuvrings must be seen not simply as an attempt to change the balance of Congress politics at the Centre. They were also aimed at restoring the stability of the U.P. administration and shoring-up his own position as Premier.

The success which Pant had achieved in controlling the left wing was, in the event, to be of only limited help to him. Beginning in April he was subject to recurrent bouts of fever, suspected by some doctors to be a sign of tuberculosis, and by September he was ordered to abstain from all work for two months. (No. 58.) He was not the only member of the administration to suffer from the stresses of the Ministry's extensive legislative and political programme. C.W. Gwynne, who as Chief Secretary had shouldered the main burden of implementing the Ministry's policies, was pronounced unfit for work in June and died on his way back to Britain in August. Haig, himself, fell victim to diphtheria at the end of August and had not completely recovered by the time he left India.

During the periods when Pant was unable to work, the role of what amounted to acting Premier was taken briefly by the Justice Minister, Dr K.N. Katju, but for most of the time by Kidwai (who himself suffered a serious heart attack in May). It was a position Kidwai clearly enjoyed and did not wish to give up. He showed considerable deference to the Governor who found him much easier than Pant to get along with. (No. 70.) At Haig's behest, Kidwai directed local Congress Committees to exercise restraint. He also authorised the issue of a circular letter to district officers on the use of additional powers to deal with violent speeches (Enclosure 2 to No. 74) although this action met with some opposition from Katju. (No. 71.) One can see considerable parallels in Kidwai's liking of power with that shown by Chakravarti Rajagopalachariar as Premier of Madras.[2]

The record of Kidwai's leadership of the United Provinces' Ministry in September and October 1939 can be studied in Chapters 3 and 4 of the Summaries of Documents. The most important issue he faced was the outbreak of the Second World War and the question whether Congress would cooperate with the British. Kidwai's information on the Congress position was valued not only by the Governor but also by the Viceroy. Kidwai, of course, did not have the standing which Pant had with the Congress high command and during this critical period the most important input into Congress thinking from the provincial ministries probably came from B.G. Kher, the Premier of Bombay. Yet Kidwai was not without influence and, according to Mushirul Hasan, Nehru turned to Kidwai during September 1939 to help plot Congress strategy on the war in the U.P.[3]

In the event Congress decided it could not cooperate with the British and the Congress Ministries submitted their resignations. Haig accepted the U.P. Ministers' resignations on 3 November. (The moving final letters between Haig and Pant are printed as Appendices 3 and 4.) Thereafter the province was administered by the Governor under Section 93 of the Government of India Act, 1935. Careful preparations had been made for this eventuality, Haig having sent the Viceroy two important memoranda on the subject in October. (Nos. 82 and 83.) A noteworthy point in them was Haig's wish (at least in the early stages) to treat Congress right wing leaders with moderation so as to retain their sympathy. He also acknowledged the possibility of a civil disobedience movement in the longer term.

It was perhaps a matter of surprise to Haig that his last month in office remained quiet. On 21 November he wrote to tell the Viceroy of a 'curious lull' in the affairs of the Province. It was like a calm ocean which could easily be whipped up under the influence of a strong gale. (No. 94.) He was able to use these weeks to tie-up certain matters. An agreement was reached with the Khaksars (Enclosure 2 to No. 93) and on his last morning as Governor he gave assent to the Tenancy Bill thus passing into legislation the single most important measure of the Congress Ministry. (No. 97.)

As Haig's time came to depart, Lord Linlithgow, the Viceroy, asked the Governor to set down in writing his thoughts on the political and constitutional situation and on the adequacy of his special powers. (See Nos. 95 and 99.) Haig's view of the British position in India at that date is of particular interest:

'For many years I have regarded our position and policy in India as that of fighting a rear-guard action. We are deliberately surrendering our power and we ought to do it with a good will; but we must not let the rear-guard action turn into a rout. There are times when we have to stand and fight, even though at the end of it we continue to retire; and I think we may perhaps before long reach such a stage.' (No. 95.)

* * *

It may be helpful at this point to draw a few conclusions on the experience of the first Congress Ministry in the U.P. These were years which are often dismissed as being of little importance, it being claimed that the Congress Ministries did not have much real power. The record of these first three volumes suggests that this criticism is not entirely fair. Ministerial office provided a valuable learning experience in constitutional government for both British and Indians. Congress undoubtedly grew in importance as a result of its time in power. Although not without their individual shortcomings, both Haig and Pant were shown to be leaders of high calibre. The ministerial experience of these years would be of use to Pant, Kidwai, Sampurnanand and others after Independence although, as Paul Brass has shown,[4] states in independent India were to be subject to much greater central control than had been envisaged for provinces in British India under the 1935 Act. Many of the problems of post-Independence India, such as corruption and nepotism in government and the posting of politically uncooperative administrators to backwaters, were already beginning to become apparent during the Pant administration.

A second general conclusion is that quite apart from the onset of the Second World War, the Congress ministries were unlikely to have lasted much longer. As Walter Hauser has argued,[5] the intervention of war was welcome as it ended the Congress stint in office at a time when the organisation was threatened by mass demands and the opposition of its own left wing leadership.

A third general conclusion is that the hesitations of the Congress Ministry on the enforcement of law and order provided an atmosphere which was conducive to the spread of radical and revolutionary ideas and movements.[6] The Ministry's ambivalent attitude to the services and a widespread feeling that the Ministry had not fulfilled all of the rather impractical promises it had made before taking up office, added to a general dissatisfaction. There were those who argued that the Congress leadership had sold out to the raj. The Ministerial years then were the time when the ideas which manifested themselves in the 'Quit India' revolt of 1942 were really bred.

This was especially true of the poorer eastern districts of the U.P. R.H. Niblett was the Collector of Azamgarh, one of the rural eastern districts worst hit by the 1942 revolt. He was an Anglo-Indian who was not unsympathetic to Congress. Niblett noted in his diary that when he took up his post in Azamgarh in December 1939 the district was suffering from the aftermath of Congress rule. He was struck by the extent to which the authority of officialdom had been weakened.[7]

A fourth and final conclusion is that there was a considerable growth in communalism in the U.P. during these years. The big conundrum is to what extent the ministry was responsible for this. The Muslim League set up its own enquiry under the Raja of Pirpur in 1938 to investigate the treatment of Muslims under the ministries.[8] This report contained considerable documentation which claimed to provide evidence of partiality against Muslims. The most that can be said is that the records are open to differing interpretations depending on one's point of view. Haig himself was consistently of the view[9] that 'the Provincial Ministry has done its best to be impartial in communal matters and with very fair success'. (No. 39.) But he was doubtful of the applicability of the Westminster model of government and opposition for India. He therefore pressed continually for some form of coalition in the U.P. because he felt that the Muslims' real grievance was that they did not exercise actual power within government. Haig expressed these views in an important interview he had with Nehru on 23 April 1939. (No. 33). Nehru was reported to have said that in the U.P. there might not be insuperable difficulties in admitting members of the Muslim League to the Ministry but it was really an all-India problem which it would be hard to handle on a provincial basis. Events were in any case to show that the Muslim League leader, Mohammed Ali Jinnah, was not at this time in favour of his party joining in the work of the ministries.

* * *

The documents in this volume are British Crown Copyright and are all taken from the following classes of material in the India Office Records:

L/P&J	India Office – Public & Judicial Department files.
MSS.EUR.F 115	Haig papers.
MSS.EUR.F.125	Linlithgow papers.
R/3/1	Prints of Viceroy's correspondence with the Governors.

I should mention that work on this volume was substantially complete before the publication of the 1939 volumes in the *Towards Freedom* series of the Indian Council of Historical Research edited by Professor Mushirul Hasan and Professor Sabyasachi Bhattacharya.

I wish to express my thanks for help and advice received from the late Anthony Farrington, who served as head of the India Office Records at the British Library. Anthony's enthusiasm for document publication (in the tradition of Sir William Foster and other India Office officials) was a constant inspiration. I am also most grateful to Graham Shaw, until recently Director of Asia, Pacific and Africa Collections at the British Library, for his interest. I owe a special debt to Ram Advani, to Dr Anne Thompson Coleman, to the late Professor K.K. Aziz and to Ramesh Dogra, M.B.E. and Urmila Dogra for advice on a wide range of issues. My publisher, Ramesh Jain, has, as ever, extended many kindnesses to me. None of the foregoing bears any responsibility for errors and omissions in the book. The responsibility for these rests solely with me.

Harrow, October 2009 LIONEL CARTER

NOTES

1. The previous volumes in this series are: *United Provinces' Politics, 1936-1937: Formation of the Ministries and Start of Congress Government* (New Delhi: Manohar, 2008) and *United Provinces' Politics, 1938: Congress in Mid-term* (New Delhi: Manohar, 2009).
2. See Sarvepalli Gopal, *Jawaharlal Nehru: A Biography,* Vol. 1, *1889-1947* (London: Jonathan Cape, 1975), p. 230.
3. Mushirul Hasan, *From Pluralism to Separatism: Qasbas in Colonial Awadh* (New Delhi: Oxford University Press, 2004), p. 189.
4. Paul R. Brass, *The Politics of India Since Independence*, 2nd edn. (Cambridge: Cambridge University Press, 1994). See especially chapters 1 and 4.
5. Walter Hauser, 'The Bihar Provincial Kisan Sabha, 1929-42'. (University of Chicago: Ph.D. thesis, 1961). Cited in Vanita Damodaran, *Broken Promises: Popular Protest, Indian Nationalism and the Congress Party in Bihar, 1935-1946* (New Delhi: Oxford University Press, 1992), p. 158.
6. The argument of this paragraph is influenced by Francis G. Hutchins, *Spontaneous Revolution: The Quit India Movement*. (New Delhi: Manohar, 1971) and Gyanendra Pandey (ed.), *The Indian Nation in 1942*. (Calcutta: K.P. Bagchi, 1988).
7. S.A.A. Rizvi (ed.), *The Congress Rebellion in Azamgarh, August-September 1942, as Recorded in the Diary of the Late R.H. Niblett, B.A.* (Allahabad: Superintendent, Printing and Stationery, U.P., 1957), p. 1.

8. See No. 39, note 48.
9. Haig maintained his view that Congress normally acted impartially in a lecture on 'The United Provinces and the new constitution' which he delivered to the East India Association in London in April 1940. A transcript of the lecture and the subsequent discussion is printed in *The Asiatic Review*, vol. 36, July 1940, pp. 423-44.

Abbreviations

A.I.C.C.	All-India Congress Committee.
A.I.R.	*All India Reporter.*
A.L.J.	*Allahabad Law Journal.*
C.I.D.	Criminal Investigation Department.
C.I.O.	Central Intelligence Officer.
D.C.	Deputy Commissioner.
D.I.	Defence of India.
D.I.B.	Director of the Intelligence Bureau.
D.I.G.	Deputy Inspector General.
D.O.	Demi-Official.
D.P.I.	Director of Public Information.
E.I.R.	East India Railway.
G.O.C.-in-C.	General Officer Commanding-in-Chief.
G. of I.	Government of India.
H.E.	His Excellency.
H.M.G.	His Majesty's Government.
H.S.R.A.	Hindustan Socialist Republican Army.
I.A.S.	Indian Agricultural Service.
I.C.	*Indian Cases.*
I.C.S.	Indian Civil Service.
I.F.S.	Indian Forest Service.
I.G.C.H.	Inspector General of Civil Hospitals.
I.G.P.	Inspector General of Police.
I.S.E.	Indian Service of Engineers.
M.L.A.	Member of the Legislative Assembly.
M.L.C.	Member of the Legislative Council.
P.C.S.	Provincial Civil Service.
P.M.	Prime Minister *or* Premier.
P.S.	Postscript *or* Parliamentary Secretary.
P.S.V.	Private Secretary to the Viceroy.
Re.	Rupee.
S.D.O.	Sub-Divisional Officer.

S. of S. *or* S./S.	Secretary of State.
S.P.	Superintendent of Police.
T.B.	Tuberculosis.
U.P.	United Provinces.
U.P.P., 1936-7	Lionel Carter (ed.), *United Provinces' Politics, 1936-1937: Formation of the Ministries and Start of Congress Government* (New Delhi: Manohar, 2008).
U.P.P., 1938	Lionel Carter (ed.), *United Provinces' Politics, 1938: Congress in Mid-Term* (New Delhi: Manohar, 2009).
U.T.C.	University Training Corps.

Glossary

Akhara	Any place of assembly; place for exercise; gymnasium; theatre.
Anna	One-sixteenth of a rupee.
Babu	A term of respect; often accorded to Indians who were fluent in English.
Badmash	A bad character; a rascal.
Bania	Trader, moneylender.
Barawafat	Anniversary of the death of the Prophet Muhammad.
Belcha	Spade, often sharpened at the edges.
Chabutra	Raised platform.
Chehlum	A Shia (q.v.) religious holiday which occurs forty days after the Day of Ashurah – the tenth day of Muharram and anniversary of the day when Husain (grandson of the Prophet) was slain at Karbala. Forty days is the usual period of mourning in many Islamic cultures.
Crore	One hundred lakhs or ten million.
Dacoity	Robbery with violence committed by a gang.
Dhoti	Garment for the lower body.
Durbar	Royal court or levee; the civil government of a Princely State.
Ghar	House.
Goonda	Hooligan, hired rascal.
Gur	Molasses, treacle, raw sugar.
Havildar	A non-commissioned officer in an Indian regiment, corresponding to a sergeant.
Holi	Hindu spring festival celebrated on the full-moon day of Phalguna (February-March). Participants throw coloured waters and powders on one another.
Id	A Muslim holy festival. Bakr-Id commemorates Abraham's sacrifice.

Jatha	An armed band or procession; a procession of religious or political protest.
Kacheri	An office where any public business is transacted.
Kharif	Grain crops sown in summer and reaped by early winter.
Khudai Kidmatgars	(Red Shirts.) Congress volunteer movement of the North-West Frontier Province started by Khan Abdul Ghaffar Khan.
Kisan	Peasant, cultivator, tenant.
Kotwal	A chief officer of town or city police; an Indian town magistrate.
Lakh	One hundred thousand.
Lathi	Thick stick, usually bamboo, sometimes bound with iron rings.
Ma bap	Mother and father.
Maulvi	Muslim religious teacher.
Mazdur sabha	Trade union.
Milad-i-sharif	Festival celebrating the birth of the Prophet Muhammad.
Mohalla	Urban residential neighbourhood.
Muharram	First month of the year in the Islamic calendar; a Muslim festival held during Muharram. The festival commemorates the martyrdom of Ali, son-in-law of the Prophet Muhammad, and of Ali's two sons, Husain and Hassan.
Panchayat	Court of arbitration (properly of five persons) for determination of petty disputes; village council.
Purdah	The custom of veiling and secluding women.
Rabi	Principal grain harvest sown after the rains and reaped in the spring season.
Rai bahadur	Title conferred by the Viceroy in the name of the British sovereign.
Ramzan	The ninth Muslim lunar month observed as a 30 days' fast during daylight hours by all Muslims.
Ryot	Landholder paying revenue to zamindars (q.v.) or directly to government.
Sabha	Association, conclave, assembly.
Sanad	A grant, a charter.
Satyagraha	*Lit.:* holding on to truth. Total self-giving; integral to Mahatma Gandhi's concept of victory achieved through non-violent resistance.

Shia	One of the two main branches of Islam (cf. Sunni); followers of Ali, the son-in-law of Muhammad.
Sir	Land held by a zamindar under title of personal cultivation.
Sunni	The majority in Indian Islam, who regard Caliphs Abu Bakr, Omar and Osman as spiritual descendants of Muhammad.
Swaraj	Self-rule, independence.
Tahsil	Revenue sub-division of a District. Tahsildar: collector of the revenue within a tahsil.
Taluqdar	Large landholder in Oudh; holder of a revenue subdivision.
Tazia	Tall, pagoda-like structures of wood or cardboard representing the mausoleums of Husain and Hassan. Tazias were carried during the Muharram (q.v.) festival procession.
Thana	Police station. Thanedar: officer-in-charge of a Thana.
Umed-war	Suitable.
Zamindar	Landed proprietor paying land revenue to government, revenue farmer.

Principal Holders of Office, 1939

UNITED KINGDOM

Secretary of State for India	The Marquess of Zetland

INDIA

Viceroy, Governor-General and Crown Representative	The Marquess of Linlithgow
Private Secretary to the Viceroy	Mr Gilbert Laithwaite
Commander-in-Chief, India	General Sir Robert Cassels

UNITED PROVINCES

Governor	Sir Harry Haig Sir Maurice Hallett (from 6 December 1939)
Secretary to Governor	Mr J.C. Donaldson
Chief Secretary to Government	Mr C.W. Gwynne Mr Panna Lal (from 18 July 1939) Mr R.F. Mudie (from 4 November 1939)

MEMBERS OF THE COUNCIL OF MINISTERS UNTIL 3 NOVEMBER 1939

Premier and Minister of Home Affairs and Finance	Pandit Govind Ballabh Pant
Minister of Revenue and Jails	Mr Rafi Ahmad Kidwai
Minister of Justice, Development, Agriculture and Veterinary	Dr Kailash Nath Katju
Minister of Local Self-Government and Health	Mrs Vijayalakshmi Pandit

Minister of Education	Sri Sampurnanand
Minister of Communications and Irrigation	Hafiz Muhammad Ibrahim

From 3 November 1939, the United Provinces was administered under Section 93 of the Government of India Act, 1935

Advisers to the Governor from 4 November 1939

Revenue, Rural Development, Agriculture, Forests, Communications and Irrigation	Mr P.W. Marsh
Education, Industries, Local Self-Government and Public Health	Mr Panna Lal
Home Affairs, Finance, Justice and Jails	Mr T. Sloan
Advocate-General	Dr N.P. Asthana

U.P. Legislative Assembly until 1 November 1939

Speaker	Shri Purushottamdas Tandon
Deputy Speaker	Mr Abdul Hakeem

Summaries of Documents

CHAPTER 1 : DOCUMENTS FOR JANUARY–MARCH 1939

Name and Number	*Date*	*Main subject or subjects*
	Jan.	
1 Haig to Linlithgow Report U.P.-213	10	Haig's stay at Allahabad; Ajodhya political conference; Nehru's remarks at conference and his longer-term objectives; appears Ministry are considering even higher reductions in rents; strengths and weaknesses of Pant; League conference at Patna; fears that communal situation will deteriorate unless Congress comes to terms with League; unrest among industrial labour; growth in volunteer armies; Pant's attitude towards police; threatened agitation against Benares State apparently averted; food situation; tube wells generally being used to maximum capacity
2 Donaldson to Laithwaite Letter 33/39-G.S.P.	16	Sends confidential notes (approved by Haig) on U.P. Ministers and Speakers and Deputy Speakers in Legislature
3 Haig to Linlithgow Tel. 195-G	22	Reports discussion with Pant on idea that pay of many Govt. servants might be cut by 10%; provides details of current budgetary position

4	Haig to Linlithgow Report U.P.-216	24	Amount of recent rain disappointing; present attitude of landlords; Tenancy Bill seems to be going through without extreme changes; does not appear that there is scope for drastic rent reductions; Pant says Ministry intends to remit all suspended arrears of rent; impression that right wing of Congress have closed ranks; Govt. and Legislature likely to move to Naini Tal in hot weather if accommodation can be found; officers in eastern U.P. do not consider that League's Patna Conference has affected communal situation; importance of admitting League representatives to Govt.; great improvement in law and order in Gorakhpur district; anxiety over possible strikes in Lucknow and Allahabad; dispute with Katju over appointment of Registrar of Allahabad High Court; situation in Benares State – talk with Sampurnanand; difficulties with Tehri-Garhwal State; proposed abolition of Commissioners
5	Haig to Linlithgow Letter D.O. U.P.-217	28	Considers possible action Ministry might take if its proposal to abolish Commissioners is turned down
6	Haig to Linlithgow Tel. 203-G	31	Doubts whether Congress would force a breakdown over position of States' subjects but Ministry would follow instructions of Working Committee

		Feb.	
7	Haig to Linlithgow Letter U.P.-219	1	Reports serious attack on police by students at Aligarh; is critical of stand taken by university authorities; may be necessary to hold enquiry
8	Haig to Linlithgow Tel. 205-G	3	Refers to No. 3; reports discussion with Ministers on budget deficit; clear they had not decided how to handle this; asks for Viceroy's views assuming Ministry wish to proceed with pay cuts for services
9	Haig to Linlithgow Tel. 208-G	4	Refers to No. 8; has now received copy of Bill to impose tax on employment; reports discussion with Pant on Bill; asks for advice on its legality
10	Haig to Linlithgow Letter U.P.-221	6	Sends names of the three Advisers he would select in a Section 93 situation
11	Haig to Linlithgow Report U.P.-222-G	8	Surprise at election of Subhas Chandra Bose as Congress President; part which Haig feels Kidwai played in this; widespread fears that Pant might have to resign but Ministry has now settled down again; speculates on attitudes of Gandhi and Nehru; Ministers' attitude to States' subjects question; possible courses which a left wing Congress Working Committee might adopt towards U.P.; Nehru now in position to dictate policy and pace to U.P. Ministry; Cabinet meeting discusses budget and proposed employment tax; marked deterioration in communal situation but Bakr-Id

			passes off peacefully; possibility of settlement of incident involving Aligarh students; situation in Benares State, Rampur and Tehri-Garhwal; increase in minimum price of sugar cane; prospects less good for hot-weather move to Naini Tal; delay in progress of Tenancy Bill; Enclosures: (1) Statement by Kidwai on Congress Presidential election; (2) Nehru's 'Independence Day' message; (3) Nehru's statement of 7 Feb. 1939
12	Haig to Linlithgow Letter U.P.-223	8	Details measures they have taken to handle situation should there be a breach with Congress
13	Haig to Linlithgow Tel. 209-G	11	Reports conversation in which Pant said Ministers would not wish to go beyond benevolent neutrality in respect of Jaipur agitation; Premier proposed asking Jaipur to return Young (I.G.P.); not impossible Congress Ministries might have to resign over States' issue
14	Haig to Linlithgow Despatch U.P.D./2	11	Sends minute by Ministers on proposed amendments to Govt. of India Act; this says that Congress has condemned entire scheme and Ministers have no observations on amendments
15	Haig to Linlithgow Tel. 211-G	17	Explains his unease at Zetland's request for an 'official report' on Cawnpore disturbances
16	Haig to Linlithgow Letter U.P.-226	23	Reports conversation with Mrs Pandit who said Gandhi was seriously ill and not expected to live long; she was evidently apprehensive Bose would appoint a left wing Parliamentary Board;

			importance of avoiding local conflicts with Indian States; incident involving Orchha State
17	Haig to Linlithgow Report U.P.-227	25	Ministry absorbed with provincial matters; Cawnpore riot – Haig considers this was well handled; Muslims have decided not to take out Muharram processions in Cawnpore; anxieties concerning Muharram; doubts whether ill-feeling between Hindus and Muslims has ever been so acute; conversation with Pant on admitting Muslims to a share of power; Pant's remarks on proposed Employments Tax; timetable for Tenancy Bill – need for parties to compromise; hot weather move to Naini Tal; his concerns about proposed Village Panchayat Bill; local problems with Indian States likely to come from Bundelkhand area; attempted train derailment near Bihar border; recent rain has done much good; Enclosure: Report of speech by Pant in U.P. Legislative Council on 18 Feb. 1939 on Cawnpore riots
		Mar.	
18	Haig to Linlithgow Letter U.P.-230	4	Sends letter from Pant and Ministers urging Linlithgow to intervene in Rajkot dispute so that Gandhi may end his fast
19	Haig to Linlithgow Tel. 218-G	6	Has received message from Pant that Rajkot situation makes it difficult for Ministry to continue particularly if anything happened to Gandhi; Ministry urges

			Linlithgow to intervene immediately to end impasse
20	Haig to Linlithgow Tel. 219-G	6	Sends report on communal riot at Benares and further trouble at Cawnpore; troops and police reinforcements brought in at Benares; they found it necessary to open fire
21	Haig to Linlithgow Tel. 219 [?220]-G	7	Refers to No. 19; in discussion Pant has said resignation would be inevitable if Gandhi died; this would most probably cause an irremediable breakdown; Pant feels need to participate in Tripuri discussions despite U.P. communal situation
22	Haig to Linlithgow Letter U.P.-231	8	Refers to No. 14; sends Note by Pant saying Ministers strongly disagree with proposed new Section 126-A of Act; this would allow Governor-General to invest Centre with all executive authority in Provinces; Pant wishes substance of his note cabled to Zetland that day
23	Haig to Linlithgow Report U.P.-233	8	Settlement with Gandhi likely to be cause of universal relief; Enclosure to No. 22 probably represents window-dressing; further outrages in Cawnpore and riot in Benares; Haig stresses again to Pant importance of giving Muslims some power; resentment among those affected by proposed Employments Tax; Srivastava appears to be attempting to organise widespread opposition to Ministry; attempted train derailment near Bihar; Pant very reasonable over Orchha and Tori-

			Fatehpur problems; talk with Sampurnanand on his discontinuance of grant to Boy Scouts Association; attempt to renew O'Donnell of Meerut College; dispute with Pant over senior public health appointment; German influence at Aligarh
24	Haig to Linlithgow Letter U.P.-234	9	Separation of executive and judicial functions of magistrates; developments on subject since May 1938; Katju has now laid provisional scheme before Assembly; Haig does not feel he could oppose scheme on ground of his special responsibility if Ministry decides to proceed with it
25	Haig to Linlithgow Letter U.P.-235	20	Sends: (1) copy of letter dated 18 March 1939 from U.P. Special Branch about new Urdu weekly *Sipahi*; (2) a review of first issue; asks whether, if necessary, he should overrule Ministry on use of Press Act
26	Haig to Linlithgow Report U.P.-237	25	Ministers show no elation on return from Tripuri; real lesson of Tripuri; Pant appears depressed and perhaps is ceasing to believe in himself; Haig considers that Ministry has lost ground in budget debates; Katju's comments on proposed cuts in pay of services; Hindu-Muslim situation still very unsatisfactory; Pant putting forward certain Gandhian ideas and Haig is beginning to lose confidence in Pant's judgement; Madhe Sahaba controversy in Lucknow has come to a head

			recently; difficulties with Shibban Lal Saksena in Gorakhpur; Cabinet considers Bills (1) to withdraw original jurisdiction of Oudh Chief Court; (2) reduce existing debts of cultivators and small landlords; Ministers have decided to write off stayed arrears of rent; hot weather move to Naini Tal will follow precedents of previous two years

CHAPTER 2 – DOCUMENTS FOR APRIL–JUNE 1939

		Apr.	
27	Haig to Linlithgow Letter U.P.-238	3	Explains way in which senior service appointments are made; Pant's influence is sometimes surprisingly wide; Haig feels it important to avoid discussion in Cabinet
28	Donaldson to Laithwaite Letter D.O. 315/39-G.S.P.	5	Sends copies of (1) Letter from Haig to Ewart dated 5 April 1939; (2) Letter from Blunden (C.I.O., Lucknow) to Ewart dated 1 April 1939; Haig contests Blunden's extremely gloomy and apprehensive picture of conditions in U.P.
29	Haig to Linlithgow Letter U.P.-240	6	Considers possible scenarios which may arise in event of war and measures they might need to take
30	Haig to Linlithgow Report U.P.-241	10	Concern for Pant's health; acute ill-feeling between Hindus and Muslims continues; four of U.P.'s five large cities unsettled; administrative measures being taken to deal with situation; idea

			of recruiting ex-Army men to police; underlying causes of the unrest; need to admit real representatives of Muslims to Govt.; Madhe Sahaba question – jails being filled by Shias insisting on reciting the Tabarra; Lucknow police avert serious riot; Cabinet discussion on Shibban Lal's activities in Gorakhpur; Congressmen disrupt anti-taxation meeting in Lucknow and assault Srivastava; Haig's talk with Mrs Pandit on indiscipline in Congress ranks; Employments Tax; resolutions of U.P. Provincial Congress Committee; Enclosures: (1) Cutting from *Leader* of 5 April 1939 giving Nehru's remarks on Allahabad violence; (2) Press report of discussion on proposed adjournment motion in U.P. Legislative Assembly on 31 March 1939; (3) Some important resolutions of U.P. Provincial Congress Committee meeting held on 7 April 1939
31	Haig to Linlithgow Letter U.P.-244	18	Sends lengthy note on the Lucknow Madhe Sahaba controversy
32	Haig to Linlithgow Letter U.P.-246	22	Describes procedure adopted by Ministers for formulation of budget; supply of U.P. budget information to Viceroy – feels it would be wrong to send detailed figures in advance of their publication
33	Haig to Linlithgow Letter U.P.-248	24	Following meeting with Agatha Harrison and contact with Mrs Pandit, has had interview with

			Nehru; outlines subjects of discussion; says Nehru was most friendly and believes interview was of value
34	Haig to Linlithgow Letter U.P.-249	25	Sends copy of resolution passed by U.P. Provincial Congress Committee; this declares that proposed legislative limitations on Provincial Govts. in time of war will not be recognised by Congress and should be resisted
35	Haig to Linlithgow Report U.P.-250	26	Kidwai (acting for Pant) was more definite and firmer; Pant still far from well – he has lost ground both with public and Congress; Press reports that Pant is being pressed to surrender law and order portfolio; Cabinet discussion on: (1) increase in police establishment; (2) draft letter to Magistrates on the handling of communal situations and riots; (3) compensation for riot victims; (4) curfew order in Benares; (5) Madhe Sahaba siutation; Sunni demonstrators force their way into Assembly Chamber; employment and petrol taxes; excise policy; no solution in sight to Hindu-Muslim troubles; believes they are reaching critical stage in affairs of U.P.; reasons which allow Haig to take stronger line with Ministry
36	Haig to Linlithgow Letter U.P-252	30	Says there has been fresh criticism of working of rural development scheme; cannot reply to Linlithgow's suggestions until he has made further enquiries

		May	
37	Haig to Linlithgow Letter U.P.-254	2	Comments on conditions in Benares State, Rampur and Tehri-Garhwal
38	Haig to Linlithgow Report U.P.-257	9	Hopes centre of gravity will move to Naini Tal for the hot weather; Pant looking better but still suffering from fever; Press report that Pant would take leave and Katju would act for him; malicious report in *Pioneer* on Haig's meeting with Nehru (No. 33); Hindus feel they are not receiving fair treatment from Govt.; Bal Krishna Sharma; Ministry's instructions to District Officers on handling of communal trouble and speeches and actions which incite; less evidence lately of left wing influence on provincial policy but Haig is concerned about revolutionary activity; *Barawafat* Day passes off peacefully in Lucknow; negotiations between Sunnis and Shias come to nothing; Govt. to take further initiative in Madhe Sahaba dispute; future meetings of Legislative Assembly and Council; consideration by Council of Tenancy Bill; possible labour trouble in Cawnpore; transfers of non-protected members of services; Enclosures: (1) Circular from Gwynne to District Officers dated 29 April 1939 on handling of communal disorder; (2) Note by Haig, dated 1 May 1939, on transfers of officers of Provincial services

39	Haig to Linlithgow Letter U.P-258	10	Comments at length on Ziauddin Ahmad's complaints against Congress administrations' treatment of Muslims; feels U.P. Govt. has done its best to be impartial on communal matters with very fair success
40	Haig to Linlithgow Letter U.P.-265	18	Reports that negotiations by Govt. with Sunnis and Shias on Madhe Sahaba and other questions have been unsuccessful; explains why he does not support Nizam's proposal for a commission appointed by Viceroy which would make an award
41	Haig to Linlithgow Report U.P.-268	24	Govt. and Secretariat divided between Lucknow and Naini Tal; Pant unable to meet Viceroy at present; Ministers appear to hope they can carry on without reshuffle; outcome of Calcutta A.I.C.C. meeting; believes it would not suit orthodox Congressmen for there to be a breach with Governor at present; Employments Tax Bill passed by Council; Discussion with Pant on Bill; Pant disposed to slip back into a reluctance to take effective action; no development in Madhe Sahaba dispute; strike in Cawnpore mills; suspension of payment by Benares Bank and its effect on Industrial Financing Corporation
		June	
42	Haig to Linlithgow Letter U.P.-273	3	Explains why he does not favour Zetland's suggestion of a statement by Linlithgow reassuring Muslims that Govt. appointments

No.	From/To	Date	Summary
			will not go unduly to Congress or 'tame' Muslims; encloses draft letter prepared previously by Haig on problems with composition of Provincial Ministries
43	Haig to Linlithgow Letter U.P.-274	10	Refers to No. 42; speculates on what might happen in U.P. if there was a split in Congress
44	Haig to Linlithgow Report U.P.-275	12	'June Week' in Naini Tal; Pant taking firmer line on Cawnpore strikes; possible reason for Pant's action; further negotiation between Lucknow's Sunnis and Shias fails; powerlessness of League in Lucknow situation; forthcoming discussions in Cabinet – an important time for planning policy; forthcoming conversations between Ministry and landlords on Tenancy Bill; Badrinath Temple Bill; Pant upset over Chintamani's knighthood; Press reactions to this honour are favourable; Home Ministers' conference at Simla; Gwynne will never work again; *Enclosure*: Letter from U.P. Industries Dept. to Mazdur Sabha, Cawnpore, dated 31 May 1939, expressing concern at Cawnpore industrial disputes
45	Haig to Linlithgow Report U.P.-277	24	Meetings with Ministers at Naini Tal; hopes he will hear no more complaints from Pant on Chintamani's knighthood; appointment of Panna Lal as Chief Secretary and strengthening of his department; further communal outbreak in Cawnpore; Sunni-Shia dispute in Lucknow; Cabinet discusses:

			(1) road programme; (2) capital projects including irrigation; (3) Industrial Financing Corporation; (4) educational policy: (5) production of power alcohol from molasses; (6) debt legislation; (7) representational scheme for villages; Legislative Council to consider Tenancy Bill – Haig assesses position; talk with Pant on combating revolutionary activities; Haig feels Ministers would give up their posts only with greatest reluctance

CHAPTER 3 – DOCUMENTS FOR JULY–SEPTEMBER 1939

		July	
46	Haig to Linlithgow Letter U.P.-282	1	Muslim attitude to Federation; believes Muslim position is vague and tactical but that they are unlikely to organise mass resistance to Federal policy
47	Haig to Linlithgow Letter U.P.-283	5	Proposes that Dible would become his third adviser in place of Gwynne
48	Haig to Linlithgow Letter U.P.-284	5	Gives account of present position on rural development schemes; recommends that Govt. of India grant be continued subject to safeguards
49	Donaldson to Laithwaite Letter D.O. 251-G.S.	7	Sends copy of tel. (No. 250-G of same date) from Haig to Linlithgow which considers three possible courses of action on Employments Tax Bill; argues that best course is to amend Govt. of India Act

50	Haig to Linlithgow Report U.P.-287	12	Tenancy Bill referred to Select Committee of Legislative Council; forthcoming meeting of Assembly; communal ill-will in Cawnpore; Police situation in Cawnpore not entirely satisfactory and change of senior officers probably needed; crime statistics; Police reinforcements; Sunni-Shia dispute in Lucknow descends into violence; Muslims from other Provinces playing important part in Lucknow dispute; idea of further negotiation with Shias; Mrs Pandit's criticism of Katju's statement on Panchayat Bill; speeches at Provincial Youth League Conference; Ministry to go on with Industrial Financing Corporation; hopes Gwynne can get to U.K.; Congress dissensions
51	Haig to Linlithgow Letter U.P.-289	12	Reports discussions with Nawab of Rampur; Haig is concerned at the effects of loss of revenue to Rampur when it enters Federation
52	Haig to Linlithgow Report U.P.-290	25	Problems at Thomason Engineering College, Roorkee; these problems precipitate crisis between U.P. Congress Assembly Party and Ministry; Haig's visit to Meerut Division – he notes that it seems not to suffer from some of the troubles occurring elsewhere in U.P.; lack of rainfall in the Division; Pant's firm line against criticisms of police firing in Cawnpore and Lucknow; believes crime figures should now return to normal; Pant's further move in Sunni-Shia dispute; Mahasabha

			actively attacking Congress in Rohilkhand Division; Talk with Muhammad Ismail Khan; anxiety of Provincial Services over proposed Employments Tax; budgetary position; possibility of a strike in J.K. Mills, Cawnpore
		Aug.	
53	Haig to Linlithgow Report U.P.-293	9	Haig has been making contact with Ministers; Pant again has fever; further information on Congress party's attack on Ministry; discussions with Tehri Durbar on Badrinath Temple Bill; apparent settlement of agitation in Benares State; hopes landlords will now settle on Tenancy Bill; Sunni-Shia dispute not resolved; subdued reaction by Ministry and Press to Haig's decision to reserve Employments Tax Bill; strikes in Cawnpore and possible strikes in Lucknow; reduction in dacoities; Gwynne's death; Enclosure: Extract from Horton's report for first half of July 1939
54	Donaldson to Laithwaite Letter D.O. 943-G.S.P	28	Ministry has altered its proposals regarding the pay of members of subordinate services on promotion; Haig is now disposed to agree to these (subject to small amendment); seeks Viceroy's agreement
55	Donaldson to Laithwaite Letter 950/39-G.S.P.	28	In view of Haig's illness sends his own account of events in U.P. in second half of Aug.: Pant's movements; Azad's attempt to mediate Sunni-Shia dispute has apparently failed; Ministry's atti-

			tude to the control of foreigners during war; Legislative Council likely to approve Tenancy Bill; Legislative Council resolves that none of its members should be an honorary magistrate; Mrs Pandit cancels visit to Cawnpore; Pant orders District Magistrates to take firm line in protecting Ministers from demonstrations; Katju unsuccessful in settling lockout at New Victoria Mills, Cawnpore; break in rains; Khaksars in Lucknow
		Sept.	
56	Haig to Linlithgow Tel. 259-G	3	Reactions in U.P. to outbreak of war; Congress and Ministry are waiting on events
57	Haig to Linlithgow Report U.P.-296	6	Kidwai (unofficially acting as Premier) has raised no difficulties with necessary war measures; Haig's message to people of U.P.; talk with Srivastava to dissuade him from starting a U.P. Defence League at present; Tenancy Bill may be passed by mid-Sept.; Azad successful in persuading Shias to suspend *tabarra* agitation; collapse of Khaksar movement in Lucknow; Govt. unable to proceed with loan flotation
58	Haig to Linlithgow Letter U.P.-299	11	Pant has been advised by doctors to do no work for two months; Kidwai will be treated as senior Minister and Pant's portfolios have been divided up; implications for any re-casting of Ministry

59	Haig to Linlithgow Letter U.P.-300	14	Suggests Viceroy sees Sapru, in addition to Chhatari and Srivastava, as representatives of non-Congress opinion in the U.P.
60	Haig to Linlithgow Tel. 263-G	17	Majority of Ministers seem to feel way will be found round Congress Working Committee's resolution on war; has told Kidwai essential that rank and file of Congress do not openly encourage anti-war activities or oppose recruitment to Army
61	Haig to Linlithgow Letter U.P.-301	17	Suggests things which might be done to utilise the desire of many people in the U.P. to help with the war
62	Haig to Linlithgow Tel 264-G	18	Refers to No. 60; in talk Katju remarked that Indians were gravely disturbed at defencelessness of their country; Haig considers that such concerns may make moderate Congress more ready to come in with Govt.
63	Haig to Linlithgow Tel. 265-G	19	Refers to No. 62; reports talk with Mrs Pandit who had seen Nehru in Allahabad; speculates as to Nehru's position on war; believes Nehru awaits invitation to see Linlithgow; leftist and revolutionary situation in U.P. becoming rapidly more difficult; need for early Congress decision on war
64	Haig to Linlithgow Tel. 266-G	21	Refers to No. 63; asks for any indication of policy as U.P. situation continues to deteriorate
65	Haig to Linlithgow Letter U.P.-303	21	Refers to No. 47; now intends to appoint Marsh as his third Adviser rather than Dible

66	Haig to Linlithgow Tel 268-G	23	In event of break with Congress, does not favour allowing opposition to form Ministry for a few months prior to an election
67	Haig to Linlithgow Tel. 269-G	23	Reports conversation with Kidwai on draft of resolution Congress were proposing Provincial Assemblies should pass; feels outlook for Congress cooperation is gloomy; hopes U.P. Ministers will agree to use of Section 108 powers by District Magistrates; is ready, as far as can be foreseen, for an emergency
68	Haig to Linlithgow Tel. 270-G	24	Considers proposal for Viceroy's Advisory Committee might be of great value if it were used on lines Haig suggests; sees great advantages in periodic meetings of Provincial Premiers and Princes
69	Haig to Linlithgow Tel. 271-G	25	Reports discussion with Kidwai on prospects of settlement with Congress; Kidwai believes Gandhi will be able to propose some acceptable solution to Linlithgow
70	Haig to Linlithgow Report U.P.-306	25	Absence of Pant not really a disadvantage; additional powers for Magistrates to allow them to act against speeches inciting to violence; Bose's tour of the U.P. seems to have fallen through; Ministry takes prompt action on profiteering; Cabinet discuses situation regarding Khaksars; general strike in Cawnpore has been avoided more than once; Sunni-Shia conversations pro-

			ceeding; Tenancy Bill passed by Legislative Council; U.P. financial position giving rise to anxiety; *Enclosures*: (1) Note by Panna Lal on development of Khaksar agitation in U.P.; (2) Press note on Khaksars issued by U.P. Govt.
71	Haig to Linlithgow Tel. 272-G	28	Katju now making trouble on proposed instructions to Magistrates; general impression that security situation has not deteriorated in previous week
72	Haig to Linlithgow Tel. 273-G	29	Refers to No. 71; Haig and Kidwai agree instructions to Magistrates; Kidwai reports that in discussions in Lucknow, senior Congress figures were strongly in favour of a settlement

CHAPTER 4 – DOCUMENTS FOR OCTOBER–DECEMBER 1939

		Oct.	
73	Haig to Linlithgow Letter U.P.-309	5	Expresses concern at effects of anti-recruitment activities in U.P.; has been hampered in taking necessary action by uncertainty as to Congress position on war; believes real feeling in U.P. is definitely in favour of helping in war; *Enclosures*: (1) Note from Haig to Kidwai dated 2 Oct. 1939; (2) Minute from Haig to Panna Lal dated 4 Oct. 1939 sending reports of anti-recruiting activities in Meerut and Etawah; (3) Extract from letter of Naqvi (D.C., Aligarh) dated 28 Sept. 1939

74	Haig to Linlithgow Report U.P.-312	8	Tandon's statement on war in Legislative Assembly; Haig believes Pant is unlikely to return to work; problems for Congress in replacing Pant; discussion with Kidwai on expanding Ministry; issue of circular to Magistrates on Section 108 powers; action against *Kirti Lehar*; substantial Khaksar activity – many arrests made; signs that Muslim opinion is taking up cause of Khaksars on communal lines; riot in Meerut City; general strike in Cawnpore – moves for a settlement; importance of Viceroy's conversations in Delhi; *Enclosures*: (1) Text of Tandon's statement of 3 Oct. 1939; (2) Circular letter, dated 30 Sept. 1939, from Panna Lal to District Magistrates
75	Haig to Linlithgow Letter U.P.-313	11	Sends tel. to Viceroy, dated 30 Sept. 1939, from Inayatullah Khan declaring that within three months he can supply him with 30,000 Khaksar soldiers for internal military defence of India, 10,000 for police purposes and 10,000 to help Turkey; Haig feels Linlithgow may wish to advise Inayatullah Khan to withdraw movement against U.P. Govt.
76	Donaldson to Laithwaite Letter 1099/39-G.S.P.	13	Sends report by Sloan on firing on Khaksars at Bulandshahr Jail on 8 Oct. 1939
77	Haig to Linlithgow Tel. 274-G	14	Does not feel formal conference of Governors' Secretaries is essential; would be disadvantaged if crisis developed while Donaldson was away

78	Donaldson to Laithwaite Letter 1109/39-G.S.P.	17	Sends extract from report of Dible indicating there was no difficulty getting cultivators in Fatehpur to enlist
79	Haig to Linlithgow Letter U.P.-314	18	Difficulties in assessing situation in U.P. but believes there is a lull in open extremist agitation; considers possible reactions of Congress to Viceroy's statement; if Ministry remains in office but break is inevitable, he may need to force early break
80	Haig to Linlithgow Letter U.P.-316	18	Sends copy of letter to Craik of same date expressing concern at invasion of Khaksars from Punjab; if this continues unabated, may have to ask Punjab Govt. to take definite action
81	Haig to Linlithgow Tel. 276-G	19	Reports talk with Kidwai who said Viceroy's Statement would be entirely unsatisfactory to Congress and seemed to contemplate early resignation of Ministry; Kidwai felt League would also find Statement unsatisfactory; he considered only faint possibility of avoiding break was to turn Statement round with emphasis on future
82	Donaldson to Laithwaite Letter 1115/39-G.S.P	19	Sends memorandum by Haig on general policy, tactics, publicity and other matters during a Section 93 regime in U.P.
83	Donaldson to Laithwaite Letter 1118/39-G.S.P	20	Refers to No. 82 and sends note by Haig on dealing with an anti-war agitation in which Congress as a whole was taking an active part
84	Haig to Linlithgow Tel. 277-G	22	Refers to No. 81; has seen Sampurnanand and Kidwai;

			former regarded break as inevitable and thought Congress would be forced to launch movement of opposition; Kidwai thought there was faint hope of compromise if Gandhi saw Viceroy; Haig has no first-hand information on League policy
85	Haig to Linlithgow Tel. 278-G	23	Briefs him on adequacy of police, arrangements to combat sabotage and arrangements for publicity
86	Haig to Linlithgow Tel. 279-G	23	Reports discussion with Kidwai on resignation of Ministry; Haig suggested resignations should be tendered on 28 Oct.; he feels strongly that further delay would be inexpedient
87	Haig to Linlithgow Letter U.P.-319	27	Found discussions with Viceroy of great value; has spoken with Khaliquzzaman who has no desire to form Govt. but is consulting Jinnah; Haig explained objections to non-official advisers; Khaliq showed marked enthusiasm for idea of War Board
88	Haig to Linlithgow Tel. 282-G	30	Ministry has tendered resignations but Haig has explained to Pant that he felt it undesirable to accept them while discussions were proceeding between Viceroy and Congress; Pant has agreed to Ministry remaining until situation clears itself
89	Haig to Linlithgow Tel. 283-G	31	Has seen Khaliquzzaman that day and asked whether he was in position to form Govt.; Khaliq will give answer next day; Khaliq suggested that if Delhi discussions were successful, an outcome might be agreement to form coa-

No.	Document	Date	Summary
			lition Ministries in Provinces; Haig is not anxious to take charge in U.P. while bound not to take vigorous action
		Nov.	
90	Haig to Linlithgow Tel. 285-G	1	Legislative Council stands prorogued; has prorogued Assembly that day
91	Haig to Linlithgow Letter U.P.-321	1	Outlines the objects of, and changes in, tenancy law made by Tenancy Bill; notes objections of landlords; proposes to grant assent to Bill; asks for Viceroy's approval at very early date
92	Haig to Linlithgow Tel. 286-G	2	Proposes to accept Ministers' resignations next day; requests sanction to go into Section 93 thereafter; indicates measures he intends to take immediately
93	Haig to Linlithgow Report U.P.-325	8	Change to Section 93 effected very quietly and smoothly; circular letter issued to District Magistrates on objectionable speeches, anti-recruitment activities and other matters; friendly goodbye to Pant; difficult final days with Ministry; agreement concluded with Khaksars; Sunni-Shia question very far from settled; Cawnpore labour situation; Haig's health; *Enclosures*: (1) Letter, dated 4 Nov. 1939, from Mudie to District Magistrates; (2) Text of agreement between Ahmad Shah and Mudie dated 4 Nov. 1939
94	Haig to Linlithgow Report U.P.-326	21	Curious lull in U.P. continues but Haig believes that eventually Congress left-wing will begin

			their campaign; cannot see what genuine further approach Gandhi could make to Viceroy; believes situation is heading for civil disobedience; District Officers have taken little action on their own responsibility; arrests of B.D. Tripathi and M.N. Gupta; Hunter's report into Bulandshahr firing; Cawnpore labour situation; conversations on Haig's idea of War Boards; Khaliquzzaman explains League's reluctance to join Boards; Sapru apprehensive at idea lest it involved conflict with Congress; need for early assent to Tenancy Bill; Katju's orders on the minimum price of sugar; Haig's health
		Dec.	
95	Haig to Linlithgow Letter U.P.-327	4	Haig's views on the political and constitutional situation as he leaves U.P.
96	Hallett to Linlithgow Letter (Unnumbered)	5	Has arrived in Lucknow; is grateful for his discussions with Viceroy
97	Haig to Linlithgow Tel. 296-G	6	After discussion with Hallett, has given assent to Tenancy Bill; sees no reason why Bill should lead to creation of large class of un-protected sub-tenants
98	Haig to Linlithgow Report U.P-328	6	Province remains quiet; unauthor-ised statement by D.P.I. that Governor had accepted charge of U.P. as a trust for Congress Ministry; Haig refuses to take part in convocation at Allahabad University as students unwilling to take down Congress flag;

			correspondence with Azad on Sunni-Shia controversy; thinks War Board idea had better now stand over; price control questions are urgent
99	Haig to Linlithgow Letter U.P.-329	6	Discusses effectiveness of Governor's safeguard powers in the U.P. during the period of the Ministry; powers remained in background but had useful influence
100	Haig to Linlithgow Letter (Unnumbered)	6	Thanks him for No. A5; believes U.P. has generally kept on an even keel and is glad they got through Ministerial period without a breakdown
101	Haig to Linlithgow Tel. (Unnumbered)	6	Thanks him for his farewell message
102	Hallett to Linlithgow Tel. 298-G	16	Comments on points made by Patel regarding Congress Ministries' treatment of minorities
103	Hallett to Linlithgow Tel. 299-G	18	Refers to No. 102; Haig has no recollection of anything remotely resembling two of the points made by Patel
104	Hallett to Linlithgow Tel. 300-G	23	Suggests Maharaj Singh for vacancy on Zetland's India Council

APPENDICES

		Mar.	
A1	Haig to Pant Letter	23	Elucidates his anxieties on newspaper *Sipahi*; notes points on which he feels they agree; exact action to be taken must await further discussion when facts are clearer

		Oct.	
A2	Pant to Haig Letter	30	Submits U.P. Ministers' resignations in view of British Govt.'s unsatisfactory attitude on India's freedom; *Enclosure*: Resolution passed by U.P. Legislative Assembly on subject
		Nov.	
A3	Haig to Pant Letter	4	Explains why he has accepted resignations of Ministers; has greatly appreciated working with him
A4	Pant to Haig Letter	14	Thanks him for No. A3; notes Haig's 'conscientious discharge of multifarious duties and responsibilities' and wishes him a well earned and active rest
		Dec.	
A5	Linlithgow to Haig Letter (Unnumbered)	5	Thanks him for No. 95 and for all the help he has given him as Governor of U.P.
		1940 *Jan.*	
A6	Donaldson to Christie Letter 11/40-G.S.P.	5	Sends confidential reports for 1939 on Tandon, Hakeem, Sita Ram and Aizaz Rasul

Map of the United Provinces

CHAPTER 1

Documents for 1 January – 31 March 1939

1

HAIG TO LINLITHGOW
R/3/1/75

Secret
No. U.P.-213

January 10th, 1939

My dear Lord Linlithgow,

I returned after my Christmas camp direct to Allahabad, and, as I mentioned in my last letter, I shall be based on Allahabad for the whole of this month. It makes a pleasant change to come here, and there is no doubt that the people generally appreciate very much this annual visit of the Governor. It is also useful to me, for it brings me in touch with the High Court, the Public Service Commission, the University, and a somewhat different atmosphere of politics and politicians to that which prevails at Lucknow.

2. The Christmas holiday was of course the occasion for important conferences and many resolutions. So far as our Provincial politics are concerned, the most important event was the big political conference held at Ajodhya near Fyzabad. I attach to this letter a copy of some of the resolutions passed and also a report of various speeches made.[1] The Ministry escaped censure, but the praise of them was very faint, and Jawaharlal Nehru, in speaking on the resolution referring to their work, said that the resolution was not for congratulating the Ministers; it only appreciated their difficulties and the work done despite them. He said that the pace of progress was very slow and they were dissatisfied with the distance they were from their objective. It might be thought from the tone of these remarks that Nehru was a hostile critic; but from conversations I have had here, I believe it to be true that in fact his influence was used to

protect the Ministry from excessive criticism and from the passing of unpractical resolutions. I think that Nehru's immediate intention is, as it was a year ago, to keep the Ministry in office and to shield them from the more embarrassing attacks made upon them by the extremists. But at the same time, I think, he does not fail to urge them on to more advanced policies. It seems to me probable, both from Nehru's utterances and from what I hear of his intentions, that he is looking forward to the time when he will secure his very comprehensive objectives by means of some movement that the British Government will not be able to resist. But in the meantime he does not underestimate the great value to the Congress cause of having Congress Ministries in office side by side with the development of Congress activities and sanctions, such as volunteers, outside the Government sphere. Incidentally, I was told a few days ago on what ought to be good authority that a movement has recently developed for pressing Nehru for the presidentship of the Congress, and that this may have a considerable amount of support behind it.

3. I am not at present in a position to judge what the effect of the Ajodhya conference will be upon the Ministry. I have, however, received one bit of information which is not very encouraging. I have written in previous letters about the left wing proposal that rents should be drastically reduced. The figure previously mentioned, which I regarded as unreasonable and unpractical, was 6½ crores, vide paragraph 4 of my letter No. U.P.-206, dated December 6th, 1938. The Ajodhya conference demanded a reduction of rents by 8 crores. I heard two days ago from the Revenue Secretary[2] that Chhatari had been told by the Premier that the left wing were demanding a reduction of 8 crores and that he would have to give them something. Chhatari's impression was that he was considering giving 6½ to 7 crores. The Revenue Secretary also tells me that the Revenue Minister had in his presence told the Finance Minister of Bihar[3] that the Tenancy Bill would cost the Government 50 to 100 lakhs in land revenue. I do not at the moment attach too much importance to this report. While the Ajodhya conference is still fresh in their minds, the Ministers are bound to be considerably influenced by it. It may be, however, that as they get further away from it, they will take a more reasonable view of what is possible. The Revenue Minister also announced at the Ajodhya conference that all the stayed arrears of rent were going to be wiped out. This however can only be done by legislation, and no Bill has so far been drafted with this object. After this public statement, however, the Ministry will I imagine have to proceed with this matter without much delay. At present the whole of their legislative time is entirely occupied by the Tenancy Bill. They

have passed about 45 clauses out of something over 300. I doubt myself whether the Bill is likely to be through the Assembly till late in February.

4. I was greatly interested in the comments you made in paragraph 3 of your letter of 22nd December 1938 on the character and attitude of Pant.[4] I myself am in agreement with Your Excellency's general estimate. I will not go into details, for I am sending you within the next few days a fairly detailed appreciation of his character in response to your request for information about all my Ministers. There is no doubt that when confronted with difficulties, he is indecisive and that he cannot make up his mind to take a firm line in opposition to the left wing. The Cawnpore situation, to which Your Excellency refers, is a very good illustration of his qualities and defects. Faced with a difficult situation during the strike he handled it, I agree, with skill and tact. But, as I think my previous letters have often pointed out, he missed opportunities at a much earlier stage of dealing with the Cawnpore situation firmly and equitably. Had he taken those opportunities, I doubt whether any strike would have materialised. One may put to his credit that on the whole peace has been preserved in Cawnpore for the last eighteen months; but Cawnpore has been in a state of constant unrest ever since he took office, and making all allowance for his good qualities, I think his own policy is very largely to blame for that. He is essentially a conciliator, and not a dictator, or even a strong democratic leader. What you say about his not having established himself in the inner ring of the Congress is, I agree, significant. But when all is said and done, we have to take facts as they are. With all his defects, he is the only possible right wing leader in this Province, and in fact he stands out head and shoulders above the others. As I said in my recent appreciation[5] of the situation, the only alternative to him is a left wing Premier. And while one is at times impatient with his attitude, it is important to give full weight to his difficulties. I very much doubt whether in any other Province the Provincial Congress Committee is largely, and perhaps predominantly, opposed to the policy of the Ministry. That is emphatically the case here. The Provincial Congress Committee is the party organisation, and when a very large proportion, possibly even a majority of them, in the sense of wanting them to go much further, are opposed to the Ministry, it does not require any argument to show how difficult the position of the Ministry becomes. A stronger man might have dealt with the situation more effectively; but that it is an exceedingly difficult situation for anybody has, I think, to be admitted.

6. [*sic*] The other Christmas conference, the effects of which are likely to be very marked in this Province, was that of the All-India Muslim League

at Patna. I need not comment on that at length, but I think it is bound to lead to an accentuation of what I have already described as aggressive leadership of the Muslims in this Province. The development is entirely in accordance with my anticipations. Unless the Congress are prepared to come to terms with the Muslim League, I think the communal situation is bound to deteriorate steadily. The Muslims, I should judge, are losing patience and losing temper. They are not prepared indefinitely to remain a minority without influence on the policy of the Government. On the other hand I see no signs at present of the Congress being prepared to make terms and in effect enter into an alliance with the Muslim League. Pant, when he took office, was I believe very definitely in favour of this line, but the policy in this matter is an all-India one and Jawaharlal Nehru threw his weight decisively against it. I doubt very much whether he has changed his views. Actually during the last few months the communal situation in the Province has been reasonably quiet, but we are now coming on to the difficult festivals, the Bakr-Id and the Muharram, and I think we shall be fortunate if we finish the cold weather without serious trouble somewhere, and perhaps in several places.

7. The general unrest among industrial labour continues, and even perhaps increases. Here, again, I see not much prospect of improvement so long as the Ministry do not take a firmer line against those who stir up the trouble. Here in Allahabad a good deal of unrest among the workers in the numerous Presses has been created by the activities of the communists. There is also some trouble about the coolies employed at the railway station. Here the view of our local officers is that the railway company is taking too stiff an attitude and that the coolies have grievances which ought to be remedied. In Lucknow an important Press has closed down owing to constant trouble with its labour, and there is even a threat of a strike at the Lucknow Electric Supply works, which would be a very serious development. I think the Ministers are watching this with close attention, and Dr. Katju realises very clearly that in the case of an essential public utility service like this the Government may have to intervene decisively, if necessary.

8. The volunteer situation appears to be developing steadily. The Ajodhya conference gave its endorsement to the movement, as will be seen from their resolution on the subject. I do not think that at this stage we can do anything to check it. There is always the possibility that enthusiasm for it may not last. Much depends on whether the volunteers are given practical work to do or not. If not, interest may gradually languish.

But those who are working the movement will, I fear, be as fully alive to this consideration as we are.

9. In paragraph 7 of my letter No. U.P.-210, dated December 23rd, 1938, I referred to the much more encouraging attitude shown by the Premier towards the police at the time of his visit to Moradabad. Since I have been here, I have heard accounts of his subsequent visit to Benares, where he held a police parade. There also he spoke on the same lines as at Moradabad and created an excellent impression on the police officers present. I hope this indicates a real change of attitude on his part. I shall be greatly interested to hear the results of the consideration you are giving to the question of "awards" as distinguished from "honours" referred to in paragraph 4 of your letter of 22nd December 1938.

10. The threatened agitation against the Benares State appears now to have been averted by a timely announcement by the Maharaja. I am very glad that this has been done. I myself shall be in Benares for a few days next week, and then I go on to Gorakhpur. On my way back I propose to visit Lucknow for one day in order to hold a Cabinet meeting and interview Ministers and Secretaries. I had hoped that I should be able to get the Ministers over to Allahabad, but they are so much occupied with the legislature that I feel it would not be fair to press them.

11. There seems to be nothing deserving much comment in the ordinary administration of the Province. The main anxiety, particularly in the western districts, is about the winter rains. They are now very urgently required, and unless we receive some good rain fairly soon, I fear the *rabi* crop will be seriously affected. The official fortnightly report gives a misleading impression of the tube well situation.[6] As I mentioned in my last letter, I spent some days in December going through a large tube well area, and I had long talks with the Chief Engineer and the other officers in charge of the tube well system. Actually, the irrigation being done this year in the *rabi* is on a very large scale and easily a record. I understand there are no general complaints about the rates, though in a few wells where there are special circumstances the rates have to be adjusted. In one district there are a number of complaints about the tube well operators. These are being investigated, and I hope the matter will soon be put on a more satisfactory footing. But speaking generally, the tube wells are being used to their maximum capacity.

Yours sincerely,
H.G. HAIG

2

DONALDSON TO LAITHWAITE
R/3/1/75

Secret
No. 33/39-G.S.P.

Camp,
January 16th, 1939

My dear Laithwaite,

With reference to your D.-O. No. 2454-G.G., dated June 17th, 1938, and subsequent correspondence, I am desired to forward confidential notes, approved by His Excellency Sir Harry Haig, on the Ministers and the Speakers and Deputy Speakers in the Provincial Legislature, for the information of His Excellency the Governor-General.

Yours sincerely,
J.C. DONALDSON

ENCLOSURE 1 TO NO. 2

PREMIER, U.P., AND MINISTER OF HOME AFFAIRS AND FINANCE
The Hon'ble Pandit Govind Ballabh Pant, B.A., LL.B.
(Appointed July 17th, 1937) (Pay Rs. 500 p.m.)

Son of Dharmanand Pant; Kumaon Brahmin; born 1886; resident of Naini Tal.

A B.A., LL.B. of Allahabad University, and a leading lawyer of Naini Tal with a large practice. Has acquired landed property in Kumaon. First came to notice in 1921 as a prominent Swarajist member of the Provincial Legislative Council. In 1928 took a leading part in the hostile demonstrations against the Simon Commission at Lucknow. In 1930 resigned from the Legislative Council on the Congress mandate, and became a recognised leader of Mr. Gandhi's followers in this Province and was convicted twice, in 1930 and 1932, on each occasion being sentenced to six months' imprisonment. He joined with Satyamurti and Bhulabhai Desai in pronouncing in favour of Council entry. He was a member of the Congress Parliamentary Board and was elected to the Central Legislative Assembly to represent the Rohilkhand and Kumaon Divisions as a Swarajist in 1934 and continued to be a member of that Assembly until he resigned his seat in 1937 after being elected to the Provincial Legislative Assembly.

In the Central Assembly he was Deputy Leader of the Congress party. He was also a member of the Congress Parliamentary Board. He was an effective speaker in the Central Assembly and showed particular grasp of financial questions.

In 1937 he was elected unopposed to the Provincial Legislative Assembly from the Bareilly-Pilibhit-Shahjahanpur and Budaun Urban Constituency. He was elected as Leader of the Congress party in the Provincial Assembly.

His own sympathies had always been in favour of acceptance of office by his party in the Provinces. In March 1937 when he refused to accept office in obedience to the party decision, it was obvious that he did not do so with a light heart, and in the events which preceded the Wardha decision, his influence was cast on the side of office acceptance. He showed, however, some hesitation in July in accepting the actual invitation to take office on account of the Governor's nominations to the Upper Chamber which had been announced shortly before.

He was reassured and persuaded to form a Ministry and four Members were sworn in on July 17th, 1937, and two more on July 28th. He himself took two portfolios, that of Home Affairs (which includes Appointments, General Administration and Police) and that of Finance. To these he added the Forest Department, in which he has a particular interest as a resident of Kumaon. The burden of these charges is really too heavy for one man, particularly as he is also consulted by the other Ministers on matters in their departments, and often interests himself in questions in other departments.

He dominates the Cabinet and no decision of importance is taken without consulting him; while he is often compelled or induced to interfere in matters of which the importance does not really merit his attention. He is a skilful parliamentarian, conciliatory, sincere, and dignified in manner, and is respected and liked by his political opponents. In the Legislature, in committees, and in meetings of his party he stands out, by force of character, as the leader. He has shown himself extremely loyal to the Congress High Command and has never let fall any hint of criticism. He has never betrayed either personal ambition, or personal jealousy. His disinterestedness and his simplicity of life have largely contributed to the respect in which he is held. He has a good brain and expresses himself readily and fluently in English, in speech or on paper. Of independent character, except where party loyalty is involved, he is a man of tenacious principles who listens willingly to argument but is slow to be convinced. Eighteen months' experience of administration, however, has modified some of his prejudices, and except where his principles or the exigencies of the political situation are involved, he is usually prepared to re-examine his views. His bent is definitely reformist and right wing, not revolutionary, but his principles and his party difficulties and his own temperament make him unwilling to take strong action against extremists. He tries to keep them in check by sweet reasonableness and personal influence. His handling of the Cawnpore strike by his own methods was a triumph for this policy, but it may yet lead him to disaster; and it is a fair comment that the situation need not have arisen, had he taken a firmer line at an early stage. Where party difficulties do not arise, as for example where communal riots threaten, he can take strong action, and even abrogate some of his cherished principles. But where his principles and the influences of left wing opinion stand together opposed to his responsibility for maintaining the peace and order of the Province he is liable to indecision and half measures. In legislation he has shown himself willing to compromise; in administration he believes in orthodox financial principles, has on the whole avoided jobbery, and has made honest attempts to reduce corruption. He has a strong sympathy for the underdog; a good conceit of himself; and a hasty temper which sometimes gets the better of him. He has some strong prejudices, is somewhat anti-European in principle and has been very suspicious of the Police, though in this respect he has shown welcome signs in the last month or two of a change of attitude. A man bigger physically and mentally than the ordinary, who on the whole is ruled by his heart rather than his head – and who is liked and respected by those members of the services who come in contact with him.

He is a tireless but unmethodical worker and has few recreations. A hillman of heavy build and unaccustomed to spending summer in the plains he finds the climate of Lucknow trying. There have been times when his health has given cause for alarm.

His Cabinet has shown no signs of disloyalty to him. He has had trouble continually with the left wing both in his parliamentary party and outside. There have been rumours from time to time that his hold on the leadership was precarious, and his position is probably less strong than it was. But outwardly he remains the undisputed leader.

ENCLOSURE 2 TO NO. 2

MINISTER OF JUSTICE AND DEVELOPMENT, U.P.
The Hon'ble Dr Kailash Nath Katju, M.A., LL.D.
(Appointed July 17th, 1937) (Pay Rs. 500 p.m.)

Son of Pandit Tribhuwan Nath Katju; caste Kashmiri Brahmin; born 1887. Educated in Jaora (Central India), at the Forman Christian College, Lahore, and the Allahabad University. He commenced practice in the District Courts at Cawnpore in 1908 and joined the High Court Bar at Allahabad in 1914. He became one of the leading Advocates at the Allahabad Bar and had a very large and lucrative practice, chiefly on the civil side, although he appeared in a certain number of criminal cases of a political nature; for example, the appeal of the Meerut Conspiracy case. He was editor of the *Allahabad Law Journal* from 1918 to 1937. In 1935 he became Chairman of the Allahabad Municipal Board. He was a member of the United Provinces Provincial Congress Committee for several years but took no open part in unlawful movements and was not imprisoned during the Civil Disobedience period.

He was not a member of the former Legislative Council. He was elected unopposed to the Provincial Legislative Assembly from one of the Allahabad Rural constituencies at the general election of 1937. His portfolio includes the departments of Law and Justice, Industries, Cooperation, Rural Development, Excise, Agriculture and Veterinary.

In the early stages of the Ministry Dr. Katju was, next to the Premier, the most prominent figure. But latterly his public importance has seemed to diminish. He is an able man and a clear and concise thinker, but of a somewhat autocratic temperament and rather brusque in manner. He has taken a large part in defending the Government policy both in the Assembly and the Council. Partly perhaps from lack of experience and partly because of his temperament he has not been successful in conciliating the Council in which his party is in a minority. They complain that he lectures them too much, and that he speaks more like a lawyer fighting a case than a responsible Minister. He is an industrious and quick worker and deals very thoroughly with his files. His advice is sought on most of the legal and legislative problems of the Cabinet. He has pressed a scheme for the separation of executive and judicial functions, and has worked hard at rural development. In matters of detail he is reasonable and practical, but in principle he seems prepared to go further than the Premier towards radical changes. He is believed to be somewhat chagrined that he was not offered a High Court Judgeship, because of his political activities when a vacancy occurred shortly before he took office. He is certainty no lover of the British or the British connection. He has made a large financial sacrifice in giving up his practice and taking office. There have been rumours of late that he was not very happy in the Ministry, and might return to the Bar. He is believed to be not very popular with the party and to have little influence in it, but his relations with the Premier are close, and the latter uses him in many respects as his right hand man. He is inclined to assert himself against the High Court and the Chief Court. He has a critical mind and in dealing for instance with appeals for mercy in death sentence cases shows himself as holding no high opinion of the way in which our Courts administer the law. But in this respect he has toned down with experience. He is personally very pleasant to deal with.

ENCLOSURE 3 TO NO. 2

MINISTER OF REVENUE AND JAILS, U.P.
The Hon'ble Mr Rafi Ahmad Qidwai.
(Appointed July 17th, 1937) (Pay Rs. 500 p.m.)

Is the son of a Tahsildar and was born about 1894. He is a resident of Masauli in the Bara Banki district and belongs to the well-known Qidwai family of that district. Graduated from the Muslim University, Aligarh, where he came under the influence of the late Mohammad Ali. He joined the Non-cooperation Movement and was convicted in 1922 in the Bara Banki district. On release he was elected a member of the United Provinces Congress Committee and became Secretary to Pandit Motilal Nehru and later to Pandit Jawaharlal Nehru. He was elected an M.L.A. in 1927 on the Swarajist ticket, but resigned in 1929. Was also Secretary of the Provincial Congress Committee. He was convicted three times during the Civil Disobedience period. Elected General Secretary of the All-India Muslim Nationalist Party but resigned in 1933. In 1934 he conducted a campaign against the Council entry programme of the Congress, as he considered it inconsistent with the principles of the "independence" resolution passed in 1929 at Lahore. At the general election of 1937 he was defeated in the Gonda North-East Muslim constituency, largely by the influence of the Raja of Jehangirabad. In April of the same year he was elected unopposed to the Provincial Legislative Assembly at a bye-election in Bahraich (S.). Up to the time when he was persuaded to take office as a Muslim representative he had opposed office acceptance, and he openly criticised the Wardha decision. As a Minister he is unimpressive in appearance and does not outwardly take a prominent part either in Cabinet or in the Legislature. But he is said really to be the most influential Member of the Cabinet after the Premier. Of the "Ward politician" type his long association with the party machinery has given him a wide acquaintance and influence with the local leaders and he is a clever wire-puller. In his departmental work he appears superficially to be indolent and casual, but he has a good deal of shrewd common-sense. He is popular with the party, and enjoys their full confidence in communal matters as one of the old established Congress Muslims. Is said to be more open to influence in personal cases than any of the other Ministers. By general reputation he is not over-scrupulous. In the Tenancy legislation which belongs to his department, the chief part in public has been taken by the Premier, but Mr. Qidwai is in close touch with all that is being done, and possibly in this, as in other matters, plays a more important part than would appear.

ENCLOSURE 4 TO NO. 2

MINISTER OF LOCAL SELF-GOVERNMENT AND HEALTH, U.P.
The Hon'ble Mrs Vijaya Lakshmi Pandit.
(Appointed July 17th, 1937) (Pay Rs. 500 p.m.)

A daughter of the late Pandit Motilal Nehru. Born about 1903. Educated for a short period at Roedean. About 1921 she eloped with Syed Husain, editor of the *Independent* of Allahabad and went through a form of marriage with him which was afterwards annulled. In 1923 she married Ranjit Sita Ram Pandit, a barrister, who is the son of a prominent and wealthy lawyer of Rajkot in Kathiawar and who had been interned for a time in Germany during the War when a student. After his marriage he took up practice at Allahabad and was imprisoned during the Civil Disobedience Movement. He is at present a member of the Provincial Legislative Assembly and General Secretary of the Provincial Congress Committee. They have two daughters. Mrs. Pandit took part in the political activities of her family and was imprisoned during the Civil Disobedience Movement in Allahabad. She was elected by a large majority to the Provincial Legislative Assembly at the general election of 1937 from the Cawnpore District Women's

Constituency in a hard fought contest against Lady Kailash Srivastava.

Her departments include Municipal, District and local boards, Medical and Public Health.

Mrs. Pandit is a good public speaker, and a woman of much personal charm. She has given some very straight talk to some of her local bodies during her tours. She does not assert herself in the Cabinet or at party meetings; but has shown great interest and energy in her departmental work and has toured a lot to see things for herself. Her outlook on ordinary departmental matters is sensible and fair. She takes the advice of the Premier on a good many of her difficult cases. Both she and her husband have a very modern outlook on questions of social reform. They live and educate their children in European style. Mrs. Pandit gets on excellently with English people and is liked by them. Politically she is naturally much under her brother's influence, but her own views are probably much more moderate, and she is a very definite supporter of the Premier. She went to Europe to recuperate from a breakdown partly brought on by extensive touring in the hot weather to inspect relief measures in districts where cholera had broken out in epidemic form. She has returned in much better health.

ENCLOSURE 5 TO NO. 2

MINISTER OF COMMUNICATIONS AND IRRIGATION, U.P.
The Hon'ble Hafiz Muhammad Ibrahim, B.A., LL.B.
(Appointed July 28th, 1937) (Pay Rs. 500 p.m.)

He is a resident of Bijnor. Said to be the son of a small Government official. His age is 46. He had a small practice as a lawyer in the Bijnor District Courts. He was a member of the last two Provincial Legislative Councils and was always a strong nationalist. He sat as an independent but acted very closely with the Swarajist party. He was elected unopposed to the Provincial Legislative Assembly at the last election from the Garhwal and Bijnor (North-West) Muslim Rural constituency. He was elected as a member of the Muslim League but very shortly after the election announced his adherence to the Congress party with which he had always been in sympathy. He was taken into the Congress Ministry as a representative of the Muslims. Shortly after becoming a Minister he accepted a challenge to resign his seat and contest it as a Congressman. He won a hard-fought election against a Muslim League candidate in which all the resources of both sides were brought into play.

His departments include Buildings and Roads, Irrigation, and Muslim Endowments.

He is the least important and least influential Member of the Cabinet. He plays a very small part in Cabinet discussions and in his departmental work he takes few decisions of importance without first referring them to the Premier. Whether this is from choice or by order is not certain, but being a recent recruit he has little influence with the Party. He is not a forcible personality, but his views on departmental matters are often practical, and he is one of the Ministers who has undoubtedly developed as the result of experience. He is considered to be a very good public speaker in Urdu. As a Minister he is earning more than he has ever made or is ever likely to make by his profession.

He has been subjected to hostile demonstrations by the Muslim League in various places, and is reported to have faced them with courage.

ENCLOSURE 6 TO NO. 2

MINISTER OF EDUCATION, U.P.
The Hon'ble Sri Sampurnanand, B.Sc.
(Appointed March 2nd, 1938) (Pay Rs. 500 p.m.)

Son of Vijayanand; caste Kayasth; born 1888; resident of Benares. Educated at Allahabad University. Acted as a Science teacher at different schools at Benares, at the Daly College, Indore, and at a school in Bikaner. In 1920 he returned to Benares. Joined the Non-cooperation movement and was convicted in 1921. He later became editor of a Hindi monthly magazine and Secretary of the Benares Congress Committee. When Shaukat Usmani was arrested, Sampurnanand's house was searched and Communist literature seized. He became a professor in the Kashi Vidyapith. In 1925 he was elected as a Swarajist to the Provincial Legislative Council. He became the Chief Organiser of the Hindustani Seva Dal, the Youth League and the Nau Jawan Bharat Sabha in the United Provinces. He was convicted three times during the Civil Disobedience period. On release he organised the all-India Congress Socialist party and became President of the Benares branch. He started a weekly Socialist paper called the *Jagran.*

At the general election of 1937 he was elected by a large majority from the Benares City Urban constituency. He was one of the most influential left wingers in the Parliamentary party, and in March 1938 on the resignation of Pandit Pyare Lal Sharma he was taken into the Cabinet as the Minister of Education with the object of obtaining more left wing support for the Ministry and quieting criticism.

His accession has undoubtedly strengthened their team. He is a useful speaker and a person with ideas of his own on education based on personal experience. In ordinary matters of detail he is reasonable and takes a practical view, but he is said to be very obstinate if a principle is involved to which he attaches importance. He fully realises the importance of maintaining discipline in educational institutions, and is prepared to take action to that end. He is particularly interested in military matters, as was to be expected from his record, and has pressed on the Cabinet the starting of military training and drill in schools. He is also a strong advocate of Hindi, and is more suspect to the Muslims than any other Member of the Cabinet. Financially he is a poor man. His ultimate aims are at present concealed, or more probably, undecided; he certainly has strongly socialistic views, and the prospect of possible mass revolution perhaps appeals more to him than to any of the other Ministers, though there have been indications of the mellowing effect of office on him.

ENCLOSURE 7 TO NO. 2

SPEAKER, U.P. LEGISLATIVE ASSEMBLY
The Hon'ble Purshottamdas Tandon, M.A., LL.B.
(Elected July 31st, 1937) (Pay Rs. 500 p.m.)

Son of Salig Ram; caste Khattri; born about 1884, resident of Allahabad. Educated at Allahabad University. Was Captain of the University Cricket Team. Was a Vakil of the High Court at Allahabad and at one time Legal Adviser of the Nabha State. He suspended practice in 1919 and became an active and ardent non-cooperator. Was Chairman of the Allahabad Municipal Board. Was convicted in December 1921 for being a member of an unlawful association; on release espoused the cause of the Kisans and later became Assistant Secretary of the Punjab National Bank. He was a member of the All-India Congress Committee. He took a most prominent part in the "no rent" campaign during the Civil Disobedience Movement and was convicted twice. In 1933 he became the President of the "Servants of the People" Society. In 1937 elected, unopposed, to the Provincial Legislative Assembly from the Allahabad City General Urban constituency.

His views in general are believed to be decidedly more extreme and socialistic than those of the Premier. His name was mentioned as a possible rival to the Premier for the leadership of the Congress party in the Legislative Assembly. When he failed to secure that, he apparently preferred not to serve as a Minister and accepted the Speakership. His election as Speaker was not contested. As Speaker he has a good control of the Assembly, knows his own mind and does not hesitate to get his own way. He has opposed the view, based on English practice, that the presiding officers of the Provincial Assemblies and Councils should not take part in politics. He asserted his intention of doing so outside the House while maintaining impartiality within it. He submitted this proposal of his to the vote of the Assembly and obtained its approval. He is much interested in the advancement of Hindi. He has encouraged the publication of Assembly proceedings and papers in both vernaculars, in addition to English, and has interpreted the rule of procedure about the language of debate in such a way as to leave it open to any member to speak in the vernacular if he wishes. He is of independent and somewhat domineering character, though pleasant to talk to. He probably still exerts a good deal of influence in the inner counsels of the party behind the scenes, but his influence appears to be less than it was, and there is ground for believing that he feels himself side-tracked in his present post. Whether he would re-emerge as a candidate for the Premiership, if Pant relinquished it, is uncertain but he might well be acceptable to the Left Wing.

ENCLOSURE 8 TO NO. 2

DEPUTY SPEAKER, U.P. LEGISLATIVE ASSEMBLY
Mr Abdul Hakeem, M.A., LL.B.
(Salary Rs. 2,000 p.a.)

A leading Vakil of the Basti district where he is wellknown and respected. Was elected at the general election of 1937 from the Basti (South-East) Muslim Rural Constituency as a Muslim Leaguer, opposing a National Agriculturist Party candidate. Before this election he had been nibbling at the Congress ticket. On 24th July 1937 he announced his adherence to the Congress party, but did not resign his seat. Was elected Deputy Speaker as a sop to the Nationalist Muslim element and has performed his duties unobtrusively. Said to be a respectable and honest man.

ENCLOSURE 9 TO NO. 2

PRESIDENT, U.P. LEGISLATIVE COUNCIL
The Hon'ble Sir Sita Ram
(Elected July 31st, 1937) (Salary Rs. 6,000 p.a.)

Caste Vaish. Comes of a landholding family of the Meerut district. Born about 1883. Educated at Meerut College. Practised as a lawyer at Meerut and for a few years in the Allahabad High Court. He was an active Member of the Indian National Congress until 1920 and left it on the inauguration of the Non-Cooperation Movement. Was a Member of the United Provinces Legislative Council under the former constitution from start to finish and was its first elected President from 1925 until its close. He was a popular and impartial President although not a remarkably strong one. He used a "pawky" type of humour with good effect. He was knighted in 1931 for his services as President. At the general election of 1937 he stood as a Liberal candidate for the Legislative Assembly from the Bulandshahr-Meerut-Hapur-Khurja and Nagina cities constituency and was defeated by a large majority by Pandit Pyare Lal Sharma, subsequently Congress Minister of Education. Sir Sita Ram was later nominated by the Governor to the Upper House, which contained few members with previous experience in the legislature. He was elected President, and has carried out his duties with the same skill and on the same lines as before. He is a man of typical Liberal views. He had lost most of his practice and is not now a wealthy man. He has a son who holds a King's Commission in the Indian Army.

ENCLOSURE 10 TO NO. 2

DEPUTY PRESIDENT, U.P. LEGISLATIVE COUNCIL
Begum Aizaz Rasul (or Qudsia Begum)
(Salary Rs. 1,000 p.a.)

Is the wife of Syed Aizaz Rasul, Taluqdar of Jalalpur Estate in the Hardoi district, who is a Member of the Legislative Assembly and belongs to the Landlord party. His estate is under the Court of Wards. Begum Aizaz Rasul is a daughter of the late Sir Zulfiqar Ali Khan of Malerkotla State. She was elected from the Sitapur-Hardoi and Kheri district constituency. Both she and her husband are young, well-educated and cultured people. Her father was a Shia, but she and her husband are Sunnis. She is popular and has apparently been an adequate Deputy President. She has developed a good deal in the last year or two.

3

HAIG TO LINLITHGOW
Telegram
R/3/1/75

No. 195-G *January 22nd, 1939*

Few days ago I heard from my Financial Secretary[7] that the Premier had asked him to examine what would be the saving if a cut of 10 per cent. were made in the pay of all Government servants on Rs. 200 and over. I understand it would be a little over 20 lakhs. Yesterday when I visited Lucknow I had some preliminary talk with Premier about the budget, and I questioned him about this suggestion. He said it was not a proposal which he wished to put forward, but that with rain holding off he felt the Province might be involved in heavy loss of revenue, and as he was worried about the situation he had wished to explore all possibilities of improving our finances. Actually at the time we were talking rain was falling and I hope there may have been reasonable rain all over the Province.

I did not get the impression that he was himself very much in earnest about this proposal, though I have heard that a Parliamentary Secretary had stated that the Assembly would not pass any new taxation unless there was a cut in pay of the services.

2. I made it clear to the Premier that if he did put forward such proposal it would raise very difficult issues and that I should have to consider matter with reference to Section 52 of the Government of India Act, apart from necessity of referring to Secretary of State in connection with all-India services. I explained that I felt we had a certain moral obligation to Government servants who have been recruited under the old constitution, and I also stressed the point that it was most important not to create widespread discontent in the services as the success of Government policies depended to considerable extent on their willing support. He showed appreciation of both these points and frankly acknowledged his dependence on the loyal cooperation of the services. I was left with the impression that it is not likely that he will raise this matter seriously; but in case he does I should be glad to know whether so far as Your Excellency and the Secretary of State are concerned, the position remains as stated in your

telegram No. 496-G.C. of December 24th, 1937.[8] I am myself strongly in favour of maintaining that position.

3. The budgetary position is still rather in the air, but the Premier did not express himself disturbed about it, apart from possible failure of the *rabi* crop. On Financial Secretary's preliminary estimates there is a deficit of 67 lakhs. This however (*a*) excludes 30 lakhs from sugar cess, which will certainly be collected. I imagine the Premier wishes to keep this in reserve; but I should guess when it comes to the point that not more than 15 lakhs would be used in this way and that we should therefore have 15 lakhs improvement on Financial Secretary's figure. (*b*) Includes a loss of 19 lakhs on further extension of prohibition policy. No decision has been taken on this and I should hope that here again we might save perhaps 9 lakhs. It is likely that a tax on the sale of petrol may be imposed which would bring in about 7 lakhs. In these ways it seems to me that deficit of 67 lakhs might be reduced to little over 30 lakhs, which would not be an alarming [figure ? word omitted], and would certainly not justify proposals for a cut in pay, especially as deficit would have been created by policy of Ministry regarding prohibition and large new expenditure. Even if a poor *rabi* crop involved remissions of 30 lakhs or 40 lakhs of land revenue, I do not consider that this exceptional and temporary calamity would justify the expedient of a cut in pay.[9]

4

HAIG TO LINLITHGOW
R/3/1/75

Secret
No. U.P.-216

January 24th, 1939

My dear Lord Linlithgow,

I have just returned to Allahabad after a short tour in Benares and Gorakhpur, including also a flying visit to Lucknow to make contact with my Ministers. I found them very friendly, and apparently satisfied with the way things are going. We have had a little rain in most parts of the Province within the last two or three days, but the amount has been disappointing, and in the Agra division where the need is greatest they have had next to none.

2. I am very much in sympathy with what Your Excellency said in your letter of 6th January about the landlords.[10] Their present position is very

unenviable, and quite apart from their attitude towards such a measure as the Tenancy Bill, they feel that the whole foundation of their position is swaying beneath them. It would be more than one could expect from human nature if they did not feel that we are in large measure responsible for this change, and that their loyalty in the past has been ill-requited. I always try to encourage them and urge them to take a less despairing view of the future, and to realise that they still have considerable power and opportunities. But many of them feel that their position is slipping away from them the whole time.

3. The Tenancy Bill continues on its course uneventfully, and it looks as if it should be through the Assembly before the end of February. It is in my opinion a very significant fact, which can be put against a good many of the more gloomy possibilities that I have been dwelling upon recently, that the Bill, which is certainly not an extreme measure, appears to be going through practically unchanged. This shows that on a major question of policy like this, moderate Congressmen are having their own way. There was some talk at one stage recently of some unpractical and dangerous provisions for giving land to landless labourers. This, however, was provoked entirely by the rather infantile sense of tactics of certain of the landlords, who thought that it was a master stroke to oppose the Tenancy Bill by attacking the Government for not having gone further and made provision for the landless labourer. The Government eventually hit back with these proposals, whereupon I fancy the landlords realised the folly of their proceedings and I think the whole matter will drop.

4. The principles for the fixation of rent have gone through practically unchanged. This is a point of great importance, for as I have mentioned in previous letters, the Ministers have been strongly pressed by the left wing to carry out drastic rent reductions, which I am assured would be impossible under the provisions of the Tenancy Bill as they stand. I mentioned in paragraph 3 of my letter of January 10th that I had had a somewhat disquieting report from the Revenue Secretary on this point, but that I was not disposed to attach too much importance to it. This attitude seems to have been justified. When I saw Pant recently in Lucknow I tackled him on this question of rent reduction, and said that it seemed to me very little rent reduction would be possible if the principles laid down in the Tenancy Bill were observed and if we were not prepared to sacrifice the financial stability of the Province. He said that he still hoped to be able to do something within those limitations. I observed that anything possible would come very short of the 8 crores which I understood had been mentioned at Ajodhya, and he replied that people at conferences were not very strong

in arithmetic. I think this conversation is very reassuring on this crucial point.

5. I also asked Pant about the statement attributed to the Revenue Minister at the Ajodhya Conference, that the Government had decided to remit all the suspended arrears of rent. I said I did not remember any Government decision on this point. He said that while it was true that a year ago there had been talk of coupling remissions of the suspended arrears with conditions about payment of the current rents, the position had changed now by the passage of time, and that it had become clear that they must remit all these arrears. They would in due course introduce the necessary legislation. I am inclined myself to agree that things have now gone so far that it is really not possible to take any other course than to remit these arrears. But there will be a great outcry from the landlords, even though I expect few of them have any expectation of ever seeing these arrears. But they will demand, and with considerable justice, that Government should refund the revenue which has been paid on the basis of these rents. There is also the danger that this action will affect the collection of current rents. These are points which I shall certainly press on the attention of the Ministers.

6. On the whole I have been getting an impression during the last fortnight that the right wing have closed their ranks and are standing more firm. I spoke to Pant about the proceedings at Ajodhya and said I was afraid they were not very encouraging for the Government. He expressed surprise and said that he had been quite satisfied. I said that according to the public reports the conference seemed to have concentrated rather on what had not been done than on what had been done; but he said that in his opinion the achievements of the Ministry had been fully appreciated, though no doubt people wanted quicker results. He spoke with a good deal of confidence, and it seems to me that in fact his position has not been at all shaken by the Ajodhya Conference; nor his policy affected. He seems to be going on precisely on the same lines as before. This is decidedly encouraging.

7. Another development which in its way points in the same direction is that of the move to Naini Tal. Last year the Ministers were decidedly in favour of it, but the Party would not have it and they had to drop the idea. Now it has been taken up again and the Party have left the decision to the Ministers. I gathered from my talk with Pant that if they can secure satisfactory accommodation for the Legislature at Naini Tal, they would almost certainly decide to move up; and indeed he asked my good offices in trying to secure the chalet building belonging to the Naini Tal Club,

which appears to be the only one that could conveniently accommodate the Legislature. I shall do what I can to help over this. The justification for going up to Naini Tal will be that it will enable the Ministry to continue non-stop with their immense legislative programme. It is generally recognised that the legislature could hardly continue sitting through May and June in Lucknow. If they move to the hills the intention will be to have the Legislature sitting throughout May, June and July and possibly into August. It will be a great thing if they do decide to move to Naini Tal. If this is not done, a great strain again will be placed on the headquarters administration, and Pant himself may well break down. The move would be a great relief to the Secretaries.

8. Another direction besides the Ajodhya Conference in which perhaps I have over-estimated the importance of speeches and resolutions is the All-India Muslim League Conference at Patna. During my tour in the eastern districts I questioned a number of District Officers and Superintendents of Police as to whether this conference had had any effect on the communal situation. They all told me it had not, and in this part of the Province at any rate they do not seem apprehensive about trouble at the Bakr-Id. There is a particular local problem in the Gorakhpur district at Zahidabad which has been a centre of difficulty for a long time. I heard a great deal about it while I was at Gorakhpur, but on both sides there was an evident hope that through the good offices of the Collector,[11] who has the confidence of both communities, they would be able to reach some compromise. It did not seem to me that there was any trace of a dangerously aggressive attitude either on the part of the Hindus or the Muslims. I had an interesting talk at Gorakhpur with a young Muslim M.L.A. who has been playing a very prominent part in the Legislature. He said to me quite frankly that what the Muslim League wanted was to have their representatives on the Government. This has always been my view, and consequently I do not think that attempts by Gandhi to reassure the Muslims against unjust treatment in the everyday administration will have any effect. During the last few days the Hindus have been showing a decidedly aggressive spirit in connection with Hyderabad Day, and here in Allahabad I am told that owing to the Hindu attitude communal feeling has become much worse.

9. I was very much gratified at the great improvement that has taken place in the Gorakhpur district generally. When I was there a year ago, the most gloomy anticipations were expressed both by officials and non-officials. Now everybody agrees that things have settled down very largely, and that such trouble as there is practically confined to the Maharajganj

Tahsil. Even there conditions are much easier as a result of the record operations which have now been in progress about a year. The Collector deserves great credit for his general handling of the situation.

10. There is still some uneasiness both at Lucknow and Allahabad about the possibility of strikes in the Electric Supply Works; but the efforts of the Labour Commissioner[12] have been successful in obtaining at any rate a postponement of the trouble, and in both places there is quite a fair chance of a settlement. If strikes were to develop, it would probably be necessary for the Government to take over the works and run them.

11. I have just brought to a satisfactory close a very prolonged tussle which I have had with Dr. Katju, the Minister of Justice, in connection with the appointment of Registrar of the High Court at Allahabad. This appointment is under the orders of the Secretary of State open both to the I.C.S. and the P.C.S. but is reserved for neither. The Chief Justice[13] had some months ago asked for sanction to raise the status of the Registrar. This was opposed by the Minister, very largely on the ground that it would rule out the appointment of a Provincial Service officer. He made it very clear at the time that he attached the greatest importance to the appointment of a Provincial Service man. I felt there was not sufficient ground for differing from the Minister and the proposal of the Chief Justice was therefore negatived. The Chief Justice soon afterwards wrote to me and said that he proposed to appoint with my concurrence a certain young I.C.S. officer who is acting as District and Sessions Judge. The position is that under Section 242 (4) of the Government of India Act the appointment rests with the Chief Justice, but the Provincial Government have to agree to placing at his disposal the officer whom he selects. I consulted Dr. Katju and he expressed the strongest objection to agreeing to the appointment of an I.C.S. officer. I pointed out to him that the mere fact that the Provincial Government had to make an officer available would not justify them in using this power to challenge the principle of the decision of the Chief Justice, and that in my opinion they could only reasonably decline to make a particular officer available if there were certain exceptional circumstances which made it administratively inconvenient. In this case there were no such circumstances, and to refuse to place the officer's services at the disposal of the Chief Justice really meant that the Provincial Government had decided that an I.C.S. officer should never be appointed to a post which the Secretary of State had declared was open to the I.C.S., and that the Chief Justice was not to be allowed to exercise the power which the Government of India Act conferred upon him. I stated all this at some length in a note; but we had three, if not four, discussions on

the subject extending over about six weeks, and Dr. Katju wrote at least three long notes shifting his ground slightly each time. Eventually, however, after I had agreed to allow him to represent by an official letter at great length his views to the Chief Justice and had assured him that the Chief Justice was not hostile to the Provincial Service, and was exercising a choice purely on merits, he acquiesced. But he showed great stubbornness, and there were times when I thought he might push his opposition very far. He also said that he had discussed the matter with his colleagues and had their support, and that it might be necessary to discuss it at a Cabinet meeting. But it did not go to this length, and I suspect that he overstated the interest of his colleagues in the matter. I found it necessary eventually to indicate to him that I had an individual judgement in the matter of making this officer's services available, and that my own opinion as to what ought to be done was quite clear. It was after this that, following another week's reflection, he finally gave in. The matter occupied an amount of time and thought quite out of proportion to its apparent importance; but I felt it necessary to take a very firm stand on the principle, and I hope that the final outcome will prove to have been of some value generally.

12. The day before I went to Benares Colonel Fisher, who is in political charge of the Benares State, saw me at Allahabad and informed me fully about recent developments in the State in connection with the agitation, and the lines on which he was proceeding. While I was at Benares I had several conversations with the Maharaja and various of his officers. They had been rather shaken by the events of December 26th, when a big demonstration of peasants said to have amounted to ten thousand had presented itself before the Maharaja at Chakia. I have written to Fisher giving him my views fully about the situation, based on my conversations not only with the Maharaja, but with various people in Benares. My own judgement is that provided the Maharaja is willing to make certain constitutional and administrative changes, which undoubtedly he is, there is no general desire on the part of Congressmen in Benares to cause undue trouble, and I hope things may gradually settle down. Indeed, before I left, I had seen the draft of a very conciliatory letter which the leaders of the agitation were proposing to send to the Maharaja, who is personally popular. He is, I fear, in a poor state of health and this arouses some public sympathy. Fisher had told me that my Education Minister, Sampurnanand, who is a Benares man, had actually drafted the ultimatum that was presented to the Maharaja. I did not get any definite confirmation of this, but I am quite prepared to believe that Fisher's information may be true. When I

was in Lucknow subsequently, I spoke to Sampurnanand about Benares, and emphasised how important it was in my opinion that a troublesome agitation should not develop there, and told him that it seemed to me the Maharaja was taking all reasonable steps. Sampurnanand expressed himself in very moderate and reasonable terms, and I hope in fact he will not further encourage the agitation, even if he were in it at one stage. I also spoke to the Premier on the same subject, and he clearly is anxious to discourage the development of trouble.

13. There has been a rather amusing development in connection with our relations with the Tehri-Garhwal State, which for some months past have been by no means satisfactory. The most acute friction centred round the conviction of a British subject named Bahuguna, who was arrested at a spot which our people maintained to be British territory, taken away to the State and sentenced on what appeared to be a trumped up charge to six months' imprisonment. The cause of these proceedings, according to our view, was that he had organised a coolie agency which was interfering with the operations of the State coolie agency, and he had incurred the enmity of the State Diwan,[14] a man whose reputation is by no means good. The Diwan is being prosecuted in our courts for kidnapping. The case gave rise at one time to very strong feelings in this Province. Recently the State High Court served a notice on Bahuguna, who was at the time in our custody in connection with the case against the Diwan, calling upon him to show cause why his sentence should not be enhanced. But we are privately given to understand that in fact if he was sent back to Tehri it was likely that his sentence would be quashed. Accordingly he was sent back and the High Court duly quashed the proceedings. I imagine that in due course the proceedings against the Diwan will also be withdrawn. There will now only remain some rather troublesome questions about boundaries, and arrangements for coolie agencies and so on, which I hope can be settled amicably by local discussion. But at a time like this it is unwise for States to take action which is justly provocative of opinion in British India.

14. When Thorne saw Pant in Lucknow not long ago, it seems that the latter grumbled a good deal about the procedure I am intending to adopt in sending up the proposal for abolition of Commissioners by a despatch to the Governor-General instead of by a letter to the Government of India. Actually I had explained the intended procedure in a note well before the Cabinet meeting at which we discussed the merits of the proposal, and while there was a very brief discussion about the procedure, it did not appear to me at the time that the Ministers took any serious objection to it.

When I saw Pant recently in Lucknow and was discussing with him the question of a cut in pay, which I have reported to Your Excellency separately, I deliberately led the conversation on to the question of abolition of Commissioners and discussed on broad lines the whole series of problems that arose in connection with the organisation and control of the Services. I wished to see whether he would take this opportunity of raising with me the procedure about which he has complained to Thorne. But he made no attempt at all to do so. I do not think therefore he can have much feeling on the subject; or if he has, he must realise that he is not on good ground. I may say that we discussed these problems about the Services in a very amicable spirit, both agreeing that they were full of complexities and conflicting principles which it was very difficult to reconcile.

Yours sincerely,
H.G. HAIG

5

HAIG TO LINLITHGOW
R/3/1/75

Secret and Personal
D.-O. No. U.P.-217

Camp,
January 28th, 1939

My dear Lord Linlithgow,

In the despatch[15] with which I have forwarded the proposals of my Ministers for the abolition of Commissioners in this Province, I have dealt fully with the merits of the case as I see it. I have not, however, thought it desirable to include in a communication of that nature consideration of the possible action that might be taken by my Ministers if in accordance with my recommendation their proposal is rejected. I think it probable that they attach very considerable importance to their proposal:

(*a*) on the grounds of principle which I have mentioned in my despatch,
(*b*) from a belief that the abolition of Commissioners would place the whole machinery of the administration much more closely under their control and would reduce the independence and impartiality of the official organisation,
(*c*) owing to the financial saving,
(*d*) owing to the political effect of making such a serious inroad into the Secretary of State's services, and the expectations that would be aroused

of further drastic changes and the not too distant disappearance of these services,

(*e*) owing to the criticisms to which they would be subjected not merely by their own followers, but by the opposition, if they do not succeed in carrying out their expressed policy. In this connection I might note my own view that a good many members of the opposition probably share the normal popular belief that Commissioners can safely be abolished, and that those who do not share that view will be quite ready to pretend they do in order to have a weapon for attacking and discrediting the Ministry.

2. The Ministry therefore will be influenced alike by their own belief in their policy and by the partisan attacks of the opposition regarding their failure to carry it out. They may therefore feel tempted to take such steps as are open to them to proclaim their belief in their policy and register their disapproval of the Secretary of State's action in refusing to accept it.

3. It appears to me that there are two lines on which they might proceed. In the first place, they might adopt a consistent policy of ignoring the Commissioners in the administration. There have been already clear signs of a disposition in many instances to cut out the Commissioner and deal direct with the District Officer. This, however, has not been part of any deliberate policy on the part of the Ministers, but merely expresses their own natural inclinations; and when attention is drawn to the more regular procedure, they have not in principle repudiated it. A difficult situation, however, would arise if they adopted a deliberate policy of ignoring Commissioners or withdrawing powers wherever possible from Commissioners.

4. In the second place, they might refuse to make financial provision for the office establishment of Commissioners and thus render it impossible for them to carry out their functions. It appears from the memorandum enclosed with Laithwaite's letter No. 634-G.G., dated March 7th, 1938, that the Governor can only prevent this by placing a somewhat strained interpretation on his special responsibility under Section 52 (1) (*c*) of the Government of India Act. It would however be necessary to take any action possible to prevent the intentions of Parliament being defeated. If this situation arose, though reliance might be placed temporarily on Section 52 (1) (*c*), it would seem most desirable that Parliament should at the earliest possible moment make the necessary amendment in the Government of India Act, which would place the position beyond doubt.

5. I think it is only right that these possibilities should be brought to your notice and that of the Secretary of State. The recommendations, however, in my despatch have been made with a full realisation of these possibilities. I trust that in the event the Ministers, if they do entertain any such ideas, may be persuaded, when they reflect on the consequences, not to carry them into effect. In any case however I would not allow these considerations to deflect us from what I regard as a crucial point of policy.

Yours sincerely,
H.G. HAIG

6

HAIG TO LINLITHGOW
Telegram
R/3/1/75

No. 203-G *January 31st, 1939*

Your telegram No. 256-S.C. of January 27th.[16] Judging situation purely on general considerations and with no inside information I should have been disposed to doubt whether Congress would attempt to force a general breakdown at this stage over position of States' subjects though I can well imagine they may conduct an intensive agitation in States. Indeed I do not quite see what reasonable justification there can be for bringing out Provincial Governments on such an issue. If however such a crisis did develop and Working Committee gave instructions to my Ministers to resign I think there is not the least doubt that they would comply. Neither the Premier's own principles and attitude to Working Committee, nor his political position, would make it possible to conceive of him opposing Working Committee. I should like however to make it clear that I believe my Ministers would be very reluctant to go out on such an issue and would use all influence they possess against such policy being adopted. Actually with Nehru now President of Provincial Congress Committee the determining voice in such matter might in effect be his, and it does not seem likely that he would be found to oppose such decision if taken.

2. With regard to general attitude of my Ministry towards agitation in States I think again one can distinguish between their own inclination and action they would take under instructions. In the case of Benares State for instance, though there is some reason to believe that Sampurnanand encouraged it, I get general impression that they are not anxious that it should spread. Indeed Nehru seems to have used his influence recently to

try and stop Satayagraha. On the other hand my Ministers would no doubt conform to any general policy formulated from the Centre, and would I think if so directed refuse to give assistance in the matter of lending staff to States and might even press for recall of officers now serving in States.

7

HAIG TO LINLITHGOW
R/3/1/75

Private and Personal *February 1st, 1939*
No. U.P.-219

My dear Lord Linlithgow,

I think I ought to inform Your Excellency of a very deplorable outbreak which took place at Aligarh on January 26th. The Aligarh exhibition was in progress, and the police had organised, as they always do, a wrestling show. Some students of the Aligarh University got into an altercation with some Seva Samiti Scouts who were on duty at the entrance, and a policeman intervened on behalf of the scouts and is said to have struck one of the students. The students went off vowing vengeance against the police. Not long afterwards several hundred students arrived in a very excitable state and demanded the punishment of the policeman who was said to be at fault. The District Magistrate[17] and the Superintendent of Police[18] argued with them most patiently, promised investigation and eventually with the aid also of some of the university staff apparently succeeded in pacifying them. Soon afterwards, however, it appears that another body of students armed with lathis and hockey sticks came to the police camp which was not far off, attacked it, beat a number of policemen and set it on fire. The accounts of what happened are most confused, but the police seem to have been caught largely unprepared and scattered, and some 40 policemen were injured. Some of the students also were hurt. The next day several hundred students again sallied forth and made a demonstration in front of the police station and also at the bungalow of the Superintendent of Police. The police were no doubt faced with a difficult situation, they were taken by surprise, and the authorities were quite properly most reluctant to use firearms in the case of university students. Nevertheless, the upshot of the matter seems to be, from what I have so far heard, that the students have behaved in an outrageous manner and with impunity, and that the authority of the police in Aligarh has been much shaken. Police reinforcements have since been sent, and the situation is said now to be quiet. One of the principal difficulties is that this outbreak took place just on the eve of Bakr-Id and that communal feeling in Aligarh has been running rather dangerously. The authorities therefore were particularly anxious not to provoke further trouble with the university students which might well lead to communal rioting. They have therefore behaved with the most extreme forbearance and have refrained hitherto from initiating a police investigation among the university students, fearing that this would lead to a further outbreak. But after the Bakr-Id this must, I think, be undertaken.

2. An extremely unsatisfactory feature of the situation is that the university authorities, so far from expressing their regret and offering their fullest assistance in having the offending students dealt with and discipline in the University restored, have publicly identified themselves with a version of the events which appears to be seriously inaccurate, and intended to create an impression that the students were not to blame. It seems clear that this matter will at some stage have to go before the Government of India, and it is on that account that I am letting Your Excellency have this information at once. Sir Shah Sulaiman[19] is coming to Lucknow on the 3rd February to discuss the situation with the Premier. If the university authorities maintain their present attitude it might be necessary for us to set up an authoritative inquiry, say by two High Court Judges, with a view to ascertain the facts unmistakably, and therefore to give us a basis to press for effective steps being taken to deal with the ring-leaders of this outbreak and to restore some respect for discipline in the university. There is no doubt, from all the accounts I get, that the students were entirely out of hand. We will not institute an inquiry of this kind without letting the Government of India know. The Government of India might find it necessary if such an inquiry were held to take action themselves as a result. We also would be able to bring some pressure to bear on the university through threatening to withdraw the grants which we give and without which they would find difficulty in carrying on. There seems to have been some hesitation to take the executive action which would normally have been taken, owing to apprehension that the Muslim League will take the matter up and try to make an important political issue out of it. But my view is that we cannot out of consideration for the feelings of Muslims allow our police to be attacked with impunity.[20]

Yours sincerely,
H.G. HAIG

8

HAIG TO LINLITHGOW
Telegram
R/3/1/75

Important *February 3rd, 1939*
No. 205-G

With reference to my telegram No. 195-G., 22nd January. Cut in pay. Yesterday budget was discussed by me with my Ministers. Budget as presented by them showed revenue deficit of 84 lakhs. They had, however, excluded proceeds of cane cess for next year which is likely to be not less than 30 lakhs. The idea apparently was not that the cess would not be imposed, but that they might avoid unpopularity of stating that it would be imposed and being attacked on (ground) that it was a tax on cultivator. I pointed out that they could hardly deal with matter on these lines and I think they will agree to putting this in their estimate of receipts, which would reduce deficit to 54 lakhs. This deficit is entirely accounted for by further sacrifice of 20 lakhs of revenue under excise for extension of prohibition and 37 lakhs of new expenditure which includes 11 lakhs for raising pay of lowest paid Government servants. This latter item they may postpone.

2. I asked Ministers how they proposed to deal with deficit. They had clearly not made up their minds. They spoke of economies, i.e. (*a*) special pay, which still awaits final discussion between me and Premier and is not likely to yield more than about one lakh (*b*) abolition of Commissioners regarding which I warned them that they could not depend on any economy while matter was not even decided. They are proposing to impose a tax of two *annas* on sale of petrol which might bring in about eight lakhs, and they are also considering other possible taxes; but it is clearly difficult to find anything that will bring in an appreciable amount. I asked them to think over the position further and it was decided to have a final discussion on February 6th. Nothing was said about a cut in pay but it seems not unlikely that on February 6th they may raise the matter formally. I should therefore be grateful if it were possible to let me have an answer to my telegram of 22nd January before that date. I fear that All-India political developments have definitely weakened position of Pant and strengthened that of Kidwai who believes in an aggressive policy.

9

HAIG TO LINLITHGOW
Telegram
R/3/1/75

Express *February 4th, 1939*
Private and Personal
No. 208-G

Reference paragraph 2 of my telegram No. G.-205, dated February 3rd. Yesterday afternoon I received a copy of a Bill to impose a tax on employment. Employment is defined as including all kinds of service, whether private or public, whether under the Crown or a local body, and whether whole time or part time; but it does not include employment in His Majesty's military, naval or air forces. Every person who is in employment in the Province as so defined and is in receipt of a salary is liable to pay a tax at rates specified. There is no tax on salary less than Rs. 2,501 a year. If salary is not less than 2,501 but not above 3,500 the tax is Rs. 90. On 3,501 to 4,500 it is 150 and so on, the percentage rising to approximately 10 per cent. For instance from 25,000 to 30,000 the tax is 2,500, and from 35,000 to 40,000 it is 3,600.

2. I discussed the Bill today with the Premier. I took the line in the first place that it seemed to me the Bill was in effect a tax on income and therefore could only be imposed by the Centre. The Bill has been drafted as a tax on employment under Item 46 of the Provincial Legislative List. Legal opinion had been taken. The Legal Remembrancer[21] had expressed a brief opinion that the Bill amounted to a tax on income. The Advocate-General[22] had given an opinion, which did not seem to me convincing, that the Provincial Legislature had power to impose this tax. Dr. Katju had agreed with the Advocate-General, and so far as the legal point is concerned I think the Ministers have made up their minds to disregard the objection. I understand from paragraph 20 of Your Excellency's letter of June 14th, 1938, that a Governor cannot properly withhold assent to a Bill on the ground that he believes it to be *ultra vires*. Nevertheless, I should be grateful if I could be informed what is the view of Your Excellency's legal advisers as to the validity of this Bill. I am sending a copy of the Bill by post, and the legal opinions recorded here.

3. In the second place, I took the point that the Bill appeared to me to be discriminatory and particularly directed against Government servants. I

could not understand on what principle it was proposed to place this heavy tax on persons in employment, while those whose incomes are derived from professions, trades and callings were to escape. The Premier's reply on this point was completely unconvincing. It amounted to little more than that persons in receipt of a fixed salary had an assured economic position and could therefore afford to pay a tax, while others could not. I pointed out that the basis for imposing a tax of this nature should be capacity to pay as measured broadly by income, and that I could see no valid ground for discriminating between the different sources of income.

4. I drew attention next to the point that the Bill seemed to me to be directed almost wholly against Government servants. The Premier argued that he hoped to secure a considerable amount from servants of local bodies, of universities, banks and well-organised industries and commercial concerns. But he admitted that the bulk of the revenue would come from Government servants. I asked him whether he had formed any estimate of the probable yield of the tax. He said it could only be guess-work, but he hoped the tax would yield about 35 lakhs, which seems to me an over-estimate. He explained that a cut in pay of 10 per cent on Government servants drawing Rs. 200 and over was estimated to bring in 25 lakhs, and he hoped that other persons in employment would yield another 10 lakhs. This gave me the opportunity to point out that in effect the Bill was really a variant on the cut in pay which he had previously been considering. I said that the Bill seemed to me to be directed almost entirely against Government servants. Unless an elaborate staff were entertained, it was probable that a very large proportion of persons in private employ would escape altogether. I then went on to call attention to my special responsibility under section 52 (1) (*c*), for safeguarding the legitimate interests of Government servants, and I said I should have to consider whether a proposal of this nature, which seemed to me so clearly discriminatory against Government servants, would not attract my special responsibility. He said that even so he understood the Provincial Government was authorised to pass such a Bill. I said that the question of my special responsibilities might arise when the Bill came for my assent, and I drew his attention to paragraph 16 of the Instrument of Instructions. He seemed a little shaken at this, but at the end of our conversation I understood that he intends to bring forward this Bill formally at our Cabinet meeting on February 6th and get the approval of the Cabinet to it.

5. In the course of our conversation he pointed out his own difficulties. He said that there was a large gap in the budget and that he considered it should not be left unfilled. The Ministry had not been backward in imposing

such taxes as had been open to them; they had put a cess on sugar cane, they had raised the Court Fees and Stamp duties against strong opposition, and they were intending to introduce a tax on the sale of petrol. I acknowledged this, but said that the gap in the budget arose directly from their deliberate action in pursuit of their policy, and could be reduced if they could postpone or modify some of their proposals. He said that it was useless for a Government to remain in office if it could not carry out its policy. They were already being attacked for having been too slow in carrying out their policy, and they must now go ahead with it. (This is undoubtedly a reflection of the left wing influence, and it does not seem to me likely that they will curtail their prohibition schemes or any of their projects for new expenditure.) I said I quite realised the difficulties that confronted them, but that they were difficulties which confronted all Governments and that no Government could ever find the money to carry out all the projects which it desired to undertake.

6. Our conversation was quite friendly and we parted on very good terms. But I think this Bill will be brought forward and that in the end I shall be faced with the necessity for deciding whether to withhold my assent or not. My own view at present is that the Bill is so clearly directed against Government servants that assent should be withheld in spite of the fact that it may provoke a serious crisis. On the other hand I have given the Premier a clear indication that such a crisis might arise, and it is just possible that he might not wish to press the matter to this issue.

7. Though on the whole I believe that the Ministers are definitely anxious to attack the pay of the Services, I think they might be induced to refrain from introducing this Bill if any alternative means of raising the money required were available. At the moment it is difficult to see any such source. While discussing what I considered to be the discriminatory scope of the Bill, I suggested that it would be much less objectionable if a tax were imposed on all income-tax payers. The Premier seemed to think that this would accentuate the resemblance to an income-tax, which is doubtless true. In fact, however, I doubt whether he would be prepared to incur the unpopularity of attempting to put a tax of this nature on all income-tax payers. It would almost certainly be thrown out by the Upper House, which might on the other hand pass a tax directed only against those in employment. A tax on the lines of that imposed in the Central Provinces (Act XIII of 1933) which is Rs. 28 a year on all income-tax payers would not bring in enough, and a flat rate could hardly be raised above the Central Provinces level. If Your Excellency could suggest any other alternative forms of taxation I should be grateful. A tax on the sale of tobacco has

been considered, but the difficulties of collecting it seem considerable and the yield not very large.

8. If Your Excellency has any suggestions for the line I should take in discussion on Monday afternoon other than that which I have already taken with the Premier I should be grateful if you would telegraph. The only decision which it is essential to take on Monday is as to the budget proper. This will determine the amount of the gap. Proposals for filling it by new taxation need not be finally determined until about the end of the month, and I shall try to persuade my Ministers not to take a final decision on this Bill on Monday.[23]

10

HAIG TO LINLITHGOW
R/3/1/75

Secret *February 6th, 1939*
No. U.P.-221

My dear Lord Linlithgow,

With reference to paragraph 2 of your telegram No. 296-G., dated February 2nd, 1939,[24] I have again reviewed the question of Advisers. The three names I had proposed in my letter No. U.P.-56, dated February 16th, 1938, were Bomford, Gwynne and Panna Lal. Subsequently, in my letter No. U.P.-57, dated February 19th, 1938, I explained that in view of Gwynne's state of health I should probably have to propose Sloan in place of Gwynne. Gwynne's health is now reasonably restored, and I think he would be quite capable of undertaking the work of an Adviser. On the other hand the sad death of Bomford has deprived me of the best of my three proposed Advisers and the only one with expert knowledge of revenue and tenancy problems. In his place I should propose to appoint Sloan who is not only a very capable officer from the general point of view, but has been working as Settlement Commissioner for the last two years and therefore has a thorough knowledge of the problems for which I should have been relying on Bomford. Gwynne, Sloan and Panna Lal would make quite a well-balanced team. I do not propose to select Marsh who now becomes senior Member of the Board of Revenue, for his qualities are in rather a different direction and he has had no experience at all of the working of Government at headquarters. Moreover, his expert knowledge of revenue and tenancy problems is I think decidedly less close than that of Sloan.

2. With regard to salaries I have considered the matter again, and I

think that the suggestion made in my letter of February 19th, 1938,[25] that the three Advisers instead of having a fixed pay should draw their present pay plus a special pay of Rs. 500 is the most convenient solution. All three Advisers actually are on Commissioners' rate of pay and would draw the same.

Yours sincerely,
H.G. HAIG

11

HAIG TO LINLITHGOW
R/3/1/75

Secret
No. U.P.-222-G

February 8th, 1939

My dear Lord Linlithgow,

I am grateful to you for three letters written on 23rd January, 2nd February and 4th February, dealing with my last two fortnightly reports and my general appreciation of the situation which I sent in December. I am very glad that you are broadly in agreement with the latter. We have had of course since I last wrote profoundly important and unexpected developments, and it must at present remain a matter of guess-work what the results are likely to be. When I wrote last on February [January] 24th, I mentioned certain factors which seemed to me to suggest that the right wing were pulling themselves together and were rather happier and more confident about their position. I think in fact this was the case, and I have since heard that they were quite reasonably satisfied with the result of the elections for the coming Congress session. The election, however, of Bose as President was to them a complete and shattering surprise. From such inquiries as I have been able to make, the election was in fact the result of a rather extraordinary conjunction of accidents combined with the fact that, as Pant himself has admitted to me, the right wing took things too much for granted and did not do sufficient canvassing. In this Province a large number of votes were turned over by the statement issued by Kidwai, the Revenue Minister, a copy of which I am enclosing, in which he openly attacked the Working Committee. It is probable that this statement was one of the important contributing causes of Bose's success, for the unexpected strength of the vote in the United Provinces which was, as I have said, largely due to Kidwai's statement, helped Bose a long way to his victory. Kidwai has always been known as representing the left wing in the Cabinet, but he has hitherto been reported as giving loyal support to Pant. On this occasion, whatever may have been his intentions (and it is suggested that he had no idea his statement would have such an important effect), he was clearly asserting a position contrary to that of Pant, and he evidently acted without Pant's knowledge.

2. When I returned to Lucknow just after the Presidential election, Lucknow was humming with excitement and rumours. There was a general idea that the position of the Ministry had been greatly shaken, that Pant might have to resign shortly, and that Kidwai might take his place. Some support was given to these views by the fact that Pant was obviously worried and depressed, while Kidwai seemed to be in an unusually expansive mood. These anticipations, however, were I think premature. Pant and the Cabinet have settled down again to the difficult problems of policy and administration, and I do not think, short of an all-India crisis on the States issue, that they anticipate any change until after the Congress session.

3. No one has ever been able to do more than conjecture what may be at any time in the mind of the Mahatma, and at this moment conjecture seems more than usually difficult. I get the impression, however, that he is seriously upset. I heard only yesterday from one of my Ministers that he had written to say that he would not be at the Congress session. I do not quite know what interpretation is to be placed on this. It is generally assumed that the All-India Congress Committee still has a definite right wing majority and that with its aid it would be possible to control the left wing. But it looks as if Gandhi's first idea at any rate was, while keeping his right wing forces in reserve, to let the left wing have plenty of rope and if possible hang themselves.

4. On the other hand the attitude of Nehru seems to me likely to be decisive. If he were to join Bose, the combination would be very powerful. Most people assume that he is so closely attached to Gandhi that he would not go against him. But his recent utterances have been very extreme. I enclose, for instance, a statement which he issued on January 26th – Independence Day[26] – and also a statement that has appeared in today's papers, which reads almost like an immediate call to arms. I have some suspicion that Nehru regards a European war as inevitable, and that immediately on its outbreak he contemplates launching a revolutionary movement in India. If war did not come, he might be disposed to hold his hand longer.

5. In the meantime Gandhi's attitude about the States is decidedly menacing, and Nehru, as you will see from his statement of today, takes

up this issue with enthusiasm. I think the present attitude of my Ministers is that they can see no kind of direct interest of the United Provinces in this movement about States subjects, and that they can hardly believe that they would be called upon to plunge the Province into confusion on such an issue. But I very much doubt whether they really know any more than we do what is going on in the mind of the Mahatma.

6. I think my Ministers are certainly uneasy as to what may happen after the Congress session and as to the action that might be taken by a left wing Working Committee. The three possibilities are:

(*a*) that they would call upon the Ministry to follow a more advanced policy, but would not seek to displace Pant;

(*b*) that they would consider it necessary to have a definitely left wing Ministry, in which case Pant would have to go;

(*c*) that they would embark immediately on a revolutionary movement and make the Provincial Ministries resign. Short of a European war, I should be disposed to think that they would not proceed immediately to (*c*), but policy (*b*) might be found to lead on fairly rapidly to this position. This is all on the assumption that the left wing secure a free hand as a result of the Congress session. If that is not so, and it is perhaps not likely, naturally the chances of a more moderate policy are increased, and I should regard it as probable that Pant would remain in office.

7. A further complication in our Provincial situation is that Nehru has just been elected as President of the Provincial Congress Committee; in other words, he is in a position to dictate policy and pace to the Ministry. I think, judging from his past behaviour, that he might be reasonable so long as he does not judge that the time for a break has come. But even so, I fear the Ministry will find themselves being urged to go faster and farther than they really consider wise.

8. The problem which has been causing my Ministers a great deal of difficulty lately is the budget. I have already in separate correspondence given Your Excellency the main outlines of the position and the proposals of the Ministry for dealing with it. At our last Cabinet meeting on February 6th they had accepted my proposal to include 30 lakhs receipts from the sugar cane cess, and by making various other adjustments reduced the revenue deficit to about 47 lakhs. They decided also to impose a two *annas* tax on the sale of petrol, which is estimated to bring in nearly 8 lakhs. This leaves a revenue deficit of about 40 lakhs. This they intended to cover by the tax on employment which I have reported separately. At our meeting on February 6th I stressed the legal point strongly with the aid of the information given in your telegram, and I think they were a

good deal shaken. Pant himself in fact has not I think any belief in it as a practical measure. Katju, however, who is said to be the author of the bright idea and who has I fear a somewhat vindictive outlook towards the higher paid Services in general, is engaged in looking up Privy Council rulings and Dominion cases, and if he can work out a plausible case (he seldom in matters like this aims at anything higher than plausibility) I think he will press the Cabinet to continue. If so, I shall open up with arguments on the merits, which at the Cabinet meeting on the 6th I kept in reserve. I tried to create the impression that really they could not depend on this source of revenue, and at the end put to Pant the plain alternatives of reducing their expenditure, seeking for another source of taxation, or leaving the deficit uncovered. He said that in view of their policy it was impossible to reduce their expenditure, agreed that it was going to be exceedingly difficult to find any other source of taxation, but revolted against leaving the deficit uncovered, for he has a strong financial conscience. Nevertheless, it seems to me at the moment most likely that that is what will happen.

9. As I mentioned in my last letter, the aggressive attitude of Hindus on Hyderabad Day produced a very marked deterioration in the communal situation just before the Bakr-Id. There was great nervousness in Lucknow, but nothing happened. Allahabad also apprehended trouble, which fortunately did not materialise. There was a riot at Bareilly directly arising out of Hyderabad Day celebrations, but the Bakr-Id itself passed off peacefully throughout the Province, which was a very satisfactory result.

10. I have written to Your Excellency separately about the clash between students and police in Aligarh. A number of Muslims have been seeing the Premier lately and urging him not to let the matter go too far. Sulaiman also has, though in a hesitating way, shown a disposition to express regret and offer some compensation and also tighten up discipline in future. On the whole I think it will be wise to settle if possible on these lines instead of having an enquiry; and in any case I feel sure that the Premier will insist on this, for he is anxious to avoid provoking a violent attack on his Government by the Muslim League. But I trust that the Government of India will look into discipline at the Aligarh University, and do what they can to have it pulled together.

11. I hope for the time at any rate conditions are quieter in Benares State. There appears to have been a serious outbreak of lawlessness which took the shape of cutting trees about the end of January. This was brought under control after a few days by outside influences, Nehru himself

apparently intervening. The Maharaja is about to announce a committee to consider constitutional reforms. He is very closely in touch with Sir Tej Bahadur Sapru who has been most helpful. We allowed one of our best deputy collectors to proceed on leave preparatory to retirement and take up the position of Chief Secretary, which is equivalent to Diwan, in the State. I hope the combination of these measures will assure a sufficient degree of tranquillity. I am sure my Government do not wish to have trouble in the Benares State, and there is a general recognition that the Maharaja is anxious to do what is reasonable. I have heard nothing about agitation in Rampur, and I understand that trouble is not expected there; nor am I aware of any movement in Tehri-Garhwal. The Diwan, Chakra Dhar Jayal, has just proceeded on three months' leave and his temporary absence (which I wish was permanent) will in my opinion reduce the likelihood of any trouble developing.

12. Hallett in a recent letter to Your Excellency mentioned sugar cane policy and referred to the fact that my Government had recently raised the minimum price of sugar cane contrary to the views of the Bihar Government. I have at various times had misgivings about the general policy, into which we entered with the very full support of the Bihar Government, of attempting to regulate and control the whole industry from top to bottom. The measures taken have undoubtedly had some valuable results, but they have also given rise inevitably to many difficulties. This year, finding sugar at the high price of Rs. 9 which the industry contended could certainly not be lowered, we fixed in consultation with Bihar a correspondingly high minimum price for sugar cane. The millowners maintained that it was too high to give them a fair profit, and not accepting the decision of the two Governments proceeded to raise the price of sugar by 8 *annas*. My Government were not prepared to allow this additional profit to the millowners and endeavoured at first to get them to reduce the price again. They argued and delayed and eventually my Ministers took the only other course that was open to them in accordance with their policy and raised the minimum price of sugar cane once more. I had not realised that in this last step they had not secured the agreement of Bihar, but in the particular circumstances of the United Provinces and given this policy of control I think the action taken was inevitable. We manufacture a very large quantity of *gur*, and the high price of sugar sent up the price of *gur*, with the result that sugar cane for *gur* manufacture was actually fetching a higher price than the minimum laid down for sugar cane supply to the mills. Normally it might have been possible to allow the cultivator to set a price above the

minimum through the ordinary operation of economic factors, but the co-operative societies through whose agency the supply of cane to the mills has been organised had entered into agreements to supply cane to the factories at the minimum price. Consequently the growers working through the cooperative societies were being made to supply cane to the mills at a price below the ruling market price. The raising of the minimum price of cane was strongly supported by our local officers. The sugar syndicate, i.e., the manufacturers, has been very indignant, but I think to a large extent they brought the trouble on themselves. I have continually pointed out to my Ministers the danger of this constant raising of the price of sugar and of sugar cane and the risk that we may cut our own throats by the process, and they appreciate the danger.

13. I fear the prospects of the move to Naini Tal are much less bright than they were. I think they have been affected by the change in political conditions. It was on the whole a right wing policy, and with the strengthening of the left wing I fancy it will be difficult to carry it through. No final decision however has yet been taken.

14. There is no expectation now that the Tenancy Bill can be completed in the Assembly during this month. The whole of March will be occupied by the budget, and it does not look as if the Tenancy Bill can be through the Lower House much before the middle or end of April. It will presumably go to the Upper House in May. There will be a very good opportunity then for compromise, and I hope this opportunity will be taken.

Yours sincerely,
H.G. HAIG

ENCLOSURE 1 TO NO. 11

CUTTING FROM THE *LEADER*,
DATED JANUARY 27TH, 1939

United Provinces Revenue Minister's Statement

The Hon'ble Mr. Rafi Ahmed Kidwai, Minister for Revenue, United Provinces, in the course of a statement to the Associated Press on the Congress Presidential Election says: "I have read the statements of Sardar Vallabhbhai Patel and the other members of the Working Committee with some surprise.[27] It may or may not have been advisable for Mr. Subhas Bose to have issued the statement he did after the retirement of Maulana Abul Kalam Azad, but surely it was not fair on the part of Sardar Patel and his other colleagues of the Working Committee to prejudice his candidature.

"In his counter-statement Mr. Bose has clarified the constitutional aspect of the question and there are many amongst us who share the Congress President's fears and apprehensions.

"Sardar Patel contends that it is the Working Committee which guides the activities of the Congress and the President is merely a figurehead, but he conveniently forgets that the Working Committee is the creation of the President, its composition depends on his will. It was a weakness on the part of both Mr. Jawaharlal Nehru and Mr. Subhas Chandra Bose to nominate Working Committees which were opposed to their politics and the situation we find ourselves in today is the result of this weakness."

Proceeding Mr. Kidwai says: "I will not go into the merits of the two candidates. But I would appeal to the delegates not to be prejudiced by the statements issued by the members of the Working Committee. We know them well enough to read between the lines. We know how they stood for wrecking the constitution. We have seen how this wrecking has been interpreted to mean the working of the constitution. This should enable us to anticipate what their rejection of the Federation would mean and our vote for Dr. Pattabhi Seetharamayya or Mr. Bose would be voting for accepting or rejecting the Federation respectively."

ENCLOSURE 2 TO NO. 11

CUTTING FROM THE *NATIONAL HERALD*,
DATED JANUARY 26TH, 1939

Almorah,
January 25th, 1939

Ready for the Order to March – "Our Knapsacks on our Backs"
Independence Day Resolve. Nehru's Call for Action
"No Peace for Us or Anyone Else"

A year ago I stood in Bannu town on Independence Day surrounded by a host of Khudai Khidmatgars and other men of the Frontier. We took the pledge together and, as was fitting, we took it in the Pushtu language. I had picked up a few words of this language during my Frontier tour and I tried to repeat the pledge word by word, together with the assembled multitude. Khan Abdul Ghaffar Khan, that gaunt and well-loved figure of the North, was the leader of this solemn chorus, and above our heads floated proudly the National Flag, emblem of that Independence to which we pledged ourselves.

Solemn ceremony. That day Khan Saheb took me to many other towns and villages and everywhere this solemn and significant ceremony was repeated and the pledge taken. The memory of that day clings to me and the earnest Pathan faces, taking that vow of freedom, form an unforgettable picture in my mind. To them it was no empty ritual, no ceremony without inner meaning, but a vital real thing, symbolising the long-suppressed desire of their hearts, which found some expression in words of promise and power. Thus we sealed our bond of brotherhood in the great cause of India's freedom.

Our success. Today I take the pledge again in another Frontier district of India, for Almora, though nearer to the heart of India, is yet one of the frontiers of this country, bordering on Tibet and Nepal. Another multitude gathers together from the distant valleys and the mountain tops, peasant folk from the borderland of Askote, a week's journey from here, and men and women from this ancient town of the Kumaun Hills, all assembled on this winter day in full view of the eternal snows, to take the pledge of independence.

Eight years have passed since we took this pledge for the first time, years heavy with sorrow for us and struggle but also with a measure of triumph and achievement. But though success has come to us, we know its meagre worth, and the promised land has yet to be reached when this pledge of ours will redeem itself.

And the world? War rages in the Far East and in Spain to the accompaniment of incredible and inhuman atrocities, and the black night of reaction covers Europe. Multitudes, tortured beyond endurance, become refugees and wander from one country to another, seeking home and shelter, and finding none.

Meaning of the pledge. What then does our pledge mean to us today, what significance does it have? Has it grown stale and meaningless through too much repetition, or is it still the vital spark of old which fired us to action and brave endeavour? Have we grown tired and complacent, tied up with offices and the petty routine of administration, thinking in terms of compromising with the evil with which there can be no compromise? Have we forgotten that we still form part of a slave empire which exploits us and keeps us embedded in dire poverty, and which strangles wherever in this world it fights for breath? Is it in this Empire that we will find redemption of our pledge?

There are some amongst us, whose memory is of the shortest, who have already forgotten the pledge they took and the many brave resolutions that they made. But we do not forget and we will not allow others to forget. We have pledged ourselves to win full independence, to put an end to imperialism in India, to sever our connection with the Empire that encircles us. By that pledge we stand.

State's challenge. We stand by it even more than we did eight years ago for that Empire has added to its sins by the butchery of democracy and freedom in Central Europe and Spain, and the crushing of the Arab people in Palestine. We will not forget this and in war or peace we shall fight this policy which hands over the world to fascism.

We stand by that pledge even more today because we have seen what petty change has come to us by provincial autonomy, and how imperialism still sits entrenched in the citadels. We see how India's will is repeatedly ignored in the interests of British finance and industry. We see from day-to-day the employment of British power to crush the people of the States. Ranpur is a wilderness today, and armed troops gather there from distant parts of India, in order to terrorise the people of the Orissa States. In Jaipur, an English prime minister[28] dares to challenge not only the people of the State but the Congress organisation itself, a challenge that will be accepted. Everywhere it is becoming apparent that the struggle in the States is not with the helpless Rulers but with the grim might of British Imperialism.

Is this the way in which the British Government seeks the cooperation of the nationalist movement in provincial autonomy and endeavours to prepare the ground for Federation? We have had enough of this foolery and the sooner it is ended the better.

Our path is clear. The time has gone by for empty and misleading talk. We are up against the hard realities of the situation and the pledge we take today tells us what path we have to tread and what our inevitable goal is. There is going to be no Federation in India of England's choosing. We will have no Federation except a Federation of a free India. To think or talk in other terms is to betray our pledge and to dishonour ourselves and our cause.

There will be no Federation, and the Provincial Autonomy of today must itself fade away and give place to an independent India, a bulwark of democracy and freedom, opposing fascism and imperialism alike. That is the meaning of the pledge.

And so we take the pledge realising its full significance and preparing ourselves for all that it involves. There is no peace or quiet for us or anyone else in the world today. We have to keep our knapsacks on our backs and be ready for the order to march. The peoples of Europe, in the vicious grip of fascism, and its allies, the Governments of England and France, stumble helplessly and seek in vain a path through the darkness that envelops them. But our path is clear.

JAWAHARLAL NEHRU

ENCLOSURE 3 TO NO. 11

CUTTING FROM THE *PIONEER*,
DATED FEBRUARY 8TH, 1939

Allahabad,
February 7th, 1939

India's "Problem of Problems"
Pandit Nehru on States Issue

"The Congress Presidential election has attracted, as it should, considerable attention," says Pandit Jawaharlal Nehru, in the course of a statement issued to the Press today, "though perhaps few people know all the facts or realise the background of this election. The Press is full of statements made by groups and individuals and the words 'Leftist' and 'Rightist' are bandied about without any regard to their meaning. There is a spate of good advice. The election will have served at least one good purpose if it serves to make us think clearly about the situation in India and abroad. Vague talk and loud assertions or criticisms do not make a 'Leftist' or 'Rightist' or help in drawing up a policy.

"*Petty matters.* It is necessary, therefore, that this talk and criticism should be confined to the narrow channels of reasoning and reality and should lead to a clear and precise definition of our policy, which should be the basis of our future action. The problem before us is the achievement of India's independence and the establishment of a free democratic state in India. It is from that point of view that everything should be judged. Yet we argue about relatively petty matters and think in terms of this office or that. Meanwhile, the world rushes ahead and bloody reaction grips it by the throat. Meanwhile India is shaken afresh by vast popular movements and at the same time disintegrating forces raise their ugly heads. How are we to meet the challenge?

"*Problem of Problems.* Today the problem of problems is that of Indian

States, of the peoples of these States who have patiently submitted too long already to autocracy and misrule. They will submit no longer and from the northern Himalayan passes to Kanyakumari in the far south millions of them are awake and moving to that freedom which has so long been denied to them. Today we face British Imperialism in one of its ugliest phases – that of patron and supporter of feudalism and slave conditions in the States. Today, as of old, Gandhiji is soft, but the iron voice of India is challenging this imperialism and preparing for the struggle with it. Everything else is secondary in this major struggle, for in its sweep it will comprise federation, provincial autonomy and other impediments to our freedom.

"Rajkot is in the grip of it already and that noble and beloved lady, Kasturbai,[29] has gone in her old age back to jail. Jaipur has accepted the challenge of imperialism, and India's faithful servant, Jamnalal Bajaj, has disappeared behind the prison walls. In Orissa, British imperialism gathers its armies to sustain the tyranny of corruption and degradation of the worst type and crush the newly arisen people in the States. In Travancore autocracy assumes Fascist colour and another struggle looms ahead. In Mysore there is the beginning of a conflict again. In the great States of Hyderabad and Kashmir popular movements are being crushed on the frivolous plea of communalism.

"We have grown complacent and petty-minded and forgetful of our great problems. But the call is coming to us again. India calls, and the call grows louder and more insistent. On your feet, men and women of India, on your feet. The time for marching approaches. On your feet."

12

HAIG TO LINLITHGOW
R/3/1/75

Private and Personal — *February 8th, 1939*
No. U.P.-223

My dear Lord Linlithgow,

With reference to Your Excellency's telegram No. 333-S of February 6th,[30] I have been carefully considering the question of our preparedness in the event of a break with the Congress, and as far as I can see, we should be generally ready.

2. The Government have just sanctioned the recruitment of 500 extra police (50 per cent civil and 50 per cent armed) on representations from

the Inspector-General,[31] which have been under consideration for some months, that this addition is essential to provide an adequate reserve to deal with the communal situation. These men are being enlisted at present and Horton anticipates no difficulty in obtaining recruits. Nor does he anticipate difficulty in obtaining whenever necessary the additional 2,000 men which he estimated as his requirements of recruits for an emergency situation, as stated in Donaldson's D.-O. letter to Maxwell (as Secretary to the Governor-General (Public)), No. 1084-G.S.P. of 28th February 1938. The other measures for strengthening the police force detailed in that letter would also be put into operation. He is, however, still short of 210 muskets and 800 bayonets out of the supply for which we indented in August 1937 to complete the equipment of the existing police force. He has been promised these by the middle of February and has been informed at the Arsenal at Allahabad that the Defence Department have issued orders that this supply is to be given priority. I trust there will be no delay about the supply of these. The importance of the matter was emphasised in paragraph 6 of Donaldson's letter to Thorne,[32] No. 1570-G.S.P., dated September 3rd, 1938. Budget provision for equipment for the 500 men now being recruited will be included in the Budget for 1939-40. That equipment has not yet been indented for and cannot in present circumstances be asked for until the Budget provision has been passed. There is, however, sufficient equipment to carry on with the recruit training of these men.

3. It is also a matter of great importance to secure provision of the reserve supply of 1,036 [?bayonets], 410 muskets, 84 revolvers and ammunition which was stated in the same letter of September 3rd from Donaldson to Thorne to be the Inspector-General's estimated requirement for the 2,000 additional police which it is proposed to recruit in the event of a grave emergency such as the revival of a Civil Disobedience campaign. These weapons were to be held in store at arsenals as a reserve for immediate issue. These are our immediate requirements, should it be necessary to expand the police force according to the plan drawn up. In Donaldson's letter to Thorne it was pointed out that it would not be possible to make an advance deposit of the cost of these reserve weapons, estimated roughly at Rs. 72,000, and that it seemed necessary that the Defence Department should manufacture them on credit and receive payment when the emergency arose. Nothing further has been heard from Thorne about this question, and a reminder has just been sent to him asking what the present position is. The provision of this reserve stock of arms is an urgent necessity and I hope that, if arrangements for its supply have not already been made, they can be put in hand at once with a minimum of delay. We

can arrange locally for the other equipment required for the expansion scheme, but must depend on the Central Government and the Defence Department for the arms and ammunition.

4. No further points have come to light in connection with the draft Section 93 Proclamation or the draft Governor's Act.[33]

Yours sincerely,
H.G. HAIG

13

HAIG TO LINLITHGOW
Telegram
R/3/1/75

Private and Personal *February 11th, 1939*
No. 209-G

I discussed today with Pant question relating to agitation against States. He said with regard to Jaipur that while the sentiments of Ministers were in favour of agitation they did not wish to go beyond policy of benevolent neutrality; but he could not agree to things being done which were in the interests of Jaipur State. He said he felt it would be necessary to take up question of Jumnalal being brought under restraint into the United Provinces (action which I should imagine was definitely illegal). He had also received reports that our Criminal Intelligence Department had been cooperating with Jaipur Police and that Young[34] had been in communication with the Superintendent of Police, Agra.[35] He has given instructions that these things should stop. I might mention that Jaipur does not at any point touch the United Provinces and it seems to me undesirable that we should be drawn into this controversy more than is necessary.

2. Pant also said he felt it was embarrassing for this Government to have Young, one of their officers, playing such a prominent part in this struggle and he proposed to ask Jaipur if they would kindly agree to his returning to the Province. I said this would require some consideration. He himself is obviously not clear about constitutional position and he therefore wishes to raise the matter only tentatively to begin with and not to recall Young. I think I shall have to let him make the proposed communication to Jaipur and indeed if later he presses the matter I doubt whether I have any authority to refuse to agree. But I should be grateful for Your Excellency's views and advice about this.[36]

3. On general question I asked Pant straight whether he was anticipating

trouble which might affect Provincial Government. He said he had no inside information and was dependent merely on statements he read in papers and conclusions he drew therefrom. He said if Gandhi felt a moral issue was involved he might press matters to an extreme point regardless of consequences and that it was not impossible that Provincial Governments would have to resign. I said I assumed he did not anticipate any very early developments in this direction. He agreed and said he did not think anything was likely to happen to affect us until after Congress Session.

14

HAIG TO LINLITHGOW
Despatch
R/3/1/75

Confidential
No. U.P.D./2

February 11th, 1939

Your Excellency,

I have the honour to inform you that in accordance with the instructions conveyed in Your Excellency's Despatch No. 159-G.G., dated January 28th, 1939,[37] I communicated to my Ministers the Secretary of State's Despatch No. 1 (Reforms), dated January 26th, 1939, on the subject of proposals to amend certain provisions of the Government of India Act, 1935. I attach herewith the observations of my Ministers who, as will be seen, prefer to make no detailed comments on the proposals.

I have the honour to be,
Your Excellency's most obedient humble servant,
H.G. HAIG

ENCLOSURE TO NO. 14

MINUTE RECORDED BY THE U.P. MINISTERS

February 11th, 1939

The Ministers have seen the proposed amendments to the Government of India Act. The Act was passed in the teeth of opposition from all sections of public opinion in India, which has declared it as being altogether unsatisfactory. The Indian National Congress has condemned its entire scheme. No useful purpose will be served by making minor amendments here and there as the situation calls for the replacement of the Act by a new constitution framed on different principles and by a different process altogether. In the circumstances the Ministers have no observations to make upon the merits of the proposed amendments.

15

HAIG TO LINLITHGOW
Telegram
R/3/1/75

Private and Personal *February 17th, 1939*
No. 211-G

Your Secretary's telegram No. 447-G, dated February 15th.[38] I have sent today fairly full information in my telegram No. 210-G,[39] which I hope will be sufficient for purposes of Parliament. I thought it advisable to show my draft to Premier. He made certain suggestions for amendment some of which I accepted.

2. I am not quite clear as to intentions of Secretary of State in regard to official report which he has asked for. I presume this means report from Provincial Government. It is possible however that my Ministers might object to making such a report particularly if they thought it was called for in censorious spirit. They may argue that they are responsible to the Provincial Legislature and not to the Secretary of State or Parliament. I am not quite clear about the constitutional answer to such a contention but it seems to me desirable if possible not to give occasion for raising this issue.

3. No constitutional objection of course could be taken to Secretary of State asking Governor to report in his individual capacity. But if this were to be treated as an official document it might again give rise to some ill-feeling on the part of Ministers. They might regard it as an exceptional course of action which circumstances hardly justified. They might point to the fact that with the Assembly in session there has been no kind of criticism from any quarter regarding effectiveness of measures taken at Cawnpore; and indeed the handling of the situation has been in marked contrast with that of the unfortunate Cawnpore riots of 1931.

4. I could easily send another telegram a few days later giving further information about the Cawnpore situation on the lines of my telegram of today if that would suffice for purposes of Secretary of State. Premier

recognises reasonableness of Parliament having full information as given in that telegram. If the matter could be left at the supply of information of this character as apart from an official report, I feel we should avoid possibility of ruffling the Ministers and creating some resentment.[40]

16

HAIG TO LINLITHGOW
R/3/1/75

Secret and Personal *February 23rd, 1939*
No. U.P.-226

My dear Lord Linlithgow,

I have seen Mrs. Pandit who returned from Wardha this morning and she gave me some interesting information and views which I pass on. I should be grateful if this is not repeated specifically to other Governors, for though Mrs. Pandit did not in any way pledge me to secrecy, I feel that she talked to me a good deal more freely than any of my other Ministers would have.

2. She said that Gandhi was seriously ill, and she doubted whether he would last more than a few months, though he might possibly go on living for a year. She felt also that he had no longer the grip on affairs that he used to have and he spoke not infrequently as if his work was practically finished. He seemed inclined not to go to Tripuri.[41] What she said suggested to me that he is no longer directing Congress policy with the same calmness and skill that he used to show, and I should guess that perhaps at the moment there is no real direction of Congress policy. Everything seems to be at sixes and sevens and no one appears to have any clear idea of what is going to happen.

3. She was evidently somewhat apprehensive in case a left-wing Parliamentary Board were appointed by Bose, as they might in that event come into conflict with the Ministries. She said that this would present difficult problems, as it would not be easy for the Ministry to continue, in opposition to the policy of the Parliamentary Board. At the same time she suggested as a possibility that the Ministry might not conform to instructions which they received from a left-wing Parliamentary Board. These are only her own personal ideas, but I should think this is probably a fair judgement of the situation.

4. With regard to the States she seemed to have no definite idea what action Gandhi intends to take. Indeed, perhaps he has not made up his

mind. She did not seem to think that Rajkot was really regarded as being of much importance, and I do not think, in spite of the statements that have appeared in the Press, she has any expectation of having to proceed there as a *satyagrahi*. She agreed with me as to the importance of avoiding as far as possible local conflicts and controversies with the States on our borders and seemed to think that if we could avoid these we should perhaps not find ourselves involved in the States issue on an all-India basis. I cannot of course be confident the Ministry as a whole would take this view, though I think that at present this does broadly speaking represent their attitude.

5. Incidentally I may mention that there has been in unfortunate affair in connection with the Orchha State which the Premier, urged on by Jawaharlal Nehru, is taking up vigorously. It seems that for some little time past demonstrations have been organised in State villages by Congress workers from British India. In this area State territory and British territory is inextricably mingled. In connection with a somewhat large demonstration of British Indian subjects organised in a State village adjoining the British village of Lohari, the Orchha State appear to have sent some armed police. They did not interfere with the demonstration, and the demonstrators dispersed. On their way back, however, a small party of the demonstrators appear to have met the force of State police, both parties being at the time in their own territory. It is said that the State police attacked the party of villagers in British territory and that a shot-gun was fired injuring some of the villagers. We are proposing to institute criminal proceedings against the State officers concerned, and the Political Agent[42] is being addressed with a request that the Durbar should cooperate. I shall discuss the whole question of this area with Pant as soon as possible, for it seems to me that the conditions are such as may very easily lead to a great deal of trouble.[43]

Yours sincerely,
H.G. HAIG

17

HAIG TO LINLITHGOW
R/3/1/75

Secret
No. U.P.-227

February 25th, 1939

My dear Lord Linlithgow,

With regard to the general political situation, I have little to add to the information which I gave Your Excellency in my secret letter No. U.P.-

226, dated February 23rd after the return of Mrs. Pandit from Wardha. The Ministers appear to be fully absorbed in their Provincial problems, and they do not seem to me to be seriously contemplating the possibility of all-India developments in Congress politics interfering with them. Pant remarked to me about a week ago that he was so constituted that he devoted himself to the matter in hand, and he certainly has had his whole attention on Provincial affairs, such as the Cawnpore riot and his budget. Kidwai about the same time told me that he did not expect that developments at Tripuri would affect us here.

2. The chief event since I wrote my last fortnightly report on 8th February was the very serious outbreak of communal rioting in Cawnpore. This started on the evening of February 11th and, except for one accidental clash on the morning of the 13th, the serious trouble was over by the evening of the 12th. That I think was a very satisfactory result, considering that Cawnpore is undoubtedly the most difficult and dangerous city in the whole of this Province, and I should judge one of the most turbulent in India. The District Magistrate[44] handled the situation very effectively and retained throughout the general confidence of the public. The military forces cooperated with the maximum of effectiveness as a result of plans carefully devised and discussed well in advance. The fact is that we have been fully aware for the last eighteen months that we might almost at any time have a serious outbreak in Cawnpore, and preparations have been made accordingly. The Inspector-General of Police[45] brought in with great promptitude substantial reinforcements of police which had to be drawn from a large number of districts. Though the actual rioting and murders were brought under control quickly, the temper of the two communities still remains exceedingly bad, and there has been a good deal of anxiety with regard to the approaching Muharram. Yesterday I heard that the Muslims in Cawnpore have decided not to take out their Muharram processions. The reason for this I am told is twofold. In the first place, it enables them to assert a grievance and to pretend that they were not receiving sufficient protection, though in fact the District Magistrate has offered them full protection for their Muharram processions. In the second place, I understand that they are really very nervous that whatever arrangements might be made, Muhurram processions might lead to a further outbreak of fighting and they do not wish to risk this. In the recent riots so far as casualties are concerned the Muslims came off the better, the Hindus having over thirty deaths and the Muslims only eleven or twelve. I gather they are somewhat apprehensive of retaliation with a view to making the numbers more even. I enclose in continuation of my report to the Secretary

of State[46] a copy of a statement made by the Premier in the Legislative Council on February 18th. The facts are practically the same as those given in my report, but he has added some timely acknowledgments.

3. The Muharram situation throughout the Province gives ground for considerable uneasiness. Practically every Commissioner comments on the aggressive and provocative nature of the Hyderabad Day demonstrations, to which I referred in my letter of February 8th, and the very serious and immediate deterioration of the communal situation which resulted. Hyderabad Day caused an immediate riot in Bareilly, and it was due to the same cause that some little time later there was a disturbance in Benares which fortunately did not spread very far. On top of this the riots at Cawnpore have created a great deal of uneasiness and ill-feeling throughout the Province. Our officers are of course very much on the alert everywhere, but it would be too much to expect that we shall get through the Muharram without disturbances somewhere. Our main anxiety, however, will be the possibility of a further outbreak in Cawnpore and Bareilly. Apart from the Hindu-Muslim trouble the Sunnis and Shias in Lucknow have during the last few days stirred up again the Madhe-Sahaba controversy, and it is by no means impossible that we shall have Sunni-Shia rioting in Lucknow before the Muharram is finished. All this means that our police resources are strained to their utmost, and I doubt if there has ever been a time when ill-feeling between the two communities has been so acute and dangerous.

4. When the Cawnpore riots had died down I took the occasion to speak to the Premier about the general underlying causes of this Hindu-Muslim antagonism, and put to him plainly my own view, that it would continue until the Congress made up their minds to admit the Muslims to some real share of power. I am perfectly convinced that nothing else will change the situation. What the Muslims resent is not any particular injustice or oppression (indeed they find it difficult to allege with plausibility any instance of this), but the fact that they are being ruled by the Hindus. Pant did not really dispute my diagnosis, but dwelt on the difficulties of forming a coalition which I recognise are considerable. Whatever the difficulties, however, I feel that sooner or later the Congress will have to accept this position, and I have little doubt that Pant will continue to ponder over it.

5. The budget was introduced yesterday and I enclose a copy of the Premier's speech.[47] I had already informed you of the main outlines and particularly of the proposed tax on employment. Pant's remarks about this are hardly likely to soothe the feelings of the Services. When he says that a tax which on the incomes of the higher paid services is practically

equivalent to an additional 2s. in the £ will not press hardly on the persons affected and that they are in a position to afford it without much inconvenience, I feel he is not taking a line calculated to soften the blow. I anticipate great antagonism on the part of the Services and also of the Cawnpore business interests which would be heavily hit by the proposed tax.

6. The Tenancy Bill is making fairly rapid progress, and with the aid of night sittings which are contemplated in March on top of days devoted to the budget debates, it is expected that the discussion on clauses will be finished about the end of March and that the Bill will be through the Lower House by the middle of April. Then comes the really crucial stage. My own view has been for a long time that it would be most desirable for the Government then to make a compromise which would enable them to get the Bill through the Upper House. I was surprised at a recent interview with Kidwai to find that he fully agreed and even went so far as to say that he hoped it would be possible to reach a compromise and that the Government would be prepared to make some concessions in order to reach that result. I hope the situation will work out on these lines. I saw Chhatari yesterday and found that he had had some conversation with Kidwai who had used much the same language to him. He is strongly in favour of a settlement if it can be reached, and I think the landlords as a whole would probably agree.

7. At a recent Cabinet meeting we discussed the question of the move to Naini Tal. This is intimately bound up with the legislative programme of the Government. They have an immense number of Bills still awaiting passage, and there seems to be rather a strong feeling that they cannot afford to give the Legislature a holiday, even for two months, though it has been sitting practically continuously since the beginning of November, but that they will have to go on with their legislative business without intermission. If in fact that were the position, the only sensible way of getting through their programme would be for the Legislature to meet in Naini Tal, and actually the Naini Tal Municipality are offering to find the necessary accommodation for them free of cost if they would come up for the whole season. This alternative is not absolutely ruled out at the moment, though I think it is unlikely that it will be adopted. On the other hand the attempt to make the Legislature work all through May and June in Lucknow may well break down, as there are limits to human endurance, and they are well aware of this danger. I think it is not impossible that in the end they will keep the Legislature sitting in Lucknow till perhaps the middle

of May and they break off for two months, allowing themselves and the much enduring Secretaries to go up to Naini Tal at that time.

8. I have recently seen the draft of the Village Panchayat Bill. Mrs. Pandit is said to be anxious to proceed with this, perhaps in consideration of the fact that her husband, R.S. Pandit, is one of the more prominent members of the committee which made the recommendations on which it is based. I hear that Pant is not particularly ready to press it forward; and if that is so, it speaks well for his political sagacity. The Bill in my opinion would stir up to the greatest degree possible the antagonism of the Muslims and the landlords, the former on account of a system of joint electorates, without even any special representation, which they will feel places them at the mercy of the Hindus in the villages; the latter on account of the loss of authority and new taxation involved. I very much doubt whether the Bill would even be appreciated by the villagers. Indeed, I think it would greatly accentuate the ordinary village feuds, and that the members of the Panchayats elected by Congress influence under the forms of extreme democracy might well find that when they attempted to exercise their powers, as they probably would in many cases, in an unjust or tyrannical way, their opponents rejecting the methods of democracy would use the argument of the lathi. The real object behind this Bill is I believe to try and rivet the control of the Congress on the villages, but as I have said I doubt whether in fact it would serve its purpose, though on paper it is exceedingly well calculated to this. One gets the impression rather of a Bill drafted by townspeople and theorists, which would not stand the test of practical application in the villages. There are also provisions in it which would affect my responsibilities.

9. I have kept you informed of the developments in our local situation as regards the States. I feel that at the moment the direction from which we may anticipate trouble is the area of little States intermixed with British territory adjoining our Bundelkhand districts. I have already communicated with you about the Orchha affair in this area.

10. We have had a report of an attempted derailment of a train on the East Indian Railway line not very far from the Bihar border and using apparently the methods employed in Bihar. The first idea was that it was a gang from Bihar that had come over to practise their activities in the United Provinces. We are prosecuting inquiries vigorously and are in touch with Bihar over this matter. I understand that some doubt has been thrown on the reality of this attempt and that it is felt that it may have been a fake. But it is too early yet to form any opinion. If it was a genuine attempt at

derailment, the Premier is exceedingly anxious to get to the bottom of this matter and pursue the inquiry effectively and vigorously.

11. The rain in the last few weeks has done much good, and though there will have to be remissions in certain areas, we shall not be faced with an abnormal situation.

Yours sincerely,
H.G. HAIG

ENCLOSURE TO NO. 17

SPEECH BY PANT IN U.P. LEGISLATIVE COUNCIL ON FEBRUARY 18TH, 1939

Rai Bahadur Babu Mohan Lal took the Chair.

Rai Sahib Lal Roop Chandra Jain: I would request the Government to make a full, detailed and up-to-date statement on the communal riot at Cawnpore and specially mentioning the points for future arrangements in the coming Muharram and Holi at Cawnpore.

The Hon'ble the Premier: Sir, I do not exactly understand what the Hon'ble Member wants to know and I am prepared to make a statement of the tragic events that happened in Cawnpore recently. But if he has anything more to ascertain that cannot be covered by my present statement, as it is necessarily to be restricted to questions of fact [*sic*]. Hon'ble Members will, I am sure, agree with me that the chief thing of the moment is restoration of confidence to return to normal, so that the citizens of Cawnpore may pursue their lawful vocations without any fear of disturbance or danger. I am sure that all Hon'ble Members of this House will share with me this desire to avoid communal acrimony and will do their best to assist the authorities and those who are exercising themselves with a view to bring about an improvement in the situation which has unfortunately undergone a deterioration during the last week. I should like to express my thanks to the Press once again for their admirable response, but for perhaps a little slip here and there, to my appeal [not] to write or say anything that would tend to hamper the growth of good feeling and that would stand in the way of the process of recuperation. Public interest centres in events at Cawnpore today and it is desirable that all those who have opportunities of influencing public opinion, whether by speech or by their writings, should exercise wholesome restraint and direct all their energies towards the achievement of the object which all lawful citizens all over this Province must at present have before them and towards which all efforts for the present should be directed and on which they should be concentrated. As I have been asked to make a statement about the recent happenings I will just say what had been the course of events. As Hon'ble Members are probably aware the riot broke out on the night of the 11th at about 8 p.m. at a place different from the area where the Bansmandi mosque is situated near which the disturbances had occurred on the 7th of February.[48]

The fighting between the communities spread to some other parts of the city and went on throughout the night of the 11th to the morning of the 12th. But for a serious clash on the morning of the 13th in Gwaltoli the situation was fairly quiet from the evening of the 12th and has been growing steadily quieter since. On the 12th, however, there were sporadic disorders accompanied in some cases, though I believe they were few, by worst features such as incendiarism. The police had to open fire more than once in the course of the day. Six platoons of the South Staffordshire Regiment, which had been mobilised as a precautionary measure on the night of the 11th, were later on posted to certain strategic points each accompanied at least by one Magistrate. The presence of troops rendered it easier for the police to carry on the normal duty of patrolling the disturbed areas, effecting arrests and dispersing the mobs. Firing, when it was necessary, was done by the police. On the 15th the situation was said to be rapidly returning to normal. The latest figures give the number of the killed as 42 and that of the injured as about 200. From the beginning of the outrage a number of arrests were made and in all some 800 persons had been arrested. In addition to the usual orders prohibiting carrying of weapons and the assembly of groups which had been enforced from the 7th February, a number of orders were issued imposing curfew and prohibiting the circulation of false rumours and shouting provocative slogans from roofs at night. As I mentioned above I invited the cooperation of the Press in refraining from saying anything that might give currency to provocative and alarmist reports or further complicating the situation and their ready and cordial response has had a salutary effect. It is reported that there is at present a rapid return to normal conditions and everywhere signs of restoration are visible. Most of the mills are working and shops are almost opening. Government were consistently in touch with the local authorities since the disturbance started on the 11th. The Commissioner of the division[49] and the Inspector-General of Police accompanied by the Deputy Inspector-General of Police[50] proceeded under instructions to Cawnpore soon after the 11th. Over 300 additional police had been drafted into

Cawnpore in addition to the full strength, and by the 13th, 750 extra police in all had been drafted. Medical assistance and stores and matresses were sent immediately from Lucknow. Prompt and effective measures were taken from the start and the situation which had the potentialities of repetition of 1931 was dealt in such a manner as to be speedily brought under control and to promote rapid restoration among the people of Cawnpore of better feelings.

Mills and shops, as I said, are opening. The *Kacheri* and courts are open today. Yesterday was a holiday. The conservancy staff are at work. And yesterday crowds enjoyed the bathing festival in a normal manner. I should like to state on my own behalf, and I believe I am here reflecting and representing the views of the Hon'ble Members of this House, when I express my appreciation of the work that the local authorities and those associated with them have done in bringing the situation under control. On all such occasions they are subjected to a very heavy strain and besides taking quick decisions they have to face difficult situations which develop quite unexpectedly in a city of the nature and extent of Cawnpore, as extensive and as varied in character as a commercial and industrial city can possibly be. I would also like to offer my thanks to all non-official bodies, the special European constabulary force, the Congress, the Sabha, the League and every other who were engaged in the work of rescue and relief. I am also obliged to the valuable assistance that was rendered by the troops. Now I hope all will agree with me that it is a sacred duty of everyone at present to devote the best in himself to the restoration of good feelings so that normal conditions may be restored and proper atmosphere may be ensured for the coming weeks which will see certain important functions in different parts of the Province.

18

HAIG TO LINLITHGOW
R/3/1/75

Confidential
No. U.P.-230

Camp,
March 4th, 1939

My dear Lord Linlithgow,

I am sending herewith a representation which I have just received this evening from my Ministers, urging that the Governor-General should intervene in the Rajkot dispute so that Mr. Gandhi's fast[51] may come to an end. I have told the Premier that I am forwarding his representation to you at once.

Yours sincerely,
HARRY HAIG

ENCLOSURE TO NO. 18

PANT TO HAIG

Lucknow,
March 4th, 1939

Dear Sir Harry Haig,

I and my colleagues view with the gravest concern the course of events which has now culminated in the fast undertaken by Mahatma Gandhi to induce the Thakore Sahib of Rajkot to honour the settlement arrived at between him and Sardar Patel on the 26th of December 1938. By this agreement the Thakore Sahib promised to set up a committee to draw up a report recommending a scheme of reforms "so as to give the widest possible powers to the people of the State consistently with his obligations to the Paramount Power and his own prerogatives as a Ruling Chief". This committee was to consist of ten members and seven of them were to be nominated on the recommendation of Sardar Vallabhbhai Patel. The letter of the Thakore Sahib dated 26th December 1938 runs as follows: "It is agreed that seven members of the committee mentioned in clause 2 of the State announcement of today's date are to be recommended by Sardar Vallabhbhai Patel and they are to be nominated by us." The Thakore Sahib went back on his solemn words some time later and not only did he modify the terms of reference to the committee but also declined to form the committee in accordance with the arrangements made with the Sardar. Mahatma Gandhi has striven his utmost to persuade the Thakore Sahib to keep his plighted word. It is a tragedy that owing to the persistent refusal of the Thakore Sahib to fulfil his solemn promise and his continued persistence in the wrong Mahatma Gandhi has been compelled to enter upon his fast for the reasons mentioned in his statement issued yesterday. From a perusal of the correspondence that was published by Sardar Patel about a month back and especially the notes of the talks that took place at the Residency on the 28th December 1938, it is evident that the British Resident[52] was annoyed over the arrangement that had been come to between Sardar Patel and the Thakore Sahib, with the result that under the influence of the Political Department the Thakore Sahib after about three weeks completely resiled from the solemn covenant mentioned above.

Apart from its political aspect and the harm done to the people of Rajkot the question has a moral aspect and Mahatma Gandhi has staked his life in order to vindicate the ethical principle, viz., that a promise made by a Prince to his people must be kept. Mahatma Gandhi's life is precious and at present his health is none too good. Anything that endangers his life is a matter of grave national concern and bound to give rise to very serious repercussions, and presumably the Thakore Sahib in adopting the present attitude feels assured of the support of the Political Department. I shall feel obliged if you will please press most earnestly on our behalf upon the Governor-General the urgent necessity of intervening in the matter, so that the Thakore Sahib may carry out the wishes of Mahatma Gandhi forthwith and the fast may come to an end.

Yours sincerely,
G.B. PANT

19

HAIG TO LINLITHGOW
Telegram
R/3/1/75

Immediate
No. 218-G

March 6th, 1939

In continuation of my telegram No. 216, March 4th.[53] I received no further communication from Premier yesterday nor did he ask to see me. This morning he has left for Benares by Air Mail in connection with serious communal riot and will return this afternoon. Before leaving he asked Chief Secretary to communicate to me verbal message to the effect that a very serious situation has arisen in which it would be difficult for Ministry to continue to discharge their responsibilities particularly if anything were to happen to G[andhi]. They therefore request me to urge Viceroy to intervene immediately to bring present impasse to an end. I hope to see Premier this evening and will telegraph again. He leaves for Tripuri tomorrow.

20

HAIG TO LINLITHGOW
Telegram
R/3/1/75

No. 219-G *March 6th, 1939*

I send for your information and communication to Secretary of State brief report on the communal riot at Benares and some recrudescence of further trouble at Cawnpore. For several weeks communal feeling had been strained at Benares. Report received on afternoon of March 4th stated that serious communal riot had broken out. The Company of troops stationed at Benares was called out and reinforcement of police totalling 580 and additional troops – one Company from Allahabad and one from Fyzabad – were sent. Situation reported under control by night of March 5th, total of casualties some 40 killed and 200 wounded. Situation quieter during night except for cases of arson and well in hand this morning. Additional District Magistrate[54] sent to assist District Magistrate.[55] Deputy Inspector-General of Police,[56] and Additional Superintendent of Police[57] also present. The precipitating cause of the riot is not known, but general cause of communal tension resulting in regular attacks of mob of one community upon another, arson, looting and murder. Six Magistrates have been drafted in for duty with Military.

Troops had to resort to firing once under orders of District Magistrate and Police also had to fire. Twenty-four hours' Curfew Order is in force. Holi is being celebrated today under restrictions, no coloured-water being allowed to be thrown.

At Cawnpore fresh trouble occurred on March 3rd – no less than 11 cases of stabbing taking place, of which 7 were fatal. Passers-by were searched for arms and 3 persons immediately arrested and convicted. Situation is well under control but there is possibility of danger owing to Holi festival. Troops as measure of precaution are patrolling street. Direct cause is not known but clearly communal in origin.

21

HAIG TO LINLITHGOW
Telegram
R/3/1/75

Immediate *March 7th, 1939*
No. 219 [?220]-G

My telegram No. 218-G of March 6th. Premier did not return to Lucknow till this morning. I have just had a talk with him. While not taking pessimistic view of possibility of fast coming to an end, he regards resignation in the event of Gandhi's death as inevitable. I asked him to consider what would happen then. Would this merely be an automatic emotional reaction which could be retraced when emotion had died down, or would it lead to a complete breakdown. He said given present exceedingly complicated situation it was more probable that breakdown would be complete and not remediable.

2. Premier will leave for Tripuri either this evening or tomorrow. He has really been detained by communal situation. He says that if anything happens to Gandhi a joint policy will certainly be devised at Tripuri and that is why in spite of communal situation he feels to go there and participate in discussions.

22

HAIG TO LINLITHGOW
R/3/1/75

Confidential Camp,
No. U.P.-231 *March 8th, 1939*

My dear Lord Linlithgow,

With reference to my despatch No. U.P.D./2, dated February 11th, 1939, forwarding the observations of my Ministers on the subject of the proposed amendment of certain provisions of the Government of India Act, 1935, I have to report that I received today the attached communication which I am informed represents the views of all the Ministers. The Hon'ble Premier has requested me to have its substance cabled to the Secretary of State today, the Government of India being also informed. I do not appreciate the necessity for sending this communication by cable to the Secretary of

State, but I forward it at once to Your Excellency and would request that it should be transmitted to the Secretary of State either by telegram or post as may seem most appropriate.[58]

Yours sincerely,
HARRY HAIG

ENCLOSURE TO NO. 22

NOTE BY PANT

March 7th, 1939

With reference to the amendments proposed to be made in the Government of India Act, the Ministers expressed the view that the situation called for the replacement of the Act by a new constitution framed on different principles and by a different process and they also drew attention to the fact that even the Government of India Act had been passed in the teeth of public opposition from all sections of public opinion in India and that no useful purpose would be served by making minor amendments. In the circumstances they hoped that the Secretary of State would at least not proceed further with the proposed amendments. It appears, however, from the reports that have recently appeared in the press of certain answers to questions put in Parliament that this is not the case. The Ministers consider it necessary therefore to express their strong disagreement with the proposal embodied in draft Section 126-A, as it tends to restrict further whatever little power the Provincial Governments possess in this connection under the Government of India Act. This proposal in substance is to invest the Centre with all executive authority in the provinces whenever the Governor-General in his discretion makes a declaration of the nature prescribed in Section 102 of the Act. In this way the authority of the Provincial Government can be completely crippled by the Central Government. The provinces will have no voice in the decision of issues relating to war and peace as under the scheme of the Act it is not even necessary to consult them in these matters. There is besides no all-India authority responsible to the people possessing an effective voice in this regard. Thus by these amendments the provincial administration may be forced to deal with matters of vital concern regardless of the wishes of the people and without exercising any choice of its own. The Provincial Government must definitely and unequivocally oppose any amendment of the Act which detracts from the authority of the Provincial Governments, already limited and crippled as it is, and tends to make it an involuntary and unwilling agent of the Central Government or transfers the executive authority in the Province to the Centre in any contingency.

23

HAIG TO LINLITHGOW
R/3/1/75

Secret
No. U.P.-233

March 8th, 1939

My dear Lord Linlithgow,

The subject that has occupied public attention almost exclusively for the last few days has been Mr. Gandhi's fast, and the news of the settlement arrived at yesterday will I think be a cause of universal relief. Whatever may be our views on the ethics of the Mahatma's fasts, there is no doubt that his death in these circumstances would have created a great wave of feeling which would have swept away the Congress Ministries and might well, as I reported to Your Excellency yesterday as the view of my Premier, have brought about a breakdown of the constitution which could not have been remedied. It is therefore very satisfactory that these dangers should have been averted, and that a settlement has been reached which I feel will be generally regarded as perfectly reasonable and which will I think enhance the position of the Viceroy in the general estimation.[59]

2. My Ministers have now all departed for Tripuri, and we must await developments there, on which I am in no position to speculate. Recent events have seemed to most observers to emphasise the fact that the Ministers are very anxious to retain office and are profoundly interested in our provincial problems. When I saw Pant yesterday the possibility of having to resign over Gandhi's fast and the consequences of such resignation weighed upon him. This being my impression, I was surprised to receive today the very strongly worded protest about the proposed new Section 126-A of the Government of India Act which I have forwarded to you separately. I was at first inclined to think this might represent a joint policy determined by the Congress and might indicate that they intend to make this particular provision in the amending Act an important issue. It is quite likely, however, that it merely represents a part of the Ministry's elaborate window-dressing which has been going on in preparation for

Tripuri, with a view in this case to making it clear that they are very advanced Congressmen indeed.

3. In my last letter I gave some account of the Cawnpore riots. Since then the continuing state of ill-feeling between the two communities, which I referred to, has issued in further outrages. There have been a number of stabbing cases which have increased the ill-feeling and distrust still more, and the authorities have to remain constantly vigilant. I hope that after the Holi conditions will gradually improve, but the underlying tension will remain. We have also had, as I reported to you in a separate telegram, a serious outbreak at Benares involving the reinforcement of our strength there by over 500 police and two additional companies of troops from outside. As happens often in these cases, the city flared up suddenly and disorders seem to have spread very widely; but within about twenty-four hours the authorities seem to have been well in control again. I have suggested to the Premier that our recent experience greatly strengthens the case of a further addition to the police on top of the 500, which he agreed to some weeks ago.

4. The Premier is greatly worried by these communal riots, as well he may be. I think there had been some criticisms on the part of his political opponents about his not going to Cawnpore when the serious riot broke out there. Anyhow, he flew over to Benares two days ago and discussed the situation thoroughly with the local officers, and has also twice recently visited Cawnpore to satisfy himself about conditions. But, however, effectively these riots may be put down, and they have in fact been dealt with well and promptly, the Government cannot but be held responsible by public opinion for the conditions of acute antagonism which are leading to so many disturbances which upset the life of the Province. I have again taken the opportunity since the Benares riots to impress on the Premier the views which I explained in paragraph 4 of my letter No. U.P.-227, datcd February 25th. He himself volunteered on this occasion that one of the great difficulties he was up against was that there was really no specific grievance either in Cawnpore or Benares the remedying of which would restore good feeling, and I pressed on him again my view that the only remedy was to get down to the root causes which to my mind are quite plain. He told me that he would be talking these things over at Tripuri, and I hope he may try to induce some change of policy on the part of the Congress which would enable us to heal our communal dissensions in this Province.

5. Before Mr. Gandhi's fast intervened, the main topic of interest in the Province was the proposed tax on employment. This has naturally enough

roused very strong feeling among those who have been singled out for this impost. The *Leader* and the *Pioneer* have been full of very damaging criticisms, the *Leader* in particular taking an extremely strong line against the tax. The *Statesman* correspondent on the other hand was content to put the propaganda of the Ministers and thus to misrepresent the real feeling on the subject. When he went so far as to suggest (at the instance, as I know, of one of the Ministers) that my assent to the Bill was expected without delay, I had the correspondent sent for and rebuked. Since then he has changed his tone. If it were not for a fairly general belief that the tax will be found to be illegal, the indignation in service quarters would I think be much more pronounced. But even as it is, there is a very strong feeling. The Inspector-General of Police mentioned to me yesterday that the Deputy Superintendents and Inspectors of Police were greatly perturbed.

6. Sir Jwala Prasad Srivastava appears to be taking advantage of the situation to try and organise widespread opposition to the Ministry. I have already mentioned in my Memorandum of the 19th December 1938, the general sense of dissatisfaction which prevails among the middle classes, shopkeepers and industrialists. This tax is a very heavy blow against the middle classes. There was at first some feeling among those who had not been directly affected, such as the professional classes or shopkeepers, that they had better keep quiet; but Srivastava is clearly doing his best to work up a general combination among the taxable classes against the policy of new and heavy taxation on which the Ministry are represented as having embarked and which they will have to pursue still more vigorously if they are to carry out their professed policy of abandoning the whole of the excise revenue. On this platform he evidently thinks it may be possible to rally all the vested interests and conservative opinion including the landlords, and I understand it is intended to have a big public meeting in Lucknow about the middle of the month, over which Sir Tej Bahadur Sapru will preside, with a view to launching an organisation to be spread throughout the Province to oppose all such taxation measures. Such an organisation might become an influence of some importance in the political world. Nobody likes having his pocket touched, and the Ministry have now gone so far in the direction of a policy of taxation all round as to have stirred up a great deal of uneasiness and opposition. It will be interesting to see whether this movement does in fact develop and provide the common ground of opposition which has hitherto been rather markedly lacking.

7. I mentioned in my last letter the attempted derailment of a train on the E.I.R. line not far from the Bihar border. When I wrote there was some

doubt whether it was a genuine case; but since then I have seen reports from the D.I.G., C.I.D.,[60] who has been looking into the case personally, and there is no doubt that it was a serious attempt and indeed that it was very fortunate that it did not lead to disaster. Our C.I.D. consider that this case, in conjunction with the recent cases in Bihar, points strongly to these derailments being the work of a revolutionary gang with their headquarters in Bihar. I understand that the Bihar police are disposed to favour the theory that these incidents are the work of discontented railway servants. But I must say that I am impressed by the arguments and facts brought forward by our own C.I.D. and I think it is more likely that we have to look for a revolutionary gang as the source of these activities. Our C.I.D. are in close touch now with the Bihar police and we are patrolling the line in the area adjoining Bihar.

8. I have been in correspondence with the Resident in Central India[61] both about the Orchha incident and the conditions in Tori-Fatehpur, and things seem at present quieter. Pant's attitude has been very reasonable, but it remains to be seen whether he can control the activities of the local Congress workers.

9. I had a talk recently with Sampurnanand, my Education Minister, about the grant to the Boy Scouts Association. He had announced some months ago his intention of discontinuing the grant. I spoke to him on the subject and suggested that provided the two Associations worked in harmonious relations, there was no reason why the Boy Scouts Association should lose their grant. Actually both Associations adopted a reasonable attitude in some conversations which were thereupon initiated, and I had some hope that the Boy Scouts Association would get their grant. But eventually the file came back from Sampurnanand with a note saying that he was afraid satisfactory arrangements could not be made and the grant could not be given. I asked him to come and see me and explain what the difficulties were. He was considerably embarrassed, and it was perfectly clear that there were in fact no difficulties, but that for political reasons the Ministry had definitely decided to withdraw the grant from the Boy Scouts Association. I said that I hoped at any rate this need not be taken as a permanent decision and he said that when feeling had changed, as it might, he hoped the matter might be reconsidered. He also explained that it had decided, though with some hesitation, to continue the grant to the Girl Guides.

10. Sampurnanand takes sometimes an unexpected view of things. The Principal of the Meerut College, Col. O'Donnell, is due for superannuation. He has an excellent influence in the college and is very popular there with

the students. There has been a strong move locally to get him an extension, but the Agra University for reasons which are said to be not solely based on principle have set their face against this. I was not prepared to interfere, though the Commissioner[62] wrote to me privately on the subject. But Sampurnanand himself wrote on the Secretariat file that he regarded it as most important that Col. O'Donnell should be kept on for a further term and asked whether I would be good enough to represent the matter to the Vice-Chancellor.[63] I have written to the Vice-Chancellor, though I doubt whether anything will come of it. But this shows that Sampurnanand is prepared to go out of his way to retain a European if he thinks he is really doing valuable work. I called his attention at the same interview to the report of a speech which he made at Agra in which he was said to have expressed some very astonishing views about the British Empire. He said that he spoke in Hindustani and that the report gave a wrong impression of what he said. I do not know whether reporters do in fact colour and misinterpret speeches made in Hindustani, but the Ministers are always inclined to explain away on this ground reports of less desirable utterances with which they may be credited.

11. An appointment which might have given rise to some little difficulty has been settled recently in a way which is very satisfactory to me. We are losing our I.G.C.H. and the senior officer available for the post was Col. Boyd, at present in Calcutta, who is very well spoken of. The Premier, however, said frankly that he would like, if possible, to have an Indian, and the next senior man was an Indian I.M.S. officer serving in Bengal who had quite good reports, though it seemed evident he was not as capable as Boyd. Brabourne[64] was good enough to give me some information about the two men, and after I had pointed out that I did not think there could be any reasonable justification for not taking the senior and apparently the best qualified man, the Premier agreed to the appointment of Boyd. I think to a large extent the position is that though the Ministers do not want to be unjust to European officers and appreciate their value in certain positions, they definitely prefer on the whole to have Indians.

12. I was very glad to get your letter of March 2nd, which gave me some interesting views about the major problems in India. You mentioned among other topics the question of German influence at Aligarh. Ewart[65] was actually staying with me when I received from the Collector the report[66] about these activities which you refer to, and I asked him whether he could let us know in due course what importance he attached to them. I have had no further information from our officers, but I will keep my ears open and let you know if anything more comes to my notice. We have

been so busy with other things lately that I have not been able to give much attention to Aligarh, but my general impression remains that the state of discipline is far from satisfactory.

Yours sincerely,
H.G. HAIG

24

HAIG TO LINLITHGOW
R/3/1/75

Confidential *March 9th, 1939*
D.-O. No. U.P.-234

My dear Lord Linlithgow,

Though I have made some passing references in our correspondence to the state of progress with the Government's scheme for the separation of executive and judicial functions [of magistrates], I have not addressed you separately about this question since the receipt (in Hallett's time) of Your Excellency's telegram No. 867-G of June 23rd, 1938, conveying the views of the Secretary of State on the points discussed in your letter of May 25th.[67] The detailed history of this question subsequent to my letter No. U.P.-75, dated May 7th, 1938, has been as follows:

At a Cabinet meeting on June 9th, 1938, my note of 6th May 1938 (of which a copy was sent to you with my letter of May 7th) and a note by Hallett dated 24th May 1938 on the same lines were considered. It was decided to appoint a special officer to work out a detailed scheme. The Cabinet decision was recorded in the following terms: "The scheme for the separation of judicial and executive functions was considered in detail and approved in main outline and it was decided to appoint a special officer to put up proposals working out the scheme in detail." This is mentioned in paragraph 3 of Hallett's fortnightly report No. U.P.-90 of June 17th. Dible, Commissioner of Agra, was the officer selected to prepare a detailed scheme. He issued a circular letter to district officers dated June 29th, 1938, explaining the lines on which he proposed to work. A copy of this circular was sent by Donaldson [?who] also had some further correspondence with Thorne about the opening sentence of Dible's circular (vide his letter No. 1545-G.S.P. of August 26th, 1938). Dible's completed report is dated 24th August 1938. A summary of the main features was sent to Thorne in Donaldson's letter No. 1580-G.S.P., dated September 7/

8th, 1938. In November 1938 the India Office asked privately for two copies of Dible's report, and these were sent to them but without the detailed appendices.

2. Hallett had some discussion with Dible at Naini Tal about his report. The Government, however, took no apparent action on it until December 1st. It was being examined in a desultory way in the Chief Secretary's department and in the Judicial department. On December 8th, Katju recorded a long note accepting Dible's proposals in the main but making one or two alterations in points of detail. He recorded his appreciation of the ability and thoroughness of Dible's report. He directed that the High Court, Chief Court and the Board of Revenue should be consulted officially on the scheme as amended by him. A letter explaining the scheme was then drafted and sent to these authorities asking for their views on various points. I may here mention that Dible's scheme had not been brought before the Cabinet and the intention was to do so at some subsequent date with the opinions of the High Court, Chief Court, &c. However, shortly before the day on which the Budget was to be presented, February 24th, 1939, and apparently in consideration of urgent political requirements arising out of the result of the Congress presidential election, there was a great drive in Government circles to introduce into the Legislature a number of Bills on various subjects which were under consideration in the draft stage. The Judicial Secretary[68] was also told to get a note summarising Dible's scheme as subsequently modified printed up as quickly as possible. The note embodying the scheme was laid on the table of the Assembly on 24th February by the Hon'ble Minister for Justice.[69] The scheme was described as "provisional" and was laid before the Legislature, as stated in the first paragraph of the note, "for information and discussion". The official report of the proceedings of that day has not yet been received, but from the journal of the House and newspaper reports it seems that there was no speech by the Minister or discussion of the scheme. I attach a printed copy of the note[70] for easy reference. Copies have already been sent to Thorne and to the India Office.

3. The note follows Dible's scheme in main outline but only explains the mechanism and does not touch on the questions of the personnel required, the cost, or whether as advised by Dible a small scale experiment should first be undertaken. The Ministry has been for a long time publicly committed to some action towards the separation of executive and judicial functions in the magistracy. Dr. Katju has made various statements on the subject from time to time, but latterly more often when reminded about the matter by questions or motions in the Assembly than spontaneously.

My impression is that there is now no real keenness among the Ministry for these proposals, but that they feel bound by their previous statements to proceed with them. Katju is probably more in favour of them than the others. The proposals are in the nature of a compromise. Dible's view of them was that if something had to be done on these lines to satisfy the "popular demand" this was the least harmful method of doing it. While reserving my opinion on certain details of the scheme – and particularly paragraph 3(*b*) of the printed book, the proposed functions of Executive Magistrates in regard to police charge sheets – my general view is that if the Ministry after ascertaining the opinion of the Legislature on these proposals show eagerness to go on with them they should be allowed to proceed with the experiment. I do not feel that with a scheme of this nature I could oppose it on the ground of my special responsibilities. The Government is not at this stage definitely committed to this scheme. Dr. Katju has informed me that it will certainly come up for discussion during the budget debates. I warned him not to commit the Government to any definite conclusions, and he has promised me that he will not. After the debate the proposals will have to be considered finally in Cabinet, and it is only after that stage that I shall be in a position to send proposals definitely to the Secretary of State for his approval. With the extensive legislative programme which is before the Ministers and their other preoccupations it may be some time before any further move takes place about this.

Yours sincerely,
H.G. HAIG

25

HAIG TO LINLITHGOW
R/3/1/75

Secrct — *March 20th, 1939*
No. U.P.-236

My dear Lord Linlithgow,

My attention has just been drawn to the publication of a new paper at Meerut under the name of *Sipahi*, which under the guise of dealing with grievances of Indian soldiers appears clearly intended to encourage disaffection among them and failure in their duty. A copy of the letter of our Special Branch, dated the 18th March, and the review of the first number of the *Sipahi* has already been forwarded to the D.I.B.'s office, but I attach copies for easy reference. I have also sent a copy of these papers to the General Officer Commanding-in-Chief, Eastern Command,[71] and have also informed the General at Lucknow.[72] I shall be taking up at once with the Premier the question of action against this paper.[73] I anticipate difficulty with him, because though he may be prepared to agree to a prosecution of the editor, if we are advised that prosecution is likely to be successful, he will, I fear, object strongly to action under the Press Act, which in my opinion is the most effective action that can be taken. His objection to the whole principle of the Press Act is so strong that hitherto he has definitely refused all proposals to make any use of it, though in fact communal incitements in the Press, which he is most anxious to put down, could be controlled far more effectively by the use of the Press Act than by the various half measures which he approves.

2. I should be glad to know as early as possible what Your Excellency's views are on this matter, particularly in the light of information about the activities of the Hindustani Fauji Mission. The real question is whether it is one on which, if necessary, I should press my view to the point of insisting on its being carried out contrary to the views of my Ministers, which would presumably provoke a serious crisis. I trust that this situation may not arise, and that the Premier may show himself responsive to argument in the special case of an attempt to tamper with the loyalty of the Army, but I think it quite possible that the Ministers will absolutely decline to make use of the Press Act.[74]

Yours sincerely,
H.G. HAIG

ENCLOSURE 1 TO NO. 25

WALSH TO GWYNNE

C.I.D., Special Branch, U.P.,
Lucknow,
March 18th, 1939

My dear Mr. Gwynne,

I forward herewith a review of No. 1, Vol. I, of the Urdu Weekly *Sipahi*, dated February 13th, 1939, edited by Kedarji and published by Thakur Kedarji from the *Sipahi* Office, Kutcherry Road, Meerut and printed by Pt. Sri Nivas Sharma at the Ajay Printing Press, Meerut.

It seems clear that this paper is being issued entirely for the benefit of Indian soldiers. This is an Urdu edition but information has been received that Hindi and English copies will also be published.

The whole tone of the paper is such as to cause disaffection amongst Indian troops and certain passages in some of the articles are particularly objectionable. *Vide* page 3, one of the objects of the paper is to protect the rights of the Indian martial classes in general and Indian military officers and sepoys in particular. On page 4 of the review in the article "Federal scheme of India and India" the threatening international situation is referred to and it is mentioned that in the event of a world war India should not help England unless her demands are fulfilled. Past experience has taught India that Britain does not keep her promises and the mistake committed in 1914 should not be repeated.

As this paper is obviously issued solely for military consumption this article amounts to incitement to Indian soldiers to refuse to obey the orders of their officers should war break out.

The article entitled "Misrepresentation of Indian History" is by Ram Manohar Lohia, a well-known communist.

These are only a few of the objectionable statements in the paper. The cumulative effect of the various articles would in my opinion certainly cause disaffection amongst Indian troops if widely broadcast amongst them.

We have as yet no information as to the extent this paper has been circulated but inquiries on this point are being made. I am told that a paper of the same name dated 19th February has appeared in Lucknow and am making inquiries about this.

In my opinion, this paper is highly dangerous and I recommend that it be proscribed.

Yours sincerely,
E. WALSH

ENCLOSURE 2 TO NO. 25

REVIEW OF THE URDU WEEKLY *SIPAHI* (SEPOY), VOL. 1, NO. 1, DATED 13TH FEBRUARY 1939

No. P.-1-32/1939

The paper is the first issue of the *Sipahi* (Sepoy) an Urdu Weekly which has been started with the object of pushing ahead the Hindustani Fauji

Mission propaganda. It announces that it will endeavour to protect the rights of Indian soldiers and officers of India's defence forces, and will fight for the removal of their legitimate grievances. The paper disapproves of the Indian as well as foreign policy of the British Government and urges Indians to prepare themselves for protecting their life and property and the honour of their women in the event of a World War which is imminent.

The paper is likely to undermine the loyalty of Indian troops. A note on each article is given below.

The title page bears a drawing of an Indian Military Officer. It also has a poem entitled "A word to the sepoy" with the refrain "O sepoy! draw the blood-quaffing sword". It says that each particle of India's dust sings the praises of the sepoy and the whole nation looks up to him with hopeful eyes. He is the hope of the oppressed and the nation is proud of his sword. (The poem is incomplete and will be continued in the next issue.)

The second page gives pictures of destructive weapons of war which have recently been invented with a view to their utility in the impending Armageddon. Page 3 reproduces messages of greetings and good wishes for the "Sipahi".

Under the caption "Comments and Opinions" there is a long article on pages 4 and 6 criticising the bona fides of the Sandhurst Committee.[75] It is said that the Military Department over which the representatives of the country have no control, has always opposed the idea of Indianisation of India's army; but the pressure of public opinion and the growing dissatisfaction in India against British troops compelled the Government of India to open a Sandhurst College at Dehra Dun in pursuance of the recommendations of the Indian Sandhurst Committee. The Committee had also recommended that five years after starting, i.e. in 1938 there should be a review of the pace of Indianisation. The Central Assembly passed a resolution at its Simla session on August 2nd, 1938, recommending to the Governor-General in Council that a committee consisting of elected members of the Assembly should be appointed to implement the recommendations of the Indian Sandhurst Committee. In pursuance of that resolution a committee has now been formed but contrary to the recommendations of the Central Assembly nominated members have been taken instead of elected members.

The paper strongly disapproves of the personnel of this newly formed committee and remarks that the nominated members are virtually the representatives of the Crown. Such a committee of puppets who dance to the tune of the Government can render no useful service to the country.

Turning to the terms of reference of the committee the paper says that the real issue – Indianisation of the Army – has been side-tracked. This has revived the suspicion which lurks in the minds of Indians in general and Indian sepoys in particular that the British Military Officers do not want to accede the right of protecting their country to Indians. This "cunning policy" of the British Military Officials is bound to have repercussions on Indian Military Officers and sepoys who are tongue-tied on account of rigid military discipline and the scant courtesy shown to public opinion is bound to prove ominous.

The leading article on page 5 introduces the *Sipahi* to the public. It points out that the Hindustani Fauji Mission movement was initiated more than a year ago and details of the activities carried on in this connection have been appearing from time to time in the columns of influential papers of the country. But in this "age of propaganda" no movement can succeed without an intensive propaganda through the Press. The *Sipahi* has been started to push ahead the propaganda of the Hindustani Fauji Mission. The paper "will protect the rights of Indian martial classes in general and Indian Military Officers and sepoys in particular. It will endeavour its utmost to get their legitimate grievances redressed. Also it will freely express its unbiased opinion in regard to other political matters of importance....The objective of the Fauji Mission is to infuse a new life in the country so that our dear motherland which is today shaking off the fetters of subjection that held her for ages, may remain perpetually free."

[*A page of the text is missing at this point.*]

alien Imperialist rulers of India have deliberately falsified Indian History to gain their ends and the history which is taught in schools and colleges today is replete with mis-statements. For instance, some historians hold that British rule was established in India a hundred and eighty years ago while others declare this period to be two centuries but the fact is that British rule in India dates from the year 1857 when the Mutiny was suppressed, which means that the British Government has been in existence in India for eighty years only. And even after 1857 there were rebellious movements in Bengal and Maharashtra. The various emancipatory struggles which have been fought under the banner of the Congress and which the Government tried to crush with violence rather go to show that India was never completely subjugated by the British Government.

Lastly, on page 15, the paper sets forth the aims and objects of the Hindustani Fauji Mission. They are:

1. To fight for the cause of Indian sepoys and their dependants.

2. To make arrangements for military training to be imparted to suitable candidates from amongst the sons of Indian soldiers.

3. To propagate patriotism in the martial classes of India.

4. To make India self-sufficient in the matter of defence.

It is pointed out that the activities of the Hindustani Fauji Mission will be confined to matters connected with India's defence forces. The Mission will also protect the rights of the martial races which supply recruits. Through the columns of the *Sipahi* the Mission will always endeavour to get the legitimate grievances of Indian Military Officials and sepoys redressed.

The paper points out that illiterate and uncivilised tribes live on the Frontiers of India and they are ever prepared to spill the blood of their brethren for petty gains. It is surprising that these tribes are regarded by British Military Officers to be the best source of suitable material for the Army. Although it is undeniable that the sepoys recruited from these warrior classes are very loyal yet the fact remains that they give and take life for a few copper coins. They do not know that their masters pay them to fight against their own brethren. The Hindustani Fauji Mission has therefore been founded to spread civilisation among the martial races and to infuse in them military spirit in the true sense of the word so that they may be able to maintain internal peace in their country and save her from foreign aggression.

26

HAIG TO LINLITHGOW
R/3/1/75

Secret
No. U.P.-237

Camp,
March 25th, 1939

My dear Lord Linlithgow,

When I last wrote, my Ministers were at Tripuri. One might have supposed that with Pant playing such an important and apparently successful part there[76] they would have returned in good heart and pleased with themselves. They returned, it is true, to meet some very damaging criticisms of their budget, and this would have served rapidly to batter them out of any undue complacency. But I certainly saw no signs among my Ministers of any elation on their return. I was myself disposed to discount a good deal of the Press propaganda representing Tripuri as great victory for the right wing.[77] It seemed to me that the real lesson of Tripuri was that there were profound differences within the Congress, that the left wing are a formidable opposition, and that on the whole the left are much more ready to face a split in the Congress than are the right. Consequently they seem to have the advantage of the initiative. This is merely speculation on my part and based on my own reflection on the published facts. But what does seem indisputable is that the Congress direction is at the moment in a state of paralysis, and I do not think the right wing can be feeling very happy about the position. I was greatly interested in what you told me in your letter of 19th March of your impressions of Gandhi in your two conversations, and also in what you said about the outcome of Tripuri and the unexpected determination that Bose has shown.[78]

2. Certainly Pant appears to me depressed and somewhat overwhelmed by his problems. The Ministry create the impression on my mind of suffering from a lack of clear thought and decision.[79] It is possibly a combination of the uncertainty of the Congress situation, the extreme hostility between the Hindus and Muslims which has resulted in riots in many places and brings discredit to the Ministry, and finally the effective and outspoken criticism on the Employments Tax and the finances of the Province, to which they have become very sensitive. Pant is perhaps ceasing to believe in himself, and on that account cannot bear to be told that he is wrong.

3. As I have indicated above, I think that the Ministry have definitely lost ground over the budget debates. Srivastava's criticisms of the Employments Tax were particularly galling, and I am told that when he enlarged on the point that the tax would accentuate unemployment, he obviously had the attention and the keen interest of the Congress members in the Assembly. I think myself that the Ministry committed a very serious political blunder in proposing this tax; and whatever the outcome of it, they will have frightened and irritated the middle classes and to a large extent forfeited the goodwill of the Services. Katju seems to have been unwise enough recently in one of the debates to take credit for having cut the pay of the Services by his own powers without the necessity of going as a suppliant to the Secretary of State. This might be an important point if it comes later to a question of refusing assent. This is what the *Statesman* reports him as having said: "Has not public opinion always considered that the public services of this country are highly paid and that salaries should be cut? If the Bill brings about a reduction in their salary, it is an additional merit. I refuse to go to the Secretary of State in supplication

and ask him to consider a salary cut when I can act on our own authority. I am looking forward to the day when all the public servants will owe allegiance to us and not to a *ma bap* Secretary of State. If by this Bill a method has been devised to bring about the wholesome result of a cut in the salaries we should receive congratulation." Another point on which the Ministers have been heavily attacked is that their policy seems to imply an endless vista of new taxation, and this I think will do them a good deal of harm. The point will no doubt be strongly elaborated at the projected demonstration to protest against excessive taxation which I believe is to take place in Lucknow towards the end of the month.

4. The Hindu-Muslim situation continues to be very unsatisfactory, though there has been no further major outbreak since Benares, and Benares itself has quietened down. It is clear from reports which have now come in that the assistance of the available company of British troops on the first day of the rioting at Benares was invaluable and that without them it might have been very difficult to bring the situation under control. With the end of the Muharram-Holi period, the likelihood of actual outbreaks is of course much diminished, but both in Cawnpore and Benares feelings are still strained. In many places in the Province rioting was narrowly averted, and much credit is due to the district authorities for their firm and impartial attitude. There were some peculiar outbreaks in the district of Budaun where communal tension had for some time been very acute. In several villages in succession Hindu crowds appear to have assembled and attacked Muhammadan houses. The situation had distinct potentialities of danger, but vigorous action was taken and I hope we shall hear no more of such developments. In one village the police had to open fire and four Hindus were killed. We have not yet had a very clear account of the facts. But these incidents illustrate a state of feeling between the two communities which, as I have said before, seems to me much more acute than I have ever known it.

5. The Premier is naturally much disturbed about these conditions, but he shows no signs of being prepared to relax the domination of his party or take any measures that would really create better feeling between the communities. I cannot help feeling that though he repeats the most admirable maxims on nationalist principles and complete impartiality, he cannot in fact escape altogether from the instincts of a Hindu. And there is no doubt that the Hindus must bear their full share of the blame for the present feeling. There have been clear indications lately of their aggressive mood. There is some reason to think that when Pant went recently to Delhi to see Gandhi he discussed with him the communal situation. Anyhow he

seems to have returned with some very unpractical Gandhian views. I have just seen unofficially some notes which he has prepared for the consideration of his colleagues. He has made some not unreasonable practical suggestions about official investigations into the handling of the recent riots and the methods by which we could take more effective measures to cheek these outbreaks at the beginning, or deal with the situation afterwards. One can always learn lessons from experience, and I have no doubt it is wise to review the facts carefully by official machinery and without publicity. But he has also written a very strange note which I think must owe its inspiration direct to Gandhi. He suggests that we should give up the attempt to regulate religious observances, processions, music, cow-slaughter, &c., that we should abandon the old practice of relying on custom and let everyone have the widest freedom to exercise their legal rights. Apparently the idea is that when, for instance, processions are not regulated by outside authority, they will regulate themselves and avoid all clashes. Hindus will show a spirit of consideration about playing music before mosques, and Muslims will not exercise their right of cow sacrifice in a provocative way. It is difficult to understand how anyone who knows the actual conditions can really put forward such ideas seriously. They are on a par with Gandhi's advice in yesterday's paper to Mr. Chamberlain to solve the present international situation by exhorting all the powers simultaneously to disarm. Another suggestion is that as communal electorates in local bodies accentuate communal differences an active policy should be pursued of substituting joint electorates, subject to some such arrangement as was approved for the Scheduled Castes. It does not seem to me that this is likely at the moment to exercise a very tranquillising effect on Muslim opinion. Another idea is to spend a lot of money on propaganda for communal concord. But propaganda not based on facts and a new spirit will be useless. Propaganda will not create the new spirit. I doubt whether these ideas after scrutiny by the other Ministers will reach me in these rather naive Gandhian forms. But it seems to me to illustrate the point that the Premier is in a state in which he has no clear and sane views of policy, and I am beginning to lose a good deal of my confidence in his political judgement. It has been suggested to me that at the moment he is suffering from lack of guidance which he used to receive from the Congress higher command. That was not my own impression. I was inclined to think that though he conformed scrupulously to certain general principles of policy laid down by the Working Committee, he was very much disposed to take his own line on the ordinary problems of provincial administration. My own feeling rather is that as he sees the difficulties around him continually increasing, his own judgement becomes less steady than it used to be, and he may be led into doing foolish things.

6. Another embarrassment of the Government is the perennial question of the Madhe-Sahaba in Lucknow. This has again come to a head recently and the Sunnis are engaged in a civil disobedience movement against the order of the District Magistrate[80] forbidding them to recite Madhe-Sahaba during the Muharram and Chehlum period. As the Government in effect promised last November[81] to give the Sunnis a fairly early opportunity of reciting the Madhe-Sahaba they are now being accused of a breach of faith in not taking the necessary steps, and the civil disobedience movement has met with a surprising degree of support. Yesterday it appears there were over 500 arrests in Lucknow. The local authorities have been anxious for some time to get some clear line of policy out of the Government. At my suggestion the Cabinet considered the matter a few days ago and we were all agreed that in the circumstances it was advisable to announce that shortly after the present prohibition under Section 144 expires after the Chehlum, an opportunity will be given to the Sunnis to take out a procession and recite their Madhe-Sahaba in public. It will bring the matter to a head. It may even lead to a riot. On the other hand it might conceivably lead to a settlement. It is really not possible to allow the present situation to continue indefinitely. Some suspicions have been expressed that the Congress have been encouraging this Madhe-Sahaba movement with a view to splitting the Muslims. The grounds for these suspicions are that Maulvi Husain Ahmad Madni who is the prime mover in the present Madhe-Sahaba agitation is a very prominent Congressman. But it seemed to me clear from my discussion with my Ministers that they look upon his activities as a grave embarrassment to themselves, and I am confident that they have done nothing to encourage him.

7. The Maharajganj tahsil in Gorakhpur is giving trouble again. The reason is simply that the Premier will not face up to his troublesome follower, Mr. Shibban Lal Saksena. Record operations have been in progress for many months and have had a settling effect. But Shibban Lal does not want a settlement. He lives by agitation, and recently he seems to have been using his volunteers for the purpose of interfering with the record operations and he justifies what he has been doing by making reckless charges of corruption against the assistant record officers who are Provincial Service men of good status supervised by a very capable young Indian I.C.S. officer. Some weeks ago the Collector[82] considered that things had reached such a point that it was necessary in order to protect the

staff from intimidation and enable the work to go on, to take action under Section 144 against Shibban Lal's activities. He asked permission from the Ministry. As usual in such cases, he got no reply; but Shibban Lal was sent for to Lucknow, and confronted with the I.C.S. record officer. I understand that Shibban Lal was reduced to silence. Nevertheless, the Ministry proposed to send down a Parliamentary Secretary to make some vague inquiry, ostensibly into the action of the Congress workers, but indirectly into conditions connected with the record operations. This seemed so undesirable that the Ministers have now been persuaded for the time being to drop the idea of sending the Parliamentary Secretary. I am proposing to take up the whole matter with the Premier as soon as possible; but at the moment he is so overwhelmed with work and in such an uncertain mood, besides not being very well, that I do not think I could get anything satisfactory out of him.

8. We have been having several Cabinet meetings lately, which are a heavy addition to the work of Ministers after attending the Assembly from 11 a.m. to 6-30 p.m. One of the matters discussed was the Bill to withdraw the original jurisdiction of the Oudh Chief Court. Dr. Katju has been for a long time a strong advocate of this, and the Ministers at one time committed themselves formally to the principle before they had even asked the Chief Court for their opinion. Since then Dr. Katju has shown himself impatient of such criticisms as I felt bound to offer, and also of any delay. When the matter came up in Cabinet, however, it was discussed on a very restrained note. The Bill was approved, and then Dr. Katju said that he assumed it should now be published. His colleagues, however, were unanimous that there was no occasion for this and it was decided that the Bill should be introduced later when the Hon'ble Minister thought it was convenient. It was quiet obvious that the feeling of the Ministers was that they had quite enough opposition on their hands at the moment and did not want to provoke more. The Bill will be strongly resisted, I think, by most of the Oudh interests. Another point of considerable interest was the decision about the Chief Court vacation. The Court at present have a two months' vacation under orders issued every year by the Local Government. This compares with two and a half months taken by the Allahabad High Court. Dr. Katju has been expressing very strong views about the excessive period of these vacations, and he had put into the Bill a definite provision to the effect that the vacation in the case of the Chief Court should not exceed six weeks. I had assumed that this like his other proposals would be accepted by his colleagues. But as the discussion proceeded it became

evident that they had no wish to introduce this matter into the Bill. It was decided that the length of the vacation should continue to be regulated by executive order, and the Clause in the Bill was omitted. With regard to the vacation for this year, it was finally decided that it should be allowed to remain at two months and should not be cut down to six weeks, the question of reducing it in the future to be left for consideration later. The lead in this direction was given by Kidwai, the only Oudh representative in the Cabinet, and it was clear that there was a feeling among the Ministers that they did not wish to ruffle Oudh feeling unnecessarily.

9. We have also discussed a Bill for reducing the existing debts of cultivators and small landlords. The Bill contained some fairly drastic provisions some of which were severely criticised by the Revenue Secretary.[83] A good many amendments were made in the principles of the Bill in consequence of this criticism, but the main provisions have been accepted and it was said that they resemble closely a measure which has already been passed in Madras. They hope to introduce this Bill in April. We shall shortly have to consider the action to be taken about the stayed arrears of rent. The Ministers I understand have quite made up their minds that these should be written off completely. This will of course be much more drastic action than is being taken on the ordinary civil debts of cultivators in the Bill I have just mentioned, and I shall not fail to point out to the Ministers the objections in principle to what they intend to do. But they are absolutely committed to this policy. It will involve legislation and they will again be very strongly opposed and criticised by the landlords. Altogether they are being driven into one measure after another which exposes them to very justifiable attack, and the time has passed when in the first flush of their victory they could brush aside and disregard all attacks upon them.

10. It has been decided after further discussion that the arrangements for going to Naini Tal should follow those which were adopted during the last two years, that is to say, officers will be allowed to recess for reasonable periods, but the Government will not officially move up. It is hoped now that the Assembly will not sit later than the end of April. In that event most of the Ministers and Secretaries will I hope be up in Naini Tal by the middle of May. It is not impossible that the Upper House may be required to sit at that time. If so, I think they will hold their session in Naini Tal. In that event the Secretaries would probably be required to move up officially.

11. I was interested in what you told me about your conversation with Raghavendra Rao regarding the handling of service questions. I will think

over the points he makes and will write to Your Excellency separately.[84] I saw him myself in Lucknow recently and had an interesting talk with him on the political situation.

Yours sincerely,
HARRY HAIG

NOTES

1. The text of resolutions passed at Ajodhya and the report of various speeches are not included in R/3/1/75.
2. Mr R.F. Mudie was Revenue Secretary at this date.
3. Mr A.N. Sinha was the Finance Minister of Bihar at this date.
4. In his letter of 22 December 1938, Lord Linlithgow criticised Pandit Pant for not having stood up to the challenge of the left wing of Congress. The Viceroy felt Pant had not performed as well as Premiers in the other Congress Provinces. R/3/1/74.
5. See U.P.P., 1938, Enclosure to No. 82.
6. The relevant portion of the Chief Secretary's Report dated 6 January 1939 reads: 'Tube well water is not being used as freely as it might be in the Western Divisions owing to complaints of the rates charged and the dishonesty of some of the operators. This aspect of the matter is engaging attention.' L/P&J/5/266: f. 21.
7. Mr W. Christie was the Financial Secretary at this date.
8. See U.P.P., 1938, No. 2 and its noting. Lord Linlithgow had said in his telegram 496-G.C. of 24 December 1937 that Ministries would be within their rights to reduce the pay scales of persons recruited or promoted after 31 March 1937. However, Governors should refuse to agree to cuts in pay of those recruited before that date. MSS.EUR.F 125/127.
9. Lord Linlithgow replied in telegram 338-G of 6 February 1939. The Viceroy said the position remained the same as stated in his telegram of 24 December 1937. He fully agreed that the situation as described in paragraph 3 of the present telegram would not justify the proposals for cuts in pay. R/3/1/75.
10. In his letter of 6 January 1939, Lord Linlithgow gave an account of a meeting he had recently been to at Darbhanga where there was a large contingent of landholders. The Viceroy said he 'could not help feeling much sympathy for these men, inheritors of a very different tradition, many of them representatives of families which have in the past served us with loyalty and distinction, now faced with a situation which they are ill-equipped to grapple with. . . .' R/3/1/75.
11. Mr J.E. Pedley was Collector of Gorakhpur at this date.
12. Mr P.M. Kharegat was Labour Commissioner at this date.
13. Sir Maurice Gwyer.

14. Rai Bahadur Pandit Chakra Dhar Jayal was Diwan of Tehri-Garhwal State at this date.
15. The despatch giving the proposals of the U.P. Ministry for the abolition of Commissioners is not included in R/3/1/75. It has not been traced elsewhere in the India Office Records.
16. In his circular telegram 256-S.C. of 27 January 1939, Lord Linlithgow asked Governors for personal assessments as to whether their Ministers would resign in the event of an instruction to that effect from the Congress Working Committee. MSS.EUR.F 125/107.
17. Mr N.C. Mehta was District Magistrate of Aligarh at this date.
18. Mr C.K. Kemp was Superintendent of Police, Aligarh at this date.
19. Sir Shah Sulaiman was Vice-Chancellor of Aligarh Muslim University at this date.
20. Lord Linlithgow minuted: 'P.S.V. – Police seem to have been badly led'.
21. Mr Harish Chandra.
22. Dr N.P. Asthana.
23. Lord Linlithgow replied in telegram 332-G of 5 February 1939. The Viceroy was advised that there was little doubt that the proposed Employment Tax was an income tax and if proceeded with, it would be necessary for the Centre to challenge it in the Federal Court. The Viceroy felt it was for the U.P. Ministry to determine how to balance the budget and it was unwise for Sir Harry Haig to make any active suggestions for taxation. R/3/1/75.

    Considerable correspondence on the U.P. Employment Tax Bill took place between Haig and Linlithgow during the first half of 1939. A principal concern was that the Ministry might resign if the Viceroy refused assent to the Bill after it had been passed by the Legislature. See Enclosure to No. 49 for the procedure eventually recommended by Haig. This procedure was followed.
24. Lord Linlithgow's telegram 296-G of 2 February 1939 was sent to the Governors of Provinces with Congress Ministries. It asked those Governors to what extent their views on the appointment of Advisers in a Section 93 situation had changed since the matter was previously discussed in the spring of 1938. MSS.EUR.F 125/107.
25. See U.P.P., 1938, No. 21.
26. Since January 1930 Congress had celebrated 26 January each year as 'Independence Day'.
27. It had been expected that Maulana Azad would be elected Congress President in January 1939 but he suddenly withdrew his nomination and Dr B. Pattabhi Sitaramayya was nominated in his place. At this juncture, on 21 January, Mr Subhas Chandra Bose announced that he would stand for re-election as President. On 23 January Bose said he was particularly concerned that Congress should have a President who was anti-Federationist to the core. He feared that the Congress right wing and the British Government might come to a compromise on the Federation issue.

These developments led six members of the Congress Working Committee headed by Vallabhbhai Patel to issue a statement on 24 January. This stressed that in the past Presidential elections had been unanimous and the signatories deprecated any controversy over the election. They also felt that it was sound policy not to re-elect the same President except under very exceptional circumstances. They argued that Sitaramayya was quite fitted for the post and they urged Bose to allow Sitaramayya's election to be unanimous.

A number of statements and counter-statements were then issued by the two sides. On 29 January Bose was re-elected Congress President. See Ravindra Kumar, *Nataji Subhas Chandra Bose: Correspondence and Selected Documents, 1930-1942.* (New Delhi: Inter-India, 1992), pp. 106-23.

28. Sir Henry Beauchamp St John was prime minister of Jaipur at this date.
29. I.e. Mrs Kasturbai Gandhi, Mahatma Gandhi's wife.
30. MSS.EUR.F 125/107.
31. Mr R.A. Horton.
32. Mr J.A. Thorne had succeeded Sir Reginald Maxwell as Secretary to the Governor-General (Public) by that date.
33. Lord Linlithgow minuted: 'P.S.V. – Perhaps all these questions re arms for police should go to Home Secretary. In any event, I shall be obliged if I may be told very early how this matter stands in the U.P. and throughout all provinces.'
34. Mr Frederick Young had been Inspector-General of Police, Jaipur since 1931.
35. Mr H.J.L. Biggie was Superintendent of Police, Agra at this date.
36. Lord Linlithgow replied in telegram 491-G of 22 February 1939. The Viceroy understood that Mr Young's deputation to Jaipur was due to end in August 1939. He agreed Sir Harry Haig had no authority to refuse to accept Pandit Pant's proposal to request Jaipur to return Young. However Linlithgow hoped Haig could dissuade Pant from making the request. Jaipur was entitled to expect that the period of the loan would be respected and the U.P. government appeared to have no authority to recall Young if Jaipur refused to return him. R/3/1/75.
37. The covering letter, dated 28 January 1939, which Lord Linlithgow sent Governors with his Despatch 159-G.G. of the same date is on MSS.EUR.F. 125/107.
38. Telegram 447-G of 15 February 1939 asked for information on the Cawnpore riots so that Lord Zetland could answer a British Parliamentary Question. In addition Zetland had asked that the Governor send an official report in due course for his own use and for Parliament. R/3/1/75.
39. A copy of Sir Harry Haig's telegram 210-G of 17 February 1939 is on L/P&J/8/580. The information in that telegram was similar to that given by Pandit Pant in Enclosure to No. 17.
40. No reply to this telegram has been traced. However in telegram 413 of 4 March 1939, Lord Zetland said he was quite content with the information

provided by Sir Harry Haig on 17 February (see note above). He would follow developments through the fortnightly reports unless the situation worsened. However Zetland could not see how, other than through a report from the Governor (via the Viceroy), he could obtain material to answer a Parliamentary Question. Such a report would naturally be that of the Governor personally. It would be an official document to be used as Zetland felt fit. L/P&J/8/580.

41. The annual session of the Indian National Congress was due to begin at Tripuri on 10 March 1939.
42. The Political Agent in Bundelkhand, with responsibility for British relations with Orchha, was Mr H.M. Poulton at this date.
43. Lord Linlithgow minuted: 'Pol[itical] Ad[viser – Sir Bertrand Glancy] may see re in particular Orchha. But the whole letter is of great interest. It will take the public some little time to spot the old man's decline, and till they do spot it, we shall have to be extremely wary, for while G[andhi] may do anything, anything he does will be right.'
44. Mr L. Owen was District Magistrate, Cawnpore at this date.
45. Mr R.A. Horton.
46. See note 39 above.
47. Not printed.
48. The order of words in this sentence has been altered to make the meaning intelligible.
49. Mr Panna Lal, Commissioner of the Allahabad Division.
50. Mr P.H.J. Measures, Deputy Inspector-General of Police, Allahabad Range.
51. Mahatma Gandhi's fast in Rajkot (a State in the Kathiawar peninsula) began on 3 March 1939. At Gandhi's request, Lord Linlithgow intervened, and the Chief Justice of India (Sir Maurice Gwyer) was asked to arbitrate between the Thakur Saheb of Rajkot and Mahatma Gandhi, who thereupon broke his fast. He later issued a statement apologising for his action in attempting to put pressure on the Thakur and the Paramount Power by undertaking a fast, which he now realised had been coercive and therefore not in accordance with the principles of non-violence.
52. Mr E.C. Gibson was British Resident at Rajkot at this date.
53. In telegram 216-G of 4 March 1939 Sir Harry Haig informed Lord Linlithgow that he was sending Enclosure to No. 18 to him. R/3/1/75.
54. The reference would appear to be to Mr J.P. Nicholson who was due to take over as District Magistrate, Benares on 17 March 1939 but was sent to the district on 6 March.
55. Mr R.V. Vernède was District Magistrate at Benares at this date.
56. Mr. P.H.J. Measures was Deputy Inspector-General of Police, Allahabad Range at this date. The Allahabad Range covered the Benares Division.
57. This would appear to be a reference to Mr E.M. Rogers who was shortly to act while the Superintendent of Police, Benares was on leave.

58. In a further letter (No. U.P.-232 of 8 March 1939) Sir Harry Haig reported to Lord Linlithgow that Pandit Pant had told him that if it was not possible for the Governor to cable the substance of his note to Lord Zetland, Pant would himself wire it to the Secretary of State. Apparently the matter had been discussed by the Cabinet some days previously but due to pressure of work Pant had overlooked it. This seemed to account for the urgent request. R/3/1/75.
59. Sir Harry Haig expressed similar views on the ending of Mahatma Gandhi's fast in his telegram 222-G of 9 March 1939 to Lord Linlithgow. He wrote: 'I think general sense here is one of relief and that there is appreciation of fact that Viceroy has been able to save country from deplorable consequences of Gandhi's action without as it would seem making any undue concessions to Congress or abandoning any general principle of policy.' R/3/1/75.
60. Mr B.G.P. Thomas was Deputy-Inspector of Police, C.I.D., at this date.
61. The Resident in Central India at this date was Mr K.S. Fitze.
62. Mr T.B.W. Bishop was Commissioner of Meerut at this date.
63. Dr P.C. Basu was Vice-Chancellor of Agra University at this date.
64. Lord Brabourne was Governor of Bengal at this date.
65. Sir John Ewart was Director of the Intelligence Bureau, Government of India at this date.
66. The Collector of Aligarh at this date was Mr N.C. Mehta. His report on German influence in Aligarh has not been traced in the India Office Records.
67. For 1938 references on this subject see U.P.P., 1938, No. 34, paragraph 8, No. 43, No. 48, paragraph 5, No. 52, paragraph 3 and No. 64, paragraph 15. India Office papers are on L/P&J/8/555.
68. Mr Harish Chandra was Judicial Secretary at this date.
69. A copy of the U.P. Ministry's provisional scheme for the separation of judicial and executive functions of magistrates is on L/P&J/8/555: ff. 66-73.
70. Not printed.
71. General Sir Douglas Baird was G.O.C.-in-C., Eastern Command at this date.
72. Major-General F.L. Nicholson was Commander, Lucknow District at this date.
73. See Appendix 1.
74. Lord Linlithgow replied on 11 April 1939. He said that he understood from the Intelligence Bureau that the 'Hindustani Fauji Mission' and the *Sipahi* were mainly the work of one man, Kidar Nath Sethi. The Viceroy felt that it would not be worth causing a crisis with the U.P. Ministers if the publication was to die and the Mission attracted no particular notice among soldiers. On the other hand if the movement had to be taken seriously, they could not acquiesce in inaction or ineffective measures. Linlithgow asked to be kept informed of further developments. R/3/1/75.
75. The Indian Sandhurst Committee, which reported in 1927, looked into the question of the training of Indians as officers of the Indian Army. The

Committee, chaired by the then Chief of the General Staff, consisted largely of Indian politicians including Mr Jinnah and Pandit Motilal Nehru (who resigned before the report). It recommended increasing the places for Indians at Sandhurst from 10 to 20 at once with further annual increases of four until 1933 when an Indian Sandhurst would open. (Dehra Dun was chosen as the venue for this.) The Indian Sandhurst would start with 33 places a year and an initial capacity of 100, expanding to 45 places a year after three years. Twenty places a year would still be open for Indians at the British Sandhurst.

76. Following the election of Mr Subhas Chandra Bose as President of Congress, thirteen members of the Working Committee resigned leaving only Subhas Chandra Bose and Mr Sarat Chandra Bose as members. At the Tripuri session of the Indian National Congress, held between 10 and 12 March 1939, a resolution on 'Congress Machinery' was passed which committed Congress to follow Mahatma Gandhi's policies. The resolution concluded: 'Congress regards it as imperative that its executive should command his [Gandhi's] implicit confidence and requests the President to appoint the Working Committee in accordance with the wishes of Gandhiji.' Pandit Pant, who moved the resolution, had played a key role in its drafting and in securing its acceptance.
77. Lord Linlithgow minuted: 'Interesting confirmation of my own instincts.'
78. In his letter of 19 March 1939 Lord Linlithgow said that his two conversations with Mahatma Gandhi had been very friendly and he believed had materially eased the position. The Viceroy was extremely surprised that Mr Subhas Chandra Bose had put up such a good fight at Tripuri. He had thought that Bose would have resigned on hearing of the majority against him. R/3/1/75.
79. Lord Linlithgow minuted: 'I shall be most interested to hear what Nehru says or does.'
80. Kunwar Jasbir Singh was District Magistrate of Lucknow at this date.
81. See U.P.P., 1938, Appendix 12.
82. Mr J.E. Pedley was Collector of Gorakhpur at this date.
83. Mr R.F. Mudie was Revenue Secretary at this date.
84. See next document.

CHAPTER 2

Documents for 1 April – 30 June 1939

27

HAIG TO LINLITHGOW
R/3/1/75

Private and Personal
No. U.P.-238

Camp,
April 3rd, 1939

My dear Lord Linlithgow,

I promised to let Your Excellency have my views on the suggestions made by Raghavendra Rao (which were mentioned in the last paragraph of your letter of 19th March), after having considered them at leisure.[1] Service questions particularly about appointments and postings provide some of the most frequently recurring grounds for differences between a Governor and his Ministers; and these personal cases, although perhaps individually they may appear to be of minor importance, when weighed against the graver issues involved in the success or failure of the new constitutional machine, yet have a far-reaching and cumulative effect on the morale of the services and their confidence in the future. Success in dealing with them obviously depends so much on the personal factor that I feel that it is not possible to adopt any very hard and fast rules of tactics. What may be suitable for one Governor with one set of Ministers might prove unwise with a different Ministry in the same Province or in another Province. Here in the case of the present Ministry owing to the preponderating influence of the Premier in the Cabinet and to the fact that the appointment department forms part of his portfolio there is I believe no question of appointments or postings of any importance on which he is not consulted by his colleagues before they take a final decision. This position has come about naturally and at present I see no advantage in trying to make more definite what appears to be an unwritten rule of Cabinet discipline of my present Ministry. To give a recent example I know that in the case of the appointment of a new Inspector-General of Civil Hospitals Mrs. Pandit's acceptance of the Director-General's recommendation was not given without considerable discussion with the Premier. He is similarly involved in the discussions which are proceeding about the appointment of the Director of Agriculture which I recently mentioned in a letter to Your Excellency. His influence on the decision of personal cases outside his own departments is sometimes surprisingly wide, and, on the whole, I fear, not very salutary. He is particularly susceptible, I am afraid, to political pressure in these matters. On the other hand I have avoided as far as possible the discussion of such cases in the Cabinet; and as far as our own circumstances are concerned I consider this to be undoubtedly wise. One early instance to the contrary was the case of the attempt to transfer Kunwar Jasbir Singh, District Magistrate, Saharanpur, in 1937 which we discussed in Cabinet, at the instance of the Premier, as I reported at the time. The effect of Cabinet discussion is generally to unite the Ministers in support of the view of whatever Minister is concerned and to make a case, which might in private discussion be argued more nearly on the merits, a matter of the prestige of the Ministry. Cabinet discussion in fact in such matters is felt to be rather a weapon of the Minister than of myself. In the recent prolonged discussions about the appointment of the High Court Registrar, which I reported to you at the time, it became clear that Katju attached a great deal more importance to the matter than did the Premier. On several occasions when Katju and I appeared to be approaching a deadlock he announced his intention of asking that the case should be taken up in the Cabinet, if I would not accept his view. He evidently hoped that the Cabinet might be prepared to make this question a matter of constitutional principle on which they must stand. Had the question been discussed in the Cabinet it was possible that that might have been the result. No move, however, was made to have it taken up as a Cabinet case and it is probable that the reason was that the Premier did not wish to commit himself to a position from which he could not retreat. I got my own way without Cabinet discussion.

2. I have been referring above in the main to personal questions, which are unfortunately far too frequent. There are of course also important general questions of service principle and procedure particularly in connection with the functions of the Public Service Commission. These are always discussed in Cabinet, and very tiresome they generally are, as one unscrupulous Minister will often succeed, if not in convincing, at any rate in influencing his colleagues. I think on the whole the underlying

principles of Raghavendra Rao's suggestions are observed here, but in our own way.

Yours sincerely,
HARRY HAIG

28

DONALDSON TO LAITHWAITE
R/3/1/75

Secret
D.-O. No. 315/39-G.S.P.

Camp,
April 5th, 1939

My dear Laithwaite,

I am desired to send you a copy of His Excellency's D.O. letter No. U.P.-239 of today's date to Sir John Ewart,[2] for the information of his Excellency the Governor-General.

Yours sincerely,
J.C. DONALDSON

ENCLOSURE 1 TO NO. 28

HAIG TO EWART

Secret
No. U.P.-239

April 5th, 1939

My dear Ewart,

I have just seen Blunden's secret letter, dated April 1st, 1939, addressed to you, giving his estimate of conditions in the Province. I understand you were worried about newspaper reports, and consequently asked him for an appreciation of the affairs of the Province which he has given in full detail. The picture he draws is one of practically unrelieved gloom and apprehension, and any ordinary person reading it might expect that the bottom would drop out of the Province tomorrow, even if it has not dropped out already. Most of his individual points are valid, though many in my opinion convey a somewhat exaggerated emphasis. He has collected together all existing and potential anxieties, past, present and future, and the cumulative effect may well be exceedingly alarming. As I am sure you will agree that no greater disservice can be done by an information officer to those responsible for dealing with a situation than to produce scare effects, I thought it desirable to write to you at once in order to introduce some perspective into the general impressions that might be derived from Blunden's letter.

2. A good deal of what it contains is merely a developed and perhaps heightened representation of the factors of anxiety which I stated in less vivid language in a memorandum, dated December 19th, 1938, containing my considered appreciation of conditions in the Province at that time.[3] It is of course perfectly true that during the last few months many of those conditions have become much more pronounced, and that the situation in the Province at the present moment is in many respects difficult. In my recent letters to His Excellency the Viceroy I have traced the changes and deterioration. The important new features in my opinion in the last two months are:

(*a*) The striking intensification of communal feeling, accompanied by serious outbreaks and continuous unrest. Now that situation cannot be taken lightly, and is indeed recognised by all thinking persons as presenting very grave problems, which are under consideration. But there is one bright feature in these events, which can be put over against the gloomy picture of depression of the Services drawn by Blunden. Actually the Services have risen to this very testing situation admirably, have dealt with it vigorously and effectively, and are quite clearly not the tired, dispirited creatures depicted. They have shown on the contrary great initiative and energy, more, in my opinion, than has ever been shown before in similar outbreaks. I understand that one of the matters which was disturbing you was an idea that during the deplorable disturbance at the Bara Dari the police were looking on unconcernedly. There were in fact no police there except a handful of traffic police. They doubtless did nothing, having no orders and no leadership and not expecting to deal with a riot. But if from that any conclusion is drawn that the Lucknow police is ineffective, nothing could be further from the truth. Only a few days after this the Lucknow police handled with great determination and success a really menacing situation in which two excited crowds of 15,000 Sunnis and 5,000 Shias were rapidly advancing towards each other in open ground. Everyone agrees that the police behaved admirably and stopped what might have been a very bloody riot.

(*b*) Disorganisation and lack of discipline within the Congress is growing, and I think probably the local Congressmen in the districts are getting above themselves and are less under control from the centre than they used to be.

(*c*) The volume of outside criticism of the Government has grown very greatly during the budget session. The Government have lost ground publicly, and they are themselves owing to this and to (*b*) somewhat perturbed and lacking in decision.

(*d*) I think the spirit of the Services has been considerably depressed by the proposal for the Employment tax and the apparent uncertainties about the outcome. That I hope will pass before long, but it is undoubtedly a factor which, added to the very strenuous time they have had in the last few months in consequence of the communal situation, is bound to affect their spirits.

3. We are at the moment witnessing some disintegration of the Congress machine and a weakening of the authority of the Congress Government. These are things which, though from many points of view unfortunate, were not unforeseen, and we have got to look at the facts calmly and judge them without panic.

4. As the matters discussed in this letter are of general importance I am having a copy of it sent to His Excellency the Viceroy for his information.

Yours sincerely,
H.G. HAIG

ENCLOSURE 2 TO NO. 28

BLUNDEN TO EWART

Secret

Lucknow,
April 1st, 1939

My dear Sir John,

This morning I prepared my usual fortnightly notes, but I must try to supplement these with a few more personal remarks.

The last few weeks have been full of troubles. Not only have communal difficulties failed to respond to the customary course of action by local authorities, but there is a widespread feeling of greater depression than at any other time since the Reforms came in. I believe that the Ministry are gravely (and justifiably) concerned over the present situation; but few people have much confidence in their power or capacity for bringing about any rapid or sufficient improvement.

Generally speaking, and my opinions are derived from a wide circle of friends in various walks of life, the attitude of the different sections seems to be as follows:

1. *Muslim Zemindars and old loyalists* – thoroughly depressed, believing that their old supporters are no longer able to help them.

2. *Hindu Zemindars and old loyalists* – similarly feeling deserted and helpless against the rising tide of Bolshevism. Disappointed by the failures and inefficiencies of the Congress administration. Fearful for their property if not also for their lives.

3. *Officials in the higher ranks* – tired out by the worries of their work; uncertain of their future; uneasy regarding the attitude of their political chiefs; depressed by the apparent falling off of all old standards of administrations.

4. *Officials of the Provincial Services* – as above, with the added worry of financial cuts directly affecting their daily lives; helpless in matters savouring of politics; inclined especially in the case of Hindus to bow down to the dominant party rather than to depend on the many tangible and other forces which have hitherto held the Services together.

5. *Businessmen* – gravely concerned by attacks from above and below; apprehensive of the financial policy now being followed; believing, justifiably in my opinion, that this Province is no place for opening fresh business; anxious to develop in States rather than in British India. All the above classes feel that prestige has been undermined.

6. *Muslims generally* – apprehensive regarding the future of their community; doubtful of the impartiality of local Hindu officials; jealous of the power wielded by the Hindu Congress; distrustful of the Muslim Ministers; agitated over the Madhe-Sahaba controversy; fearful for their lives, property and rights during festivals.

7. *Hindus generally* – afraid of the power of Congress; sympathetic with nationalism which means their domination of the whole of India; nervous to excess when communal troubles break out; probably still willing to vote for Congress.

8. *Students* – filled with vague communistic notions; unbalanced; undisciplined; nationalistic to extremes and sympathetic to all means of attaining so-called freedom; restive of all right wing influences. Latterly there have been fewer incidents, but chiefly because authority has ceased to come into conflict with its pupils.

9. *Officials of lower grades* – steadily trimming their sails; not yet lost their morale, but tired and tending to avoid action; depressed by their share in the loss of general prestige.

10. *Members of Boards* – communal; beyond guidance by officials; anxious to obtain power and notoriety; careless of the well-being of the Province.

11. *Congressmen of lower grades* – gaining power and local influence; dominating in manner; disappointed still at not having more from the acceptance of office; alleged frequently to be making money for themselves as well as for the party; tending steadily towards the Left.

12. *Peasants* – still quietly waiting for something beneficial; getting out of the control of the Zemindars and into the hands of semi-professional Congressmen who have little sense of responsibility, even to the tenets of Mr. Gandhi; not yet entirely carried away by the wild oratory which is now delivered with impunity, but tending steadily to become contemptuous of the authority of local officials. The last few months have been busy, for agriculturists, but conditions may quickly change for the worse. Many rural people find their way into the Army and Police; so far, when well led they have all given of their best, but one must consider the cumulatively undermining effect of an atmosphere of antagonism or indifference to authority in their homes.

13. *Criminals* – crime varies seasonally; so far apart from dacoities things might be worse; preventive action is difficult and men take shelter behind Congress; the taking away of policemen from rural thanas to fund district and range reserves is according to the I.G.P. responsible for adverse effects on crime work; officers find it not worthwhile always to investigate cases with their old zeal, especially when politicians may be interested or may foster complaints. There have been recently two cases in the east of the Province which have all the appearance of being revolutionary crimes.

14. *Low grade Government employees* – so far loyal, but less inclined to depend on their officers; communally minded; noticing the benefits derived by strikers in other spheres of work.

15. *Industrial workers* – unsettled by Bolshevist intelligentsia posing as union officials; conscious of their grievanccs and inclined to direct action on provocation or otherwise; gaining something from strikes and becoming undisciplined. Much has, however, been done lately by Labour officers to prevent direct action and remedy genuine grievances. Quiet lately for communal reasons, but likely to give trouble again during the summer.

I have often said that we are not unfamiliar with trouble in this Province, and we have gone through much, in 1921-22, in 1924, and in 1930-32; but nowadays there are many features which indicate that things have become dangerous. Communal riots recur, criminals go free, authority is flouted,

Bolshevism has spread in all directions. Prestige has been undermined, and there seems no sign of responsible opinion growing up in its place. Power should breed responsibility – but our Ministry are surrounded by difficulties of all kinds, and they are tending to pander to subversive elements.

Formerly, the most vociferous critics of the old régime, the Congress Ministry are now impatient of all criticism; but they are gravely concerned and on the whole have adopted a very proper attitude in communal matters – fundamental clashes between great communities cannot easily be stopped; local troubles and squabbles have recurred and do not respond to the old methods of persuasion and argument, chiefly because of the decay of the prestige of those responsible for local peace.

An attitude such as that displayed in the Lucknow meeting convened to protest against the Government's financial policy, when Indian and European gentlemen of position were roughly handled, is a significant sign of the times.[4] The statement published by Pandit Jawaharlal Nehru indicates his own fair-mindedness, but at the same time shows that Congress has conjured up forces which it cannot control.

This Province is so large that administrative problems would occupy the full attention of a first-class Ministry with no party or other distractions. As things are, allegations of administrative inefficiency have great force. I doubt whether the Ministry is enhancing its prestige; but it seems determined to cling to power, regardless of ultimate or immediate consequences to the seething population. At the moment, it is difficult to see any rays of hope, while the dark clouds of agrarian unrest may soon arise and cause infinite difficulties.

Yours sincerely,
A.C. BLUNDEN

29

HAIG TO LINLITHGOW
R/3/1/75

Secret *April 6th, 1939*
No. U.P.-240

My dear Lord Linlithgow,

I am writing in answer to Your Excellency's secret and personal letter of April 2nd, 1939,[5] regarding the situation that might arise in the event of an outbreak of war. I take up the three main alternative possibilities as given in your letter.

2. The first is (*a*), refusal of my Government to cooperate, followed by its demission of office, leading to Government under Section 93. The following points require consideration:

(*i*) I understand that in the event of war the draft Defence of India Ordinance would be issued at once. In the case of a Section 93 situation arising otherwise than as a result of war, we have ready the draft Revolutionary Movement Act. I am not altogether clear regarding the relations between these two measures, and in particular whether the Defence of India Ordinance will give us all the powers that are given in the Revolutionary Movement Act, and in as convenient a form. I have not yet had this matter examined in detail, as I think it probable that Your Excellency has already had this point under your consideration and detailed thought has been given to it. A cursory examination leads to the conclusion that the Defence of India Ordinance gives powers which are at any rate very comprehensive. But I should be glad to know as soon as possible what is the view on this point held by those who have drafted the two measures, and whether it is contemplated that the Defence of India Ordinance will be sufficient by itself. It is likely that in the situation contemplated we should sooner or later require maximum powers.

(*ii*) Much will depend on whether, as you say in your letter, the attitude of Congress is actively hostile or merely passive. I should imagine that in the early stages at any rate the official Congress attitude would not be actively hostile to the principle of war, but that they might merely refuse to lend any assistance. But even so, there would be a very considerable extremist wing in this Province which would not accept that policy and would definitely try to create the maximum of embarrassment. Even now they are not under very good control by the Congress Ministers. In the event of the Ministry going out, they would certainly in my opinion not submit their actions to control directed to observing a moderate policy. It is possible even that the extremists would definitely gain the upper hand in the Provincial Congress Committee. I think therefore it may be taken as certain that within a short time at any rate of a resignation of the Ministry caused by war we should be faced with dangerous and widespread activities on the part of the extremists, and those activities would have to be dealt with vigorously. This in itself would arouse the criticism and opposition of the more moderate Congressmen who in any case would feel that they had to do something in the way of agitation and protest in order to save themselves from complete political eclipse. I think therefore so far as agitation by the Congress is concerned, the situation would be likely steadily to deteriorate, and it would be one for which we should require all our resources and powers.

3. It is difficult to forecast the influence of the acute antagonism at present existing between the Hindus and Muslims; but this is a factor which might have very profound effects on the situation. We may I think start from the premise that the Indian Muslims have no sentimental attachment to the British connection, though the recollection of a long period of friendly relations will not be without its influence. They have at various times supported the British strongly against revolutionary movements, but that support has been given on a calculation of their own interests and was based on the view that a victory by the Congress over the British would mean the establishment of complete Hindu domination in the country. The temper of the Muslims since the assumption of office by the Congress Governments has become not only increasingly anti-Hindu but increasingly anti-British. The reason is that they feel they have not had the protection against the Hindus which they had expected as a result of their past support of the British against the Congress. The British are accused of having entered into an alliance with the Congress. The Muslims feel to some extent that they have been betrayed. They are in a bad temper, and in such a frame of mind they might take unwise decisions. If, however, it came once more to an open struggle between the British and the Congress, as it well might under the conditions we are considering under head (*a*), then I should hope it might be possible to rally the support of the Muslims, for I think their present master passion is a hatred and distrust of the Hindus. But it is possible that their support would only be given on terms, and the British Government will have to consider very carefully how far they are prepared to make certain political concessions to the Muslims in order to secure that support.[6] We can hardly expect the Muslims to support us, only to find at the end that they are put back again under the domination of the Hindus.

4. An incalculable factor in the Muslim situation is their liability to be carried away by waves of religious fanaticism which may originate with events outside India, which are to some extent beyond our control. The Palestine situation in this connection may clearly be crucial, or feelings might be stirred up by a big pan-Islamic movement, and everything that is likely to sow distrust of the British policy will be sedulously fostered by German and Italian propaganda.

5. Altogether the Muslim situation is in my opinion the key to the whole position, and it seems to me vital to do everything possible to prevent the Muslims siding against us in the event of war. It might seem inconceivable that in the present state of feeling Hindus and Muslims would unite against us. But it is not necessary to contemplate a Hindu-Muslim alliance. It is not impossible, if the situation were unwisely handled, that we should find the Hindus fighting us on their policy, and the Muslims on theirs. A situation like this would be very difficult to hold.

6. The second situation (*b*) contemplated in Your Excellency's letter is that in which Congress Governments while protesting against the participation of India in the war would remain in office and carry on ordinary duties of administration under protest, possibly interposing such obstacles as they could to the effective participation of their Province in war work. You say that you recognise that in such circumstances a break might easily come at short notice which would necessitate recourse to Section 93. I think in fact these conditions would lead to a Section 93 situation very rapidly. Indeed, we ourselves clearly could not tolerate such a situation for long and we might even have to force a break ourselves.

7. The third possibility (*c*) is a situation in which Congress Governments would accept the *bona fides* of His Majesty's Government and the potential importance to India of the ideals which would underlie our action. I think it is not unlikely that this might in effect be the first phase. From such brief conversations as I have had with individual Ministers I get the impression that they fully realise the dangers that threaten the world from the dictator countries, and that they know that their own interests as well as their general principles would naturally carry them into a war of this nature on our side. But they feel that it is hardly consistent with their conception of national dignity to have to enter it without their consent and under the domination of Britain, and to take part, as they might say, rather as slaves than as free men. There is also the deeply rooted instinct of the Hindu not to do anything for nothing, and they will certainly attempt to drive some sort of political bargain as the price of their voluntary support. In such a situation it would be necessary to consider very carefully the effect on the Muslims of any political concessions given to the Congress.

8. I think that even with the Congress Governments cooperating we should be faced with many grave difficulties, arising from extremist activities, which in this Province the Ministers would not be able to control by their influence and would be reluctant to control by administrative action. These conditions might indeed lead before long to a break-down.

9. With regard to the question of being fully prepared for war conditions, the point that has to be considered I think in the main is whether we are ready to deal with a Section 93 situation. Subject to what I have said in sub-head (*i*) of paragraph 2, I think we are administratively reasonably ready, but of course the occurrence of such a situation would involve some very intensive work at the beginning. With regard to situations (*b*) and (*c*), the question of legal powers and administrative problems has, I think, already been thought out in connection with the proposal for amendment of the Government of India Act. The main problems, however, that are likely to arise in these conditions are those of political judgement in handling a difficult situation.[7]

Yours sincerely,
H.G. HAIG

30

HAIG TO LINLITHGOW
R/3/1/75

Secret *April 10th, 1939*
No. U.P.-241

My dear Lord Linlithgow,

I have come away from Lucknow for two or three days' holiday at Easter and am writing this from a very pleasant canal bungalow right in the forests and not far from the headworks of the Sarda Canal. I am glad to say that my Ministers have also for the most part taken an Easter holiday. Pant, whose state of health has been giving rise to considerable anxiety lately, has at last agreed to go away to the hills for about a week. He has been suffering from low fever combined with over-work, and the Civil Surgeon told me some days ago that if he did not take a holiday he might break down seriously. It is quite obvious that he has been very far from his normal self. His temper and judgement have been uncertain, and at Cabinet meetings he has been sitting for the most part silent and has only taken his share when I have deliberately brought him in.

2. The acute ill-feeling between Hindus and Muslims continues to dominate the provincial scene. In Benares, in spite of vigorous administrative measures, occasional stabbings and short-lived panics take place. The Superintendent of Police,[8] an excellent Muslim officer, broke down completely a short time ago and has had to proceed on leave. He was not

in a good state of health when the riots broke out and was on the point of proceeding on long leave. The strain of the riots was great, and as soon as the acute phase was over the Hindus started a campaign of attacks on him (quite unjustified) for communal prejudice. I fancy he felt these a good deal. At Allahabad there have been some disturbances and stabbings which at one time created a great deal of nervousness. There again, however, administrative action has been prompt, vigorous and far-reaching, and I hope that the situation has practically returned to normal. You may be interested to read the comment of the *Leader* on those disturbances, and I enclose one of their articles. The *Leader* is of course published in Allahabad, and it is interesting to see how greatly they appreciate the action of the authorities. Cawnpore, I fear, is still in an unsettled state, and there has been great tension in Lucknow, though that is due to the controversy between Sunnis and Shias and not between Hindus and Muslims. I will refer to that later. But the result is that in four out of our five large cities (Agra being the one exception) extreme vigilance is required in order to prevent outbreaks of rioting. I mentioned in my letter of March 25th that there had been some unusual communal outbreaks in the district of Badaun. The situation there has been brought under control, but there is uneasiness in some of the neighbouring districts, and Muslim villagers are said to feel that they may be attacked.

3. So far as concerns administrative measures to deal with this situation, the action that is being taken or contemplated is in my opinion generally suitable. I mentioned in my last letter that it was proposed to appoint an official committee to look into the handling of the riots and to see whether any lessons could be drawn from their experience. The committee will consist of three or four officials with the Chief Secretary presiding, and they may be able to make some useful suggestions for the future. In the second place a letter is to be sent to all District Magistrates, summarising and calling their attention to all the general orders and principles of the past for dealing with these communal situations, and giving practical suggestions and instructions. The draft of this letter will be considered in Cabinet when we reassemble after the Easter holidays, and I propose to put certain considerations plainly before the Ministers, in particular the necessity of making full use of our powers to control inflammatory speeches and writings, and the importance of letting our officers feel that they will have the confidence and support of government and will not be liable to unreasonable attacks, and possibly arbitrary transfer subsequently, as a result of prejudiced complaints. So far for the most part these communal outbreaks have been handled by European officers, and the Ministry have

been good about supporting them. But in the ordinary administration it has been borne in on me a good deal lately that in the case of the non-protected services, for instance the provincial and subordinate civil services and police services, transfers and threats of transfer are setting up demoralizing conditions. The remedy is of course in the hands of the Ministers. All they have to do is to refuse to lend a ready ear to every suggestion and complaint, based on personal or political grounds, which comes to them from their supporters. But instead of ignoring these they appear to welcome them, and I fear in some cases officers are beginning to be afraid to do their duty if it is likely to offend anyone who has any political influence with the Ministers.

4. Another important matter which I raised in Cabinet shortly before I left Lucknow and will pursue further when I return, is the possibility of recruiting immediately for the police on a temporary basis a considerable number of ex-Army men who have finished their time in the reserve. The idea is that men of this type could immediately on enlistment be entrusted with the more ordinary routine duties at present carried out by the armed police, and would thus set free an equivalent number of armed police for the more difficult duties of maintaining order. We need a considerable addition to our strength, both as punitive police in Cawnpore and Benares and if possible, to create a regular formed central reserve. Ordinarily I should have hoped to get a satisfactory decision on a matter like this by the Premier, but in his present state of mind and health I felt it would be useless to discuss the matter with him as we should get nowhere. Consequently, I wrote a minute for the Cabinet and brought it up at our last meeting with the result that the Inspector-General of Police, whose scheme it is, was authorised to make immediate inquiries as to the possibility of being able to recruit men of this class. I think in matters like this the Ministers generally would be prepared to take a reasonable attitude. I have in fact recently found it more and more desirable to take important matters direct to the Cabinet, as my feeling is that Pant has lost grip to some extent. Consequently I took the initiative in asking the Cabinet to face the Madhe-Sahaba situation, I have raised with them this question of enlisting additional police, and I took up with them the question of action in the Maharajganj tahsil of Gorakhpur which I shall mention below.

5. While, as I have said, I think the administrative action at present in contemplation to deal with the Hindu-Muslim situation is adequate, my mind runs constantly on the underlying causes. We cannot afford indefinitely to have these conditions persisting; but unless something is done to deal with the underlying causes, I fear the present feeling will not

only continue, but even grow worse. To my mind there is no doubt that the root cause of the trouble is that the Muslims look upon the present Government as Hindu raj and to a very large extent the Hindus also have the same feeling. In these conditions it does not require any striking and obvious examples of injustice, which indeed are really lacking, to keep alive the flame of communal animosity. The Muslims, feeling themselves politically impotent, stir up religious issues. The Hindus, feeling themselves on top, tend to show an aggressive and intolerant spirit; and apart from these religious irritants the intrigue and petty political jobbery which is so prevalent gives the Muslims a sense of grievance and unfair treatment. As you know I have held these views about the fundamental causes of the Hindu-Muslim trouble for a long time, but I reproduce an extract from the last fortnightly report of the Commissioner of Meerut,[9] dated March 27th, 1939, which makes the same point. He wrote: "I would not like to exculpate the organisations of either community. But the root of the matter seems largely to be that the Hindu rank and file think that now they can assert themselves and disregard Muslim susceptibilities to a greater degree than previously because in their view they have now a Hindu Government."

6. I can myself see no cure for these conditions short of admitting to the Government real representatives of the Muslim community. As you know, I have raised this matter with Pant more than once, but he does not seem to be considering it seriously. The point was raised also publicly in the Budget debates and elicited from the Government an unfavourable response. Circumstances have rendered it out of the question hitherto for Governors to take any effective action in regard to including members of important minority communities in their Cabinets in accordance with paragraph VII of the Instrument of Instructions. The inclusion of two Congress Muslims in my Cabinet is of course not the slightest solace to the feelings of the Muslim community as a whole, who regard the present Ministry as a Hindu administration, the Congress as a Hindu body, and the Congress Ministers as renegades. If, however, present tendencies continue, Hindu-Muslim antagonisms increase, and general opposition to the Government grows, the time may it seems to me come when the Governor of this Province may be in a position to insist that the Cabinet should be recast and should include representatives of the Muslim League. Meantime I shall continue to make clear my views to Pant.

7. The Madhe-Sahaba question is still causing great trouble in Lucknow, though the position has now been entirely reversed. When I last wrote, the Sunnis were engaged in a rapidly growing civil disobedience movement because they were not allowed to recite Madhe-Sahaba. Orders were issued

by the Government to the effect that the Sunnis would have an opportunity every year of taking out a Madhe-Sahaba procession on the Barawafat day, and in view of the commitments already made last November, I considered that this was a reasonable conclusion. It has the great merit of giving a precise order about the Madhe-Sahaba claim instead of leaving it indefinitely in the air, and in fact under the conditions that will be laid down by the Deputy Commissioner this procession once a year ought not to be objectionable. It was foreseen that these orders would provoke a strong reaction by the Shias, and this has come at once. The Sunnis called off their civil disobedience movement and the prisoners were released. But the jails are now being filled up again by the Shias who are insisting on reciting the Tabarra. This has always been regarded as a much more objectionable thing than Madhe-Sahaba, cursing as against praising. The Shias will not be satisfied unless they are allowed to take out some procession indicating their views though not actually reciting the Tabarra, and it seems to me not impossible that eventually a settlement may be reached on those lines. In the meantime I am receiving numerous telegrams from Shia bodies urging me to intervene against the orders of my Government allowing the Sunnis to have a Madhe-Sahaba procession. The Barawafat day is early in May and the matter will be brought to a head then. I propose to discuss policy further with the Cabinet as early as possible.

8. The Lucknow police have behaved admirably and in particular averted what might have been a very serious riot, a few days after the orders of Government were issued. 15,000 Sunnis had assembled at the Tila Mosque and 5,000 Shias were at the Imambara closeby. The Shias began issuing from the Imambara shouting the Tabarra. The Sunnis at the Tila Mosque were greatly excited and the two mobs began moving towards each other across open ground. The police who were stationed there in strength between the two mobs were gradually being forced back, when the Superintendent of Police[10] seeing the situation was critical ordered a volley to be fired. This had the desired effect and both mobs retreated. Had he not acted at once, the mobs would have come to grips and there would probably have been considerable loss of life.

9. In my letter of March 25th I mentioned the situation in the Maharajganj tahsil in Gorakhpur. As it seemed to me difficult to get anything satisfactory out of the Premier, I recorded a note on the case, circulated it to all the Ministers and had the matter up in Cabinet. On the first day some of the Ministers asked for a few days' delay in order to study the papers, to which I agreed. Before the question was taken up again Shibban Lal

Saksena appears to have been sent for by Nehru, and I should imagine talked to somewhat severely. Anyhow before the Cabinet meeting took place I had heard from Gorakhpur that the situation had greatly improved, that Shibban Lal had gone off to Lucknow, that the record operations were proceeding without interference, and the situation was no longer formidable. At the Cabinet meeting I made the point that this was really a matter between the Ministers and Shibban Lal. He was resisting not the local officials but the Ministers' own policy, and I suggested that they must make it clear that it was their policy and that they intended to see it through. They accepted this, but said that there were certain matters of detail in connection with the revision of records which required to be set right and that when a settlement had been reached about them, as they hoped it would be shortly, they would certainly see that the matter was carried through and would not tolerate further interference by Shibban Lal. I hope they will stick to this determination. Anyhow for the moment Shibban Lal appears to have been eclipsed and the work is proceeding smoothly.

10. I have mentioned in earlier letters the intention of the opponents of the taxation policy of the Government to hold a big meeting of protest in Lucknow. This was fixed for the 29th March and a very representative gathering had been assembled, with Sir Tej Bahadur Sapru to preside. There had been rumours for a day or two before in Lucknow that the Congress intended to break-up the meeting, but no special arrangements had been made to give police protection. This I think was due partly to some negligence on the part of the organisers of the meeting and partly to the great preoccupation of the police with the Sunni-Shia position. Congressmen managed to secure entrance to the hall and occupied the first two rows, and as it was evident that they intended to interrupt the proceedings the organisers, and in particular Sir J.P. Srivastava, asked the Congressmen to withdraw as admission was only by ticket and the meeting was not open to the public. The Congressmen refused to withdraw and were then hustled out; but I understand there was no question of their being assaulted or injured in any way. A few minutes after they had been removed, a mob of Congressmen outside the Bara Dari, broke the windows and eventually forced their way into the hall and in particular deliberately assaulted Sir J.P. Srivastava. The whole affair was exceedingly discreditable, and to my mind the worst part of it all was the attitude of levity and unconcern adopted by the Premier. When I think of the number of discourses I have heard from him on the subject of civil liberties and the necessity of not interfering with freedom of speech, I am amazed at his

indifference to the action of his own followers in forcibly preventing the exercise of freedom of speech by their political opponents. I am told that prominent among those who assaulted Sir J.P. Srivastava were two or three ex-Kakori prisoners.[11] An attempt was made to raise the matter by a motion for adjournment, but this was ruled out of order on technical grounds. I enclose a newspaper account of this, and also of the remarks made by the Premier regarding the incident. I am glad to say that the promoters of the meeting have decided that it should still be held and it is to take place at the Baradari on Sunday the 16th April. I understand no risk will be taken this time of having the meeting disturbed by Congressmen. As a number of Europeans from Cawnpore who were attending the meeting took a prominent part in removing the Congressmen and also in defending the Bara Dari against the subsequent attack, the local Congress Press made every effort to give the whole matter a racial tone. I think, however, their efforts were only partially successful. Jawaharlal Nehru issued a fairly reasonable statement on the subject and did not attempt to gloss over the fact that whatever might have been the circumstances, Congressmen were to blame in regard to their actions.

11. I had an interesting talk recently with Mrs. Pandit who was lamenting the state of indiscipline in the Congress ranks. I fancy in fact that this is a very serious embarrassment to the Ministry. So much has the spirit of independence spread that everyone seems to regard himself as equal to any one else, and consequently the leaders are finding it very difficult to secure obedience to their policy. Mrs. Pandit appeared to think that the only remedy for these conditions lay in a dictatorship within the Congress organisation, and she seemed to think that in Bombay with Vallabhbhai Patel that dictatorship was in fact in operation and working successfully. I suggested to her that her own brother would naturally be cast for the part of dictator for the United Provinces. She agreed entirely and said he was the only man who was capable of doing it, but that at present he seemed disinclined to assert himself and was proceeding on ultra-democratic lines. I have little doubt myself that Nehru is the only man who could control the Congress in this Province, and I am inclined to think that unless he assumes control the disintegration which has clearly set in already may spread with rapidity.

12. I was very glad to hear from your letter of 29th March that you were hoping to let me know before long your conclusions about the Employments Tax as a result of your correspondence with the Secretary of State. I think that the uncertainty as to the outcome of the Government's proposal is exercising a depressing effect on the services generally. The Bill is likely to be through the Lower House by about the 20th April. I still do not know

what its reception will be in the Upper House. The Tenancy Bill also is expected to be through the Lower House by the end of April.

13. Since writing the above I have seen a newspaper report of some of the resolutions which have just been passed by the Provincial Congress Committee under the presidency of Nehru, a copy of which I enclose. The earlier resolution about the disruptive forces that are at work represents, I have no doubt, a definite conviction in the mind of Nehru and others who can look ahead; but whether in fact it will be possible to check them is doubtful. I am particularly interested in the latter resolution, which appears to suggest that Congressmen should not concern themselves with the appointment, dismissal or transfer of Government officials "for personal reasons". The resolution may be read in conjunction with the remarks I have made in paragraph 3 of this letter. I imagine the Provincial Congress Committee, under the guidance of Nehru, are approaching this matter from a realisation that these petty intrigues are demoralising to the Congress, and that they are not concerned with the fact that the situation is also demoralising to the administration. But at any rate it gives me a text for urging my Ministers to disregard undesirable representations of this nature.

Yours sincerely,
H.G. HAIG

ENCLOSURE 1 TO NO. 30

CUTTING FROM THE *LEADER* OF APRIL 5TH, 1939

"All investigations indicate", says the District Magistrate[12] in connection with the so-called communal trouble at Allahabad in one of his communiqués, "that the assaults are the work of hooligans". Mr. Jawaharlal Nehru has stated that "these stabbings have been largely done by a few professional *goondas*, probably very few".

He further observes: "Compared to previous communal disturbances, Allahabad is singularly free from the tension and mass excitement that usually prevails under such circumstances. This shows that there is no real basis for the trouble which is largely the action of a few persons."

Formerly cases of individual assaults and stabbing led to a general communal excitement and rioting, and thus the purpose of the evilly-disposed persons was served. But this time, thanks to the good sense of the law-abiding members of the two communities and to the prompt and energetic measures of the authorities, the *goondas* have failed to bring about a commotion. The situation might have deteriorated if those entrusted with the maintenance of law and order in the town had not won public confidence by the very capable manner in which they have handled the situation. We doubt if ever before the executive acquitted themselves in such a splendid manner in grappling with communal troubles. It is due to their timely action and vigilant attitude that a number of alleged assailants were arrested without loss of time. This by itself has had a deterrent effect. But it appears that drastic measures are needed for dealing with communal terrorism in Allahabad and other towns in the province, such as Benares and Cawnpore. They may not be necessary if the people of both the communities cooperate with the authorities in bringing the offenders to book. Cowardly and murderous assaults on innocent passers-by cannot be altogether stopped unless those who indulge in them feel that they will not get protection in any quarter. It is not in the interest of either community that assaults on communal lines should continue. They are not only shocking but utterly senseless. The terrorists, to whatever community they belong, should be regarded as public enemies.

ENCLOSURE 2 TO NO. 30

NEWSPAPER REPORT OF ADJOURNMENT MOTION MOVED IN U.P. LEGISLATIVE ASSEMBLY ON MARCH 31ST, 1939

Attitude of Government towards right of free speech and meeting by lawful citizens opposed to its policy

The Deputy Speaker then informed the House that he had received notice of an adjournment motion from Mr. Muhammad Ishaq Khan to discuss a matter of urgent public importance namely, "the disgraceful incidents which took place on the forenoon of March 29th, at the Kaiserbagh Baradari and which were cleverly pre-organised and pre-arranged, and to express the sense of acute dissatisfaction of the House at the utter indifference of Government in the exercise of the right of free speech and meeting by lawful citizens opposed to its policy and its manifest failure to prevent its supporters and followers from trespassing into a private place and interfering with the holding and conduct of meetings and further to discuss the wholly unsatisfactory and evasive reply of the Premier on Thursday in pleading ignorance of an affair of common notoriety."

The Deputy Speaker: What is the specific matter that you want to discuss?

Mr. M. Ishaq Khan: The issue which I want to raise before the House is already mentioned in the terms of the motion.

The Deputy Speaker: There is more than one thing in this motion.

Mr. M. Ishaq Khan: The specific issue to which I want to draw attention is the right of free speech and meeting by lawful citizens opposed to the policy of Government. I also want to discuss the disgraceful incidents and injuries received on both sides and the action of the parties on that particular day. Further on Thursday a question was put to the Premier and the Premier replied that he knew nothing officially about the matter. We want to discuss this unsatisfactory reply by the Premier.

The Deputy Speaker: You want to discuss two things – incidents in the Baradari and secondly the unsatisfactory reply of the Premier. Rule 66 says that an adjournment motion can only be in respect of one single matter.

Mr. Ishaq Khan: Before you give your ruling the Premier may be called upon to give his view. That is done usually in the Central Assembly.

The Deputy Speaker: The Speaker has first to see whether the motion is in order. If the motion is in order he will admit it and call upon the Premier to say whether he has any objection to it or not. I think that the matter is not in order and I would therefore rule it out of order.

Referring to the incident the Premier said: "I regret very much that such an incident should have happened. I am sorry that things should have taken the turn they did. I wish people who hold different views from the Government to be given an opportunity of expressing their views freely. I know their number is very small, and by bearing their tom-tom they can make it out that they have a large number. They may be allowed to meet in their drawing-rooms or in a barricaded place, and they should not be given an opportunity of giving people the feeling that they have a grievance when a realistic state of affairs would expose them more than any pretensions which can be made under such circumstances." (Congress cheers.)

ENCLOSURE 3 TO NO. 30

TEXT OF SOME IMPORTANT RESOLUTIONS PASSED BY U.P. PROVINCIAL CONGRESS COMMITTEE HELD AT LUCKNOW ON APRIL 7TH, 1939, PANDIT NEHRU PRESIDING

The Council regret that disruptive forces are at work in the country which come in the way of national unity and divert people's attention from the central issue of freedom for the people. The Council are firmly of opinion that all such tendencies and efforts even though they might appear sometimes to be for good causes, are to be deplored and avoided as they injure the cause of the country as a whole and thus injure also the cause of any group or part of it.

In this dynamic age of transition and change, when world war threatens and the fate of millions hang in the balance, no one who cares for the freedom and the progress of the Indian people can afford to get entangled in mutual controversy and conflict or in petty issues. The only call that every Indian should listen to today is the call of India demanding her freedom. That call requires mutual forbearance and tolerance, discipline, courage and sacrifice. To answer that call the Council pledge themselves afresh, on behalf of the Congressmen of these provinces.

While it is the duty of all Congressmen to keep a vigilant eye on the welfare and rights of the people and to report cases of oppression, it is not their business nor is it in consonance with their dignity to interfere in any way in matters of administration, more specially those relating to appointments, transfers and the like. The Council, therefore, lay down the rule that in future no member of a Congress Committee should make any recommendation to Government officials for appointment or dismissal or transfer for personal reasons. The Council realise that much injustice is often done in such cases but, in their opinion, it is better to put up with this temporary injustice rather than to waste our energies in petty personal matters and thus lower the ideals of the Congress. This rule must be strictly adhered to, both by members of Congress committees, as well as Congress members of the Legislature.

In cases of oppression or maladministration, it is the duty of Congressmen to inquire and make a report. In all such cases, if any contact with State officials is rendered necessary, the only person who should do so should be some one authorised by the District or City Congress Committee or of the Provincial Congress Committee. No other members of subordinate committees should approach State officials for this purpose. They may, however, report to the District Congress Committee concerned or directly to the Provincial Congress Committee. Members of the Legislature may also report instances of oppression and the like in their constituencies to the Government officials concerned.

31

HAIG TO LINLITHGOW
R/3/1/75

Secret *April 18th, 1939*
No. U.P.-244

My dear Lord Linlithgow,

I have had occasion frequently in my fortnightly reports of the last two years to refer to the Madhe-Sahaba controversy at Lucknow. The whole question has now come to a head, and I think Your Excellency may find it useful to have a connected account of the problem. I have accordingly written a note which summarises the history of the controversy and the steps taken up to the present time, and I send it herewith for Your Excellency's information. I am also sending a copy of this letter and of the note to the Secretary of State for his information.

Yours sincerely,
H.G. HAIG

ENCLOSURE 1 TO NO. 31

NOTE BY HAIG

April 18th, 1939

The Lucknow Madhe-Sahaba controversy

The Madhe-Sahaba controversy in Lucknow originated about the year 1906. The Shias who are very numerous and influential in Lucknow held that the three Khalifas who immediately succeeded the Prophet and who were succeeded by Ali, were usurpers, that they were guilty of acts of tyranny and oppression against Ali and his wife Fatima, who was the daughter of the Prophet, and that the result of their policy was the terrible tragedy at Karbala when Hasan and Hussain, the sons of Ali, were massacred. This massacre is mourned at the period of Muharram. The Sunnis on the other hand regard the first three Khalifas as rightful rulers, and hold them in profound respect and regard them as men of great honesty, virtue and courage.

2. About the year 1906 disputes arose in Lucknow between the Sunnis and Shias about the celebration of Muharram, and the Sunnis began to

recite verses in praise of the first four Khalifas whom they described as friends and comrades of each other and of the Prophet. These are the recitations which have now crystallised into what is known as the Madhe-Sahaba or praise of the Companions. The Shias retaliated by employing the Tabarra, that is, curses on the first three Khalifas for their inhuman treatment of the descendants of the Prophet.

3. As a result of these demonstrations serious rioting took place between Sunnis and Shias in Lucknow in 1907 and 1908, and in 1908 the Government appointed a committee under the Chairmanship of Mr. Justice Piggott, a High Court Judge. The conclusions of the committee were that the attempt to transform the *tazia* processions of the Muharram into processions in honour of the first four Khalifas was an innovation, and recommended that there should be a general prohibition against the organised recitation of such verses on three days, viz., Ashra (the 10th day of Muharram), Chehlum and the 21st of Ramzan. The Shias contended that the recitation of such verses was highly offensive to them at all times. The committee thought that the question of the public utterance of verses in praise of the first three Khalifas at times other than the three days mentioned should be left to the operations of the ordinary law. The Government accepted the prohibition on the three days mentioned and left the question of prohibition on other days to some extent open. The Government resolution of 1909 said: "The desire of the majority of the committee, which is entirely shared by the Lieutenant-Governor,[13] is to correct this abuse (i.e., converting a Muharram procession in commemoration of the martyrdom of Hussain into an untimely demonstration in favour of the first three Khalifas) without interfering beyond what is absolutely necessary with the right which the Sunnis of Lucknow share with all classes of His Majesty's subjects to express at suitable times and in suitable places the distinctive doctrines of their faith." The desire of the Shias was to secure a pronouncement from the Government that the public recitation of the praises of the first three Khalifas was at all times a provocation and an offence against the public peace. The Government resolution says that it is obviously impossible for the Government to issue any such pronouncement because the Sunnis have as much right as the Shias to hold the distinguishing doctrines of their faith and to assert the same in the proper time and manner, with due regard to the provisions of Section 298 of the Indian Penal Code.

4. Soon after the issue of the orders of the Government in 1909, when there was great excitement in the city over the prohibition of the recitation of Madhe-Sahaba on the Chehlum day, the Deputy Commissioner of the

time issued a proclamation pointing out that the recitation of praises of the first three Khalifas was not entirely prohibited, but that restriction had been imposed only for the three days, and that on other days the verses could be recited after a licence had been obtained under the provisions of the Police Act. It is said that this proclamation was subsequently withdrawn under Shia agitation. But while the theoretical position adopted by the authorities doubtless was that there should be no general prohibition of the Madhe-Sahaba, in practice no public recitation was ever permitted and in fact the Shias secured their object.

5. The controversy remained in abeyance until 1935 when on the day of Chehlum some Sunnis defied the order and recited the Madhe-Sahaba. In 1936 a much stronger and more troublesome Sunni movement developed and a regular practice was started every Friday of disobeying the orders and reciting the Madhe-Sahaba. Attempts were made to take out processions. This state of things continued for more than three months and a considerable number of arrests were made. As the course of events was seriously disturbing the tranquillity of Lucknow, efforts were made to bring about a settlement. I agreed to receive a deputation from Sunnis and Shias separately. In the meantime the movement of defiance by the Sunnis was called off and those who were in prison were released. I received these deputations in November and December 1936 and appealed to both parties to reach some agreement among themselves. Every effort was made for the next month or two through official influence to secure some agreement, but both sides remained uncompromising. My Government then appointed a committee consisting of Mr. Justice Allsop, a High Court Judge, and Mr. Ross, Collector in charge of the Jhansi division, to consider whether the principles and policy laid down by the Government Resolution of January 7th, 1909 required any modification, and whether the practice adopted by the district authorities in Lucknow with regard to these matters required any modification. The committee reported on June 15th, 1937.

6. The committee reviewed the past history of the case elaborately and also examined the principles of law. They came to the conclusion that the prohibition of assemblies and processions for the Madhe-Sahaba on the three days had been rightly imposed. They then said: "We have already expressed our belief that it was not the intention of the Government that the recitation of Madhe-Sahaba on other days should necessarily be prohibited" and went on to point out that "the real question is whether Madhe-Sahaba recitations in public can fairly be considered as deliberate attempts at insult and annoyance." Further they observed: "If at any time it could be inferred that the recitation of Madhe-Sahaba was a perfectly

independent religious observance having no concern with the Shias or any Shia ceremony, we do not think the Shias could reasonably object to it. The question is largely one of intention, but intention can be inferred only from conduct and when we examine the conduct of the Sunnis in 1935 and 1936 we are forced to hold that their desire to recite Madhe-Sahaba arose out of a feeling directed against the Shias." Their conclusion is: "When we take the facts as a whole into consideration we cannot avoid the conclusion that the movement was essentially directed against the Shias and as such was rightly opposed by the authorities"; and later: "We do not think that it should be assumed that the public recitation of Madhe-Sahaba is always in all circumstances objectionable but we are bound to say that the authorities will have to take similar action in similar circumstances in the future, particularly if the Sunni agitation is continued."

7. The general effect therefore of the Allsop Committee's report was, while reasserting the theoretical right of the Sunnis to recite the Madhe-Sahaba, to hold that in the circumstances that existed in Lucknow it was a provocative action and should not be allowed.

8. The report was presented after the new constitution had come into force and came under the consideration of the minority Ministry. They were reluctant to deal with this thorny question and left it alone. The present Ministry also tried to avoid tackling it and for some months the position remained quiescent. But the Sunnis were not content to leave the matter indefinitely without a decision, and eventually on March 28th, 1938, the present Government published the Allsop Committee's report and their conclusions on it. The operative part of the resolution runs as follows: "The United Provinces Government devoted most careful and anxious consideration to the arguments and conclusions so clearly set forth in the report and accept the Committee's findings. They wish to make it clear that the Sunnis' right of public or private recitation in praise of the three Khalifas is not in dispute. This right they undoubtedly possess. What is in dispute is merely the method and circumstances in which it had been sought to make such recitations in Lucknow. Where there is a conflict between the tenets and points of view of different communities it becomes the duty of the Government to intervene in order to ensure public tranquillity and to maintain the balance of public convenience. The Committee's findings are based on these well recognized principles."

9. The Sunnis were dissatisfied with this conclusion and were continually bringing pressure to bear on the Ministry to allow a recitation of the Madhe-Sahaba under threat of starting a civil disobedience movement. Both my Muslim Ministers are Sunnis and thus personally inclined to favour the

Madhe-Sahaba agitation. The matter was handled on behalf of the Ministry by one of the Muslim Ministers, Hafiz Muhammad Ibrahim. During November 1938 while I was on tour, Hafiz Muhammad Ibrahim apparently with the approval of his colleagues issued a Government Press communiqué, a copy of which is attached. In this it was said: "For some time past Government have been intending to allow Sunnis to have public recitation of Madhe-Sahaba in the manner mentioned above (i.e., special meetings and processions) provided there is peaceful atmosphere in the town of Lucknow. But Government regret that sometimes on account of threats of civil disobedience and sometimes for other reasons no such peaceful conditions could establish themselves." The communiqué then went on to say that the Government were having talks with the Shias and Sunnis to bring about an amicable settlement and ended with the words: "Either the talks will lead to some fruitful result or Government will in the near future make an announcement of their decision." The result of this communiqué was that the threatened Sunni civil disobedience movement was postponed, but it was generally interpreted as a promise by the Government that they would before long allow a public recitation of Madhe-Sahaba.

10. Discussions and negotiations went on and eventually the Sunnis about the beginning of March 1939 launched their civil disobedience movement. This met with a very considerable and growing degree of support. Large numbers of Lucknow Sunnis were arrested and *jathas* were organised from many other districts. The district authorities were becoming very restive under these conditions. For many months past relations between the two sects had been gravely strained, and it was only by the utmost vigilance that disturbances between them had been averted. The situation had not only become chronic, but seemed to be getting steadily worse. The Sunni agitation was encouraged by the knowledge that the Ministers were in favour of making a concession to them, and the district authorities felt that they were fighting a losing battle which would end in the granting of the Sunni claims after the agitation had got out of control. They therefore pressed for some definite decision of policy. I felt the force of these arguments and was anxious also to avoid a repetition of a decision being taken in direct negotiation with the Sunni leaders of the agitation without the Ministry as a whole having had an opportunity of considering the matter. Accordingly I raised the question at a meeting of the Council of Ministers on March 22nd, 1939.

11. At this meeting it became clear that the Ministers were considering a concession to the Sunni demand, and felt themselves committed to giving

the Sunnis an opportunity to recite the Madhe-Sahaba publicly some time during this year. It was decided that the whole question should be discussed by the Minister with the district authorities, the Commissioner[14] and the Chief Secretary. The upshot of this decision was a proposal that the Sunnis should be allowed to hold a procession and meeting to recite the Madhe-Sahaba on the Barawafat day each year. The intention was to prescribe a route for the procession far removed from any Shia population, and in fact to have the meeting on the other side of the river and outside the city. The advantage of this plan from the official point of view was that it would remove the perennial uncertainty as to whether Madhe-Sahaba would or would not be allowed, and would limit the recitation of the Madhe-Sahaba definitely to one day in the year. The question was raised what would be the reaction of the Shias; but though it was known that the decision would be bitterly resented by the Shias, and that the Shias might demand as a *quid pro quo* a procession to recite the Tabarra, or at an rate the praise of Firoz who had killed one of the three Khalifas, neither the district authorities nor the Ministers had any idea that the Shia reaction would be of a very striking character.

12. After further negotiation with the Sunnis, a communiqué was accordingly issued on March 30th, 1939, of which a copy is attached, stating that the Sunnis will in any circumstances be given the opportunity of reciting Madhe-Sahaba at a public meeting and in a procession every year on the Barawafat day, subject to the condition that the time, place and route thereof shall be fixed by the district authorities. The communiqué was issued by the Ministers in some haste, and the intention which had previously been expressed that the Shias would be informed beforehand of what was intended was not carried out.

13. The result of the communiqué was that within a day or two the Sunnis called off the civil disobedience movement. But the effect on the Shias was far greater than had been anticipated. It appears to have been an overwhelming blow to them. Their view was that they had the authority of two separate committees and the practice of thirty years in support of their position. They had also been recently ingratiating themselves with the Congress in order to make their position stronger. It appears not to have occurred to them as a possibility that this permission would be given to the Sunnis. The sanction of the Madhe-Sahaba has set up among the Shias conditions of intense emotional hysteria. It is particularly strong among the women. Civil disobedience was at once started and very large numbers of Shias have already gone to prison. In contrast to the Sunni civil disobedience movement in which those offering themselves for arrest were generally the riff raff, Shias of the most respectable families and

standing have been reciting the Tabarra and going to jail, and it is reported that if the Madhe-Sahaba is actually recited *purdah* ladies of high family will come out into the streets, recite the Tabarra and go to jail. This might create feelings of intense excitement. Shias of the very highest standing have said privately that it will be impossible for them not to offer themselves for arrest, and Shias outside Lucknow and even outside the Province seem to be seriously disturbed. Mr. Kidwai, one of my Muslim Ministers, told me that he had been to see the prisoners in jail both during the Sunni civil disobedience and during the Shia civil disobedience, and he was very greatly struck by the difference in the class of prisoners. This difference seems to have made a great impression on his mind.

14. It is difficult to know exactly how far politics have played a part in the accentuation of the Madhe-Sahaba controversy.

I think there is no doubt that the trouble to begin with at any rate was in fact encouraged by the Congress in order to split the Muslims. It must also be remembered that the Congress Muslims are mainly Sunnis, and that this agitation had been adopted vigorously before the present constitution came into force by the Ahrars who are under the influence of the Congress. It is freely asserted that Maulvi Hussain Ahmad Madni who has been the leading figure in the movement for a long time is in the pay of the Congress, and it is difficult to believe that they could not control him if they wished to. Nevertheless, my Ministers speak as if Maulvi Hussain Ahmad represents a force that cannot be controlled and is in fact a considerable embarrassment to them. If in fact the Congress have been playing a double game in this matter, it appears they have over-reached themselves. While the Sunni agitation was going on the Shias took great pains to conciliate the Congress, and the Muslim political movement as a whole was appreciably weakened. The effect of the orders now passed about the Madhe-Sahaba is to swing over Shia opinion in the most violent way against the Congress. They feel that they have been betrayed and that a gross injustice has been perpetrated on them. At the same time the Sunnis, other than Congress Sunnis, are not likely to be in the least grateful to the Congress, and there are even traces of a feeling that the whole matter has gone too far and that something should be done on the part of the Sunnis to waive their rights in view of the tremendous strength of opinion shown by the Shias.

15. The Ministers are perturbed at the result of their orders about Madhe-Sahaba, and are genuinely anxious that the tension should be relaxed and that a settlement should be reached. Various possibilities are at the moment under close consideration. The Barawafat day is on the 2nd or 3rd May.

H.G. HAIG

ENCLOSURE 2 TO NO. 31

PRESS COMMUNIQUÉ ISSUED BY
U.P. GOVERNMENT ON NOVEMBER 10TH, 1938

Question of the Recitation of the Madhe-Sahaba

[*The full text of this communiqué is printed in* United Provinces' Politics, 1938, *Appendix 12.*]

ENCLOSURE 3 TO NO. 31

PRESS COMMUNIQUÉ ISSUED BY
U.P. GOVERNMENT ON MARCH 30TH, 1939

Question of the Recitation of the Madhe-Sahaba

"Government in their statement of November last stated that the Sunnis could recite Madhe-Sahaba in their houses, mosques and on the occasion of Milad-i-Sharif without any interference. What then remained to decide was when the Government would give the Sunnis an opportunity to recite Madhe-Sahaba at a public meeting or in a procession. As regards this they said that they were intending to do so, but as at that time talks with the Shias and the Sunnis were in progress, it was not desirable for the Government to announce their own decision.

"Since then the matter has been engaging the earnest attention of the Government but, on account of the unsatisfactory and disturbed atmosphere in Lucknow on the one hand and their desire for an amicable settlement between the two sects on the other, they could not carry out their intention expressed in November last.

"During this period in some quarters a doubt has been expressed as regards the three days' ban. Government do not feel it necessary to reconsider this point as the Sunnis' right of public recitation of Madhe-Sahaba without the exception of any days has already been recognised in the aforesaid statement. This right, like so many other civil rights, is only subject to control by the district authorities in the form of restraint or regulation to be exercised solely in the interest of the maintenance of law and order. This restriction is unavoidable and no section of the public can escape it.

"Therefore, in continuation of the Press statement of November last, Government hereby announce that the Sunnis will in any circumstances be given the opportunity of reciting Madhe-Sahaba at a public meeting and in a procession every year on the Barawafat day subject to the condition that the time, place and route thereof shall be fixed by the district authorities."

The above communiqué was issued as a result of correspondence between the Premier, Pandit Govind Ballabh Pant, and Mr. Muhammad Ismail, M.L.A., President of the Anjuman-i-Ahrar. Mr. Muhammad Ismail wrote to the Premier:

"It is already within your knowledge that the Sunnis are carrying on civil disobedience in Lucknow to defy Government order as regards the public recitation of Madhe-Sahaba. This movement is gaining ground and becoming widespread every day. *Jathas* from outside are pouring into Lucknow daily to join the movement. More than 2,000 have so far already courted arrest and thousands more are waiting for their turn. This state of affairs should not be allowed to continue. I do not know Government's mind on this question but from their statement of November last it is evident that they intended to allow the Sunnis to have recitation of Madhe-Sahaba in public meetings or processions. Why the Government did not so far carry out this intention is not known. May I know it from you now in answer to the questions I put below?

"1. Do Government really intend to allow the Sunnis to recite Madhe-Sahaba at a public meeting or in a procession in Lucknow? If so, when?

"2. Do Government intend to lift the three days' ban regarding the Ashra and the Chehlum days and the 21st Ramzan? I think I need not point out to you here that this ban is against the religious code of the Sunni sect and makes it obligatory on them to recite Madhe-Sahaba in defiance of it.

"In order to elicit this information I tabled a cut motion on the grant relating to the General Administration, which I am sorry could not be reached so far. Nor is there any likelihood that it will be reached at all. I wish you would clear the position as regards this matter at your earliest and, if possible, issue a Government communiqué on this matter."

The following was the Premier's reply:

"I am sending to you herewith a copy of the Government communiqué which is being issued. From it you will fully know the position as regards the right of the Sunnis of reciting Madhe-Sahaba, but I want to make it clear that Government will not be able to translate their intention of allowing the Sunnis to recite Madhe-Sahaba into action if the present civil disobedience movement is not called off without delay. This movement was started quite unnecessarily as the Government had already expressed their intention to meet the wishes of the Sunnis as far as they could in the statement issued in November last. I am publishing this letter along with yours and the Government communiqué."

32

HAIG TO LINLITHGOW
R/3/1/75

Confidential
No. U.P.-246

Camp,
April 22nd, 1939

My dear Lord Linlithgow,

I have taken a little time to consider Your Excellency's letter of 15th March 1939 as the matter did not appear to be of pressing urgency, since the proposals concern the budget for 1940-41.[15] On referring to the correspondence that has taken place between us this year on the United Provinces Budget I think the information supplied is very much what your letter contemplates. I would refer first of all to my telegram No. G-195 of January 22nd, 1939, in which I gave an account of the discussions with Pant on the previous day and my Finance Secretary's[16] preliminary estimate of a deficit of 67 lakhs. The probable imposition of the tax on petrol was mentioned, and the Premier's answers to my enquiries about a rumoured intention to put forward a 10 per cent cut on salaries. In replying to this telegram of mine, Your Excellency asked urgently for an abstract of the Budget and the Revised with brief notes on the lines which have been proposed in the memorandum attached to your present letter. My Secretary accordingly on January 27th, 1939, sent Laithwaite two printed copies of the Finance Secretary's first cast of the Budget and Revised, with notes on some of the more outstanding points.

2. The Budget meeting of the Council of Ministers took place on February 2nd, 1939, and I reported its results to you in my telegram No. G-205 of February 3rd, 1939, in some detail. That telegram mentioned the decision of my Government to impose a petrol tax. After it was sent, on the same day, I received information for the first time about their intention to introduce the tax on employments, and I secured a first draft of the Bill. This was reported to you in my telegram No. G-208 of February 4th and copies of the draft Bill and other connected papers were sent by Donaldson to Laithwaite with his letter No. 93/39.G.S.P. of February 4th. The results of further Cabinet discussions on the Budget and on these taxes on February 6th, 1939, were given to you in paragraph 8 of my

fortnightly report No. U.P.-222 of February 8th. The Budget was introduced into the Legislative Assembly on February 24th. The Premier's speech was in draft up to the day previous, and was in fact not written and not fully settled in details until about that day. A copy of his speech, with a short further comment on the Budget, was enclosed with my fortnightly letter No. U.P.-227 of February 27th (see paragraph 5 of that letter).

3. The conclusions I draw from my own experience hitherto are:

(*a*) That the Government owing to many preoccupations and the difficulty of making up their minds put off decisions on the Budget till the last possible moment. This year, for instance, the Finance Secretary was considerably perturbed at being unable to get orders earlier, and I had to press on the Ministers more than once the necessity for not delaying our Budget discussions too long.

(*b*) Before the actual Budget discussions in the Cabinet it is possible to get the Finance Secretary's preliminary estimates, vide paragraph 3 of my telegram No. G-195, dated January 22nd, 1939. I agree that it is desirable that a communication should be made to Your Excellency, as in that telegram, giving a general picture of these estimates.

(*c*) There may well be proposals which the Ministers deliberately hold back till the last moment, but they have normally to be disclosed at the time of the main Cabinet discussion on the Budget. This was the time when the Employments Tax proposals came forward. The Cabinet discussion must, on account of arrangements for printing, take place about three weeks before the introduction of the Budget. It is of course possible that Ministers would at this stage only settle proposals for normal revenue and for all expenditure and would leave a deficit uncovered, and not disclose their proposals for covering it until a few days before the introduction of the Budget. If this were done deliberately it would not, I think, be possible to prevent it.

(*d*) I have some doubts about the proposal that Governors should forward to the Governor-General an abstract of the first edition of the Budget and the Revised estimates, and that the figures given in these estimates should be kept up to date by further information. My own feeling is that while it is clearly of general interest and may be of profound importance that the main features of Provincial Budgets should be known to Your Excellency, it is not at first sight appropriate that detailed figures prepared in the Provincial Secretariat should be forwarded in advance by the Governor. Neither the Governor nor the Governor-General have any special responsibility for the finances of the Provinces, and if it became known that the Governor was supplying detailed information in advance to the

Governor-General I think the Ministers might very reasonably protest that it indicated some intention to invade the sphere of their responsibilities. I do not know what degree of importance Your Excellency attaches to a scrutiny by your staff of these detailed figures, but clearly the Ministers would have serious cause to complain if the figures were communicated to the Finance Department of the Government of India. The financial interests of the Provinces and of the Central Government may in some matters be in opposition, and I think my Ministers are entitled to claim that their financial proposals and difficulties should not be communicated to the Central Government until they face the world with them in the Budget speech.

4. My general conclusion therefore would be that it would be sufficient for Governors to provide Your Excellency with a general account of:

(*a*) the preliminary estimates;

(*b*) the main features of the Budget proposals as they begin to emerge;

(*c*) the Budget proposals as they are finally settled at the Budget meeting;

(*d*) any subsequent modifications or additions of importance.

I would hope that it might not be necessary, and I think it is of doubtful expediency so far as the Governor is concerned, that the detailed figures referred to in the memorandum attached to your letter should be furnished.[17]

Yours sincerely,
HARRY HAIG

33

HAIG TO LINLITHGOW
R/3/1/75

Secret and Personal *April 24th, 1939*
No. U.P.-248

My dear Lord Linlithgow,

A few days ago Miss Agatha Harrison[18] came to see me and was talking a good deal about Hindu-Muslim troubles in this Province which she said were causing Gandhi great anxiety. She then got on to the subject of Jawaharlal Nehru, with whom she had just been staying, and said she felt it was a great pity that a man who counted for so much in the Congress movement should be out of touch with the higher Government authorities. Ministers were in the closest relation with Governors, Gandhi had made an effective contact with His Excellency the Viceroy, but men like

Jawaharlal Nehru were left rather in the air. She spoke of him as being the natural successor to Gandhi. I said that I myself regretted that I had not been able to come in contact with Nehru, but I had always supposed that he was not anxious to establish contact and he might be unwilling to come to Government House to see me. She said there might be difficulties, and we left the matter there.

2. After reflecting on this conversation I came to the conclusion that it was not unlikely that it was a definite feeler for me to see Nehru, and as I considered there would be advantages in my making contact I wrote to Mrs. Pandit saying that I had been thinking a good deal lately about the communal situation in the Province. So far as administrative measures were concerned the Government had under consideration every aspect, but when all possible administrative action had been taken there still remained the underlying causes which have given rise to this acute ill-feeling, and unless something was done to deal with these underlying causes we could hardly expect any permanent improvement. Though there were grave difficulties in any attempt to deal with these intractable factors, nevertheless thought and discussion might open out some way that is not just now apparent. I said that it had occurred to me that from this point of view it might be helpful if I could have a talk with her brother and that if he would care to see me for such a purpose it would give me great pleasure to have the opportunity of meeting him. I had a reply from Mrs. Pandit the same evening saying that she had been speaking to her brother on the telephone when my letter arrived and that he would be in Lucknow on the 23rd and 24th and would be happy to meet me. Accordingly I saw him on Sunday evening (23rd).

3. I had only once before met Nehru for a few minutes at a garden party and had only a very superficial impression of him. When he came on the 23rd I was at once struck by his great resemblance both in appearance and in manner to Mrs. Pandit. He had great charm of manner, spoke in a very quiet and moderate way and was most friendly. It was in fact difficult to picture him as the fiery speaker or the author of eloquent incitements to revolution which had been my chief mental image of him hitherto. There have of course been clear signs for some time past that he has changed very considerably from that implacable attitude which appeared to characterise him some years ago, and I have speculated whether we should not discount a good deal of his public utterances as being the essential trappings of his position. I had wondered whether in the last year or two the real man was more essentially represented by his trumpet calls to revolutionary action, or by his sensible and courageous re-proofs of the

excesses in the field of labour agitation, educational indiscipline and so on. It would be rash to form an opinion after a single interview, but I am certainly more inclined than I was before to feel that at bottom he wishes to establish a reasonable system of administration and is not looking, as some of his utterances might suggest, to a revolutionary change.

4. With regard to Hindu-Muslim relations he was disposed not to take too seriously present conditions which he thought would improve rather than deteriorate. His contention was that on both sides people were beginning to get tired of these conditions. He also seemed to have some belief in the Muslim mass contact movement, though we did not actually discuss it, for he said that Muslims in the villages mainly voted for Congress because they supported the agrarian policy of the Congress, though in the towns the Muslims were steadily in favour of the Muslim League. We had some discussion about the possibility of admitting representatives of the Muslim League to the Ministry. He pointed out the obvious objections, which I accepted, but he said that so far as this Province was concerned the difficulties might not be insuperable, meaning no doubt that some prominent Muslim Leaguers in this Province are very strongly nationalist in their views. But he said it was really an all-India problem, and it would be very difficult to handle it on a provincial basis. We also had some talk about joint electorates, and he expressed a great desire for their establishment in local bodies. I was pleased to find, however, that he had no idea of trying to impose this solution on Muslims (though there have been indications of Congressmen in this Province apparently thinking on those lines). He was quite clear that it could only be done by consent. He spoke also of the problem in the villages in connection with the scheme for village panchayats, and said that it would be a deplorable thing to introduce separate electorates in the villages. He stressed the point that the Muslims in this Province are for the most part dwellers in towns and that in the villages they are usually a very small minority.

5. I asked him about the resolution which I referred to in paragraph 13 of my letter No. U.P.-241 of April 10th that was passed recently by the Provincial Congress Committee that Congressmen should not concern themselves with the appointment, dismissal or transfer of Government servants for personal reasons. I said that I had been uneasy about these developments recently which I felt were demoralising to the administration, and that I hoped it was with the same idea of keeping the administration intact, whoever might be in power, that this resolution had been passed. He showed at once that he fully agreed on this point and said that the effect of the resolution would be not only to discourage these activities of Congressmen in districts, but to make it easier for Ministers if they did get

any such representations to refuse to have anything to do with them. This was in very refreshing contrast to the normal attitude of Pant on these matters.

6. We also got on to the subject of international affairs and the probabilities of war. Here again he spoke very sensibly and moderately. A little over a year ago when Lothian[19] was in Allahabad he had a long talk with Nehru and afterwards told me that Nehru was inclined to take the line that the British Empire was finished and would not be able to defend itself against Germany and Italy, and therefore it was doubtful whether India had anything to gain by supporting the British. Yesterday his attitude was quite different. He volunteered the remark that the resources of the democracies were so great that in the long run Germany and Italy were bound to beaten. We did not get to grips regarding the attitude of India in the event of war, but he certainly did not suggest that there need necessarily be trouble. On the other hand, he has in public been denouncing strongly the amendment of the Government of India Act in connection with war conditions, and the Provincial Congress Committee under his presidentship passed recently a bellicose resolution urging the Provincial Government in the event of war to disregard the restrictions imposed upon them. Here again one is left with the choice between his moderate attitude in conversation and his very vigorous utterances in public.

7. I feel that this interview has been of value. Nehru is certainly the most influential man in the Province and it is an advantage that we should know each other and have established what I hope are friendly personal relations. He is President of the Provincial Congress Committee and in that capacity has a very considerable influence on provincial policy. If Pant were to break down, which is a contingency that might happen at any time, Nehru's influence on the reconstitution of the Ministry would obviously be great, and it would be an advantage if I could be in touch with him over this. There is even perhaps the outside chance, though it may not seem very likely at present, that he might himself take on the Premiership if he were to judge that this was the only way in which the Province could be kept in hand. If he has any such idea at the back of his mind, I feel sure that it will have been an advantage that we have been able to have a look at each other with, I think, satisfactory results.

8. I am sending a copy of this letter to the Secretary of State for his information. But apart from this I should be grateful if you would kindly treat it as strictly secret and personal.

Yours sincerely,
H.G. HAIG

34

HAIG TO LINLITHGOW
R/3/1/75

Confidential *April 25th, 1939*
No. U.P.-249

My dear Lord Linlithgow,

I received two days ago from the Hon'ble Premier a copy of a resolution passed by the Executive Council of the Provincial Congress Committee at its meeting held on the 7th April 1939 regarding the attitude of the Provincial Government towards the limitation of their powers in the event of war proposed in the amendment to the Government of India Act. The Hon'ble Premier requested that I should send a copy of this resolution to the proper quarters.

2. I took occasion today to question the Hon'ble Premier regarding the attitude of the Provincial Government to this resolution. I pointed out to him that the resolution was in the form of a recommendation to the Provincial Government to act in a particular way. He informed me that the Ministry would feel bound to carry out the Congress policy whatever it might be. He was not in a position to put any authoritative interpretation on the resolution, but expected that he would receive instructions from the Congress as to the action to be taken if an occasion should arise. He explained, however, that in his view the meaning of the resolution would be that action taken by the Central Government in accordance with the powers newly conferred upon them by the amendment to the Government of India Act would not be recognised as binding on the Provincial Government.

3. I have informed the Hon'ble Premier that I am forwarding this resolution to Your Excellency for information.

Yours sincerely,
H.G. HAIG

ENCLOSURE TO NO. 34

RESOLUTION PASSED BY EXECUTIVE COUNCIL OF U.P. PROVINCIAL CONGRESS COMMITTEE, PANDIT NEHRU PRESIDING, AT ITS MEETING ON APRIL 7TH, 1939

In view of the attempt that is being made by the British Government to amend the existing statute with a view to restricting in the event of war the already limited powers of the Provincial Governments, the Council wish to declare that no such limitations will be recognised and every attempt by the Central authority to impose the policy of the British Government on this Province should be resisted. The Council trust that the Provincial Government will act in accordance with this declaration and, in the event of war, will follow the policy of the Congress regardless of any restrictions imposed on them.

35

HAIG TO LINLITHGOW
R/3/1/75

Secret
No. U.P.-250

Camp,
April 26th, 1939

My dear Lord Linlithgow,

When I last wrote I was away for a few days' holiday at Easter and Pant was in the hills. I returned to Lucknow on April 10th and the Ministers, with the exception of Pant, reassembled about the same time. He did not arrive until a week later, and during this period Kidwai was acting for him. I found that he was much more definite and firm than Pant. He passed an unequivocal draft promising support to the District Magistrate of Gorakhpur[20] in the event of further trouble in Maharajganj. He announced in the Assembly that action under the Press Act would be taken against six papers in Lucknow which had been stirring up trouble between Sunnis and Shias. He appears to have rung up the Premier on the telephone and got his agreement to this. But I think had the Premier been here he would have found some excuse for avoiding this action. Kidwai told me that he himself saw no reason why the Press Act should not be used and why a much more vigorous line should not be taken against dangerous communal speakers.

2. When Pant returned he was still far from well. He has not yet shaken

off his fever, which persists every day. He goes about his work, however, and writes his usual notes of great length. The Civil Surgeon has strongly advised him to get back to the hills as soon as possible and stay there for at least two months. But instead of that he is going to Calcutta for the All-India Congress Committee meeting, leaving here on April 27th, and on his return he thinks he may have to stay in Lucknow for another week or more. It is true enough that there are many problems of the utmost difficulty and importance crowding in upon him, and that it is difficult for a man of his temperament who likes doing everything himself to stand aside and let others handle them. I fear, however, that he may at any time break down seriously. I have spoken to him more than once about the importance of going to the hills, but he says it simply cannot be done just yet. One factor which no doubt makes him feel that he cannot go away is that in public estimation he has lost a great deal of ground lately. Public opinion has begun to hold him responsible for the conditions of disorder that have unfortunately been so prevalent in the last two months or so. Not only general public opinion, but his own Party seems to have become very critical of him. They feel that he has shown weakness in handling the Muslim agitation. He has certainly been weak with both sides in the sense of shrinking from taking action to control dangerous speeches and writings.[21]

3. There have been reports in the Press that the Party have become so dissatisfied with him that they wish him to surrender the law and order portfolio. I fancy there is considerable truth in these reports, but he himself appears to be putting up a strong opposition to any such ideas. He is a man with a good conceit of himself, fond of power, and possessed of an unbounded optimism. I think he is not likely to be prepared to make way for someone else in charge of law and order unless circumstances, physical or political, force this upon him.

4. We had Cabinet meetings on April 18th and April 21st. On the 18th I raised again the question of an immediate increase to the Police force. Pant said that very difficult problems were involved, that he would have to study the old files and give the proposals detailed attention. I emphasised the fact that the situation was dangerous and that in my opinion some action ought to be taken without delay. It seemed to me clear, knowing Pant's methods, that he was intending to procrastinate. I therefore pressed him to reach certain interim conclusions at once, and I suggested that it would at any rate ease the situation greatly if he could agree to the immediate recruitment of 1,000 Army reservists in place of the 2,000 that the Inspector-General of Police had asked for. I got him to promise to

reach conclusions before our next Cabinet meeting, and at the meeting on the 21st he said that he agreed to the immediate enlistment of 1,000 men while the complete proposals of the Inspector-General would be examined in detail and carefully. I thought this was a very satisfactory result, and orders were issued to the Inspector-General at once. I hope therefore that within a very short time we shall have a real addition to our resources of 1,000 men.

5. We also discussed at some length a draft letter to District Magistrates about methods for handling communal situations and riots. On the whole I think this is a sensible and useful letter and enjoins upon District Magistrates to take vigorous and effective action. With regard to the control of newspapers and pamphlets Pant was very anxious to confine action to the issue of orders under Section 144 with prompt prosecution for breaches of such orders, which he maintained would be practically effective. He is a great enthusiast for Section 144, and said that in civil disobedience days he considered we could have made far more effective and extensive use of it. I argued, however, that the Press Act provided a much more rapid and effective procedure. He agreed in the end that District Magistrates should be told that in special cases they could recommend action to be taken under the Press Act. He would not have agreed to this a few weeks ago. He is moving under the pressure of public opinion and also, I think, the views of some of his colleagues. But he moves reluctantly and slowly.

6. Pant also brought forward himself a proposal to amend Section 15-A of the Police Act so as to provide that action could be taken to compensate persons who had suffered from the consequences of a riot within a period of four months instead of one month, as laid down in the Act. One object of this amendment is that compensation should still be assessed for the damage done in Cawnpore. It was decided to introduce an amending Bill, of which I enclose a copy.[22] This has been already passed by the Assembly. There is also a proposal under consideration to take by legislation powers to extern by executive order those who are believed to be promoting communal trouble, and also power to impose collective fines on localities where there have been communal outbreaks.

7. Another topic which gave rise to considerable discussion was the order passed recently by the District Magistrate of Benares[23] imposing a 24 hour curfew on the Hindus for three days. This was done because two Muslims had been found stabbed. The curfew order was imposed not merely on the locality where these stabbings had taken place, but on the whole city, and in my opinion was a very ill-judged order. The actual results of keeping people shut up in their houses for three days in the

month of April, allowing them out only for one hour in the morning and one hour in the evening, can hardly have been appreciated by the local authorities. The whole life of the city was interrupted, great hardship was caused to thousands of people, and my Education Minister (Sampurnanand) who had been to Benares came back with a really horrifying report of the various consequences that had ensued. Apart from the actual effects, the order seems to have created great resentment, as it was felt to be not unlike martial law and to have inflicted humiliation on the whole Hindu population. It was decided to call on the District Magistrate and the Commissioner[24] to give their explanation with reference to the detailed report of Mr. Sampurnanand. The District Magistrate is an Anglo-Indian holding a listed post. He is a very vigorous officer and was in fact specially selected by the Premier for the appointment a few weeks ago when the District Magistrate[25] who had handled the riots went home on leave. But I think on this occasion he used the iron hand without discretion. The Commissioner who had concurred in this order is a Hindu, who is lacking in independence of judgment.

8. The Madhe-Sahaba situation is giving rise to great anxiety in Lucknow at present. I sent Your Excellency recently a full report of the whole Madhe-Sahaba controversy bringing it up to date. We discussed the matter in Cabinet on the 18th April and at that time the Muslim Ministers were hopeful that the Sunnis might be prepared to surrender their right in order not to carry the controversy too far. Opinion, however, had seemed to be hardening again and the critical Barawafat day, which is the 2nd of May, was approaching. I therefore wrote a full note for the Cabinet, bringing out the various considerations and possibilities, and this was discussed fully yesterday evening. I found it desirable to take a somewhat definite line myself, as there seemed to be some hesitation among the Ministers as to what should be done.[26] But the conclusions we reached were concurred in by all and I think in fact caused them some relief of mind, as they laid down a clear policy. In the first place, it was decided that as the Sunnis had been given the right of taking out their procession on the Barawafat day it was essential to see this matter through. The District Magistrate[27] has been instructed to prepare his plans in full detail for preventing interference with this procession, which should not be a matter of any particular difficulty, and for dealing with what is likely to be a far greater embarrassment, the demonstration of the Shias on this day in other parts of the city reciting the Tabarra. Trouble is anticipated in particular from the activities of Shia *purdah* ladies who appear to be determined to come out on this occasion and demonstrate in public. The best method of dealing

with them will receive the most careful consideration. Arrangements will be made to have an ample body of Police available and to warn the military. In the second place, it has been decided that it would only complicate the situation further at the present moment if the Shias were allowed to make any recitation of their own doctrines, short of Tabarra, which certainly could not be allowed. The Shias themselves would at the moment be content with nothing short of Tabarra, and the idea of putting them eventually on an equality again with the Sunnis must be left for consideration after the Barawafat. In the third place, it is agreed that every effort should be made to induce the Sunnis to make a concession which would pacify the Shias. Active conversations are in progress at the moment. The Muslim League appears at last to be taking a hand, and a good deal is hoped from the intervention of the young Raja of Mahmudabad who has been the chief financial support of the Muslim League in this Province and at the same time is a prominent and very devout Shia. Best of all would be that the Sunnis should voluntarily surrender altogether their right of reciting Madhe-Sahaba. This is not altogether impossible, but is unlikely. It is possible that the Sunnis might be got to declare that after this one recitation of Madhe-Sahaba they would not exercise the right again. At the moment the Shias are not disposed to accept this, but they might be got round to regard this as a reasonable settlement. Indeed, some months ago there was no doubt that the Shias were prepared to accept this proposal. Another possibility is that the Sunnis would merely declare that in view of the strong feeling of Shias they did not want to recite the Madhe-Sahaba on the Barawafat day this year. That would give a whole year's respite and would at any rate greatly ease the immediate position. There is yet another proposal, to which I am myself very definitely opposed, and that is that the Sunnis should say they did not wish to recite the Madhe-Sahaba on the Barawafat day but ask for permission to recite it on some other day which may be fixed by the District Magistrate. This would simply have the effect of keeping the controversy alive and perpetuating the uncertainty to remove which was the main object of the present orders. I fancy some of the Hindu Ministers had been encouraging this idea with a view to conciliating the Sunnis on political grounds. But I was glad to find that both my Muslim Ministers were against it, though they are Sunnis. There the matter rests for the moment, but at any rate we have a clear programme.

9. There was a very deplorable incident two days ago when a band of some 30 to 40 Sunni demonstrators (part of a crowd of 4,000 to 5,000) forced their way into the Assembly Chamber when the Assembly was sitting and interrupted the proceedings. I discussed the whole matter with the

Premier yesterday and also referred to it at the Cabinet meeting. The incident brings the administration into serious discredit, and the Ministers themselves feel this acutely. They are as anxious as I am that effective action should be taken to re-establish their credit. Though the Premier seems to have made some weak promises about the demonstrators not being arrested, in fact three of the ringleaders who did not take part in the demonstration but had organised it from behind have been arrested, and 7 of the actual demonstrators. Probably more arrests will be made, and these people will all be proceeded against vigorously. It is also not unlikely that one of the most troublesome leaders of the Sunni Madhe-Sahaba agitation will be proceeded against under Section 107. Orders are being issued that in future no demonstrations will be allowed within a certain distance of the Council House. An urgent enquiry is being conducted by the Chief Secretary, which will probably be finished today, to ascertain the responsibility for the apparent failure of the Police to prevent the invasion of the Council House, and to deal with it adequately. Finally, and this is a matter which I hope will have some considerable effect on the whole Sunni-Shia controversy, it is being announced that punitive Police will be imposed at once in Lucknow for a period of one year and that the cost will be levied from the Sunnis and Shias of Lucknow. It is also to be stated what that cost will be, and I hope that the figure will cause the Muslims to reflect on the unwisdom of prolonging this useless controversy.

10. I have written to Your Excellency about the Employments Tax. The Upper House has just taken action which I had not expected, but which I think will fit in well with our general plans. It has decided to refer the Bill to a select committee, and though I have not yet got any definite information about the intention, I assume that this is likely to mean a delay of a month or two in proceeding with the Bill. As soon as I get definite information I will telegraph to Your Excellency. With regard to the Petrol Tax the Upper House reduced the rate from 2 *annas* to 1 *anna* 6 *pies* per gallon. The Assembly has now restored the rate to 2 *annas*. This will presumably lead up shortly to a joint session.

11. A striking commentary on the excise policy of the Government is contained in the annual report of the Excise Commissioner[28] which has recently been published. I do not quite understand how the Ministers allowed some of the statements which are really very damaging to their policy to remain in it. I attach extracts.[29] I have no doubt that these extracts give a true picture of the facts. I fear it is plain that our excise policy is not only leading the Province straight to bankruptcy, but has little chance of achieving the objects aimed at by the reformers.

12. I am very grateful to Your Excellency for your letter of 17th April[30] and your various comments. We are certainly in these Hindu-Muslim troubles up against a problem of which no solution is in sight. I quite agree that the suggestions made by Muslims for meeting the difficulties do not carry us far. I will, however, be dealing with the problem a little more fully in answer to your letter about Zia Uddin's representation.[31]

13. As you will have understood from the general tone of this letter, I think we are reaching a critical stage in the affairs of the Province and that we may expect important developments within the next few weeks. There may be some recasting of the Ministry, or the Ministry may in connection with the Employments Tax or on some more general issue resign. It is impossible really to anticipate the future, but we must be prepared for anything. I am however confident that if it came to resignation I should be able to carry on and I hope that it would be possible to tone up the administration fairly quickly. I have said nothing about the all-India complications, but they are of course also considerable and may not be without their influence on what happens in this Province. Meantime my relations with my Ministers continue normal and friendly. We do not discuss the Employments Tax, and we endeavour to tackle in a practical way the immediate problems of urgency, such as strengthening our resources in connection with Hindu-Muslim trouble, facing the Madhe-Sahaba situation, and so on. I have recently been taking a much stronger line with the Cabinet and they have shown no sign of resentment. The reasons which have enabled me to do this will be apparent to Your Excellency from my recent letters. They are these:

(*a*) The problems of immediate urgency are those of law and order in which they recognise that I have a definite responsibility.

(*b*) These problems have disturbed public opinion in the Province and have somewhat shaken the Ministry. Consequently they are much more prepared to accept guidance from me than they were some months ago.

(*c*) The Premier himself who is generally a supporter of half measures and conditional policies has come in for strong criticism both from his own Party and from public opinion for these very defects, and is consequently easier to move than he used to be.

(*d*) Several other members of the Cabinet who probably have a more practical and vigorous outlook on these matters than the Premier are beginning, I think, to make their influence felt, and though they say little, I feel that they are often more in agreement with me than with the Premier.

Yours sincerely,
HARRY HAIG

36

HAIG TO LINLITHGOW
R/3/1/75

Confidential *April 30th, 1939*
No. U.P.-252

My dear Lord Linlithgow,

I am much obliged for your very helpful letter, dated April 18th, 1939, regarding the Government of India grant for rural development in this Province.[32] As Your Excellency has observed, I have not so far been asked by the Ministers for my personal intervention with a view to having this money made available. I think this has been due to their preoccupations with many other urgent and difficult problems, but in conversation a few days ago with the Finance Secretary[33] I heard that the Premier, who is Finance Minister, was beginning to stir about the provision of something under 2 lakhs which has been put in our budget this year as the expected contribution from the Government of India, and is anxious to know whether this will be available. Ordinarily therefore I should at once take up this question on the basis of the suggestions contained in your letter and see whether it was possible to get an agreement on these general lines. There has, however, recently been some public criticism of the working of the rural development scheme and allegations that money is being wasted. I am not at present in a position to form an independent opinion about this. I am proposing, however, to make such enquiries as are open to me. These will necessarily take some little time. For this reason I may not be in a position to reply to your letter very early; but I hope you will understand that I have the matter very much in mind, that I am grateful for Your Excellency's suggestions, and that if I am reasonably assured about the present administration of this scheme I am hopeful that we could reach a settlement about the method of expenditure of the Government of India grant.

Yours sincerely,
H.G. HAIG

37

HAIG TO LINLITHGOW
R/3/1/75

Secret and Personal *May 2nd, 1939*
No. U.P.-254

My dear Lord Linlithgow,

I am very grateful for the information contained in Your Excellency's secret and personal letter, dated April 15th, 1939, which makes clear the general policy in regard to Federation and to conditions, administrative and constitutional, in the States.[34] I am glad also to receive copies of the periodical reports made by Your Excellency to the Secretary of State about events in the States.

2. I have been, as you know, in pretty close contact with the Benares State where there has been a troublesome agitation, which is I fear sure to revive before long. I am myself satisfied that all that is reasonable is being done by the authorities there, both on the administrative and the constitutional side. But unfortunately that is no guarantee against agitation being stirred up by self-seeking and unscrupulous persons. That seems to me to be one serious problem in connection with the States – how to keep under control with the resources of a little State an unscrupulous and unreasonable agitation organised from outside.

3. I am glad to say that in Rampur, where there is I think no reasonable complaint either on the administrative or constitutional side, everything appears to be quiet. In Tehri-Garhwal there probably are grievances which require to be looked into, and there are perhaps indications that agitation might start there unless the grievances are remedied.

4. I mention these three States, with which I used before the present constitution to be myself connected, as representing three different sets of conditions.

Yours sincerely,
H.G. HAIG

38

HAIG TO LINLITHGOW
R/3/1/75

Secret
No. U.P.-257

Camp,
May 9th, 1939

My dear Lord Linlithgow,

I am writing this letter from Naini Tal. I left Lucknow on the night of May 6th and was up here on the morning of the 7th. It is a very pleasant change, and I hope before long the centre of gravity will have shifted from Lucknow to Naini Tal, and will remain here till the middle of July. At present the Legislature is still in session, but the Premier has told me that he has every intention, if he can possibly manage it, of coming to Naini Tal some time this week, and the Chief Secretary will I hope be up here within a day or two as he has been feeling the heat somewhat lately. I was very glad to hear from your letter of 28th April, for which very many thanks, that you have been enjoying your time at Dhikala and finding it something of a relaxation from the incessant pressure of the last few months. It is certainly a peaceful and beautiful place.

2. When I last wrote I was a good deal worried about the state of Pant's health, and his approaching visit to Calcutta did not seem likely to do him any good. Curiously enough, however, since his return from Calcutta he has been looking better, seems to have recovered his grip, and is altogether much more like his old self. He is, however, still suffering from fever, and it is quite clear that the sooner he can get away to the hills for a change of climate and some rest, the better. I do not think he has any intention of allowing himself to be laid on the shelf. I saw a telegram recently in the *Statesman* from Allahabad which asserted that Pant was going to take leave and that Katju was to act for him. I imagine that constitutionally there is no possibility of a Premier taking leave; but as I say I do not think that even informally he is going to lay himself up.[35] I do not know whether this telegram owed its origin to Katju, but he was certainly in Allahabad at the time it was despatched. I hope that soon after the middle of this month all the Heads of Departments and Secretaries to Government and some at any rate of the Ministers will have assembled in Naini Tal. It is hoped that the Assembly will have finished its work by the 16th May. The Legislative Council will go on somewhat longer, but I think they too will have finished before the end of May. There will perhaps be a tendency on the part of

Ministers to go to their homes rather than come to Naini Tal. Pant of course will be here, and I think Katju. Kidwai prefers the plains. Ibrahim will probably go to his home in Bijnor. Mrs. Pandit will spend most of her time at Mussoorie, where her children are, and Sampurnanand I fancy will not be a great frequenter of the hills. However, from time to time it will clearly be necessary to have Cabinet meetings and call them together.

3. When I last wrote the Government were somewhat submerged under a great wave of criticism. The criticism is still there, but I think they have got their heads above water. When it was at its height the *Pioneer* published what I am afraid I must regard as a deliberately malicious invention regarding my interview with Jawaharlal Nehru. I think it was a piece of tactics by Sir J.P. Srivastava. It was represented that Nehru was greatly upset at the failure to maintain order in the Province, that he had sought an interview with me in order to discuss the matter, and that he and I were fully in agreement that firmer action should be taken. This was all quite clearly designed to discredit the Ministry and Pant. At the same time suspicion was also to be roused against Nehru by representing that he had sought the interview with me, that he was more or less in my pocket, and that he had committed the deadly Congress sin of accepting my hospitality. I sent for Pant as soon as this article appeared, and having ascertained that he regarded it as definitely damaging and would welcome a statement by me, I put out a short communiqué which seems to have had the effect of killing this propaganda at once. I enclose copies of the *Pioneer* article and my communiqué.[36] Mrs. Pandit whom I saw a day or two afterwards said she was very grateful for my communiqué and for meeting the allegations so directly.

4. Though the Government continues to be subjected to much criticism in regard to its policy over the Madhe-Sahaba agitation, the fact that it saw its orders through without hesitation and that no kind of disturbance occurred in consequence has I think served to restore its credit a good deal. The Hindus remain very critical of the Government on the ground that the Ministers are through weakness favouring the Muslims. A number of factors contribute to this feeling. The Hindus think that on the whole in the big communal riots they had the worst of it. It certainly was so in Cawnpore and in the present state of public opinion they interpret that as being due to deliberate bias on the part of the officials in favour of the Muslims. Much feeling also was created by the very severe curfew order against the Hindus in Benares which I referred to in my last letter. This was regarded as a most unfair and arbitrary act of discrimination against the Hindus. The Government themselves had also put out a very foolish

piece of propaganda for the Muslims, enumerating the cases in which they had taken restrictive action against Hindus, and this was seized upon by the Hindus as evidence that Government were not treating the Hindus fairly. All this has given rise to a good deal of feeling which has been worked up by the Hindu Mahasabha and by the many Hindus who for various reasons are now opposed to the Congress. Even Congress Hindus joined in the attack and there was a remarkable onslaught on the Government in the *Pratap*, perhaps the most widely read vernacular paper in the Province. This took the form of a signed article (enclosed)[37] by Pandit Bal Krishna Sharma, its editor, the President of the Cawnpore City Congress Committee, a man whom I mentioned in my letters of December 6th and December 23rd, 1938, as an influential, ambitious and unreliable person, who is more responsible than anyone else for the conditions of unrest and disorder that have prevailed so long in Cawnpore. The Ministry have always been afraid of him and he has now requited their forbearance by accusing them of inability to maintain order. If they had taken firm action against him, we should have been spared a great deal of the trouble in Cawnpore.[38] Bal Krishna Sharma encourages both communism and communalism. At the moment he seems to be trying to mobilise Hindu discontent against the Ministry.

5. Though the feeling between Hindus and Muslims is as acute as ever, we have been free from disturbances since I last wrote. But the last fortnightly reports from Commissioners are disquieting with their references to constant and even increasing tension between the communities. Much harm is being done I should judge by the Hyderabad agitation, which is deliberately provocative on the part of the Hindus. At the same time, as I have indicated in the previous paragraph, Hindu feeling is being worked up on the lines that they are not receiving fair treatment from the Government and Hindus are beginning to regard themselves as aggrieved. I mentioned in my last letter that instructions were being issued to District Magistrates giving them guidance and enjoining upon them vigorous action in connection with communal trouble. I enclose a copy of this letter,[39] which was discussed in Cabinet, as it will give Your Excellency some idea of the attitude that the Ministers are now adopting. I also enclose a copy of another circular letter which has just gone out dealing with action against speeches and writings.[40] This was originally intended to refer only to communal speeches and writings, but at my suggestion and after a certain amount of hesitation the Premier agreed to widening its scope to include all kinds of incitement to class or communal hatred, not excluding attacks on Europeans, and if the Government back up their

officers in carrying out the instructions they are now giving them, there should I think be a real improvement in the situation.

6. The result of the Congress meeting in Calcutta[41] must I think be regarded as satisfactory from our point of view. I have been seeing less evidence lately of the left wing influence in our Provincial policy, and I think the outcome of Calcutta should be an encouragement to my Ministers to pursue their own policy without being too nervous about left wing opinion. I should judge that Nehru feels it is necessary to keep the left wing pretty strictly under control in the United Provinces if the Government administration and consequently the Congress is not to find itself involved in discredit, and with the right wing entrenched again in the higher command it should be possible to carry through such a policy. A great deal depends I think on Nehru's attitude, but I believe that to be reasonable and indeed in practice stiffer than that of Pant. I took occasion a few days ago to speak to Pant about specifically revolutionary activities in this Province, and I told him that I was uneasy about the reports we were getting which suggested that we might be moving from the stage of talk and agitation to the stage of organisation and action. I found him quite responsive to these ideas and anxious to know what particular organisations or individuals might be regarded as dangerous. We decided to ask the D.I.G., C.I.D.,[42] to let us have a special report in this connection as early as possible. With this before us it may be that I shall be able to induce him to take some definite action in certain directions, and in any case we ought to take stock of the position now.

7. Since I last wrote the matter which has roused much the most intense public interest and feeling has been the Madhe-Sahaba dispute. I mentioned in my last letter the conclusions of policy which the Government reached. In pursuance of these decisions elaborate precautions were taken for maintaining the peace on the 3rd May. Five hundred additional Police were drafted into Lucknow and the military authorities gave their fullest cooperation. A march of a large body of Police through the city a day or two before the date of the procession had a marked effect on public opinion. It was realised that Government intended to maintain the peace and had the means to do it. At the same time a state of considerable nervousness prevailed in Lucknow, and I think this was not without its effect in making the Shias behave in a more reasonable way than at one time seemed likely. It was a great relief to everyone when the project of bringing out the Shia *purdah* women was abandoned. The Sunnis having gained their object were anxious that there should be no trouble on the Barawafat day. Some efforts were made beforehand by the more troublesome sections of the

Sunnis to object to the route and restrictions laid down by the District Magistrate; but good sense prevailed and the procession went off quite peacefully and Lucknow heaved a very great sigh of relief. The lowest estimate given in the papers of the numbers in the procession was 30,000, and on the whole I should think that is about accurate. In spite of the large numbers it was a very orderly procession. The district authorities deserve great credit for the arrangements and the sense of security was enhanced by the presence of a number of pickets of British troops at important places.

8. Negotiations for some kind of settlement which would have meant a voluntary surrender by the Sunnis of their right at any rate to repeat this procession continued right up to the 3rd May, but led to nothing. I think it is true to say that the great majority of reasonable Sunnis would have been very glad to reach such a settlement, but the Sunni masses were really out of control of any leaders. No one could answer for them. The Muslim League might have been able to do something had they taken a strong line, but it appeared that on the contrary the League were so nervous about their own organisation being disrupted by this controversy that they would take no line at all, and I was told even that Jinnah had threatened ex-communication to any Muslim Leaguer who should try to intervene. I have read in the paper today that Jinnah suggests that the Muslim League may find some solution, but I am disposed to doubt whether this means anything. If Your Excellency hears again from the Nizam on this subject, perhaps it would not be unfair to ask him whether he would propound a solution which owing to his great authority in the Islamic world might be expected to win acceptance. In fact a Shia did suggest this to me. But I fear His Exalted Highness would follow the same policy as Mr. Jinnah.

9. As soon as the Barawafat was safely over, I discussed the situation fully with the Premier and the two Muslim Ministers. We were all agreed that the time had come to make a strong effort to settle the controversy. The most satisfactory settlement of course would be a voluntary one between the Sunnis and Shias; but it seemed that there was no chance of the Sunnis, owing to absence of leadership, taking the necessary initiative. Consequently we agreed that the Government should concentrate on the only other feasible alternative, namely, to put the Shias back on an equality with the Sunnis by allowing them also to recite publicly their distinctive doctrines, provided language was not used which was deliberately offensive to the Sunnis. In other words our view was that no form of Tabarra should be allowed, but that the Shias might be allowed to declare their own beliefs in this matter without abusing the three Khalifas. It seemed clear that unless the Shias got a concession of this kind, which in itself was entirely

reasonable, they would not abandon their Tabarra agitation. Though they kept quiet on the Barawafat day, we are none of us under any illusion as to the depth of their feelings, and the Ministers believe that if no settlement is reached, the Shias who already have something like 8,000 persons in jail will be able to put in another 8,000. The women also are sure to join the agitation before long if it continues. At a Cabinet meeting the day before I left Lucknow we discussed the situation, and the policy as indicated above was accepted. The Ministers were very busy when I left negotiating with the Shias, but I have not heard what the outcome of these conversations has been. At any rate I am convinced that the Ministers are very anxious now to bring the Shia agitation to an end and to close down, if possible, the controversy which is so profoundly disturbing the life of Lucknow and has shown signs of spreading widely outside. If the Shias are given an opportunity of taking out their procession, it is not unlikely that both sides will voluntarily abandon these processions. The District Magistrate, Jasbir Singh, who is a good officer, a brother of Sir Maharaj Singh, has been feeling very much the strain of the last few months, and now that the Barawafat is over has said that he feels he must have two months' leave. There is no choice but to give it to him, for he is definitely over-strained. But it will not be easy to replace him. The Superintendent of Police, Parkin, has done admirably throughout this difficult time, has kept his head and has made excellent arrangements.

10. I have been in correspondence with Your Excellency about our attitude towards the Employments Tax Bill. It is very difficult to get a clear idea of the programme contemplated by the Ministers. Indeed at times it almost seems as if they have no programme. At present matters stand as follows. The Assembly is expected to finish its work about the 16th May, and on that assumption I have summoned a joint sitting of the two Houses to consider the Petrol Sales Bill on the 17th May. The select committee on the Employments Tax Bill has to report by the 13th May; but for some reason which I was unable to understand Katju told the Legislative Council when they separated about a fortnight ago that they will meet again about the 22nd, which seems to me from the point of view of the Government unnecessarily and inconveniently late. In connection with the date of the joint sitting of the two Houses I suggested that the Legislative Council should meet again on the 18th or 19th, as members will have to be in Lucknow on the 17th for the joint sitting, and this I understand will be done. When the Legislative Council reassembles it will have before it the select committee's report on the Employments Tax Bill, and though the Ministers talk in a vague way of a possible settlement

with the Upper House, it seems to me inevitable that there will be some disagreement between the two Houses. But by the time the Legislative Council have registered that disagreement, the Assembly will have been prorogued, and when I put this point to Katju some time ago he spoke vaguely about a joint session perhaps not taking place till July. On the whole I think the Ministers have drifted into this position without realising what they were doing. I feel that they are getting a little tired of the Employments Tax and doubtful whether anything will ever come of it, and it is possible that they are not unwilling to put out of the way for the moment an unpleasant subject. It would of course be possible for them to deal with the anticipated disagreement between the two Houses by resummoning the Assembly for the end of May. But I think that would be an unpopular move.

11. Another matter of uncertainty is the line that will be taken by the Legislative Council in connection with the Tenancy Bill. This will come up before them when they reassemble. There is a good deal of talk on both sides of the possibility of a compromise, and I am sure that this would be the wisest course both from the point of view of the Government and that of the landlords. I think there will be important conversations before long, but the immediate question is what action the Legislative Council will take. They can either take the Bill into consideration clause by clause, or they can refer it to a select committee. The Government were disposed to regard the proposal to refer to a select committee as an obstructive move, and indeed the landlords had this very much in mind. But in fact I am inclined to think that reference to a select committee might provide the best opportunity for conversations and a settlement which could be put into the report of the select committee and that perhaps this would be a wiser course than to discuss the Bill clause by clause in the Council which would involve long controversies over many points of little importance. If the Council decide to refer the Bill to a select committee they can disperse as soon as they have finished with the Employments Tax Bill and their session will be over well before the end of May. If on the other hand they take the Tenancy Bill into consideration, there is some idea that they should sit for that purpose in Naini Tal. You will realise that the whole programme of the Legislature is still very uncertain.

12. I fear that as soon as one trouble subsides a little, another emerges, and it looks to me likely that we shall have some serious anxieties during the next month in Cawnpore arising out of the labour situation. During the communal trouble in Cawnpore labour kept quiet, but a strike has now developed at the New Victoria Mills and the omens for settlement are not

good. Labour is still in an uncertain and restless mood, and the Mazdur Sabha have no influence except for mischief. If labour trouble starts again it may well be the signal for a serious recrudescence of communal rioting. I look upon Cawnpore therefore with considerable anxiety. I hope, however, that if trouble does start again in Cawnpore, the Ministry can be induced to take a much firmer line with regard to the communists and labour agitators than they have before.

13. I have mentioned before my feeling that a good deal of harm is being done by transfers of the non-protected Services based on complaints or suggestions from members of the Legislature or local Congressmen. I decided to raise the matter definitely in Cabinet, and I wrote a note recently, a copy of which I enclose,[43] which was circulated to all Ministers as a preliminary to discussion.[44] I put plainly to them the ill effects of such tendencies, and I referred to the resolution of the Provincial Congress Committee passed on April 7th which deprecated activities of this kind. I raised the subject in Cabinet on a restrained note, though making the points clearly. I had anticipated that they might argue that my apprehensions were over-stated or that the evil was exaggerated. But to my surprise and satisfaction I found that they accepted practically everything I said, and fully agreed with me about the dangers of such developments and the inevitable weakening of the Services. They said that the Provincial Congress resolution had actually been inspired by themselves and that they were entirely in agreement with it. I took the occasion to emphasise the elementary point that the Ministers laid down policy and passed orders and the Services have to carry these out, and that there was no place in such a scheme for what I described as little Ministers in the districts. This was very well received. It will be too much to expect that the abuse will be altogether stopped; practice will not always conform to precept. But as we have had this formal discussion and got the policy of the Ministers on record, I hope that at any rate there will be a considerable diminution in such political transfers, and I certainly found the attitude of the Ministers extremely sensible and reassuring.[45]

Yours sincerely,
HARRY HAIG

ENCLOSURE 1 TO NO. 38

GWYNNE TO ALL DISTRICT OFFICERS

L/P&J/5/267: ff. 108-11

Confidential
No. 72/III-1939

Lucknow,
April 29th, 1939

Sir,

The Provincial Government are greatly perturbed by the growing bitterness of the relations between Hindus and Muslims and the dire results of the wave of communal frenzy that has swept over certain parts of the Province this year. It is not proposed in this letter to dwell on its deeper causes – be they political, social or religious – nor to attempt to apportion blame for what has happened. Communal disorder is no new feature of life in this province and there is a long series of Government orders on the subject which should be within the knowledge of all District Magistrates. Government are anxious that the tension should be immediately relieved, so that mutual confidence, amity and goodwill may be restored. There can be no two opinions about the supreme importance of this problem and Government earnestly desire that it should receive the special attention of everyone who is associated with the administration of public affairs in the Province. It is difficult to set forth at length the disastrous consequences which follow communal strife. The serious effect which communal bitterness exercises on the provincial finances and on the social and political life of the Province cannot be over-emphasized. The extra expenditure involved in dealing with riots has to be met from the provincial revenues. The police has been subjected to continuous heavy strain during the last few months and an increase has already been sanctioned in the strength of the armed police. Unless communal peace and harmony are restored it will be necessary to make still further additions, and even though the cost is partly met by the imposition of additional police it will fall in any case on the people of the province and is not remunerative expenditure. As regards social and political life, ill-feeling between Hindus and Muslims results in serious loss to trade and commerce and impairs credit. There can be no doubt that communal disorders detract from the efficiency of administration and bring it into disrepute. In the circumstances all possible measures should be adopted by district officials to promote harmony between different communities and they should be particularly on their guard to see that nothing is done that may tend to worsen the situation further. A great deal depends on the personality of the District Officer and on the watchful care ceaselessly exercised by him. An efficient and energetic officer who knows how to handle the situation with tact, firmness and promptitude can do a lot to avert trouble. As has been pointed out before, it is essential that executive officers should observe an absolutely impartial attitude and they should be particularly careful where questions of a communal character call for decision. The District Officer should make it a point to impress upon his subordinates that any one found guilty of communal bias will be regarded as having committed a serious breach of discipline, and wherever such cases are noticed prompt and effective action should be taken, so that the contagion may not spread to other ranks. The District Magistrate should himself preserve a calm and equable attitude as any display of panic or a want of confidence on his part encourages the same feeling in others. He should keep in touch with the sensible and responsible people of his district and should endeavour to induce them to be reasonable and tolerant; and whenever fair-minded persons of goodwill are available and willing to exert themselves in the cause of communal harmony he will appoint peace committees or conciliation boards. He should encourage every activity which conduces towards better feeling and greater friendliness and should discourage all attempts likely to exacerbate feelings or to embitter relations between the different communities. His task will be greatly facilitated by his reputation for impartiality and the confidence he enjoys among the different sections of the community. After these general observations I am to address you on the attitude that should be adopted by district officials in regard to communal differences and the steps which should be taken when signs of communal tension become manifest and the measures which should be enforced effectively when once a communal disturbance has broken out in spite of every effort to prevent it.

2. Orders have been issued from time to time as to the maintenance of the records of local customs, usages and rights. The District Magistrates should examine these records and, if they find any deficiencies, they should make every endeavour, if they can do so without giving cause for any fresh controversy, to bring them up-to-date. It is difficult to lay down instructions that would meet every conceivable case. It may, however, be helpful to give a synoptic view of the position and to indicate the broad lines of approach towards such problems. They may be summarized as follows:

(*a*) It is the paramount duty of executive officers to maintain public tranquillity and public order and they are required and expected to adopt all means that may be necessary towards the achievement of this supreme purpose. Subject to this, they must make every endeavour to enable communities and individuals to enjoy their religious and social rights and any restriction or interference on their part should not exceed the requirements of the situation which must be determined by the circumstances of each case.

(*b*) It is no part of the normal functions of the executive officers to pronounce upon questions of religious right or usage, and where there has been a definite declaration by any civil court of competent jurisdiction the executive officers should make every endeavour to ensure the enjoyment of the rights recognized by the judicial tribunals. Only in cases where there is an imminent danger of a breach of the peace should an interference with such rights be allowed.

(*c*) Where the record of a local custom has been properly maintained the executive officers should stick to it. If the existence of any such custom is disputed and considered by the District Magistrate to be doubtful he should give due weight to the legal rights normally enjoyed. His decision can only be of a summary nature and the inquiry should not be prolonged as any conclusions reached in an atmosphere of excitement and growing bitterness are likely to make his task even more difficult. Any party that is not satisfied with his orders should be advised to seek the arbitrament of the proper civil courts.

(*d*) A party should not be deprived of its rights on account of any threat held out by its opponents. After the District Magistrate has reached his decision as to what is just and proper he should use his resources to give effect to his decision and if there is any danger of defiance or disorder from any quarter he should not hesitate to take effective action against those from whom mischief is apprehended to prevent them from doing so.

(*e*) In abnormal circumstances the District Magistrate, while paying due regard to past practice and normal rights, may still find it necessary to pass orders of regulation or restriction if he has a reasonable apprehension that peace cannot be maintained otherwise, as the preservation of public order must receive precedence over any other consideration.

(*f*) Settlement by negotiation and agreement is the best method of dealing with these problems, as any decision, however, just and sound, cannot be expected to meet fully the conflicting points of view. Where sentiment is the governing factor, as it is in such cases, reason is at a discount, and in the circumstances an arrangement by consent alone can be an ideal solution. But if parties refuse to come to terms the District Magistrate should not fight shy of his responsibility and should make it abundantly clear that having once given his verdict he would see it through.

(*g*) When communal feelings are excited people are particularly sensitive and objections may be raised on very slender grounds or even without any foundation. On such occasions fantastic assertions may be made and restrictions which were never imposed may be insisted upon. Due caution should be observed not to interfere with the normal practice, especially when conditions are disturbed in any locality, and care should be taken not to hold out any hopes that may not be ultimately fulfilled.

3. I am now to turn to the measures which should be taken in the early stages when signs of communal strife are becoming manifest. The approach of a festival season is in itself a signal for care and forethought on the part of the District Magistrate whatever the political conditions may be; but it also happens that festivals provide an occasion for the display of communal rivalry which is deliberately exploited by those who should know better. Whenever there is an outbreak of communal disorder on a large scale, the religious emotionalism of the masses is easily and skilfully aroused and manipulated by leaders anxious to obtain an extensive following amongst the people and to key them up to action which will be most embarrassing to Government and to the opposite party. When this state of feeling exists, there are usually:

(*i*) a deterioration in the tone of the press;

(*ii*) a large number of meetings on a communal-cum-political basis at which very wild and inflammatory speeches are delivered;

(*iii*) the issue of leaflets, pamphlets, songs, etc., in vast quantities throughout the country with a view to stir up communal feeling and the free use of communal slogans;

(*iv*) the dissemination of false rumours and a growing insistence on ceremonial observances and an increasing fear of interruption from the other party which lead to general panic and absence of confidence; and

(*v*) as a result of the above, the closing of shops.

When this statc of affairs exists not only communal leaders but members of the two communities take up with increased bitterness somc of the burning questions of religious controversy such as cow-sacrifice, music before mosque, *tazia* processions, throwing of coloured water on the occasion of the Holi and the like. Then is the time for precautionary measures. The District Magistrate must maintain, as stated above, an attitude of courage, firmness and impartiality. He must be prompt and strong in action. His mental attitude at this stage should be to prevent trouble occurring; if still it does occur he must be prepared to crush it quickly.

During this period it is necessary for him to deal firmly with newspapers and pamphlets preaching communalism and with speakers. This he can do by the use of Sections 107, 108 or 144 of the Criminal Procedure Code. If a paper offends after the issue of a notice under Section 144 it can be prosecuted under Section 188 of the Indian Penal Code. The order under Section 144 of the Criminal Procedure Code should be served not only on the editor and manager but also on the proprietor of the paper. Where recommendation is made to Government for prosecution under Section 158-A of the Indian Penal Code action may also be taken in advance by the District Magistrate under Section 107 or 108 of the Criminal Procedure Code and preliminary orders for demanding security may be sought. If such offence is again repeated the security can be forfeited even during the pendency of the proceedings. Pamphlets which are unauthorized news sheets should be confiscated, and those which though not unauthorized but are incitory should be dealt with under Section 144, or other provisions of the law. Moreover if a District Magistrate is of opinion that security should also be demanded from the publisher of a newspaper or the proprietor of a press under the provisions of the Press Act he may in special cases make such a recommendation to Government.

As regards meetings, the District Magistrate must not hesitate to prohibit them if this is considered necessary for the maintenance of peace, and to take action freely under Sections 144, 107 and 108 of the Criminal Procedure Code.

As regards the dissemination of rumours, he should issue suitable orders under Section 144, and prosecute promptly in cases where breaches of these orders are committed.

The difficulty in dealing with shopkeepers who refuse to open their shops is considerable, but it is very important that they should be persuaded, if possible, to open them as nothing restores order more quickly than the appearance of normality. Recent experience has shown that where shopkeepers have been prevailed upon to open their shops, trouble stops more quickly.

In addition the District Magistrate will be well advised in taking the two following measures which past experience has shown to be most beneficial:

(*a*) Recognized *badmashes* and *goondas* should be rounded up and the free use of Sections 109 and 110 of the Criminal Procedure Code should be encouraged so that the situation is well under control during the festival season.

(*b*) Lists of persons, who might be considered as suitable in each ward or *mohalla* of a city, for appointment as special constables, should be prepared and kept ready for use should the situation deteriorate and require the calling out of these men.

The measures recommended above must be regarded as suggestive rather than exhaustive. It need not be assumed that it is necessary to adopt all these measures simultaneously. Government are not attempting to prescribe for every communal situation that may arise. The District Officers are the best judges of the situation and they may with their experience introduce or follow such methods as may be most suitable in the circumstances in which they are placed.

4. It is conceivable that if vigilant control is exercised and the measures mentioned above are put into effect in time, the occasion for any sanguinary conflict may not arise. But if, in spite of their best endeavours, disturbances take place, the District Magistrates would be well advised to act on the lines mentioned below.

The action already described should continue to be taken, but obviously it is not sufficient in itself and should be amplified as follows:

(*a*) Special constables – a list of suitable persons should be, as stated above, already available – should be appointed.

(*b*) In cases of assaults, stabbing, murder or arson the wrong-doers, failing them suspicious persons unable to explain their presence in the locality, should be arrested immediately. It is highly desirable that the first symptoms of lawlessness should be effectively suppressed. If any peaceful procession or assembly is attacked the assailants should be forthwith arrested and adequately punished. If aggressors are not properly dealt with it is bound to give rise to panic on one side and hooliganism on the other.

(*c*) Searches for weapons and firearms should be made of the locality where disturbances take place.

(*d*) Orders under Section 144 should be freely issued in order to end everything which leads to danger or to the promotion of bitterness – the gathering together of persons in numbers, curfew orders, the carrying of arms or weapons or lathis, the spreading of false rumours, the holding of meetings at which communal feelings will be roused, shouting of offensive slogans, etc. Care should, however, be taken not to cause undue hardship to innocent people.

In this connexion I am to emphasize that any action taken for preventing or controlling communal tension or communal disturbance should be taken solely with the desire of preserving law and order and maintaining public tranquillity. Such action is not meant primarily as a method of punishment of any community or section of the public supposed to be guilty or supposed to have taken active part in the furtherance of these communal disturbances. The task of meting out proper punishment is for the courts of judicial enquiry. The task of an executive officer is to preserve law and order and ensure it. With this end in view suitable orders under Section 144, Criminal Procedure Code, may be passed and curfew orders imposed, but the orders must not exceed the requirements of the situation, and care must be taken that any restrictions imposed under the curfew orders or any orders issued under Section 144, do not operate too harshly on the public at large which must necessarily include a very large number of presumably innocent, peace-loving and law-abiding citizens. A curfew order restricting movements at night will often be justified, but a 24-hour curfew order must be considered to be a very severe measure justified only by extremely exceptional circumstances, and curfew orders for periods exceeding 24 hours, such as two or three days continuously, should normally never be passed. In passing these curfew orders it may be desirable to consider whether its full purpose would not be served by limiting it to the disturbed locality rather than to make it applicable throughout large towns and cities. Further, whenever a curfew order is passed, no matter of what duration, scrupulous care should be taken to soften its rigour as much as possible and to afford ample facilities for movements in real cases of need such as calls for medical help, the performance of religious worship, etc. Whenever a 24-hour curfew is imposed the District Magistrate must personally see to it that the townsmen and particularly the poor classes have ample facilities for purchasing foodstuffs, for calling medical help and for the adequate supply of pure water for domestic purposes. Prevailing climatic conditions must also be borne in mind and it may be indefensible to compel people to spend days and nights shut up in close, stuffy and small quarters.

5. Investigations should be expedited, trials held speedily and exemplary sentences pressed for without delay. It is important that if trouble does not quickly subside, additional police should be imposed on disturbed areas of the city, town or countryside and the members of the community which is primarily responsible for the disorder, loss and injury to life and property should bear the cost of such police and pay compensation to the innocent sufferers. The Hon'ble Premier made the position clear in his speech in the Assembly when he said:

"If a large number of Muslims are killed then Hindus should be made to pay for them. If the property belonging to Muslims is damaged then Hindus should be made to pay for it. Similarly, if a large number of Hindus are killed or the property belonging to them is destroyed then the other community should be made to pay for it. In a place (*mohalla* or ward) where a particular community predominates it should be the duty of the members of that community to see that the members of the other community are allowed to live in peace and are not in any way hurt. It is their moral duty to look after their protection and if they do not do that they fail in the discharge of that duty."

6. Ample warning should be given to the Deputy Inspector General of the range concerned if and when police reinforcements are required. It is important that as far as practicable arrangements should be made whereby pickets and patrols can obtain relief and at the same time it is essential that sufficient police should be available for the discharge of their ordinary duties of controlling crowds and arresting those who break the law. Riot schemes should be re-examined with a view to readjust them, wherever necessary, in the light of present circumstances and to improve them in any other way considered desirable.

Troops should be called out when the situation demands it. The presence of troops has a great moral effect and they are able to perform picket and patrol duties along with the police, thus setting the police free for their more legitimate duties of controlling the crowds and effecting arrests.

Mobility is essential and for this purpose where police motor lorries are insufficient, lorries should be hired and utilized. Loud-speakers may be used in order to restore confidence by giving correct information, contradicting false and malicious rumours, etc.

If troops are employed, magistrates should invariably be deputed to work with them. If the supply of magistrates is insufficient, Government should be requested to despatch additional magistrates immediately. The Commissioner and the Deputy Inspector General will in every serious case be well advised to proceed to the place at once. They will be able to appreciate the needs of the situation, and they can point out to Government any further measures that may be required.

District Magistrates must see that adequate medical facilities are available.

7. It is the duty of every citizen who has the welfare of his country at heart to come forward fearlessly on the side of reason and toleration. Government hope that this result, after the experience of 1938-39, will come about. But in view of the past history of this evil and of the consequent fear that trouble may again arise, they wish to make their own intentions clear. They intend that peace should be kept by means of all the resources at their command. They will support District Officers and Police Officers in all reasonable action taken to this end and trust that district authorities

will not hesitate to take disciplinary action against any one guilty of dereliction of duty. If disorders occur, they will not only prosecute the offenders against whom evidence is available, but impose additional police if the conduct of the inhabitants of the locality justifies this measure. They intend that measures should be taken not only against those who actually participate in riots, but against those who foment them by violent speeches, or by the publication of inflammatory and incitory leaflets, songs, etc., or against newspapers adopting a communal and inflammatory attitude, and against those who make false charges against local officials with a view to stirring up or continuing communal trouble.

I have the honour to be, Sir,
Your most obedient servant,
C.W. GWYNNE,
Chief Secretary

ENCLOSURE 2 TO NO. 38

NOTE BY HAIG
R/3/1/75

May 1st, 1939

Transfers of Officers of the Provincial Services

Item 4

I have formed the opinion for some little time that the transfers or discussions of transfers of officers in some at any rate of our Provincial Services are giving rise to a great deal of uneasiness in the Services and are tending to undermine the independence of officers. I understand that a considerable number of officers are transferred on complaints which originate with members of the Legislative Assembly or members of District Congress Committees. If this is in fact being done it cannot but set up most demoralising conditions. It means that our officers in the districts on whom we rely for even-handed and impartial administration and whom we expect to take firm action in accordance with the merits of cases will be driven continually to asking themselves, if in pursuance of their duty they take action which is displeasing to any local Congressman, whether they may not find themselves as a result of some complaint transferred. Or there is another and equally deplorable contingency. Once it is believed that official orders are being influenced by the favour or disfavour of local Congressmen, there will always be certain officials who will endeavour to conciliate the favour of these Congressmen in order to benefit themselves. Such conditions are demoralising to our officers. They also destroy the credit of our administration, create distrust in it and weaken it seriously.

2. It is not only from the official side that there is talk of these demoralising conditions. The Provincial Congress Committee itself is evidently aware of them and very definitely deprecates them. In a meeting on April 7th the Provincial Congress Committee recorded a resolution on this subject. I reproduce the full text of this resolution as published in the papers:

[*There follow the last two paragraphs of Enclosure 3 to No. 30.*]

3. A copy of this note should be circulated to all Hon'ble Ministers, and I wish thereafter to discuss the matter at a meeting of the Council of Ministers.

H.G. HAIG

39

HAIG TO LINLITHGOW
R/3/1/75

Secret
No. U.P.-258

May 10th, 1939

My dear Lord Linlithgow,

I am afraid I have taken some time to reply to Your Excellency's letter, dated April 13th, 1939,[46] forwarding Sir Ziauddin Ahmad's complaints against the Congress administrations in the United Provinces, Central Provinces and Bihar. As these complaints ranged over such a wide field, I thought it might be necessary to deal with them at considerable length. But when I came to look into them closely, I reached the conclusion that they do not really merit any very elaborate answer. The complaints which have been made under the head "General" represent an indictment of the general policy and administration of the Congress Ministry. While I am far from suggesting there is not plenty of ground for criticism, and indeed many of these matters have caused me at various times and in varying degrees a great deal of anxiety, there is nothing specifically Muslim in all this. The general political criticisms are the stock-in-trade of the opposition, voiced by non-Congress Hindus just as much as by Muslims, while my own anxieties connected with these matters have related to general administrative conditions and not to specifically Muslim problems. They are only represented as Muslim grievances because the Muslim community as a whole is in political opposition. I have dealt with all these matters so constantly in my fortnightly reports that I do not think you will wish me to attempt in this connection the task of a general review of the Provincial administration. I will therefore confine myself to a very few remarks under the "General" section.

2. The so-called "dual system of administration" has in my opinion appreciably diminished since the early days when the Ministry first took office. I do not say that local Congressmen have not still more power and influence than is good for the administration, and are not in some districts a considerable nuisance. But they are beginning to be recognised as such by the Ministers. What I reported in paragraph 13 of my fortnightly letter No. U.P.-257, dated May 9th, as regards transfers is of interest in this connection. The real grievance of Muslims under this head is that they have no political pull. That is inevitable in present circumstances, and even if petty political jobbery was reduced to smaller proportions than exist at present Muslims would still feel that they were left out in the cold until they themselves formed part of the Government and could share in the little jobs. In any case they have not the same powerful and widespread organisation in the districts as the Congress, and consequently are bound in the matter of exploiting real or unreal local grievances or personal cases to be at disadvantage.

3. I come now to what are called the special complaints of Muslims and deal with them under their separate heads.

(*a*) There have been troubles in the villages of landlords of all communities. I think it is true that in special cases the Congress have tried to stir up trouble in the villages of those landlords who are their prominent political opponents and Muslims to a large extent come under this category. But they are not attacked *qua* Muslims but *qua* opponents of the Congress. Thus Muslim landlords who choose to pay blackmail to the local Congressmen (and one of the largest of the Taluqdars undoubtedly does this) have little or no trouble from their tenants. But Hindu landlords suffer in exactly the same way. It is no doubt possible that in some cases the communal issue is raised as well as the ordinary issue of tenant *versus* landlord, but I think such cases are rare. On the whole however at present, apart from special circumstances, a sympathetic and reasonable landlord of whatever community can maintain not unsatisfactory relations with his tenants, though of course they are very different to what prevailed before the general election.

(*b*) and (*c*) These are the allegations that are made freely by the communalists on both sides, and considering the volume of the allegations, which incidentally pretty well cancel each other out, I think there is very little substance in them. The Hindu counterpart of Sir Ziauddin is to be found for instance in a long petition I received a week ago from the Hindu Sangh of Cawnpore, one sentence of which ran as follows: "Sir, this is a historical fact that the Hindus are proverbially mild and that the Muslims are blessed with an aggressive mentality." This kind of thing takes us nowhere. As for communal riots being started by Hindus, it was really aggressive action by Muslims which started the chain of events that led straight to the recent Cawnpore riots, and judged at any rate by casualties the Muslims had decidedly an advantage over the Hindus. In Benares on the other hand the Hindus seem to have started the trouble. Sir Ziauddin refers to Marehra, a small town in the Etah district. There the ill-feeling seems to have started through a Congress flag pole having been bent by a *tazia*, perhaps accidentally. The next stage was some brick throwing by Hindus on a *tazia* procession, and then the Muslims broke out, killed several Hindus, looted their shops and desecrated a temple. Whatever the provocation, the Muslims were undoubtedly the aggressors in the riot. There are allegations that since the riot the Hindus have been taking revenge on the Muslims in the villages round about by cutting crops and damaging their property. There is probably some truth in this, but the matter has been receiving attention and punitive Police are being imposed. Incidentally the District Magistrate[47] of this district is a Muslim. More serious in my opinion were the incidents which I mentioned in paragraph 4 of my letter No. U.P.-237, dated March 25th, 1939, in the Budaun district, when in a number of cases Hindu crowds collected and threatened or injured Muslims and their property in villages. On the other hand this supervened on trouble in the town of Budaun, where the Muslims had behaved aggressively. The fact is that in the present temper the community that feels itself strong is apt to be assertive. The Muslim strength is mainly in the towns. In the villages they are at a disadvantage.

(*d*) The enquiry Report[48] (p. 25) devotes some space to this and has produced very little in the way of solid fact in its support as far as the United Provinces is concerned.

(*e*) There has been a lot of criticism that the Rural Development scheme does too little in the way of practical work and too much in the way of propaganda. I am looking into these criticisms, which I am inclined to think are certainly a good deal exaggerated. According to an answer given in the Assembly on the 19th March 1938, out of 789 rural development organisers 20 per cent are Muslims. This is not a remarkably low percentage seeing that these men have to be taken from the rural classes and that the Muslim population in the Province is so largely concentrated in the towns.

(*f*) The general remarks under (*b*) and (*c*) apply to this. In the case, however, of the enquiries made by the anti-Corruption Office in the Police department, which have given rise to much discontent and distrust, it was I think the case in the beginning that an unusually large proportion of Muslims were the target of these inquisitions. It was not so much that the officers who got into trouble did not have a reputation for corruption as that among a very large number of officers of this class those who were selected for attack were usually those who had made themselves obnoxious to the Congress, and these tended to be to a considerable extent Muslims. Direct communal feeling was also not absent. This feature, however, attracted attention and criticism, and I do not think it is true now to say as a rule that Muslim officers are specially attacked. But it is a matter that always requires attention.

(*g*) In this Province we have two Muslim Ministers out of six, and had at the outset 3 Muslim Parliamentary Secretaries out of 13, though one of them has now resigned. The Deputy Speaker of the Legislative Assembly and the Deputy President of the Legislative Council are also Muslims, and one of the two Deputy Directors of Publicity is a Muslim. The Muslim Ministers are certainly not unmindful of Muslim interests, but they are distrusted by the majority of Muslims and denounced by the Muslim League. I dealt with this matter in paragraphs 5 and 6 of my fortnightly report No. U.P.-241, dated April 10th, 1939, and I need not repeat what I there said.

(*h*) This has been the subject of constant questions in the Legislature, and the facts elicited have not substantiated these charges as regards appointments under the Government.

4. In general I think it is correct to say that the Provincial Ministry has done its best to be impartial in communal matters and with very fair success. Their good intentions have not, however, saved them from ceaseless attacks on communal grounds from both sides, and as I have brought out in my fortnightly report of the 9th May, at the present moment the Hindus are exceedingly loud in their complaints against the Government on the ground that they show undue favour to Muslims. The one substantial grievance of the Muslims is that they have no part in the Government. This is true, and it is a serious matter, but administratively they have little to complain of except that they do not have the general political influence, and the pull in petty local matters, that the supporters of the Ministry have. In essence

the grievance is not a religious one, though it assumes an intensely communal form. It is political, and is due to the fact that the community is in opposition. It would largely cease to exist if the Muslim League had a share in the Government.

Yours sincerely,
H.G. HAIG

40

HAIG TO LINLITHGOW
R/3/1/75

Confidential *May 18th, 1939*
No. U.P.-265

My dear Lord Linlithgow,

Many thanks for your telegram No. 1095-G, dated May 13th, 1939, repeating a copy of a telegram from the Nizam about the Madhe-Sahaba controversy.[49] I have waited a few days before answering it, as my Ministers were at the time very closely engaged in important negotiations and I wished to see what was the result of these and, if they did not lead to agreement, how the situation was likely to stand.

2. I think before dealing with the Nizam's telegram it would be convenient that I should now place Your Excellency in possession of the latest developments. As I explained in paragraphs 8 and 9 of my letter No. U.P.-257, dated May 9th, there appeared to the Ministers and myself to be only two real possibilities. The first was a direct settlement between the Sunnis and Shias. This seemed at the moment very unlikely. The second was action by the Government to place the Shias on a reasonable equality with the Sunnis. This objective was adopted by the Cabinet, and when I left Lucknow the Ministers were busy exploring the situation with the Shias.

3. The Premier himself took a leading part in these conversations and did not merely leave them to the Muslim Ministers. He stayed in Lucknow for an extra day or two in order to try and bring the negotiations to a conclusion. I was of course not aware of the details, but I received from the Premier on May 15th the papers, of which I enclose a copy, which he had hoped represented a settlement. These papers consist of a draft communiqué, a draft letter from Saiyid Ali Zaheer and the Premier's draft reply.[50] The communiqué follows very closely the main lines settled in

Cabinet. The only new point is a good one, namely, the proposal of Government to set up a committee with a view to arrive at a settlement with the consent of the parties concerned. The intention of the Premier, as explained to me subsequently, was that there should be some official of high standing, either administrative or judicial, to preside over the committee which should otherwise consist of an equal number of representatives of Sunnis and Shias, that there was no intention of their submitting a report unless they could arrive at agreed conclusions, but that if they could arrive at agreed conclusions and report them to Government, the Government would accept them. In other words, this committee was merely intended to provide a means of conciliation which might, if the circumstances were favourable, be successful. It was not intended to pronounce an authoritative award such as the committee proposed by the Nizam. I think myself that the proposal of the Government is entirely on right lines and might be of value when the proper time comes, i.e. after the Shias have been put on an equality with the Sunnis.

4. I do not myself much care for the explanatory correspondence, in particular the statement that the Shias would be allowed to offer fair and legitimate criticisms of the historical personages of Islam, and I mentioned to the Premier that I thought this might lead to trouble from the Sunnis. He told me, however, that he had shown the drafts to certain moderate Sunnis, including Chhatari, who were quite satisfied, and of course the two Muslim Ministers who have been taking part in these conversations are themselves Sunnis. Actually the Premier's draft letter leaves the final decision about the nature of the recitations by Shias to the district authorities and safeguards the position against unreasonable or provocative recitations.

5. The Premier told me that the Shia leaders with whom these conversations had been conducted had practically accepted this settlement, but they said that they must consult one or two others before finally agreeing. As usually happens on such occasions, the more intransigent people raised objections and the more reasonable allowed themselves to be overruled. Consequently, though when the Premier left Lucknow he thought he had got an agreement, it has since become apparent that the Shias have refused to accept this settlement. There the matter stands at the moment.

6. The Premier said he felt it was necessary to stand quite firmly on two points, namely that the Government communiqué of the 31st [30th] March[51] should stand unless it is modified by a mutually agreed settlement between the Sunnis and Shias, and secondly that no form of Tabarra should be allowed. The Government therefore can go no further to meet the Shias

than is proposed in these papers. I am entirely in agreement with the Premier on these points. The question then arises whether it would be wise for the Government to issue the draft communiqué without the correspondence, as stating and clearing their own position. The Premier thinks this would not be wise, for at the present stage the Shias having rejected this offer would be bound to criticise and attack it, and consequently would find it impossible at a later stage to accept it, which is a possibility that must not be ruled out. If there were public discussion of this communiqué now, the Shias would subsequently if they wanted a settlement require some further concession, and Government are unable to give any further concession. These agreements [?arguments] seem to be sound.

7. The intention therefore is for the moment to leave things alone. The fact of these negotiations and the general line of the proposed settlement are well known. It seems to me unlikely that after this the Shia agitation will continue with much vitality, for reasonable Shias know that they could have had a reasonable settlement. It is not impossible that after a few weeks the Shias will come round and ask for the terms they are now rejecting. In the meantime if their agitation continues it is likely to command less public sympathy than before. In the beginning there was a fairly general feeling of sympathy with the Shias. After their rejection of these terms there will be little sympathy left.

8. I now come to the Nizam's telegram. My intention in what I said in paragraph 8 of my letter of May 9th had been that the Nizam might be asked to use his influence directly on his co-religionists for purposes of a settlement between themselves, but I felt it probable that like Jinnah he would shrink from this, and refuse to jeopardise his position by making definite proposals for a settlement or endeavouring to arrange terms. As a most influential Muslim he might take a part in what everybody recognises as the only true solution of the matter, namely an agreement between the Sunnis and Shias. But he is not prepared to do this, his suggestions for action to be taken by the Government, though deserving of careful consideration, carry no particular authority.

9. At the last Cabinet meeting in Lucknow the possibility of setting up another committee something on the lines of the Piggott or Allsop committees had been raised by one of the Ministers and was discussed. We felt this was not likely to be wise. So far as the legal aspects were concerned we had already had two committees presided over by High Court Judges which had gone carefully into the law. The issues to be decided were really administrative issues relating to the city of Lucknow. We were not likely to receive any better guidance from a third committee than had

already been given by the two previous committees, which had in fact dealt with the whole problem very fairly and thoroughly. It was not considered that the Government could possibly surrender its responsibility for decision to any committee, for the enforcement of the decision might involve the Government in very far-reaching action. On the other hand if it retained its own executive judgement it would have to reach conclusions after considering the report of this third committee, which it was in as good or even better position to reach without the intervention of a committee. Indeed the appointment of a committee would really put the matter back again where it was three years ago. Everything that has been done would be reopened, and we should probably have to go through the whole agitation once more; for if one thing may reasonably be taken as certain, it is that the pronouncement of such a committee, or rather of its presiding officer, would not be accepted by both sides.

10. For these reasons which appear to me to be sound I do not think the suggestion of another committee at this stage is helpful, except in so far as it may be regarded as a method of conciliation, and this is already provided in the Government's scheme. As I have explained in the earlier part of this letter, we have now in my opinion reached the final stages of this controversy, and I should hope are not very far from final decisions. It would be very unwise to throw the matter open again to discussion *ab initio*. I quite recognise that the idea has from certain points of view attractions. If both sides could be got to agree that they would accept the decision of such a commission, the whole controversy would be solved. But I confess I see no possibility of this. The controversy concerns religious rights and claims and rouses intense feeling. Neither party are likely to submit their religious rights to the arbitration of an outsider, however, eminent. Moreover one of our chief difficulties throughout has been to find any persons who can really answer for either side.

11. I need not go into the probable attitude of my Ministers to a suggestion that a commission should be appointed by Your Excellency. But apart from all questions of constitutional prestige, I think it would be decidedly unwise to attempt to deal with this matter as a general question between Sunnis and Shias all over India. It is in terms still a dispute regarding conditions and action at Lucknow, and it seems to me exceedingly important to keep it as far as we can on that plane.

Yours sincerely,
H.G. HAIG

ENCLOSURE TO NO. 40

DRAFT COMMUNIQUÉ

Confidential

Government deeply regret the continuation of discord between the Shias and Sunnis in Lucknow which has resulted in disobedience of the law and the arrest and imprisonment of a large number of persons. They have endeavoured to bring about an amicable settlement, realising that only such a settlement, as carries with it the goodwill of the parties concerned, can be an abiding one. That endeavour has so far not succeeded but Government still hope that the two communities will be able to come together and to reach an understanding on a mutually satisfactory basis. With this end in view and in order to promote harmonious relations between the two communities, Government propose to set up a committee at an early date. The objective of this committee will be to endeavour to arrive at a settlement with the consent of the parties concerned. Any such mutually agreed settlement will be welcomed by Government and will be given effect to.

Government wish to declare that the decisions embodied in their communiqué of March 31st [30th], 1939, remain unaltered. They trust, however, that the rights thus recognised, like all rights, will be exercised with a view to avoid ill-feeling as far as possible and in an atmosphere of friendliness and goodwill.

Government understand that certain misapprehensions have arisen in the minds of the Shias in regard to the exercise of their religious rights. Government take this opportunity of affirming that the Shias have the same right to declare the distinctive articles of their faith as any other community and may exercise them in a like manner. But Government are unable to permit the public recitation of Tabarra, or any statements which are not permitted by law. Subject to this reservation, all communities have an identical freedom to practice their religion in public or private. Government are prepared to give facilities to the Shias, similar to those given to the Sunnis, for the exercise of an equivalent right.

Government trust that this clarification and the fresh attempt to find a solution will lead to a final and satisfactory settlement of the problem, so that goodwill might prevail and public peace and tranquillity be ensured. They invite the cooperation of all concerned in this endeavour to end a conflict which is injurious not only to the two communities but to the nation at large.

41

HAIG TO LINLITHGOW
R/3/1/75

Secret *May 24th, 1939*
No. U.P.-268

My dear Lord Linlithgow,

Not a great deal has been happening during the last fortnight, though various problems that confront the Government are developing. In any case it would have been difficult to take any important decisions, for both the Government and the Secretariat have been divided between Lucknow and Naini Tal. At the moment we have in Naini Tal the Premier, who arrived on May 13th, and Sampurnanand, who is up for a short time. Mrs. Pandit is in Mussoorie. Kidwai who had a serious heart attack is laid up in Lucknow. Katju is doing most of the work of Government in Lucknow. The Secretaries have for the most part arrived in Naini Tal. But the Revenue Secretary[52] is still down in Lucknow owing to the legislative business, which is going on which consists of Agrarian and Debt Bills in bewildering numbers. The Premier's health appears to be better. He told me when I saw him a week ago that the mere sight of the lake made him feel a different man, and he has certainly been busy noting on files. He is going daily to the Ramsay Hospital for treatment, and I gather that there is probably nothing seriously wrong with his health. The difficulty I foresee in the next few weeks is to get the Government together and get any decisions out of them on important matters. It is unfortunate that at this moment Gwynne, the Chief Secretary, who has been decidedly unwell for the last few weeks and whose condition was affected by his move to the hills, has had two days ago to go into hospital and will have to stay there, keeping very quiet, for ten days.

2. When I saw Pant last week, I had some talk with him about the possibility of his going to Simla, as suggested in paragraph 3 of your letter of 13th May.[53] He said that he himself had for some time been anxious to meet Your Excellency and was looking out for an opportunity of doing so, but he clearly could not attend this conference of Home Ministers, for apart from the fact that he really needs as much rest as possible just now, it would interfere with the treatment he is receiving. But I was glad to find how anxious he seemed to be to make personal contact with Your Excellency.

3. There does not seem to have been much further talk about the possibility of a reshuffle of the Ministry. I think so far as the Ministers themselves are concerned, they are anxious to carry on and not land themselves in the difficulties which would attend any attempt at re-constitution. Rumours about bringing in representatives of the Muslim League seem to have died down, and with a general slackening of public criticism of the Ministry they seem to be hoping to carry on as usual. But recent events have revealed very clearly their weaknesses, and not the least among them is the weakness of ill-health.

4. I was interested in what you said in your letter of May 13th about the result of the All-India Congress Committee meeting in Calcutta.[54] I quite agree that we must suspend judgement as to its ultimate results. I think too, as you say, that the split is probably deeper than it has been before in our experience. It seems to me a pretty clear parting of the ways. The Premier, when I asked him what he thought of the prospects of Bose attracting support in this Province, spoke with his usual optimism and said that he thought he would not have much of a following; and so far it appears, if one can judge from his meetings, that he is likely to attract only the revolutionaries, who I fear may be getting active, and the extreme Kisan agitators who may of course under the influence of his party be stimulated to considerably greater activity than they have been showing lately. Men with a name in the Congress movement seem at the moment to be holding aloof from Bose. I expect this is to a considerable extent due to Nehru's influence.

5. One general conclusion I should be disposed to draw from this situation is that it would not at all suit the policy of the orthodox Congressmen that there should be a breach between the Ministry and the Governor leading to resignation.[55] Such a situation would, as it seems to me, play straight into the hands of Bose and greatly strengthen the left wing as against the right. This general consideration perhaps has its bearing on the probable attitude of the Ministry to the difficulties arising out of the Employments Tax Bill.

6. The Bill, as I have already informed you, has now passed the Council with only such amendments as are acceptable to the Government and will come before the Assembly again on some date not yet determined in the first half of June. When the Assembly has accepted the amendments the legislative procedure will be complete, and the Bill will come to me. The passing of the Bill in this form by the Legislative Council means a considerable reversal of the Council's attitude when the Bill first came before it, and a crumbling of the united front that Sir J.P. Srivastava and

others had laboured to build-up in their Baradari meeting. So far as I can judge this result has been brought about by skilful use of the Government of their tactical position. They have been able to appeal to the separate interests of the opposition. The landlords have been told that if they withdraw their opposition to the Employments Tax Bill, they will have a better chance of getting a compromise on the Tenancy Bill. The Banias have been told that at the same price they will receive some concessions in connection with the Debt Bills now before the Legislature. And in general an attack on the pay of the Services is not an unpopular measure except in Service circles and those middle class families which are largely dependent on Government service for their support. Not many care to come forward as champions of the pay of the Services. It is therefore perhaps not surprising that the Legislative Council opposition has crumbled away. The general anticipation now appears to be that the matter will be decided one way or the other by the Federal Court. When I last saw the Premier, however, I thought it well to give him an indication that the Bill might lead to serious difficulty. I said that the public discussion which had taken place had only served to confirm me very strongly in the views which I had expressed about the tax when he first communicated the proposals to me namely, that it was illegal, inequitable and practically the equivalent of a cut in the pay of the Services. I also said that it seemed to me that the finances of the country could not be worked if the Centre and the Provinces were allowed to impose competitive income-taxes. The Premier did not really attempt to answer any of these arguments except by reiterating that the tax should not be regarded as a cut in pay. But he did not express any surprise at my views or at my statement that I was afraid the Bill might give us serious trouble. He did not appear particularly disturbed at what I said, but one can draw no conclusions from his attitude, for in these matters he is inclined very much to keep his own counsel.

7. I fear that the Premier having got away now from the great volume of criticism with which he was assailed some weeks ago and finding conditions for the moment peaceful again, is disposed to slip back once more into his attitude of complacent optimism and reluctance to take effective action. The question of satisfying the full demands of the Inspector-General of Police for additional strength, which I referred to in paragraph 4 of my letter No. U.P.-250, dated April 26th, 1939, is now up for final consideration. I am hoping to discuss the matter before long with the Premier and the Inspector-General of Police. But in the meantime the Premier has written a long note advancing numerous reasons for doing nothing more, and his general attitude is shown by the following extract

from his note: "But for the Shia-Sunni dispute at Lucknow the Province seems to be on the whole quiet. I am hoping that nothing untoward will happen at least for the next four or five months." This is at a time when our Commissioners are warning us that communal tension is still extremely serious, a matter which is in any case obvious. It is I fear only when he is up against disorder that he gets alarmed and is prepared to take action, and I think it is a good thing that I struck fairly hard a few weeks ago in Lucknow when the iron was hot. It has now cooled. His attitude in regard to the *Sipahi* newspaper, about which I had separate correspondence with Your Excellency some time ago, also tends to be unsatisfactory. The paper it is true has not come out for a considerable time and there is some possibility that we shall see no more of it; but his attitude remains rather irritatingly casual in spite of my having written a strong note on the subject.

8. I have nothing further to report about the Sunni-Shia trouble subsequent to the long letter I wrote to Your Excellency on this subject on May 8th. The *Pioneer* had an article recently which seemed to me deliberately designed to keep the controversy alive. I suppose as you say the temptation to embarrass the Ministers on any pretext is too great to be resisted. But when I saw Sir J.P. Srivastava yesterday I told him I thought this was going beyond what politics would justify. He is greatly dissatisfied about the attitude of the Ministers in regard to the strike in his mills, and I think it is true that Pant is simply pursuing a course of drift. Sir J.P. Srivastava had a long discussion with Pant, but the upshot is apparently nothing. He complains a good deal about the picketing by the Mazdur Sabha, which he maintains makes it impossible for work to be resumed. He contemplates closing down the mills altogether, and thinks that if he does this, after a couple of months or so the men will be glad enough to come back to work.

9. The recent suspension of payment by the Benares Bank may have important results on the Industrial Financing Corporation which the Government launched eight months ago. This is an institution with capital subscribed by the public and a guarantee of a considerable annual subsidy by the Government. The Government nominate certain directors to the Board. The object of the Corporation is to lend money to small industrialists who would not be able to secure loans from a bank. It was provided that the Corporation should not proceed to allotment unless ten lakhs were subscribed by the public. Actually the public subscribed little more than four lakhs. The Government were not prepared to admit that their scheme had failed to obtain public support and considered certain dubious expedients for getting the remaining six lakhs. Eventually they appear to

have persuaded the Benares Bank to take up the shares on some promise that Government would help them to dispose of them to the public. I am not sure how far the exact transactions between the Ministers, the Corporation and the Benares Bank will stand public examination which I think they may before long receive. Anyhow whether or not the crisis in the affairs of the Bank was precipitated by these shares being pressed upon them, it seems highly probable that the Financing Corporation will not secure now its minimum capital, as I understand only 25 per cent had been paid-up on those shares which are held by the Benares Bank. Consequently the whole position of the Corporation must come under very close consideration, and I have already advised the Ministers to face the situation and weigh it up most carefully, and warned them that otherwise the Government may find themselves later on involved in an unfortunate financial scandal. My own belief is that the wisest course would be to wind up the Financing Corporation as quickly as possible. It seems to me the project is clearly going to fail.

10. I shall be greatly interested to see what the decision is about the move to Simla. Our own indecisive arrangements, combined particularly with the prolonged sitting of the Legislature in Lucknow, are unsatisfactory from the point of view of Government business, though I hope by the end of the month all officers who are coming up will be here. Naini Tal in fact seems very full at present, and next week is the "June Week" which always attracts a great many people. The heat in the plains has from all accounts been most trying since I left.[56]

Yours sincerely,
H.G. HAIG

42

HAIG TO LINLITHGOW
R/3/1/75

Secret
No. U.P.-273

Camp,
June 3rd, 1939

My dear Lord Linlithgow,

In paragraphs 5 and 6 of Your Excellency's letter, dated 26th May 1939,[57] you asked my views about the Secretary of State's suggestion that the Governor-General should issue a statement directed to reassuring the Muslims that Government appointments would not go unduly to Congress or "tame" Muslims, but that the non-Congress or "good" Muslims should receive their fair share of what was going. I do not myself think that in the sense in which the Secretary of State views the matter there is really any problem or injustice. Appointments of any importance are made on the advice of the Public Service Commission. The main function of the Ministry in this connection is to decide how many Muslims should be appointed – a matter on which I can see that decisions are reasonable. The Public Service Commission are then asked to recommend the names of say five Muslims for a particular service. These men are selected by the Public Service Commission entirely on their merits. There is no question of their being "tame" or "good", and the Ministry would be in no position to put forward names of their own in consideration of the fact that they were connected with their supporters.

2. Theoretically in the lower grades of Government service, such as clerks in district offices, which are not recruited through the Public Service Commission, the Ministers could bring pressure to bear of the kind which the Secretary of State envisages. But in practice they would not do anything of the kind, and I do not think there is any reason to suppose that Collectors and other officers who have the appointment of these lower grade Government servants would be influenced in favour of Congress as against non-Congress Muslims. There may have been some reason for complaint in connection with the appointment of rural development organisers. This, however, was a very special case, in which appointments (not only of Muslims) were admittedly made on improper principles, and new appointments have now been put on a proper footing.

3. Any grievance that the Muslim community may have in this matter is not I think as regards actual appointments to Government service, but consists rather in what I have described in my letter No. U.P.-258, dated May 10th, 1939, about Sir Ziauddin Ahmad's complaints as the absence of political pull, particularly in local matters. It is probably the case, for instance, that in the selection of honorary magistrates the "tame" Muslims may have an advantage over the "good" ones, but that is not a matter in which it seems to me to be possible for the Governor to interfere.

4. The primary grievance of the majority party among the Muslims in my opinion is not that they do not get their fair share of Government appointments, but that they have no part or lot in the Ministry. I do not remember public complaints that the right type of Muslims are not getting Government appointments. But Muslim League platforms have rung with accusations that the Governors have neglected the duty placed on them by their Instrument of Instructions and have wrongly accepted in their Ministries "tame" Muslims instead of "good" ones.

5. About three weeks ago I drafted a letter to you discussing the whole situation from the point of view of the composition of the Ministries and making some tentative suggestions for the future. I was doubtful, however, whether this would be of much practical value to you, and I consequently put it on one side. But as it is clear that you and the Secretary of State are closely considering the whole problem of the attitude of Muslims, I think it is worthwhile to send a copy of this draft letter which accordingly I enclose. Though it does not deal with the problem of appointments, it does discuss the problem whether the Muslims can be regarded as represented by Congress Muslims, which really underlies the present reference of the Secretary of State, and I think it has a good deal of relevance to the general issues which are perplexing us.

6. As you will have gathered from what I have said above, I think that the problem of recruiting particular types of Muslims for Government service is not one which is giving rise to any difficulty, and consequently that there will be no advantage in making a pronouncement about it.

Yours sincerely,
HARRY HAIG

ENCLOSURE TO NO. 42

DRAFT LETTER BY HAIG

Undated

In several letters which we have exchanged lately we have discussed the extremely unsatisfactory condition of Hindu-Muslim relations, and the general position and attitude of the Muslims not only to the Hindus but to the British, and you have asked me more than once whether I have any practical suggestions to make for easing the situation or meeting the apprehensions of the Muslims. The question has arisen in connection with:

(*a*) the Hindu-Muslim disturbances in this Province and the possibility of creating some relaxation of tension,

(*b*) the all-India situation that might arise in the event of war (my letter No. U.P.-240, dated April 6th, 1939, and Your Excellency's reply, dated April 12th), and

(*c*) the situation that arises with the approach of Federation.

2. So far as concerns the provincial situation, it has long been my view that the root of the trouble is that the Muslims as a community have no part in the Government. Now it may be argued that there is no reason why

they should, that the Government should be formed on party lines based on political or economic principles, and that such parties should receive the support of considerable sections of all communities. That no doubt is the ideal, but it is perfectly plain that present conditions are in flagrant contradiction with this theory, and the question is whether there is any prospect of our gradually moving towards it. Jawaharlal Nehru in his recent conversation with me clearly indicated his anticipation or hope that the present acute communal phase would not last, that the economic factors would have their natural effect, and that if we were patient we should find that the present Hindu-Muslim antagonism might cure itself. Hallett in his letter about Ziauddin's complaints,[58] which I have seen, seems to think there is some possibility of the Muslim masses in Bihar being attracted by economic policies and leaving the more communal upper class Muslims stranded. I cannot myself think that such developments are likely in this Province; nor I should have thought in India as a whole. It was recognised when the constitution was being framed that separate electorates created a very difficult problem in regard to fitting the minority communities into the general scheme of responsible government. It was clear enough that separate electorates would tend to encourage communities to think communally, and when they think communally with sufficient vehemence, they are not going to be disintegrated by economic or other general policies. That I think is precisely what has been happening ever since the introduction of the present constitution. There was a time when the Congress Ministry took office in July 1937 when a new direction could have been given to this problem. The Congress had since the general election been flirting with the Muslim League and suggesting some form of coalition. These conversations resulted in the Muslim League holding aloof from my minority Ministry. But when the Congress took office they decided to reject the idea of a coalition with the Muslim League and to pursue instead a policy of direct approach to the Muslim masses. Had they entered into a coalition, I cannot help feeling that Muslim solidarity would soon have been undermined. There are bound to be differences between Muslims on the main agrarian and economic issues. The Muslims in office would have to make themselves responsible for definite policies in regard to these matters; they would have received the support of some Muslims and aroused the opposition of others. Nothing seems to be so effective in disintegrating a party as the taking of office.

3. The Congress, however, chose the opposite course, and from that time it was easy to work up strong Muslim communal feeling, for the community as a whole had a grievance in being excluded from a share in

the Government. More and more the Muslims have come to regard themselves as a separate nationality, and I do not think at this stage those ideas and that organisation are going to be disrupted by economic policies. The Muslim League have usually an answer to economic policies sponsored by the Congress. They can, being in opposition, go one better. An illustration of this came before me recently. My Ministry introduced a far-reaching Bill for the relief of agricultural and other poor debtors. In the report of the select committee, there are a number of minutes of dissent by the Muslims who all take the line that this measure is quite inadequate and that far greater relief ought to be given to these debtors. This of course is a particularly easy line for them to take in connection with this subject, as the creditor class are Hindus. It is, however, a good illustration of the limitations of the economic appeal to the Muslim masses. A responsible government can only go a certain distance in proposing measures, and an opposition which has no prospect of coming into power can quite safely advocate and promise far more sweeping measures.

4. My conclusion therefore is that the present conditions are not going to cure themselves, or be cured by the process of appealing to the economic interests of the Muslim masses. We can only escape from this dangerous and growing sense of separate nationality based on intense religious feeling by adopting the course which the Congress rejected in 1937, namely, admitting the Muslim community as a whole to a share of power.

5. The importance of including representatives of the minorities in the Ministries was present clearly enough to the minds of those who framed the constitution. It was not I think merely because the Muslims so vehemently demanded it, but because it was realised that a denial might set up very difficult conditions, that provision was made that so far as practicable the Governor should include in his Council of Ministers members of important minority communities. It is interesting to look back to the discussions of the Joint Parliamentary Committee. In paragraph 71 the Committee clearly recognised the obstacle imposed by religious antagonisms to majority rule strictly on the British model. The corrective was felt to lie in the independent power of the Governor. But looking back at those ideas in the light of our experience of the actual working of the constitution, it seems to me that the Committee's report contemplates the Governor being in a much stronger position than in fact circumstances have permitted. The Committee were apprehensive that it might be difficult to establish strong Ministries based on well-organised parties. They recognised in paragraph 112 that the representation of minorities in the

Ministry would be an element working against cohesion. They did not wish to rouse the distrust of minorities and recognised the importance of the provision for finding representation for minorities in the Ministry. But they were clearly afraid that this might prevent the development of strong and united Ministries, and they were perhaps more impressed with the danger of the Governor by his action unduly weakening the Ministry than by the possibility that by his inaction he would fail to give the minorities the protection which was required.

6. Actually the Governors in Congress Provinces found themselves faced with a well-organised and homogeneous party with overwhelming strength in the Legislatures and in a position to insist on the Governors accepting the composition of the Council of Ministers which they proposed. If a Governor had stipulated that the Ministry must include representatives of the Muslim League, the Congress would have refused office and he would have found himself without a Ministry at all. Moreover, the wording of paragraph VII of the Instrument of Instructions is very cautious. The Governor is enjoined to include so far as practicable members of important minority communities. He is not enjoined to include representatives of the preponderating opinion of these minority communities, and this is a very fundamental distinction. When the minorities were pressing for this safeguard they probably had it in mind that the members, for instance, of the Muslim community included in the Cabinet should be fair representatives of the Muslim community as a whole. The matter is to some extent discussed on that basis in paragraph 112 of the Joint Parliamentary Committee's report, where they point out that the Ministry may be a composite one, and that a Ministry formed in accordance with the Instrument of Instructions must tend to be the representative not, as in the United Kingdom, of a single majority party or even of a coalition of parties, but also of minorities as such. But whatever may have been the intention, it was clearly sufficient compliance with the wording of the Instrument of Instructions if the Governor secured the inclusion in the Ministry of a reasonable proportion of Muslims, whether they were or were not representative of the community. The inclusion of even an unrepresentative Muslim is not without its importance, for whatever his political views, a Muslim remains a Muslim, and my own Muslim Ministers have certainly not been unmindful of the interests of the community in such matters as appointments and fair play generally. But the Muslims are now organised as a communal political party, and it is no satisfaction to that party that two Muslims entirely unrepresentative of it are included in the Ministry.

At the general election only one Congress Muslim was returned to the Legislative Assembly, and he was returned by a university constituency. It is true that subsequently a certain number of Muslims elected on the League ticket transferred their allegiance to the Congress; but it is clear enough that the inclusion of two Congress Muslims in the Ministry, while it complies with the literal terms of the Instrument of Instructions, does not in any adequate way give representation to the Muslim community.

7. The British Parliamentary system may be said to have worked well under the domination of the Congress party. Indeed in some respects it has worked too well. The majority has been entrenched firmly in power. We have had a homogeneous executive strong in the support of a well-organised party, and therefore prepared to carry through without hesitation a definite policy. But in proportion to the exaltation of the executive has been the suppression of the opposition. That would not matter if the opposition were able to profit by the natural fickleness of the electorate and the mistakes of the Government and to look forward to the time when they in turn would be in power. But that is not the case. The opposition is a permanent communal minority, and faced with this position of permanent political inferiority it stresses more and more its communal unity, its antagonism to the governing community, and the religious claims which give it the enthusiastic support of the masses.

8. If I am right in this diagnosis, there is no cure for the present conditions of Hindu-Muslim antagonism in this Province short of including in the Ministry real representatives of the Muslim community, that is, at the present time representatives of the Muslim League. Both from the point of view of establishing tolerable and peaceful conditions in the Province and from the point of view of his responsibilities for safeguarding the interests of the Muslims, I think that the Governor should use the influence he possesses in order to work towards that solution. Hitherto I think it has been the accepted policy that Governors should feel that they have fulfilled their obligations if they have secured that a reasonable proportion of Muslims are included in the Ministry. I would suggest for consideration that Governors should now be directed consciously to try and secure that the Muslim members of their Ministries should be really representative of the Muslim community as a whole. I do not say that much, if anything, can be done at once; but I think if that policy were accepted it would not be without its effect gradually. Opportunities arise which might be utilised. In paragraph 6 of my letter, No. U.P.-241, dated April 10th, 1939, I said that if present tendencies continue, Hindu-Muslim antagonisms increase

and general opposition to the Government grows, the time may come when the Governor of this Province may be in a position to insist that the Cabinet should be recast and should include representatives of the Muslim League. Actually Nehru in his conversation with me indicated that such a development might not cause insuperable difficulties in this Province; but he stressed the point that it was really an all-India problem. Accepting that position, it would clearly be easier to gain our end, if that is accepted as a desirable end, if all Governors were using their influence in the same direction.[59]

9. I have no further suggestions to make so far as the Provincial Governments are concerned. But it is clear that similar problems are going to arise in connection with the Federation, and it would seem that at present the Muslims will not be prepared to accept Federation if there is to be any danger that the Muslims in the Federal Ministry will merely be Congress nominees. It seems clear that Congress are planning and working to dominate completely the Federal Ministry. It seems doubtful whether the Muslims in view of their experience in the Provinces would be content with any vague assurance that the Governor-General would do his best to secure for them real representation in the Ministry. Practical political forces may render such anticipations impossible to fulfil unless the position is defined more clearly. If therefore at a later stage there is any intention of making a concession to the Muslims or reassuring them, it might perhaps most easily take the form of an amendment of the Governor-General's Instrument of Instructions. It might go far to reassure the Muslims if in place of the words "members of important minority communities" in paragraph VII of the Governor-General's Instrument of Instructions were substituted "representatives of important minority communities". The word "representative" is already used in connection with the Federated States, and though it may have been used merely as a convenient drafting term, I imagine the States also would regard it as important that the Ministers drawn from the States should be really representative of opinion in the States and not merely be States' representatives who are prepared to accept the policy of the Congress. It is in fact as it seems to me necessary to face the question whether in forming the Federal Executive it is intended, in spite of the consequent lack of homogeneity, to include real representatives of State opinion and of Muslim opinion, or to accept in fact a Congress Ministry with such State and Muslim elements as can most conveniently work in harmony with them.[60]

43

HAIG TO LINLITHGOW
R/3/1/75

Secret *June 10th, 1939*
No. U.P.-274

My dear Lord Linlithgow,

Many thanks for your secret letter of 6th June.[61] My draft letter dealt rather with general considerations and tendencies, and it was not my intention to go into any detailed anticipations of what might happen in the event of a re-grouping of political parties. My arguments dealt on the whole with a situation in which the Congress remained the dominant party and would be faced in consequence with a more or less united Muslim opposition. I certainly agree, however, about the possibilities of a considerable split in the Congress which would inevitably lead to a substantial regrouping of forces. It was with reference to that possibility that I suggested that Governors should bear in mind the importance of securing in any re-constituted government a reasonable representation of Muslim opinion. One possibility is, as suggested by Your Excellency, that the right wing of the Congress might wish to take in landlords, including Muslims. On the other hand, I should be inclined to guess that if the Congress were weakened the Muslim League would be encouraged to hold together and that the Muslim landlords would find it difficult to break away at that stage from the main body of the Muslim League. Moreover, the elements in the Muslim League other than the landlords are in general outlook much nearer the Congress than are the landlords, and it might be that Congress would find it easier to establish a coalition with them. For these reasons I should be inclined to anticipate that if the right wing in the Congress found it necessary to strengthen themselves in this Province they might do so by a coalition with the Muslim League rather than with the landlords as such. It is, however, very difficult to make any anticipations with confidence. The Hindu Mahasabha may prove not to be a negligible factor. Possible combinations are endless. One cannot perhaps hope to do more than examine certain general tendencies.

Yours sincerely,
H.G. HAIG

44

HAIG TO LINLITHGOW
R/3/1/75

Secret
No. U.P.-275

June 12th, 1939

My dear Lord Linlithgow,

The last fortnight has been a period when the hills have been a very desirable place of refuge from the great heat in the plains, and Naini Tal was very full for the "June Week". A large number of officers were up, some on normal recess, others on casual leave. A cheerful spirit prevailed, and I took the opportunity of the Club dinner, which had a larger attendance than we have seen for years past, to advise officers not to allow themselves to be unduly worried about the prospect of the Employments Tax.

2. Ministers have been moving about, and I have been in touch with Katju, Sampurnanand and Mrs. Pandit. Pant suddenly made up his mind towards the end of May to go down to Lucknow for a few days. It was partly in connection with developments on the Tenancy Bill, partly to get in touch with the Sunni-Shia situation again. But he told me that his main object was to discuss the labour situation in Cawnpore and announce a new policy. This was to me a very agreeable surprise. I knew that he had recently had a three-hour inconclusive conversation with Srivastava and he seemed disinclined to budge from his old position of waiting on events and refraining from doing anything that would displease the Mazdur Sabha. Before he left Naini Tal, however, he told me that he had come to the conclusion that it was necessary to take a firmer line with the Mazdur Sabha and make it clear that Government did not approve of lightning strikes, and that he proposed to issue instructions that picketing in the form of lying down and obstructing ingress and egress should be stopped by the police and dangerous speeches should be checked. He said he intended to make this new policy quite clear to the Mazdur Sabha. He was as good as his word, and I enclose a copy of an official letter, dated May 31st, which was sent to the Mazdur Sabha. The immediate result of this action was the calling off of the strike in the New Victoria Mills, and though one or two more small strikes in Cawnpore have developed since, I feel reasonably confident that if Government maintain this policy firmly there is a prospect of labour conditions steadily improving.

3. It is a matter of speculation what was the cause for this sudden change

of policy. I can hardly think it was a case of delayed conversion resulting from the long discussion which he had with Srivastava, and though the Ministry are I am sure disturbed at the idea that as a result of their policy the prosperity as well as the peace of Cawnpore have been impaired, there have been no striking new events which would account for their suddenly translating a latent conviction into definite action. I am inclined to wonder whether they did not receive some instructions from the higher command who may well have felt that the time had come when an effort should be made to put a stop to the progressive deterioration in labour conditions in Cawnpore and the progressively evil effects on the prosperity of this great industrial and commercial centre and incidentally of the Province. On the whole the suddenness and definiteness of this action suggest to me instructions from outside.

4. I had described to you the termination of the negotiations between Government and the Shias on the Madhe-Sahaba and Tabarra agitation. When these conversations had broken down, the two parties turned once more to the only other possible alternative, namely, a direct settlement between themselves. For a time there seemed to be some hope that a settlement might be reached. The Commissioner[62] initiated conversations and prepared a note as a basis of settlement, the ultimate decision to be that the Sunnis should not exercise their right to hold a public Madhe-Sahaba procession and meeting and that the Shias would agree that the recitation of Tabarra would definitely cease. There were difficulties about the preliminary stages that would lead up to such an agreement, but the Shias were obviously anxious to reach a settlement on these lines and many of the more reasonable Sunnis were also prepared to consider it and were working for a settlement. Meantime a joint appeal suggesting similar conclusions was issued from Simla by a number of important Shia and Sunni leaders, and a statement was also put out by Abul Kalam Azad. These statements, obviously inspired by the best intentions, provoked a most uncompromising rejoinder from Zafar-ul-mulk, who is one of the two men who have the greatest influence with the Sunni mob in Lucknow, and who had in any case been holding back from these negotiations with the Commissioner; and at the moment there has been a definite setback to the prospects of settlement. I think the Shias are undoubtedly getting tired of their agitation. It has been encouraged lately by contingents of civil resisters from other Provinces. In particular some very troublesome Punjabis made their appearances and seemed disinclined to conduct the agitation on the gentlemanly lines initiated by the Lucknow Shias. Their behaviour began to disturb the peace of the city and in consequence the

district authorities took the initiative and ran in nearly one hundred of them under Section 107 of the Criminal Procedure Code. This action was very effective. I hear that some of these Punjabis were at any rate in part responsible for the disturbance subsequently at the Benares camp jail when a Parliamentary Secretary visited it, but I have not had confirmation of this.

5. I think for the present we must continue to see how matters develop. It is interesting to observe the powerlessness of the Muslim League to bring about a settlement between two sections of its own supporters. It seems to me that the Muslim League, like the Congress in the past, is really strong only in opposition. Then [?When] faced with a necessity for positive action and policy, it seems to be unable to secure agreement and has no adequate leadership. This confirms my view that if the Muslim League were to take office in this Province, it would soon lose its solidarity, just as to a large extent Congress are doing now.

6. The Ministers, with the exception of Kidwai, will all be assembled in Naini Tal for the next week or fortnight, and I hope we shall be able to get through a good deal of Cabinet business. We are having our first meeting today when we shall discuss a number of important issues. One of these will be the future of the Industrial Corporation. Katju is disposed to take the line that the attacks on Government in this connection are malicious; but I told him that in my opinion there are some very weak points in the Industrial Corporation and that he should not be surprised if his opponents concentrated on these points. The Government appear to regard their political credit as being involved in the maintenance of the Corporation, but we shall no doubt talk all these matters out fully at our meeting. Another very important matter which will come up is the ambitious programme of new roads to cost 1½ crores. The scheme, if it proves to be practicable, should undoubtedly be of great economic advantage to the Province. The financing of it requires careful consideration and all the relevant factors will be before the Cabinet at their meeting. Another very important topic will be the comprehensive proposals for the reorganisation of education as a result of the report of a representative committee. One of the chief questions of principle will be whether Government should assume control of primary education, which is at present gravely hampered by the intrigues and inefficiency of the district boards. The Education Minister is strongly in favour of Government assuming control, and I think the Council of Ministers will back him up. Nothing is more likely in my judgement to improve our education. Another committee which is dealing with the engineering services will I understand before long propose that the

maintenance of district board roads should be entrusted to the Public Works Department – a reform which would be of great value from the point of view of efficiency. But if the district boards were deprived of the powers to mismanage education and roads there may be little left for them to do, and the interference with vested interests would be considerable. These issues therefore may raise somewhat acute political difficulties. I understand also before the end of the month we shall have some discussion on the very far-reaching proposals for the establishment of village *panchayats*. This will therefore be a very important period from the point of view of planning policy. So far as the Legislature is concerned the Council is to meet on the 3rd July and the Assembly probably a little later in July. It is hoped that Assembly business will be concluded by the end of July and that we shall then have a rest from legislative business until the beginning of October, except in so far as there may be discussions on the Tenancy Bill proceeding in the Council.

7. Conversations will open shortly in Naini Tal between the Ministers and the landlords regarding the Tenancy Bill. The position is that the Council have not committed themselves to the choice between taking the Bill into consideration clause by clause and setting up a select committee. A decision will be taken when the Council meets again on the 3rd July, and this will depend on the result of the previous conversations in Naini Tal. Chhatari seems fairly hopeful that an agreement may be reached, and from what he told me it does not seem as if the landlords are likely to make unreasonable demands. My impression is that the Ministers will be anxious to reach a compromise if they feel it is politically possible. I should certainly myself be very glad to see a compromise reached and the Bill passed.

8. I have had separate correspondence with Your Excellency about the Badrinath Temple Bill, and received a few days ago a copy of the memorandum of claims made by the Maharaja of Tehri. I have passed this on to the Ministers for their comments. I have no doubt these comments will be severe, for it seemed to me on a somewhat hasty perusal that the Maharaja must be putting forward a number of claims which he had either not raised at all, or had waived, at the time of the conversations with the Ministry. There have been various paragraphs in the papers suggesting that the delay in giving assent to this Bill was likely to involve a crisis with my Ministers. As a matter of fact the Ministers, though very anxious that assent should be given at the earliest possible date, have been quite reasonable in their conversations with me, and would not wish to make this *casus belli*. But I think they are disposed to feel very much aggrieved at the attitude of the

Maharaja, and they would certainly not be likely to acquiesce in concessions to him which they would regard as unreasonable.

9. When I saw the Premier last Friday he started at once on the topic of the award of a Knighthood to Chintamani. He was clearly upset and for three quarters of an hour I listened patiently to his complaints and representations. He refused to regard Chintamani in any light other than that of a political opponent, and would not admit any broader considerations based on his outstanding position in the life of the Province, or as a journalist. He declared that this honour would greatly weaken the position of the Government. He made it clear how acutely he feels and how bitterly he resents political criticism – a matter which I had come to realise during the budget debates last March. It also seemed pretty clear that he feels that this criticism is exceedingly damaging to the Government. He regards Chintamani as a man who has done the Government much harm, and therefore objects to his being publicly honoured. I suggested that in fact he was exaggerating this aspect and that the criticisms of the opposition were not likely to make much impression on his supporters. But he said more than once that there was a very large body of middle opinion, and he evidently feels that this has been appreciably affected by the opposition attacks. He even expressed the view that the conferment of this honour was going to injure the position of the Government in the Legislative Council, and that it would be felt that rewards in the shape of honours might be available for those who oppose the Government; while he spoke with quite unnecessary depreciation of the powers of the Government to offer to waverers inducements of similar potency. Actually I believe that the Government have shown no kind of scruple in trying to secure the support of members of the Legislative Council by means of such inducements as it was in their power to offer. But it was interesting to find him apparently believing sincerely that Legislative Councillors of doubtful views might vote against the Government in the expectation that they might thereby qualify for a Rai Bahadurship. I did my best to disabuse the Premier of these ideas, and indeed, to do him justice, I do not think he felt for a moment that I was inspiring any opposition to the Ministers. But he felt that this might be the judgement of public opinion, and he repeated, as he has so often said before, that in his opinion it was essential that the Governor and the Ministers should so far as the public are concerned appear to be acting in harmony. This is a point which I have always had in mind in connection with the possible reactions of Pant to various lines that might be taken on the Employments Tax, and it confirms me in my view that the more remote the issue may be from one directly between myself and the

Ministers, the more likely it is that they will not feel compelled to resign.

10. I had realised that the bestowal of the Knighthood on Chintamani was not likely to be agreeable to my Ministers. It has certainly been rather unfortunate that since the recommendation was made opposition attacks on the Ministry, in which the *Leader* has taken a prominent part,[63] have become much fiercer than before, in connection with the budget and the Employments Tax. But I do not myself in any way regret the recommendation, which indeed seems to have been very well received by the principal newspapers, including the *Hindustan Times*. I said at the time that I hoped Congressmen would have the fairness to acknowledge the eminence of Chintamani in public life, even though they differed from his politics, and that is the line taken by the *Hindustan Times*. I hope the Ministers here will soon get over their indignation, though they may wish to raise some general questions of principle about the grant of honours. You will remember that Pant's attitude hitherto has been to say that he wants to have nothing to do with them, and know nothing about them. I draw from Pant's long representation two conclusions:

(*a*) that he takes an exceedingly personal view of politics, and finds it difficult to forgive political opposition;

(*b*) that the Ministry are more anxious about their political strength than I had supposed.

11. I am grateful for your very interesting letter of the 26th May with its comments on various problems and possibilities of the future. I was glad to hear that the Home Ministers' Conference had proved such a success, and it seems to me that their conclusions in regard to such matters as action against newspapers, &c., may be of considerable value. I hear our Parliamentary Secretary, who is certainly the most troublesome and unpleasant in our team, did not make a good impression in Simla. If that is so, I am not surprised.

12. Gwynne's condition I fear is very serious.[64] There is no chance of his ever returning to work. His loss will be a very great one to the Provincial administration, he had exactly the qualities that enabled him to get on with Ministers and particularly the Premier, who had a real friendship for him, and at the same time he acted as a most effective brake on their less wise proposals, and was able to give much sound advice which was accepted. The selection of his successor will be a matter of considerable difficulty. We shall certainly not get anyone who will be his equal in the combination of these invaluable qualities, and it is evident that the Premier and I are likely to find difficulty in agreeing on the selection. I have recently accepted the views of the Ministers about the appointment of an I.C.S.

officer as Director of Agriculture. The appointment will, I have no doubt, make for efficiency, which is of special importance in view of the Ministers' policy of expansion of agricultural activities, but there will be memorials from the I.A.S., and of course Richards who has been officiating for a long time will be bitterly disappointed.

Yours sincerely,
H.G. HAIG

ENCLOSURE TO NO. 44

LETTER FROM SECRETARY, U.P. INDUSTRIES DEPARTMENT[65] TO SECRETARY, MAZDUR SABHA, CAWNPORE

No. 3456/XVIII *May 31st, 1939*

I am directed to say that Government have observed with deep concern the recent outbreak of industrial disputes in Cawnpore. Over 4,000 workers have now been without work for over three weeks and the amount of suffering and privation which this must have caused to the families of those affected cannot but fail to evoke general sympathy. The industry in Cawnpore cannot yet have recovered from last year's unrest, and from the dislocation of business resulting from the recent riots. It is of the utmost importance in the interests of the industry as a whole, employers and labour alike, and of the commercial prosperity of the city of Cawnpore that normal conditions in industry should soon be firmly re-established and should not be lightly disturbed from time to time, so that the industrial development of Cawnpore, of such vital importance to the Province as a whole, may continue unhampered.

2. It is needless to say that Government have the welfare of labour at heart and are anxious to bring about by all legitimate and sound means a lasting improvement in the conditions of labour. With that end in view many matters were investigated last year by the Cawnpore Labour Enquiry Committee and its principal recommendations were given effect to, and those remaining are still under the active consideration of the Government and will be suitably implemented without any avoidable delay. To promote collective bargaining, and to avoid unhappy prolongation of industrial disputes, which may ultimately lead to strikes and dislocation of industry, by a process of conciliation and arbitration, a Trade Disputes Bill has been drafted and will soon be sent to you and to the employers for their comments. It is expected that the Bill will be found satisfactory and will

put conciliation and arbitration on a statutory basis and will prove a powerful and efficient instrument for maintaining peace and harmony in industry. Government are aware that the conditions of labour in shops and commercial establishments also stand in need of considerable improvement. A private Bill dealing with this subject was introduced last year in the Assembly, but its examination has disclosed that it is somewhat incomplete. Government propose to introduce shortly a much more comprehensive measure for the consideration of the Legislature. Meanwhile Government would impress upon you the urgent necessity of labour doing nothing which may be calculated to introduce an element of strife or excitement in Cawnpore. Government are aware that over certain questions differences of opinion have arisen between the employers and workmen, but Government earnestly wish that the existing machinery for conciliation set up by Government should be utilised on all such occasions for an impartial investigation into, and settlement of, such differences. There is no doubt that strike is a powerful weapon which can be wielded by labour when the exigencies of the situation demand it, but there can also be no doubt that strikes should not be lightly resorted to and should be considered only when all other ways and methods for the settlement of disputes have been fully pursued and exhausted. There may be legitimate grievances, but no grievances can justify a lightning or a stay-in strike and such strikes, Government think, should be invariably deprecated. Government feel sure that the Mazdur Sabha itself recognises that the workers of the New Victoria Mills, by going on a lightning strike, did not act either with propriety or wisdom. This strike has now continued for nearly four weeks and must have caused deep distress and misery to the workers and their families, and Government earnestly hope that steps will be found to terminate this strike as soon as possible so that these regrettable consequences may soon come to an end.

3. In addition to the misery and hardship which a strike entails, it leads to further evil and unforeseen consequences. It leads to unrest and excitement and causes commotion in the city. In such a contingency Government's primary duty is to ensure that public tranquillity is not disturbed and law and order is maintained and the enjoyment of civil liberties by all persons, strikers and non-strikers, alike, is assured as far as it lies in the power of the Government. Such civil liberties obviously include the unobstructed use of public highways and the right of egress and ingress in regard to private premises by all persons entitled thereto.

4. Government would also strongly deprecate the making of speeches containing, directly or indirectly, incitements to violence or tending to

create unhealthy excitement or class hatred. Government hope that they may rely upon the cooperation of the Mazdur Sabha in this matter.

5. Government hope that the principle that there shall be no strikes without previous efforts at amicable settlement will be rigorously followed in the future, and that the present differences will be resolved quickly in a spirit of mutual goodwill. For attaining this end Government are always willing to assist the industry in every possible way.

No. 3456 (1)/XVIII

Copy forwarded to the Labour Commissioner, United Provinces, for information. He will please discuss the matter with the employers, if necessary, and he may tell them the gist of this letter, if he thinks fit. Government are very anxious that the New Victoria Mill strike should be settled as soon as possible, without any further delay.

By order.

45

HAIG TO LINLITHGOW
R/3/1/75

Secret
No. U.P.-277

Camp,
June 24th, 1939

My dear Lord Linlithgow,

Since writing my fortnightly report on June 12th I have been in Naini Tal, except that yesterday I came out for a week-end, which is a pleasant change though hardly a holiday, to Almora the headquarters of one of our Kumaun districts, and about 80 miles from Naini Tal by road. During the last fortnight I have seen a good deal of my Ministers. Kidwai is still out of action and I believe has been taking a sea trip from Calcutta to Bombay. Mrs. Pandit too, who was to have been in Naini Tal, stayed in the Nehrus' very pleasant estate near Almora for most of the time, as unfortunately she was running a temperature. The other four Ministers, however, have been in Naini Tal continuously and I have held no less than four Cabinet meetings at which we disposed of a large amount of business. I have also been able to discuss other matters with the Ministers individually. In my last letter I gave you a long account of Pant's protest about the Knighthood conferred on Chintamani. In spite of my constant talk with the Ministers since, both individually and in Cabinet, not a word has been said on this subject by any of them, and I am inclined to hope that Pant having discharged his feelings has realised that the matter is not of such importance as he had supposed and that there is another side to it, and that possibly the other Ministers are not greatly interested. So I hope I shall hear no more of it. I had been playing a good deal of tennis in the Naini Tal tournament which had been in progress for some ten days,[66] and on the last day of the tournament I found all the Ministers there among the spectators and took the opportunity of going over and chatting to them. As a rule they do not appear at public functions of such a frivolous character; so I take this as a good sign.

2. After very thorough discussion with the Premier I have settled the matter of a new Chief Secretary. We have decided on Panna Lal, who acted for six months while Gwynne was on leave last year. This decision is agreeable to the Premier, on the whole less so to me, though after very careful consideration I came to the conclusion that the choice was inevitable. Hallett under whom Panna Lal worked for some months is quite satisfied with the decision. I have taken the opportunity, however, of strengthening the Chief Secretary's branch. We have at present one Deputy Secretary,[67] who is a Muslim officer of the I.C.S., and is a steady though not brilliant worker. But both Gwynne and Panna Lal have continually been complaining that they need further assistance, and we have given it to them in a somewhat unsatisfactory way by drafting in junior officers of the I.C.S. for limited periods. I thought it was advisable to stipulate that we should have a second regular Deputy Secretary, and Pant agreed to a temporary appointment being made for a period of one year. He also accepted my selection, which was that of a very capable and independent British officer of the I.C.S. who has been District Magistrate of Bareilly and has been doing excellent work recently in keeping that troublesome city in order.[68] The fact that there is a British officer of some standing and character in the Chief Secretary's department will I hope be a source of reassurance to the British element in the I.C.S. and the Police. Gwynne's health continues about the same. He has lately been a little better, but it seems unlikely that it will be possible to send him home.

3. In my last letter I reported the marked improvement in the Cawnpore labour situation, which has continued. Unfortunately we have now had another communal outbreak in this unrestful city. The actual disturbance was brought under control promptly, but it will leave a legacy of communal ill-feeling for some time, and there have been several isolated stabbing assaults, which seem nowadays to be the almost inevitable aftermath of a riot. The Premier is worried and I believe has gone to Cawnpore on his

way to Bombay. The root of the trouble is the exceedingly provocative communal attitude of both sides, and I think it is typical of the situation that a so-called Unity Board appears, according to the papers, to have done nothing in the direction of promoting unity except to express a united view that the Police had failed in their duty. In fact so far as my information goes the Police acted with great promptitude and resolution, and I do not believe for a moment that they showed any lack of impartiality.

4. The Sunni-Shia controversy drags on its dreary course, and I think there are signs that everyone is beginning to get rather tired of it. The punitive tax in Lucknow amounting to a lakh is being assessed, and the realisation that the luxury of sectarian strife has to be paid for is perhaps having some effect. The local Shias are reported to be tired and despondent, and the Tabarra movement is being kept going to a large extent by Shias from the Punjab and other Provinces. These, however, I am told are not very happy at being kept in jail, as they had been led to believe that the movement would quickly be victorious and that they would be let out after a short period. Discussions proceed in a desultory manner, but I think at the moment it is wise for Government to do nothing and await further developments.

5. Our Cabinet business has included the following subjects:

(*a*) The approval of a road programme costing 1½ crores, to be carried out over a period of three years, though it will doubtless take nearer five. Thirty lakhs has been provided in this year's budget and the means of financing the programme have been considered carefully. The money can certainly be found, unless we subsequently throw away further revenue resources by our prohibition policy.

(*b*) We decided to raise a loan of 2 crores this year, and I am glad that we have since received the approval of the Government of India. The greater part of the money is required for capital expenditure on irrigation works and roads both for last year and this year, for we raised no loan last year. An important scheme has been approved and will be started at once for extending the Sarda Canal. It has been found by the experience of a number of years that there is surplus water available in the upper parts of the canal. This by means of widening one of the main branches will be carried down to the tail-end and will be of the greatest value there, enabling irrigation to be extended in areas which need it greatly. The scheme will also yield a very good return. We are also providing for a new steam generating station for our big western electric grid system, the demand on which continues to expand rapidly. In all these matters the Ministers are very anxious to press forward with sound development schemes.

(*c*) We discussed the future of the Industrial Financing Corporation at some length. I suggested to the Ministers that they were making a mistake in accepting the position that was being thrust upon them by the opposition, that the credit of the Province was involved in the success of this Corporation. I pointed out that on the contrary it was never intended to be more than an experiment to see whether the public would assist in such a scheme, that the scheme was not in fact theirs but had been inherited by them from their predecessors, and that if they were now to close down the Corporation on the ground that the public had not shown sufficient interest they need not lose credit either politically or financially. They considered these arguments for some time, but eventually have decided to make all possible efforts to keep the Corporation going. This means that they have got to find purchasers for the large block of shares held by the Benares Bank, the allotment money of which cannot be paid by the Bank. If they cannot find purchasers for these shares, I think they will decide to wind up the Corporation.

(*d*) We had discussions on educational policy which will result before long in the issue of a Government resolution. The most important question of principle was whether primary education should be withdrawn from the District Boards and placed directly under the Education Department. This was the view of the Education Minister. On the other hand, the Local Self-Government Minister (Mrs. Pandit) was largely committed to an opposite view by the elaborate report of a committee on Local Self-Government which had been set up by her. It was decided that it was necessary to get Mrs. Pandit over from Almora to discuss this matter and they finally settled between themselves what appears to be a satisfactory compromise, namely, that the District Board will retain the nominal control, but all questions regarding transfer, punishment, &c., of teachers, which are at the root of much of the present inefficiency and intrigue, will be placed in the hands of the officers of the Education Department. In practice they should be able to ensure that sound policy is followed and that efficiency is maintained. I think that this change should have a great effect on our standards of primary education.

(*e*) We also approved a scheme in conjunction with the Bihar Government for the production of power alcohol from molasses, and I hope that this will receive the cooperation of the Government of India. I think it is conceived on sound lines, and that from many points of view, not the least that of war time insurance, it is desirable that this industry should be established. The proposal is to legislate so as to make it compulsory that 25 per cent of power alcohol should be mixed with all petrol in the two Provinces of United Provinces and Bihar.

(*f*) We also discussed various proposals dealing with debt legislation. The Ministers had no hesitation about approving the Bill which finally extinguishes the claim to sue for the arrears of rent which were stayed originally by executive order almost immediately after the present Ministry assumed office. I think the zamindars have made up their minds that these arrears are lost, and though I pointed out that I should have to consider the principle of the Bill somewhat carefully when it comes to me for assent, I think in fact it will be necessary to let it go through. On the other hand, a comprehensive Bill for the regulation of agricultural credit was postponed after some brief discussion, and I think it is clear that for reasons which I shall explain in connection with the Tenancy Bill the Ministers were anxious not to commit themselves at the moment to the details of a Bill which is going to affect the moneylenders seriously.

(*g*) We did not discuss the Village Panchayats Bill, which I think I have mentioned more than once before; but as a long statement had appeared in the Press which purported to give the views of Dr. Katju, I mentioned the matter in Cabinet and enquired whether these views indicated generally the attitude of the Cabinet. It was evident that the matter had formed the subject of discussion among the Ministers, and the Premier expressed his general agreement with Dr. Katju's suggestions. The matter has not come up for formal consideration by the Cabinet, but as these views seem to me an immense improvement on the very dangerous and unwise proposals of the Local Self-Government committee which had been reduced to a draft Village Panchayat Bill, I told the Ministers I was attracted by Dr. Katju's ideas and I congratulated them on suggestions which might well prove to be the solution of the difficulties of village administration. The main point of Dr. Katju's suggestions is that we should get away from the very dangerous and embarrassing proposals for introducing an electoral system into every village. This would not only be extremely unsuitable in itself, but it was quite clear that it was going to raise in an acute form the question of joint or separate electorates for Muslims and other minorities. Dr. Katju proposes to cut away from all this electoral machinery by saying that a co-operative society should be formed for each village unit consisting of the heads or representatives of each household. This would form a body of manageable size, perhaps two hundred in number in a fairly large village, which would meet from time to time and discuss the village affairs, and would be able by its own methods to appoint or elect a panchayat representing the society. In this way it is hoped that instead of creating or accentuating divisions in the villages, which would be the inevitable result of a regular electoral system, the unity of the village would from the start be emphasised. Moreover, the intention is to limit the functions of the society to purposes which are of real practical interest to the village. The Village Panchayat Bill, prepared by townsmen for villagers, was modelled on the Municipalities Act and proposed to entrust to village panchayats absurdly unsuitable functions. If the ideas which the Ministers at present hold can be developed into a practicable scheme, I feel that we shall have avoided serious dangers which would have been created by the original village panchayat proposals, and that in fact a really practical and helpful organisation may be given to the villagers. One point which was specially stressed in our discussion was that advantage should be taken of the fact that the village is a small unit. Therefore it can be dealt with by a small assembly consisting of the villagers themselves reduced in numbers by the device of having only one member to represent each household, and we can get away from the defects and difficulties of representative government which is a device necessitated by the existence of large communities.

6. Recently the main interest in Naini Tal has been the progress of negotiations between the Ministers and the representatives of the landlords in the Upper House in regard to the future of the Tenancy Bill. On the landlord side the negotiators have been a committee of members of the Upper House, but they have been advised from the background by the principal representatives of the British India Association and the Agra Zamindars' Association, and I understand they are in a position to take decisions definitely on behalf of the whole body of landlords. They have put their demands clearly before the Ministers, though no doubt they would be prepared to modify or abandon some of them. The Ministers I understand have given no indication of their attitude. The Premier has promised the landlords that he will give an answer when he comes back to Naini Tal from Bombay about the 29th June. He has given as his reason for delay that he must consult the Revenue Minister, Kidwai, whom he expects to meet in Bombay. But apart from that, I have little doubt that he will take the opportunity in Bombay of consulting the higher command. The Ministers are not without some hope that they may be able to secure a bare majority in the Upper House, and the landlords think that the Ministers may hold back their final decision until the very eve of the meeting of the Legislative Council on 3rd July, when it will be known definitely how the voting will go. If, however, as the landlords believe, the Ministry will find themselves in a minority, then it seems likely that they will make such concessions as are sufficient to bring about a settlement. The landlords do not seem to me to be in an unreasonable mood, and I think would be glad

enough to settle on anything that would meet some of their main points. It will be seen that the decisive question is the voting strength in the Upper House, and it is in this connection that the votes of a considerable number of Bania members of that House have assumed a great importance. A party of about 14 Banias seems to have been formed which is likely to support the Ministry in return for concessions about the debt legislation. On the other hand, the Banias are a little nervous of antagonising the landlords too much, as they fear that if they do, the landlords may refuse to pass the concessions in the debt legislation which the Government might be prepared to give them. The whole situation is thus very uncertain.

7. In paragraph 6 of my letter No. U.P.-257, dated May 9th, I mentioned that I had discussed with Pant the revolutionary activities in this Province and that we had decided to ask the D.I.G., C.I.D., to let us have a special report as early as possible. The report[69] has taken a little time to prepare, but it reached me a few days ago, and I was able to discuss it with Pant before he left for Bombay. The report gives a good summary of the existing position and includes, as I had requested, suggestions for any practical action that might be feasible. Though the Youth League is clearly being used as a means for spreading revolutionary doctrines, we were agreed that direct action cannot be taken against it. It is also clear that a conspiracy case at this stage would not be useful. The two main directions in which effective action could be taken would be in instituting prosecutions for violent and revolutionary speeches and in proscribing and forfeiting revolutionary literature. In this connection I had a frank talk with Pant, who has shown a reluctance practically amounting to refusal to agree to any prosecution for violent speeches. He admitted that he had been extremely reluctant to agree to any such prosecutions, but said that now he was prepared to consider them in special cases, and we agreed that certain recent speeches should be examined definitely with a view to prosecution. I hope I shall be able to keep him up to this resolution. He also said that he had been examining certain books and pamphlets recently and was prepared to agree to proscribe two of them. This, at any rate, is a beginning, from which he has for many months been holding back. I think he is at last coming to realise that these speeches and writings are dangerous and are having effect. With regard to overt criminal actions, on the whole we seem to be dealing with these not unsuccessfully. The C.I.D. report mentions by name several M.L.As. who are alleged to be supporting the revolutionary movement and I spoke to Pant about these cases. He expressed, as I had expected, great surprise at the allegations made, but promised to discuss the facts more closely with the D.I.G. He said that if

he were really satisfied about the truth of these charges he would take action to make clear the disapproval of the Congress organisation, and added that persons who were really pursuing a policy of this nature had no place in the Congress party. Altogether so far as the conversation with Pant went his attitude was satisfactory, but I think it will be necessary continually to maintain pressure on him.

8. You will see from the information I have given in this letter how deeply involved and how keenly interested my Ministers are in numerous constructive policies. I cannot believe that they would give up these activities save with the greatest reluctance.

Yours sincerely,
H.G. HAIG

NOTES

1. In paragraph 6 of his letter of 19 March 1939, Lord Linlithgow said that Mr Raghavendra Rao had suggested in conversation that it was very desirable to involve provincial Prime Ministers in every service case of importance. He also thought that Governors should press for the discussion of all service cases in the Cabinet. The Viceroy wondered to what extent these suggestions were already established practice in the U.P. R/3/1/75.
2. Sir John Ewart was Director of the Intelligence Bureau, Government of India at this date.
3. See U.P.P., 1938, Enclosure to No. 82.
4. See No. 30 below, paragraph 10 and Enclosure 2.
5. In his circular letter of 2 April 1939, Lord Linlithgow asked Governors of the extent to which they felt they were fully prepared for a war situation. The Viceroy was particularly interested in the likely attitudes of the Congress Ministries. MSS.EUR.F 125/107.
6. Lord Linlithgow minuted: 'Any specific suggestion?'
7. Lord Linlithgow minuted: 'P.S.V. – This is a gloomy letter! Sec. 93 is evidently going to lead to an immense amount of cogitation! – if not much else!'
8. Mr S.K. Raza was Superintendent of Police, Benares until 1 April 1939.
9. Mr T.B.W. Bishop was Commissioner of Meerut at this date.
10. Mr G.D. Parkin was Superintendent of Police, Lucknow at this date.
11. These were persons who had taken part in dacoities (some involving murder) in 1924 and 1925. The last incident took place at Kakori. Those remaining in prison had been released in the first months of the Congress Ministry.
12. Mr G.W.M. Whittle was District Magistrate of Allahabad at this date.
13. Sir John Hewett was Lieutenant-Governor of the United Provinces in 1909.
14. Mr G.M. Harper was Commissioner of Lucknow in 1939.
15. In his circular letter of 15 March 1939, Lord Linlithgow said he had been

considering the extent to which he was kept in touch with the preparation of provincial budgets. The practice varied considerably from province to province but developments could occur which had all-India implications. The Viceroy sought Governors' views on a memorandum which he enclosed. MSS.EUR.F 125/107.

16. Mr W. Christie was Finance Secretary at this date.
17. The Viceroy replied on 24 April 1939. He said he would see whether there were any other points which could be put to Governors in the light of their representations. R/3/1/75.
18. Miss Agatha Harrison was Secretary of the India Conciliation Group. She paid three extended visits to India in the 1930s and came to know Mahatma Gandhi well. She acted as an intermediary for him during his Rajkot fast.
19. Lord Lothian had been Parliamentary Secretary, India Office, 1931-2.
20. Mr J.E. Pedley was District Magistrate of Gorakhpur at this date.
21. Lord Linlithgow minuted: 'I seem to remember saying something of the same sort myself, but without much encouragement, if I recall aright!'
22. Not printed.
23. Mr J.P. Nicholson was District Magistrate of Benares at this date.
24. Mr J.L Sathe was Commissioner of Benares at this date.
25. Mr R.V. Vernède was the District Magistrate who had handled the Benares riots in March 1939.
26. Lord Linlithgow minuted: 'Shabash'.
27. Kunwar Jasbir Singh was District Magistrate of Lucknow at this date.
28. Mr B.V. Bhadkamkar was Excise Commissioner at this date.
29. Not printed. This portion of the Excise Commissioner's report related to the Ministry's temperance policy on alcohol. The Commissioner said that 'in some places illicitly manufactured liquor is supplied to customers with the regularity of milk from a dairy.' He felt that 'in spite of the general public opinion in favour of temperance it is unfortunately a fact that so far as the detection of excise offenders is concerned the general public is apathetic if not some time actually hostile.' A very definite public opinion would need to be created against the illegal liquor producers if the Ministry's policy was to be successful.
30. Lord Linlithgow's letter of 17 April 1939 is on R/3/1/75.
31. See No. 39 below.
32. See U.P.P., 1938, Nos. 63 and 72. In his letter of 18 April 1939 to Sir Harry Haig, Lord Linlithgow said that he felt much importance must still attach to the close association of the District Officer with the spending of the Central Government's rural development grant in the U.P. Linlithgow suggested that they might secure their object by providing that District Officers should arrange for the inspection of works sanctioned by District Associations from Central Government funds and should certify to audit that the money had been properly spent. R/3/1/75.
33. Mr W. Christie was Finance Secretary at this date.

34. Lord Linlithgow's circular letter to Governors of 15 April 1939 forwarded a copy of a speech he had made to the Chamber of Princes on 13 March. The covering letter summarised and developed points made in this speech. MSS.EUR.F 125/107.
35. Lord Linlithgow minuted: 'Heaven knows what this means!'
36. The article and communiqué are on L/P&J/5/267: ff. 100-3.
37. The article is ibid: ff. 104-7.
38. Lord Linlithgow minuted: 'I hope the G[overnor] has told Pant this.'
39. See Enclosure 1.
40. This second circular letter sent by Mr Gwynne to district officers is on L/P&J/5/267: ff. 112-13.
41. See No. 26, note 76. In accordance with the terms of the Pant Resolution, Mr Subhas Chandra Bose consulted Mahatma Gandhi on the formation of his Working Committee. However Gandhi wrote: 'Pandit Pant's resolution I cannot interpret. The more I study it the more I dislike it. . . . I cannot, will not, impose a Cabinet on you.' (Letter to Bose of 10 April 1939.) Gandhi had earlier advised Bose: 'I am of opinion that you should at once form your own Cabinet fully representing your views, formulate your programme definitely and put it before the forthcoming A.I.C.C. If the Committee accepts the programme, all will be plain-sailing. . . . If, on the other hand, your programme is not accepted you should resign and let the Committee choose its President.' (Letter to Bose of 2 April 1939.)
    The Collected Works of Mahatma Gandhi, vol. 69 (New Delhi: Government of India, 1977), pp. 96-8, 125-7.
    Bose reported to the meeting of the All-India Congress Committee held at Calcutta from 29 April to 1 May 1939 that he had failed to form a Working Committee. He therefore tendered his resignation. The Committee then elected the right winger, Dr Rajendra Prasad, as President for the remainder of the year. It also appointed a predominantly right wing Working Committee.
42. Mr J.C. Weymouth was Deputy Inspector-General, C.I.D. at this date.
43. See Enclosure 2.
44. Lord Linlithgow minuted: 'P.S.V. – Our Dictator moves from strength to strength!'
45. Lord Linlithgow minuted: 'P.S.V. – Full of interest and with some points of encouragement – vide circular to D.Os.'
46. Sir Ziauddin Ahmad was a distinguished mathematician and served as Vice-Chancellor of Aligarh Muslim University 1934-46. From 1938 he was Secretary of the Muslim League in the Indian Central Legislature. Lord Linlithgow's letter of 13 April 1939 enclosed a summary of Ziauddin Ahmad's complaints. The general complaints were: (a) dual system of administration; (b) interference with the judiciary and reversal of High Court decisions; (c) financial inequilibrium – loss of income under various heads like land revenue; (d) dislocation of law and order in villages; (e) interference in the work of the executives; (f) corruption; (g) forcible suppression of free speech.

Ziauddin Ahmad said the special complaints of Muslims were: (a) trouble in the villages of Muslim landlords; (b) rewards to Mahasabhaist officers who had done injustice to Muslims; (c) communal riots were started by Hindus; (d) forcing Hindi and non-Muslim culture on Muslims; (e) wasting enormous sums on self-propaganda under the name of rural uplift and employing only non-Muslims; (f) unfair enquiries in the case of Muslim officers; (g) C.P. and Bihar Ministries had no Muslim Minister; (h) Muslims did not get a fair share in public appointments. MSS.EUR.F 125/107.

47. The District Magistrate of Etah was Mr Rafi-ul-Qadr Khan at this date.
48. The reference here is to the Report of the Inquiry Committee under the Presidency of the Raja of Pirpur, appointed by the Council of the All-India Muslim League to inquire into some Muslim grievances in Congress Provinces. (Delhi: The League, 1938.) The Pirpur Report is reprinted in: K.K. Aziz (ed.), *Muslims under Congress Rule, 1937-1939: A Documentary Record*, vol. 1 (Islamabad: National Commission on Historical and Cultural Research, 1978), pp. 307-86.
49. In his telegram on the Madhe-Sahaba dispute, the Nizam of Hyderabad said: 'In my opinion the best course of deciding the issue will be to refer the matter to a Commission appointed by Your Excellency, whose President should of course be a European Judge of the High Court, while the other two members should represent their own communities respectively whose status may be recognised. Whatever the decision the Court may give, should be binding on both parties concerned . . .' R/3/1/75.
50. See Enclosure for the draft communiqué. The draft letter of Mr Saiyid Ali Zaheer (Shia spokesman) and Pandit Pant's draft reply are not reprinted but are included in R/3/1/75.
51. See Enclosure 3 to No. 31.
52. Mr R.F. Mudie was Revenue Secretary at this date.
53. Lord Linlithgow minuted: 'It would be as well to break the news as to our intentions on Employment Tax before this happy meeting?'
54. In his letter of 13 May 1939 to Sir Harry Haig, Lord Linlithgow said there was no doubt that the Calcutta session of the A.I.C.C. was a decisive victory for the right wing of Congress. The Viceroy felt that the split between right and left was based more on a real difference of approach than on a difference between leading personalities. R/3/1/75.
55. Lord Linlithgow minuted: 'I saw signs of the same feeling in Munshi's mind.' Mr K.M. Munshi was Home Minister of Bombay, 1937-39.
56. Lord Linlithgow minuted: 'I hope our plan may prove of help. I see no reason why it should not, with appropriate modifications, suit the U.P. quite well.'
57. Lord Linlithgow's letter of 26 May 1939 to Sir Harry Haig is on R/3/1/75.
58. Sir Maurice Hallett was Governor of Bihar at this date. His letter of 8 May 1939 (685-G.B.) to Lord Linlithgow on Muslim grievances is on R/3/1/19.
59. Lord Linlithgow minuted: 'And as much in non-Congress as in Congress Provinces!'

60. Lord Linlithgow minuted: 'P.S.V. – This is interesting, though I find in it no new ideas. Haig seems to give little or no weight to the possibility that a Congress split may come, along the line of "haves" and "have nots", with the probable result that the right of Congress will have the full support from landlords, including Muslim landlords. I suppose he has sent S. of S. a copy of this draft letter.'
61. In his letter of 6 June 1939, Lord Linlithgow put to Sir Harry Haig the point made in the preceding footnote. The Viceroy added that perhaps Haig felt that this was not a likely contingency. R/3/1/75.
62. Mr G.M. Harper was Commissioner of Lucknow at this date.
63. Sir Chirravoori Chintamani was editor of the *Leader* at this date.
64. Lord Linlithgow minuted: 'I am so very sorry.'
65. Mr N.C. Mehta was Secretary of the U.P. Industries Department at this date.
66. Lord Linlithgow minuted: 'I hope H.E. won the finals!'
67. Mr S.H. Zaheer was Deputy Secretary in the Chief Secretary's Department at this date.
68. Lord Linlithgow minuted: 'What is the British O[fficer]'s name?' Mr D.S. Barron was the officer appointed as second Deputy Secretary.
69. Mr Weymouth's report has not been traced.

CHAPTER 3

Documents for 1 July – 30 September 1939

46

HAIG TO LINLITHGOW
R/3/1/75

Secret *July 1st, 1939*
No. U.P.-282

My dear Lord Linlithgow,

In Your Excellency's letter, dated 10th June 1939, you asked for my views generally about the attitude of the Muslims towards Federation.[1] I have taken a little time to reply, because it is a matter on which I myself feel somewhat uncertain, and I have tried in the interval to clear my ideas by conversations with such Muslims as I have been meeting. But even now I feel that there is a considerable element of speculation in the views I express.

2. The first question I put to myself is whether the Muslims have any fundamental objection to Federation, and that question can be viewed in two aspects:

(*a*) Federation as a further step in the process of self-government for India.

(*b*) Federation as a detailed scheme in which there are certain obvious disadvantages for the Muslim community.

3. These two aspects really represent an essential antinomy in the Muslim position. As Indians the Muslims want a greater degree of power and self-government. They do not wish to be governed by a foreign race. On the other hand, as a communal minority they know that their interests and their authority in the country depend to a large extent on the support of the British and that it is to their interest to back up the British so long as the British are likely to exercise an effective restraining influence on the power

of the Hindu majority. In practice the Muslims seem to have reacted to these conflicting considerations by expressing, even with some vehemence, a theoretical demand for wider self-governing powers for Indians, coupled with a practical lack of enthusiasm for extensive political changes. It would not be unnatural therefore if the Muslims combined these two positions by opposing Federation, not on principle or in respect of the wider powers it confers, but on the grounds of its practical disadvantages to the Muslim community.

4. I think this is probably the basis of the Muslim position. It is a tactical attitude resting on what they conceive to be the interests of the community. It is not an attitude that is likely to lead them into very strong or fervent opposition to Federation as such, but is likely to involve rather the putting forward of certain tactical demands as the price of their consent. There is of course the possibility that certain demands might be evolved which would be regarded as a sort of charter of Muslim security and would in that light develop into a serious battle-cry. But it might in practice prove very difficult for Muslims to reach agreement about such demands.

5. Still viewing the matter as one primarily of Muslim tactics, there is the question as between an all-India Federation and a British India Federation. So far as I can judge at the present moment these federal issues are left very largely in the hands of Jinnah. I have been told that when Jinnah attacked Sikander Hayat[2] for his speech pledging the support of the Punjab in the event of war, Sikander reacted very strongly and said that if any interference were attempted by the Muslim League in Punjab affairs he would go out of the League; but if the Muslim League kept their hands off provincial matters then provincial Ministers would leave Jinnah a free hand in regard to all-India matters, and that this in fact is the kind of working arrangement that at present prevails. If that is so, we must naturally expect these federal issues to be handled almost entirely on a tactical basis, for that is the essential quality of Jinnah's politics. I gather that Jinnah thinks he would be in a stronger position in a British India Federation than in an all-India Federation, and I have had similar views expressed to me by Muslims here. On the other hand if the Congress, rather than the Hindu community, is regarded as the enemy, then the Muslims might in fact find themselves in a better position in an all-India Federation than they would in a British India Federation, which would undoubtedly be dominated by the Congress. As between these two possibilities I am disposed to doubt whether it would be easy to work up strong Muslim feeling in favour of a British India Federation rather than an all-India Federation. In any case I feel that whatever may be the present working arrangement among

Muslims, when it really comes to any crucial decisions about their attitude towards Federation, Jinnah will not be left in undisputed control.

6. I am afraid all these views are very vague, but the situation itself seems to me essentially vague. Muslims do not really know their minds. They have not fully faced up to the problem. When they do face up to it, I should doubt whether they would carry their opposition to Federation or to particular forms of Federation to the point of organising mass resistance. But they may make a strong bid to get certain changes made in the scheme. You ask in your letter whether it would be possible for the Muslim community effectively by itself to impede or hold up the introduction of Federation. I do not know whether, if we looked at Federation as a matter of machinery, they could stop its introduction or working, but it would clearly be a very formidable and indeed disastrous development if the Muslims were to proceed to the length of active mass resistance. I do not think it is likely to come to this; but with reference to your specific enquiry I think it is only right to state this opinion.

Yours sincerely,
H.G. HAIG

47

HAIG TO LINLITHGOW
R/3/1/75

Secret
No. U.P.-283

July 5th, 1939

My dear Lord Linlithgow,

With reference to the correspondence ending with my letter No. U.P.-221, dated February 6th, 1939, on the subject of Advisers, it is necessary for me now to find a third Adviser to take the place of Gwynne who I am afraid can never return to duty. I am left still with Panna Lal and Sloan. Of these Sloan has been intended by me to handle Finance and Revenue, and Panna Lal what are generally called the nation-building departments. I have been depending on Gwynne for the general law and order departments.

2. Though Panna Lal is now going to be Chief Secretary I do not propose that in the event of a Section 93 situation he should handle law and order. He will be much more useful to me in the nation-building departments. Similarly Sloan, though he would be quite capable of handling law and order, would be more useful in the departments for which I had intended

him. I therefore need a third Adviser who will be able to handle law and order. I do not think that either of the Members of the Board of Revenue, Marsh and Mehta, have quite the qualities of vigour and decision that would be required. I have carefully considered the qualifications of the Commissioners and I have come to the conclusion that the most suitable will be Dible. I therefore propose that he should be appointed as the third Adviser. Dible is at present on leave. He would have to be recalled immediately if the necessity arose. I would not contemplate putting in anyone for the short time pending his arrival.

Yours sincerely,
H.G. HAIG

48

HAIG TO LINLITHGOW
R/3/1/75

No. U.P.-284

Camp,
July 5th, 1939

My dear Lord Linlithgow,

I am afraid that I have taken some time in replying to Your Excellency's letter of 18th April, about the question of the old and the new schemes of Rural Development and the conditions on which the Government of India grant might be continued. I explained the reasons for the delay in my letter No. U.P.-252 of April the 30th, and since then I have discussed the question at length with Chaturvedi (I.F.S.), the Rural Development Officer. I have also while in Naini Tal had the opportunity of getting from a number of Commissioners and District Officers, who have been up here, their views on the way in which the scheme has been working in the particular areas with which they are familiar.

2. In my letter of April the 30th, I mentioned that the Provincial Government had provided something under 2 lakhs in our Budget this year as the expected contribution from the Government of India. This statement however, was based on incorrect information and the figure should have been 4 lakhs round (or exactly, as entered in the Budget, Rs. 3,81,827). The actual sum which will be due from the Government of India is, however, I understand, still the subject of correspondence. According to the two schemes approved by the Government of India the annual amount provided by the Government of India should be 5.34 lakhs;

and the Provincial Government contribution to the same schemes 1 lakh (this to be for staff). The reason for the Government of India contribution for 1939-40 being estimated at the lower figure of 4 lakhs round is that there is still a balance in hand from the previous Government of India grant of 15 lakhs which will be sufficient to make the total up to 5.34 lakhs. The total annual expenditure of 6.34 lakhs covers the pay of the staff employed in the centres under the original Rural Development scheme (270). It also covers a discretionary grant of Rs. 5,000 per annum placed at the disposal of each District Officer for expenditure in those centres. It also covers certain separate allotments made to each district on a population basis for expenditure on three specified purposes, improvement of water-supply, improvement of rural communications and improved seed supply. The allotments to each district for each of these purposes are fixed. The expenditure on the first two is controlled by the District Officer while the expenditure on seed supply is controlled by the Director of Agriculture.

3. The Provincial Government has its own more extensive scheme covering some 780 centres. In framing that scheme the scales of salary for the staff were made lower than those under the original scheme; and the salaries of the staff employed under the original scheme are being reduced to the same level. The Provincial Government's new scheme is administered by District Rural Development Associations. District Officers have been advised to spend their discretionary allotments under the old scheme in consultation with these District Associations. The expenditure from the discretionary grants is to be utilised for small works of public utility, such as the construction of *panchayat-ghars*, the improvement of village sanitation, the supply of material for games or physical culture, &c. This expenditure is confined to villages situated in Rural Development Circles. The expenditure from the separate grants for water-supply, &c., on the other hand is not confined to villages so situated. In practice the staff under both the new and the old schemes is now amalgamated and all is controlled by the Rural Development Officer through the District Associations. The old and the new centres are similarly under unified control. The Provincial Government budgeted in 1938-39 for an expenditure of 75 lakhs on various schemes which formed part of their Rural Development Programme, and which were distributed among the various departmental budgets. They found it impossible, however, to spend anything like this sum and I believe that at least half the amount provided lapsed. In the current year the total amount provided for their various Rural Development Schemes is 33.97 lakhs.

4. The result of my enquiries has on the whole been reassuring. A great

improvement has taken place since the appointment of Chaturvedi. With regard to the alleged political activities of the staff he said that he had been working against great difficulties, but he claimed to have effected much improvement. He said that he had got rid of 6 or 7 out of the 10 Divisional Superintendents, and that over 100 organisers had also been weeded out. These were the men who were doing no practical work but devoting themselves to politics. The Chairman of the District Associations, who are nearly all Congressmen, are in most cases devoting themselves genuinely to Rural Development work. He recently circularised these Chairmen and asked their opinion as to how the system of having a Deputy Collector as Secretary was working. Something like 40 out of the 48 Chairmen definitely supported the system and acknowledged its advantages. Chaturvedi speaks highly of the work of the Deputy Collectors who are Secretaries of the District Associations. He also finds that District Officers are taking a practical interest in the work and giving valuable co-operation.

5. In his opinion the actual expenditure of money is being very strictly scrutinised, and the money is only being spent on approved objects. He considers that these approved objects are of real value. He has been concentrating largely on the establishment of Better Living Societies through which the practical work in the villages is being conducted. He has also been encouraging the erection of *panchayat-ghars* which are felt by the villagers to belong to themselves and to provide a visible centre for all Rural Development activities. A good deal has also been done in starting *akharas*. Much work has been done in the improvement of water-supply; and the Public Health and Agriculture Departments are carrying on activities in connection with sanitation and agriculture. The latter includes the establishment of 379 Seed Stores, run by the Agriculture Department. Nothing has yet been done for the improvement of communications, as there are no funds, but this is a matter for which the villagers clamour, and on which a good deal of the funds supplied by the Government of India could be spent with great advantage.

6. The opinions of the Commissioners and District Officers to whom I spoke varied; and there is no doubt that there is a good deal of variation from district to district depending to a large extent on the character and ability of the Chairman and members of the District Association, as well as on that of the staff. Officers in general consider that a great deal of useful departmental work is being done. They are more dubious about the work of the Organisers and Inspectors. There is no doubt that a certain amount of political propaganda has been done by members of this staff

and that some of them have shown more interest in political and agrarian agitation than in their proper duties. There is also undoubtedly a good deal of eye-wash about the work carried on in some places. There have been complaints about political propaganda at training camps, flag hoistings, and so on, and about some literature provided for the village Reading Rooms. At the same time there seems to be no doubt that there is quite a lot of solid work being done and that there are in many though not all of the centres signs that the villagers are beginning to take a genuine interest in the work and that it is establishing permanent roots.

7. I definitely consider therefore that the two schemes should be amalgamated; and that the Government of India grant should be continued, and will be profitably expended, for the purpose for which it was originally made, the benefit of the rural population and the creating in them of a desire and will to better their own lot. I consider that the proposal made in Your Excellency's letter that the grant should be continued subject to safeguards is eminently sound. The safeguards and conditions which I should suggest are as follows:

(*i*) The Government of India grant should be given for specified objects. No portion of it should be spent on staff. In my opinion, with which Chaturvedi agrees, it might well be limited to the following:

(*a*) Improvement of water-supply.

(*b*) Improvement of communications.

(*c*) The paving of village lanes.

(*ii*) All works should be on a contributory basis. The selection of works and allotment of money should be made by the District Rural Development Association, which should inform the District Officer regularly of the action thus taken.

(*iii*) The Government order placing a lump allotment at the disposal of each Rural Development Association shall specify precisely the objects on which and the conditions under which it may be utilised. The grant once made to the Association will not lapse at the end of the year.

(*iv*) The Association will be held responsible for seeing that the money is properly expended. The District Officer, himself or through his staff, may in the capacity of a visitor at any time inspect and check work while it is in progress.

(*v*) The Examiner Local Fund Accounts who has been entrusted with the task of auditing the accounts of the Rural Development Associations will be made responsible for the auditing of the accounts of these district grants. He will not, however, be able to audit all the accounts. His audit will be of the nature of a test audit from time to time.

(*vi*) The Secretary of the Rural Development Association concerned will furnish to the District Officer a completion certificate for each work constructed from this grant, as it is completed.

(*vii*) At the end of the year the District Officer shall furnish a certificate showing all works completed from funds provided out of this grant, and certifying that the work has been satisfactorily constructed and is value for the money spent on it. This he can ascertain by local inspection when on tour himself or through his staff. It should, however, be clearly understood that this certificate does not commit him to guaranteeing the accuracy of every *anna* and *pie* in the accounts. To do so would be to strangle the whole organisation in red tape. The certificate ought however to be a sufficient guarantee that the money has been profitably expended or at any rate that an honest attempt has been made to expend it profitably. It must be remembered that petty works carried out by villagers for themselves or through small tradesmen and contractors may sometimes fail through bad design or through misfortune. The District Officer in such cases should have power to write off the loss and his certificate that he considers that reasonable precautions were taken and that no one should be held to blame should be held a sufficient bar to further enquiries except such as may arise in the ordinary course of audit.

8. The measure of control by the District Officer which I have suggested would serve the useful purpose of giving him definite functions in relation to the District Associations and definite points of contact with and of interest in their work. Officers have been taking different views about this work under the new conditions and while many of them have maintained their interest in it some have been disposed to stand on one side and leave the responsibility entirely to the District Association. This has in some cases been the result of the attitude of a particular Association or of its Chairman and of the fact that the District Officer had no definite duties which brought him into regular contact with the Association.

9. I believe that the Minister responsible, Dr. Katju, would welcome a continuance of the grant on conditions such as I have described. I also believe that its continuance on these lines would be the best way in which the Government of India could help to consolidate the results already secured and to cooperate with the Provincial Government in the latter's genuine desire and effort to improve conditions in the rural areas.[3]

Yours sincerely,
HARRY HAIG

49

DONALDSON TO LAITHWAITE
R/3/1/75

Secret | Camp,
D.O. No. 251-G.S. | *July 7th, 1939*

My dear Laithwaite,

With His Excellency's permission I send this telegram by special messenger on account of its length and in order to ensure accuracy.

Yours sincerely,
J.C. DONALDSON

ENCLOSURE TO NO. 49

HAIG TO LINLITHGOW

Telegram
No. 250-G | *July 7th, 1939*

Your telegram No. 1361-G, dated July 5th. Employments Tax. There are as it seems to me three possible courses:

(*a*) To deal with Bill by an amendment of the Government of India Act by Parliament. Though in past discussions we have contemplated that that course would be accompanied by refusal of assent by Governor-General, on further reflection this does not seem to me to be a necessary part of this course of action and for reasons explained below I consider that refusal of assent would be inexpedient. The first course therefore would involve Governor-General merely refraining from passing any order until announcement of intended amendment has been made, after which Employments Tax Bill would naturally lapse without any definite order refusing assent.

(*b*) Refusal of assent by the Governor-General either on grounds given in alternative (2) of paragraph 1 of your telegram No. 1139-G, dated May 24th,[4] or on grounds suggested in paragraph 3 of your telegram of July 5th,[5] or on ground of protection of Services.

(*c*) Reference of unassented Bill to Federal Court.

2. It is clear that there is no easy way out of our difficulties and that whatever course is adopted will involve dangers and disadvantages. We

have to choose that course of which the dangers and disadvantages appear to be least. The first course involves certain political difficulties in Parliament and possible retardation of Amending Bill. The second involves grave risk of resignation of my Ministers which might lead on to a serious crisis in the working of the constitution in India generally. The third course presents itself to my mind as gamble. If successful, it would be the most satisfactory of all. If unsuccessful, it would present us again with a choice between the first two courses under circumstances appreciably less favourable.

3. I have lately been trying to estimate the effect on my Ministers of the possible courses of action. The Premier has at many times and in many different connections emphasised his view that he can only work the constitution successfully if there is a general belief that he and I are not in serious disagreement. He has not tried to use this as a weapon against me, indeed he has often given way to my view on this account. Refusal of assent to an important Government Bill by the Governor or I think by the Governor-General would probably be held by my Ministers to destroy the position to which Pant in particular has attached so much importance and would be regarded by them as an affront, and unless on all-India ground they were prohibited from resigning by the Congress high command they would I think resign. It is probable, however, that Working Committee attach great importance to non-exercise of power to refuse assent. They would therefore perhaps not oppose Ministry on this point. Of course we cannot admit that power of disallowing Bill should never be exercised, merely because it will provoke conflict with Ministers. If there were no other means of stopping this Bill I should have no hesitation in saying that it should be disallowed. But if there are other means, then it may be unwise to take that course which is most likely to lead to ministerial resignation. If the difference of opinion were confined to constitutional issues and if it were resolved by the authority which is alone in a position to pronounce ultimately on such issues, namely, Parliament, I do not think there would be appreciable danger that the Ministers would wish to resign. Reference to Federal Court would be regarded I imagine as a perfectly legitimate constitutional action and I do not think could give rise to any danger of resignation. My conclusion therefore is that course (*a*) and course (*c*) would not involve resignation of Ministry, but that course (*b*) probably would.

4. To come to details of proposals contained in Your Excellency's telegram of July 5th. My view is that quite apart from the probable reaction of my Ministers to any refusal of assent by the Governor-General, refusal of assent on the grounds explained in alternative (2) of paragraph 1 of

your telegram of May 24th is open to very serious objection for the reasons stated in Your Excellency's own telegram of May 24th and my telegram No. G-242 of May 25th. Refusal of assent on the broad general ground that Employments Tax would endanger the financial stability of the Federal Government would be much less open to attack. I agree that it could not be based technically on the provisions of Section 12 (1) (*b*) of the Government of India Act, but it might be argued that apart from technicalities the Governor-General clearly must regard himself as responsible for the financial stability of the Government of India and that in the last resort he would be justified in refusing his assent to a measure which was clearly going to endanger its foundations. But the Employments Tax only points the way to a danger, owing to the probability that other Provinces would follow suit. It could hardly be said that this particular measure in the United Provinces by itself would lead to such results. In any case we come back to what I regard as the central point of this problem, namely that it cannot be considered a normal function of the Governor-General to interfere with constitutional processes merely because those constitutional processes are dangerous, but that it is the duty of Parliament, recognising the danger, to amend the constitution and place it on sound lines. If the Governor-General is to refuse assent I suggest he should base his action partly on the argument of financial stability and partly on protection of Services, for latter is extremely valid point, though it may make little appeal to general public in India. The considerations affecting Services are stated in draft B attached to my letter No. U.P.-247, dated April 24th.

5. With regard to reference to Federal Court as I have said the matter presents itself to me as a gamble, and I am not aware what are the odds. This depends on the legal views with which I am not acquainted. If the odds are very decidedly in favour of success it might be a chance worth taking. But in the event of failure it seems to me that the difficulties remain as stated in my telegram No. 253-G, dated 2nd May. If the Bill is declared valid either the Governor-General would have to refuse assent, and I have no doubt that refusal at that stage would involve resignation of Ministry, or the Secretary of State would have to take action at once to amend the Act. Would the Secretary of State be prepared to do this? If Federal Court refuses to deal with the reference we are again faced with alternatives (*a*) and (*b*).

6. To sum up, of the three courses open I would definitely advise against (*b*), namely refusal of assent by Your Excellency as I feel that would almost inevitably involve resignation of my Ministry and a serious crisis. Course

(*c*) has the advantage of postponing the problem for two or three months and in the general uncertainty of the international situation this may have some advantage. But unless we get from the Federal Court the decision we want, we shall at the end of that time be in a more difficult position than if no reference had been made. In spite therefore of the considerations stated in paragraph 1 of your telegram of July 5th I am driven to the conclusion that the only reasonably satisfactory course is to face the Parliamentary difficulties involved in amending the Government of India Act. These might perhaps not cause greater embarrassment to the Secretary of State than the resignation of Provincial Ministers. The course I would very strongly suggest is as follows. I need not be in any great hurry in taking action on the Bill and in any case would not do so until I have returned to Lucknow on the 25th July and have had an opportunity of talking to my Ministers and warning them of what I am going to do. I would then about the end of July reserve the Bill for Your Excellency's consideration. There would be no necessity for Your Excellency to announce a decision with any promptness. The matter obviously requires careful consideration and the Federal Court would not be sitting. At some time that would best suit Parliamentary tactics the Secretary of State might announce his intention of making the amendment in the Government of India Act. As soon as that intention was announced there would be no obligation on Your Excellency to pass any orders on the Employments Tax Bill. It would merely remain pigeon-holed until such time as the amendment was passed by Parliament. I would urge that this course of action should be seriously considered by the Secretary of State. I venture to think that constitutionally it is the right course and that politically if we look at conditions in India it is the wisest.[6]

50

HAIG TO LINLITHGOW
R/3/1/75

Secret — *July 12th, 1939*
No. U.P.-287

My dear Lord Linlithgow,

Since I last wrote, I have not seen much of my Ministers. The Premier returned to Naini Tal from Bombay for a few days before going down to Lucknow, but by the beginning of July all the Ministers had left and were concentrated in Lucknow where the Legislative Council met on the 3rd. I have had no first-hand accounts of what happened behind the scenes in connection with the Tenancy Bill, but I think it is quite clear that the Ministry finally found that they could not muster a majority against the landlords, and consequently they had to accept with such grace as they could the Opposition motion for a Select Committee. The landlords have shown wisdom in not trying to use the Select Committee for purposes of delay. As some of them seemed to think that the longer they spent over discussions in the Legislative Council, the longer would the Bill be delayed, I pointed out to them that a joint sitting cannot be held before April next year, i.e. twelve months after the Bill reached the Legislative Council. Whether that interval is spent in discussions in the Council or in merely waiting is from their point of view immaterial. It has now been agreed between the Ministry and the Opposition that the Select Committee should report by the 10th August, which is a reasonable date, and discussion in the Select Committee will afford a convenient method of reaching an agreement, if agreement is possible. Before the meeting of the Council the Ministry buoyed up by the hope that they might secure a majority were I think inclined to be rather stiff. Now I hope they may be more accommodating, and I think the landlords would be satisfied with comparatively few reasonable concessions. The Ministry certainly will not like to let this Bill hang on till next April.

2. The Legislative Council has now adjourned and the Assembly will meet on July 12th. I hope the session will be over before the end of the month. The first item of business will be the Employments Tax, regarding which I have recently sent you my views in detail.

3. In my last letter I mentioned the unfortunate fresh communal outbreak in Cawnpore. Disorder was brought under control very quickly, but it has left behind a legacy of extreme ill-will between the communities. The City Muslim League passed some very foolish resolutions urging the community to a systematic campaign of agitation, largely directed against the Police. The Hindu Sangh have been giving vent to attacks not only on the Police, but on the Ministry, whom they hold responsible, owing to their alleged pro-Muslim policy or at any rate weak handling of Muslims, for this recurrence of trouble. Actually I consider that there is nothing wrong with the attitude of the Ministry. They try to deal with these matters impartially, and back up the local authorities who are doing their best to hold the balance even. But everything is distorted by communal prejudice on both sides. There is a rather widespread rumour that this communal trouble is fomented by some of the Indian millowners who are said to

think that this acts as a good lightning conductor, saving them from labour trouble. It is undoubtedly the case that some of the important Hindu millowners are strong supporters of the Hindu Sabha, which is a very communal organisation and which, whether its activities lead to communal riots or not, is at any rate a serious political embarrassment to the Ministry.

4. I have recently had a talk with the D.I.G. of Police[7] who went to Cawnpore immediately on the outbreak of the recent trouble and examined conditions thoroughly. I am afraid the Cawnpore Police are not as effective as they should be, and I think it is probable that on the recommendation of the D.I.G. and the I.G. of Police, we shall before long change both the Kotwal and the Superintendent of Police.[8]

In the days before the present constitution our larger cities were to a great extent kept in order by the personality and authority of the Kotwals. They were often men of no great scruple and of no great honesty, but they were indubitably effective and they knew how to keep turbulent characters in order. When the present Ministry came in, Pant said that it was necessary to get a new type of Kotwal for the large cities, and in spite of the experience of the past with which he was well acquainted, he insisted on a policy of posting as Kotwals young, well-educated men who had been recruited directly. In some cases this policy has answered well, but in Cawnpore it has been very far from a success. When the present Ministry took office the Kotwal of Cawnpore was a typical example of the old style Kotwal, a man who had kept Cawnpore in order for many years but whose methods certainly did not stand examination. It soon became apparent that he and the Congress Ministry could not co-exist, and as he was at the end of his time he retired. As Cawnpore was felt to be a special case he was replaced by an experienced officer whose qualifications were midway between those of the old style Kotwal and the new style that Pant wanted. He was doing fairly well when the unfortunate attack was made by the Muslims on the Minister, Hafiz Muhammad Ibrahim, who was going in procession very unwisely through a Muslim quarter. The Ministry felt they had been disgraced. They considered that the Kotwal ought to have prevented the attack, and eventually after many months of consideration, much discussion and two meetings of the Cabinet they insisted on transferring him. Following out the new policy a comparatively young man took his place in whom the Police never had much confidence, but there was no one else of this type available. I gather that though the recent disturbances were handled strongly and effectively when they broke out, there is some ground for the complaint that the intention of the Muslims to attack the Hindu procession should have been known beforehand, and if the Kotwal had

had the authority and the knowledge of the old type Kotwal he would have been able to prevent the attack ever taking place. It is pretty clear that we must get now a more effective Kotwal for Cawnpore. Apart from this, the discipline of the Cawnpore Police has for some considerable time not been altogether satisfactory. They have had to contend with difficult and disheartening conditions, and the D.I.G. and the I.G. of Police both think that discipline has been unduly relaxed. We shall probably move the present Superintendent of Police and put in a stricter disciplinarian to try and pull them together.

5. While on the subject of the Police I may as well refer to the question of crime statistics which Your Excellency has mentioned in one of your recent letters. You will see that in our official fortnightly report enclosed with this letter it is said that dacoity figures are considerably down, being 46 as against 72. I have discussed this matter generally with some of the D.I.Gs. and the I.G. of Police and their view is that the main reason for the recent increase in dacoity has been the depletion of our Police strength in the districts in order to cope with the riots in the cities. The situation is now being rectified rapidly owing to the arrival of the 1,000 ex-Army reservists whom I got the Ministry to agree to recruit temporarily a few months ago. The official view is that as the relief due to these reinforcements makes itself felt, dacoity figures are likely to return to the normal. I am not pressing any further the demand of the I.G. of Police that we should sanction 2,000 Army reservists instead of 1,000. For one thing it is clear that we should have difficulty in raising the men. For another we shall now before long have the benefit of the 500 additional men who were enlisted on a permanent basis early in the year and whose training will be finished before long. I think these additions to strength will have a generally encouraging effect all round. The I.G. of Police also stresses the necessity of some headquarters reorganisation to relieve him of the excessive burden of office work. I hope we have now devised a scheme which Pant is going to accept and which will enable the I.G. of Police to get round the Province more frequently and find out on the spot where the administration needs tightening up.

6. The Sunni-Shia trouble has recently broken out into violence in Lucknow and the Police had to fire, though apparently only one man was killed. Here again, as in Cawnpore, the Muslims are using this opportunity to agitate strongly against the Police and against the Ministry. Before Pant left Naini Tal we agreed that the time had come for Government to take a stronger line against those who are organising the Tabarra agitation, particularly against the Punjabis who are now playing an important part in

the organisation and I think have imported into it ideas and methods of violence. I have not yet heard whether we have in fact taken the action which the Premier was contemplating, but I am sure it is high time we did take it. I had a letter recently from Cunningham[9] in the North-West Frontier Province who told me that he had been able to prevent a large incursion of Turis from the Kurram who were proposing to descend upon Lucknow. The *jatha* had been reduced to 40, and he had warned a *jirgah* of Turis that they should not take part in this agitation. He had also told all his Deputy Commissioners to try and restrain their people. I wrote to Craik in the Punjab and asked him whether Sikander could do anything by means of his influence to discourage reinforcements of Shias from the Punjab, and Craik has told me that he is confident Sikander will do all he can.[10] There is no doubt that at the present stage the movement depends to a great extent on the strength it derives from outside sources, particularly the Punjab.

7. Newspaper editors with their short cuts to wisdom are now beginning to say that as peace is not likely to be restored unless the Madhe-Sahaba and Tabarra are both given up, the Ministry should withdraw their communiqué allowing the Madhe-Sahaba procession. This simple solution, however, does not take account of two factors. The first is that the Ministry would be very seriously discredited if as a result of this agitation it changed its orders and conceded to the Shias what it has repeatedly said it will not concede. The second is that as soon as the Ministry admitted that the Shia agitation had defeated them and had caused them to change their orders, the Sunnis would inevitably start their civil disobedience movement, with a view to regaining what had been given them by the communiqué. It is quite clear that no solution is to be found along the line of vacillation. I have, however, recently written to the Premier and asked him to consider whether the time is not approaching when he might try once more to renew the negotiations with the Shias, which were very nearly brought to a successful conclusion about the middle of May, the result of which would be to give the Shias a right roughly equivalent to that given to the Sunnis, the ultimate object being that the two sects having been put on an equal footing would eventually agree to surrender these rights. In any case an agreement with the Shias would mean the calling off of the Tabarra agitation. It has become quite apparent that while the Tabarra agitation continues, there is no possibility of direct negotiations between the two sects. The Sunnis are adamant on this point. The Nawab of Rampur who has been staying with me for the last few days has told me how perturbed he is over this general situation. He is fully in agreement that the right line

of action is to pursue the negotiations with the Shias. I told him that the trouble was that while a large section of the Shias accepted the Premier's suggestion, at the last moment others refused. He said that he believed that the Shias could now be got to speak with one voice, and that he would be very glad to use all his influence to that end. He may perhaps overestimate his influence, but I think it may be of use. I do not, however, want him to come too much into the open, for his position as the Shia ruler of a Sunni State is not too easy, and it would be a great misfortune if a Shia-Sunni controversy developed in Rampur.

8. I mentioned in my last letter Katju's Press statement about the Village Panchayats Bill and how I had raised the matter at a Cabinet meeting and elicited Pant's general support for Katju. Recently Mrs. Pandit has replied with an equally elaborate Press statement criticising Katju's views and supporting those of the Local Self-Government Committee. This is rather an amusing situation and I do not know how Pant will deal with it, but he is skilful at arranging compromises and keeping his Ministry together. Mrs. Pandit is I think in matters like this very much in the hands of her husband and her Parliamentary Secretary who were both leading lights on this exceedingly unpractical Local Self-Government Committee.

9. Your Excellency mentioned in paragraph 4 of your letter of 24th June the meeting in Unao of the Provincial Youth League Conference and the objectionable speeches there made. These were among the speeches which as I reported in paragraph 7 of my letter of June 24th Pant had agreed to have examined with, I hope, some practical intentions. I have not yet had the result of the examination.

10. The Ministry have persuaded some financiers to take over all the shares of the Industrial Finance Corporation held by the Benares Bank. So that embarrassment is out of the way, and they intend to go on with the Finance Corporation.

11. Gwynne's health has been improving lately to a surprising extent. Some weeks ago the doctors had little hope of being able to get him Home. But now they think it will be possible, and I hope he may start some time this month.

12. I have heard nothing directly about the Congress dissensions, but it is clear from the newspapers and from reports that the cleavage is going very deep, and it seems to me that it may before long begin to have important effects.

13. I am very grateful for your two letters of the 24th June and the 3rd July. I leave here on the 14th, and after a short tour reach Lucknow on the 25th. I hope the monsoon will have re-established itself. After a very strong

and early start it has faded away in this Province for the last ten days or so, and it is high time it returned.

Yours sincerely,
H.G. HAIG

51

HAIG TO LINLITHGOW
R/3/1/75

Confidential *July 12th, 1939*
No. U.P.-289

My dear Lord Linlithgow,

The Nawab of Rampur has been staying with me for a few days lately, and I have had some interesting talks with him about conditions in his State. As you know, we have always in the United Provinces taken a considerable interest in Rampur, which is an island entirely enclosed by our territory, and during the last six years or so, since it became apparent that administrative conditions in Rampur were unsatisfactory and urgently needed rectification, we have done a great deal by advice and the lending of officers to help the Nawab to bring his administration up to a standard that could reasonably compare with ours. The justification of this policy has I think been very clearly shown during the last year. If Rampur conditions had at all resembled those which prevailed there in 1934, when Hailey took the matter up seriously, I think there is little doubt we should have seen a most embarrassing agitation there lately. As it is things seem to have been perfectly quiet.

2. The Nawab tells me he has been having discussions with Your Excellency at Simla about the terms of entry into Federation, and he is a good deal upset at the possibility that he may have to lose something like 8 lakhs a year from the income that he derives at present from the sugar excise. He has of course put all his arguments before Your Excellency, and I do not wish to express any opinion on the technical merits of his case. But I think there is force in the general consideration that it is, broadly speaking, to our interests and I think the interests of this Province that the Rampur State should continue the excellent development work on which it has embarked, and which if continued should before long raise the level of prosperity among the Rampur cultivators very much to the same standards as those of the surrounding British districts. We have lent them

some good men and I believe work of real value is being done. I should judge that there is reason in the Nawab's contention that if his income is cut down so drastically, he will find it very difficult, and perhaps impossible, to continue his development work on its present scale.

3. I hope you do not mind my having written about a matter which you may think does not concern me; but my excuse must be that during the whole of my period here I have felt myself very much concerned in the question of developing and improving the administration of Rampur State both from the point of view of the State, while it was under my charge, and from the point of view of our own provincial interests, as agitation in the State is bound to be disturbing to us.[11]

Yours sincerely,
HARRY HAIG

52

HAIG TO LINLITHGOW
R/3/1/75

Secret
No. U.P.-290

Camp,
July 25th, 1939

My dear Lord Linlithgow,

Since I last wrote on July 12th, I have spent most of my time on tour in the Meerut division which I had not visited for some time. I left Naini Tal on the 14th and arrived in Lucknow this morning (25th). The first place I visited was Roorkee, where I presided at the annual Convocation of the Thomason Engineering College. This college, which is the source of supply for our Engineering Services and has to provide us now with men to take the place not only of their Indian predecessors, but of the diminishing body of European officers in the I.S.E., has always been recognised as a most important factor in the Province. It has had a very fine history and turned out many first class engineers. Latterly, it has been going through a period of difficulty, which I hope may not prove to represent a permanent deterioration. The late Principal[12] who had held the post for about six years and retired a few months ago was not a man who seemed to impress his personality either on the students or the staff, and lately in particular a regular faction had been established among the staff working in opposition to the Principal and headed by a certain Professor Raja Ram, who I understand is an exceedingly unbalanced person with no sense of discipline or loyalty and who had got into serious controversy not only with the Principal but with the Director of Public Instruction.[13] When the late Principal retired Raja Ram appears to have been the senior member of the staff. It was felt to be quite out of the question to put him in as Principal even in an officiating capacity, and we were glad to be able to secure the services temporarily of Major Reed, R.E., who was working on the staff. On this appointment being made Raja Ram in a moment of pique tendered his resignation from Government service accompanied by an insubordinate letter, and though he subsequently asked to be allowed to withdraw his resignation, the Education Minister who was well aware of the harm Raja Ram was doing in the college held him to it. There had also been some acts of indiscipline among the students of no very great importance which had unfortunately been magnified by an unwise speech of the Education Minister himself made at the college a few months ago which seemed to justify the action of the students. Major Reed thought that if I visited the college it would have a generally tranquillising and encouraging effect, and consequently I agreed to go. I spent an interesting day there, and I think my visit was of some value and I was myself glad to get some first-hand impressions. It was obvious that all was not well and that the college was not likely to settle down until we can get a really good permanent Principal; but I see no reason why it should not then be pulled together.

2. I have given these details because, as you will have seen, the affairs of the Roorkee College have since precipitated a crisis between the Provincial Congress Assembly Party and the Ministry which went so far that the Ministry had to threaten resignation. The Party appear to have taken up with enthusiasm the case of Raja Ram, who is a Congressman; the racial issue was raised acutely and the very mild administrative action taken to enforce discipline among the students was attacked as inconsistent with Congress principles. I am very glad that the Ministry stood firm against this attack, which indeed had it been successful would have meant an abdication of functions by the Government. They have declined to allow their ordinary administrative actions to be dictated to them by the Party, and I understand they have no intention of allowing Raja Ram, who clearly contrived this attack, to return to Roorkee. This outburst appears to have been the culmination of a policy of self-assertion by the Party M.L.As. which has been in evidence since the Legislature resumed sitting this month. They claimed the right of modifying the policy of the Ministry in regard to village *panchayats* and control over District Board education, but I fancy in both these cases the modifications were not of a very important character and there was a division of opinion among the Ministers

themselves. But when the Party claimed to interfere in the administration of the Roorkee College, it was high time it was pulled up, and I hope the result of this incident will be in the end to strengthen the position of the Ministry as against the Party. In various ways recently the Ministry have been resisting the improper influence and jobs which the M.L.As. are always trying to press on them, and it is possible that this attack originated in resentment on this account. The Party must, I presume, realise clearly enough that there is no possibility of finding alternative Ministers who could run the Government with the slightest hope of success. The incident, however, gives one an illuminating glimpse of the difficulties that the Ministry have to contend with from their own followers. It is rather interesting that this attack should have been provoked by the action of Sampurnanand who before he joined the Ministry was regarded as more extreme than any of the others. As a matter of fact I have always found him reasonable and realistic in administrative questions. I am sorry he was unable to go to Simla for the Education Conference and that consequently Your Excellency did not have an opportunity of meeting him.

3. The Meerut division is on the whole fairly peaceful and does not seem to suffer from some of the more troublesome manifestations that exist in other parts of the Province. The local Congress leaders seem for the most part to be persons of reasonable outlook, and though the landlords complain of the difficulty of realising rents, it seems evident that relations between landlords and tenants and agrarian conditions generally are a good deal easier than they are in the east. I was talking recently to one of our Indian Collectors who has just come to a district in the Meerut division from a district in the Gorakhpur division, and he said he found the contrast most marked and he did not feel here anything of the tension and ill-feeling that exists in the east. The division has been free from the recent Hindu-Muslim outbreaks, though feeling cannot be said to be very satisfactory. Such trouble as there has been, has been caused mainly by the parading of *jathas* for Hyderabad which seems to have been done on a widespread scale. There is also a good deal of ill-feeling between the Ahrars and the Muslim League. Just before I arrived in Meerut the District Magistrate[14] found it necessary to issue an order under Section 144 prohibiting all processions for a month owing in the main to the Hyderabad agitation. But this was accepted without protest, and indeed with some general relief.

4. The division is ordinarily one of the most prosperous in the Province. It suffered from a very poor monsoon last year followed by an almost complete failure of the winter rains; but the large area irrigated by canals

and by tube wells enabled it to come through without very serious loss. Remissions of rent and revenue have been given on a scale which is probably unnecessarily liberal, and if the monsoon is reasonably favourable this year conditions should be perfectly normal again. It was fortunate that exceptionally large profits were made on the sugar cane crop which is really the most important crop in the division.

5. The Ministry was subjected to strong attacks in the Legislature on account of the firing by the police at Cawnpore and at Lucknow. The attacks which were of an unreasonable and unfair character were made in both cases by the Muslims. I think it may interest you to see the newspaper account[15] of the Premier's reply in both these cases. I think you will agree that he took a very firm and reasonable line.

6. With reference to the question of increase in crime I send copies of extracts[16] from the most recent reports of the Inspector-General and the Deputy Inspectors-General of Police regarding dacoities. These bear out the general view which I expressed in my last letter that with police forces in the districts restored to their full normal strength it should be possible to bring dacoities back to more normal figures. In some places the police have had considerable successes in arresting gangs of dacoits and working out cases. The Unao district appears to me to be in a somewhat disturbed state. I have been making enquiries into several different matters, including the speeches that had been made there recently, and hope to take this up more effectively now that I am back in Lucknow.

7. In my letter of July 12th, I mentioned that I had written to the Premier and asked him to consider whether the time was not approaching when he might try once more to renew the negotiations with the Shias which were very nearly brought to a successful conclusion about the middle of May, the result of which would be to give the Shias a right roughly equivalent to that given to the Sunnis. The Premier replied saying that he fully agreed and that in effect the offer of last May was a standing offer which was always open to the Shias. After the debate in the Assembly regarding the firing in Lucknow, one final effort was made to bring the Sunnis and Shias directly together. They met the Premier, but the result, as before, was entirely negative. On my arrival in Lucknow today the Premier told me that he had been pursuing actively this idea of a direct settlement with the Shias, and he showed me a draft communiqué which he said was acceptable to all sections of the Shias. The communiqué is very close to the one that had been prepared last May, but it embodies also the points which had been brought out in the supplementary correspondence and states certain matters rather more definitely. It is of course not necessary to get the

agreement of the Sunnis to an arrangement which is one between the Shias and Government; but from every point of view it is desirable, if possible, to avoid doing anything that would seriously upset the Sunnis. The Premier therefore has been in communication with Chaudhri Niamat-ullah, an ex-High Court Judge, who appears now to have got control of the Lucknow Sunni movement and to be in a position to restrain the two principal Sunni firebrands. He intends to show the communiqué to Niamat-ullah and, subject to any modification that may appear desirable as a result of this conversation, he and the rest of the Ministry are prepared to issue it. The two hopeful new signs in what the Premier has told me are that the Shias appear at last to be speaking with a united voice, and that a reasonable man is in a position to control the Sunnis. I think myself that this line of approach is the only one which holds out any prospect of escape from the present deadlock. The grant of the "equivalent right" enables the Shias to call off the Tabarra agitation without loss of face. It also puts them in an equal position with the Sunnis for purposes of negotiation, and it is a part of the Government scheme that a conciliation committee should be set up as soon as possible after the Tabarra agitation has been called off with a view to getting a direct settlement between the Sunnis and Shias. The Shias will not want to exercise their right until it is quite clear that the Sunnis are going to exercise their right again next year, so there is plenty of time for counsels of moderation to prevail. I sincerely hope that these developments will really lead to a settlement of this unfortunate controversy.

8. When I passed through Bareilly on leaving Naini Tal, I heard that the Hindu Sabha have been very active in the Rohilkhand division in attacking the Congress. Many meetings have been held, particularly in Bareilly city, to express non-confidence in the Congress Ministry. This is a development which may prove in time to be of some importance. There is no doubt that the Hindu community have been getting very restive under this prolonged strain between Hindus and Muslims, and it is easy to persuade them that the Congress are not paying due regard to Hindu interests and are allowing themselves to be frightened by the Muslims. This Hindu feeling and antagonism to the Congress is certainly growing and is a factor of which account must now be taken.

9. The other side of the picture is illustrated by an interesting talk I had recently with Muhammad Ismail Khan, one of the chief leaders of the Muslim League in the Legislative Assembly. He is a man with a long record of political activities, essentially moderate-minded, but very definitely a nationalist in the old days [?ways]. He was always looked

upon with considerable suspicion by the ordinary conservative Muslims as a man who put Nationalism above Communalism. I found that though he used moderate language, he seemed now quite to accept the position adopted by the more extreme Muslim Leaguers, that there really was little prospect of any accommodation between Hindus and Muslims, that their culture and ideas were fundamentally different, and that it was difficult for them to unite into a nation so long as the barrier created by the exclusive Hindu social customs remained. He also explained the distrust of Muslims for the Federal scheme. They are afraid that the Federal centre, which must be under the control of the Hindus, will be able to interfere too much with the Muslim Provinces. Therefore they wish to reduce the power of the centre as far as possible. They are also afraid of the Hindus getting control over the Army and using their influence to diminish the proportion and importance of Muslims in the Army. I have no doubt this represents Punjab views with which Your Excellency is well acquainted; but coming from this particular source I thought it might be interesting to pass on this conversation.[17]

10. It is my normal practice when I visit a district to interview all deputy collectors together. I have interviewed recently in this way the deputy collectors of Saharanpur and of Meerut. In both cases when at the end I asked them whether they had anything special to say, they raised the question of the Employments Tax. They spoke with considerable apprehension and bitterness. They resented the ingratitude of the Congress Government who had rewarded the loyal and exceedingly arduous work that they had been doing for it by this measure, and they commented severely on the disingenuous method by which their pay was being cut, and said that if it had to be cut they would much rather that it had been done in a straightforward manner. I have no doubt that these two bodies of deputy collectors represent the general feeling of this important class throughout the Province and also of many hundreds of other Government servants outside the ranks of the All-India Services. Pant in his speech in the Assembly is reported to have said that the Government expected that the Services were willing to accept this sacrifice. I am afraid he must have been well aware how far removed this statement was from the truth. In the same speech he made some optimistic remarks about our financial position. He of course takes credit, by what is little more than a guess, for 30 lakhs from the Employments Tax. If we leave this out of account the budget shows a deficit of 38 lakhs, and in consequence of the very large remissions of land revenue, and disappointments under other revenue heads, combined with extra expenditure on police and jails owing to the special conditions

of the last few months, it looks to me as if the budget might work out to a deficit of something like 80 lakhs.

11. Premier tells me there is some possibility of a strike breaking out at Cawnpore in the J.K. group of mills. The management applied a little time ago in the case of the jute mill for a reduction of wages. Their case was after examination rejected by the Labour Commissioner.[18] Thereupon they decided to close down one section of the mill and discharge 1,400 employees. The Premier considers that the management have acted most unwisely, and I am disposed to agree with him. The workers naturally consider that the case for a reduction of wages having been rejected the management are trying to force down wages by this threat of reduction of staff. The management contend they are losing money on the mills, though it seems hard to believe it at the present moment in the case of a jute mill. The Premier is bringing such influence as he can to bear on Mr. Padampat Singhania, the proprietor of this group of mills, to reconsider this drastic reduction of staff, and he seems to think there is some possibility of Padampat proving open to reason. If there is a strike on this issue, I cannot help feeling that public opinion will be definitely against the J.K. mills, who are in any case reputed to be among the least satisfactory employers in Cawnpore.

Yours sincerely,
HARRY HAIG

53

HAIG TO LINLITHGOW
R/3/1/75

Secret *August 9th, 1939*
No. U.P.-293

My dear Lord Linlithgow,

Since I wrote my last report on July 25th I have been throughout in Lucknow and have been glad of the opportunity of making contact again with my Ministers who have all been here most of the time except Dr. Katju, who went to Allahabad after the Assembly rose, and has remained there in consequence of the death of his mother. We have been getting rain fairly regularly and the weather has been by no means unpleasant. On the 10th August I go off for a ten-day tour to Jhansi and Agra, from which I shall return again to Lucknow. I fear the climate does not suit Pant. He has once more developed recurrent fever, which while it does not keep him in bed or prevent him doing his work, clearly makes him feel off colour. I have not myself during this last fortnight found him difficult to deal with, but I get the impression from the Secretariat that he is not at his best. He would be glad to get away for a short time to Naini Tal, and I hope he may be able to.

2. When I first returned to Lucknow I heard a good deal about the revolt of the Party against the Ministry, which I mentioned in my last letter. While the Ministry stood firm when attacked, I am rather afraid they may have been somewhat shaken by the attack and may be a little nervous of provoking more opposition from the Party. They are certainly under the impression that they have not heard the last of these attacks, though for the moment quiet has been restored as the Assembly is not sitting. The revolt was widespread, and I have been told on good authority that the majority of the Parliamentary Secretaries voted against the Ministers, which indicates a poor sense of Party loyalty or possibly nascent ambitions. I gather the Ministers prefer to ignore the behaviour of the Parliamentary Secretaries; but if it is repeated I should imagine they would be forced into action. Sampurnanand, and to a certain extent Mrs. Pandit, appear to have been the principal targets of the attack. While a good deal of temporary feeling was worked up over the Roorkee College case, the underlying causes of the attack on Sampurnanand, as far as I hear, were, firstly, that he is brusque in manner, says what he means, and if he has to give a negative reply to M.L.As. does not wrap it in pleasant words; and secondly, that he has made himself responsible for, and is pressing, the exceedingly unpopular policy of depriving District Boards of control over primary education. I am told that this has raised very strong feeling, for it cuts at the root of the political power and patronage which members of District Boards are at present enjoying. District Board teachers are regarded as a most important factor in electioneering. The policy is as unpopular with the Opposition as it is with the Government benches, and it remains to be seen whether Government will have the considerable courage required to go through with a reform which is on merits entirely justified and will do more than anything else to raise the standard of primary education, but which will rouse such strong political and selfish opposition. I am not quite sure why Mrs. Pandit should be an object of attack except that she is also inclined to speak her mind freely and to take very non-political decisions. She is perhaps considered not to have fought strongly enough the battle of the District Board members for retention of their vested interest in primary education, and also to have compromised over the Village

Panchayats Bill, which is likely in consequence to be a more reasonable measure than if it had been left entirely to the theoretical enthusiasts who sponsored it. There is a move to attack her also because she agreed several months ago to the appointment of Colonel Crawford Boyd as our new Inspector-General of Civil Hospitals, whereas according to the back-benchers she ought to have insisted on the appointment of an Indian, who was one of the three whose names were considered, even though he was junior to Colonel Boyd and less well qualified. With the rank and file there is no attempt to conceal the demand that Indians should be put into all positions of authority quite regardless of considerations of equity or efficiency. Kidwai is of course back again after his prolonged rest due to illness in the hot weather. In his character of "party boss" he probably has a stronger hold on the M.L.As. than any of the other Ministers, and I think he is inclined just now to throw his weight about a good deal, not normally for the best of purposes. He is a rather baffling figure, unscrupulous to a degree, extreme in general outlook, but a shrewd judge of what is practical, and sometimes as a result surprisingly on the side of the angels.

3. About the end of last month we had a very successful conference between the Ministers and representatives of the Tehri Durbar on the vexed question of the Badrinath Temple Bill. The Maharaja came to Lucknow himself and appreciated being asked to stay at Government House. After some slight difficulty on questions of dignity on both sides two interviews were arranged at the end between him and Pant, and certainly did good. Skrine came and stayed with me and also Burnett,[19] and their influence was most valuable in promoting a reasonable agreement. I hope we may regard the matter as now really settled. It would be greatly appreciated by my Ministers, and in particular Sampurnanand, if I could as early as possible give my assent to the Bill. Sampurnanand has of course lost some little credit by the delay in getting assent to his Bill, and at the present moment I want to strengthen his hands and to let it be seen that he can get his policies through. He was by the way I believe very helpful in getting a settlement of a distinctly troublesome agitation that had developed in the Benares State. Pant decided to do all that he could to stop this agitation which was of course being promoted from Benares city, and by means of Sampurnanand seems to have succeeded.

4. The Tenancy Bill discussions have now narrowed themselves to the single point of the formula to govern ejectment in default of payment of rent. The landlords have been offered by the Ministry two alternatives, and either of these in the view of my Revenue Secretary,[20] which I accept, would be satisfactory and would give the landlords the practical assurance

that they will be able to collect their rents. With the moment of decision approaching the landlords of course have begun to hesitate about committing themselves, but I hope very much that when they reassemble in Lucknow in a day or two they will close with the Government offer. In that case we might hope to have the Bill through pretty soon. There are, however, always the die-hards who partly from conviction and partly from personal ambition wish to take a different line. They are the same sort of forces that make a settlement with the Shias so difficult.

5. In my last letter I mentioned that the Premier was very hopeful of getting a settlement of the Sunni-Shia question, but once more hopes were disappointed. He had told me that all sections of the Shias had agreed to certain proposals. Within a day or two the Shias had split again and conversations fell through. Nevertheless I feel we are slowly drifting towards a settlement. In spite of the obstinacy and incompetence of many of the leaders, there is no doubt that on both sides there is a general feeling of fatigue and disillusionment and the pressure of events must be making itself felt. But whenever the movement looks like dying down from natural causes we can depend on our neighbours to galvanise it once more into action, and the latest threat comes from the Khaksars who have been for some time proclaiming by a series of ultimatums, which are postponed one after the other, that they intend to come to Lucknow and stop the dispute by force. August 11th is the next date fixed for the invasion. It is difficult to know whether they will really attempt anything: but if they do, it looks as if there might be some serious disorder and they will have to be dealt with very firmly.

6. I have as you are aware reserved the Employments Tax Bill for Your Excellency's consideration. I was not sure how the Premier and the Ministers were likely to take the news, though I did not anticipate at the most more than a protest at this stage. Even that, however, was not forthcoming. When I informed Pant of my decision and reminded him of the views I had consistently expressed about the Bill from the beginning and said that I was afraid this was a matter in which our views differed, he did not attempt to argue; nor did he express surprise, nor make any enquiries. The whole subject in fact was disposed of within five minutes and we went on to discuss a variety of other topics. The same line has been taken in newspaper comment. It is quite clear that the Ministry have desired that as little as possible should be said about this action, and that it should be treated as a move which was expected and not unnatural. This is the line, for instance, taken by the correspondent of the *Statesman* who

is in the closest possible touch with the Ministers and represents their views. The *National Herald* carrying this line a little further did not even, as far as I can see, publish the news at all. This very quiet attitude affords perhaps confirmation of the view which Your Excellency expressed in your letter of the 1st August (for which many thanks) that the embarrassments of the right wing may well be making them realise that there is advantage in avoiding too much difficulty with us. At the same time it must be remembered that this is only an intermediate stage, and that we cannot expect the same degree of acquiescence in the next stage.

7. The threatened strike at the J.K. Mills in Cawnpore, which I mentioned in my last letter, started in a half-hearted way and was quickly stopped by a compromise under the influence of the Government. On the other hand, what seems to have been an unpremeditated outbreak in the New Victoria Mills has led to the mill being closed until a better spirit prevails. The Mazdur Sabha were for a time seen in the unusual part of dissuaders of strife, but feeling obviously embarrassed in such a position they soon slipped back into their normal attitude. Cawnpore on the whole continues in its state of uneasy truce. We have been threatened here in Lucknow in the last few days with a strike at the Municipal Water Works and at the Electric Supply Company. These strikes had they materialised would have been a formidable menace to the life of the town. Certain precautionary plans were made in consultation with the military authorities for running the Electric Power House if necessary and precautions were also taken with regard to the running of the Water Works. However, both these strikes have now been postponed and I hope they will not in fact come to anything.

8. Our dacoity situation has continued to improve, and I attach an extract from the report of the Inspector-General of Police for the first half of July. The monsoon of course discourages these activities, but I think there is no doubt that the police now have the situation well in hand.

9. I am glad Your Excellency's visit to Cuttack went off so well. I have always understood that in the rains it is one of the least pleasant of climates, but this does not seem to have deterred you at all. You will have seen the sad news that Gwynne died on his way Home. It was always a matter of considerable doubt whether he would be able to get through the Red Sea. But in any case the doctors gave him a very short time to live, and he was himself most anxious to try and get Home. He is a great loss to the administration. He had established relations of great confidence and friendliness with the Premier which were of particular value in these two difficult years when we were engaged in bringing the constitution into

operation and establishing new working arrangements. I shall miss very greatly his advice and assistance.

Yours sincerely,
H.G. HAIG

ENCLOSURE TO NO. 53

REPORT OF THE INSPECTOR-GENERAL OF POLICE, U.P., FOR THE FIRST HALF OF JULY 1939 (EXTRACT)

A comparison of the figures for the first half of each month of this year shows that, with the exception of the figure (28) for the first half of January 1939, the figure of 31 for the first half of July is so far the lowest recorded, and, incidentally, it coincides with the figure for the first half of July 1938. On the whole, as the reports of all the three Ranges show, there is a marked improvement in the dacoity situation of the Province attributable to the fact that police hitherto deputed elsewhere for emergent [emergency] duty are now available for duty in their own districts, to excellent work in rounding up gangs and to the break of the monsoon.

54

DONALDSON TO LAITHWAITE
R/3/1/75

Secret — Camp,
D.O. No. 943-G.S.P. — *August 28th, 1939*

My dear Laithwaite,

In His Excellency's secret D.O. No. U.P.-196 of November 16th, 1938,[21] he informed His Excellency the Governor-General of the Provincial Government's proposals for reduced scales of pay for new entrants to the Provincial services. He went on in paragraph 3 of that letter to mention that they also proposed to apply these new scales when officers were promoted to selection posts outside the time-scale of the service to which they belonged. Sir Harry wrote further on the same subject in his secret D.O. No. U.P.-197 of November 19th, to which His Excellency the

Governor-General replied on 7th December, and we were sent information about how they had handled the same problem in Madras.

2. Sir Harry had discussed the proposal about promotion with the Ministry in a Cabinet meeting on November 15th, but they reached no final decision. The Cabinet, however, approved the new scales of pay proposed for new entrants. Subsequently, as the Ministry desired to bring these new scales into effect at once, from 1st January 1939, they issued orders applying them to new entrants only. At the same time a Press communiqué was issued which stated that the question as to what extent these revised scales would apply on promotion was still under consideration.

3. After considering the Madras rules Sir Harry took the view that whatever had been done in Madras these proposals should be resisted here as being a direct invasion of a principle which had hitherto been strictly maintained, namely, that officers in all the services should be protected in the enjoyment of the rates of pay which were open to them when they were recruited. This principle had been discussed in general terms in the Governor-General's telegram No. 496-G.C. of December 24th, 1937, and Sir Harry was in full agreement with the conclusions reached. He drafted a letter to the Governor-General in January 1939 in which after setting out in detail some inequalities and anomalies which would result from the proposal and the bad effect on the confidence of the services he wrote: "I have no doubt in my own mind that a stand should be made on this point of principle. If I were now to concede the point merely because it has already been conceded in Madras, it would I think be impossible for such proposals to be resisted in any of the other Congress Provinces. But I see no reason why a stand should not be made now in the case of the Congress Provinces other than Madras, and I strongly suggest that this should be done. The rule which I propose to maintain is that which has been in force ever since the revisions of pay in 1931, and it sccms to me entirely equitable. If an officer is promoted to a new service, then he would have to come on to the new scale of pay. But in the case of posts borne on the cadre of his service or deemed to be reserved for that service he would on promotion receive the old rate of pay. This is the position, I understand, accepted in paragraph 2 of your telegram No. 496-G.C. of December 24th, 1937. I should be glad to know whether I would have the support of Your Excellency and the Secretary of State in telling my Ministers, if necessary, that I am unable to agree to their proposal. It may be that when I have clearly indicated my dissent from their proposals, they will not press them,

as they may prefer not to be definitely overruled. But once I express my view I must be prepared to see it through, and in the last resort to exercise my individual judgement contrary to the advice they may give. I should be acting under Section 52 (*c*) of the Government of India Act."

4. It was pointed out that the anomalies and injustices caused by the application of the Ministers' proposal would be much more numerous and difficult in the case of the subordinate services for which new rates had still to be framed. This was because of the very varied pay rates and organisation of those services. It was thought that it might prove very difficult to apply the proposal at all to them, and Sir Harry finally decided not to send his letter but to wait for the proposals of his Ministers after they had tackled this problem as they might possibly see reason of themselves. That result has occurred, although it has taken some time.

5. Preliminary proposals about rates of pay for the subordinate services were drawn up but they were not found satisfactory and were referred to a sub-committee of the Cabinet. That sub-committee has now come to a decision on the principle to be followed about this question of promotion. This decision is an abandonment of their original idea, for the time being. Abandonment had been strongly advocated by the Finance Department, and its view has prevailed.

6. The new decision is that pay on promotion should continue to be governed by the same rule which was followed at the 1931 revision of rates of pay in this Province. This applies in the case of all persons who were substantively appointed to Government service before July 1st, 1938. From that date all entrants had been warned that the scales of pay then in force were liable to revision. Under the rules in force from 1931 officers on pre-1931 scales of pay were allowed the pre-1931 scale for the post to which they were promoted if it was a post on the cadre of their service or reserved for that service. If promoted to a new service, they got the post-1931 rate for that service. Under the present proposal they will continue to enjoy the same rights and will therefore in certain cases still be entitled to pre-1931 rates on promotion. Persons who were appointed before July 1st, 1939, on the post-1931 scales will be entitled to those scales, as at present; and not only on promotion to posts reserved for their cadres, but also on promotion to any new service they will get the post-1931 scale and not the new 1939 scale. Officers will also get similar scales if appointed to a new or temporary post which is on an existing cadre. For example, there are two permanent Superintending Engineers in the Buildings and Roads Department. A third temporary post of Superintending Engineer has just been created to deal with the road expansion programme. The

holder of that post will get the same rate of pay which he would have got in one of the permanent posts. On the other hand, if a new and detached post is created, not belonging to any existing cadre, and to which an existing Government servant is appointed by open selection, he will get whatever rate may be fixed for that post under the 1939 rules, or by the Government, if it is not included in those new scales.

7. This proposal has been accepted, although with a certain amount of reluctance, by the Cabinet sub-committee and by the Cabinet, because of the numerous anomalies and hardships which they see from experience in their departments that an application of the rules followed in Madras would produce. These are particularly evident in the case of officers at present on the pre-1931 rates of pay, since in many cases these are now drawing a higher scale in a junior post than they would draw on promotion to the next senior post if paid on the 1939 scale. The three scales are shown in the printed schedule of which I attach a copy.[22] The Cabinet's reluctance is shown by the imposition of a time-limit. The sub-committee's decision is stated as follows: "The committee came to the conclusion that the proposal made by the Finance Department should be accepted but that it should be operative only for five years, that is, from January 1st, 1939, to December 31st, 1943. During this period all persons in service on July 1st, 1938, promoted to other posts and appointed to hold new permanent or temporary posts should be allowed pay in accordance with the proposals made by the Finance Department and that persons promoted or appointed after December 31st, 1943, should get such pay as may be prescribed for them by the then Government after taking into consideration the rates of pay then drawn by persons who would be due for promotion to higher posts. It is highly probable that by then many of the persons on the old rates of pay, in whose case the application of the post-1939 scale or any intermediate scale of pay would have caused distinct hardship, would have been provided for and a majority of the Government servants would then be drawing pay in the reduced post-1931 scales who would accordingly benefit by promotion in the intermediate scale suggested above or even in the post-1939 scale. However, the question should be reconsidered in 1943. In the meanwhile the rule and announcement containing the Finance Department proposal should contain a clear provision that it will apply only to persons promoted or appointed before December 31st, 1943." The Ministry do not consider that their decision attracts Sir Harry's individual judgement, since it makes no change in the existing position. Sir Harry agrees, except to the extent to which it may be considered to prejudge the case when reconsidered in 1943.

8. He is of opinion that he may safely accept the present proposal, subject to a clear statement on the file that the Governor reserves judgement with reference to his special responsibility for securing the rights and safeguarding the legitimate interests of members of the public services in regard to any proposals that may be made at the end of 1943 to alter the rules. The rule and announcement should not take the form recommended by the sub-committee but some such form as: "The pay of officers on promotion shall be regulated as follows up to 31st December 1943. Thereafter the position will be examined further."

9. In view of the importance to the services of the principle involved and having regard to the previous correspondence Sir Harry thinks that he should report the position to the Governor-General and obtain his agreement before committing himself. As he is ill he has asked me to write this letter to you. The Ministry are anxious to get the rules out as soon as possible.[23]

Yours sincerely,
J.C. DONALDSON

55

DONALDSON TO LAITHWAITE
R/3/1/75

Secret
No. 950/39-G.S.P.

August 28th, 1939

My dear Laithwaite,

As His Excellency will not be able to write a fortnightly report for some time, I thought that a brief summary of provincial events might be useful.

His Excellency was on tour in Jhansi from the 11th to 15th August and at Agra from 16th to 20th. He was feeling troubled by a sore throat and temperature at Agra on the evening of the 20th, and arrived at Lucknow on the 21st morning with a temperature of 103 and a very inflamed throat. He went straight to bed. By 11 a.m. on Wednesday the case had been definitely shown to be diphtheria by bacteriological examination, and I telephoned to you. So far it seems to be a mild case. The temperature is a good deal down, and the throat clearing up as a result of treatment. Sir Harry is very much himself again, except that he is not allowed to talk very much. He can, however, take an interest in what is going on and attend to necessary business. As strict precautions have to be taken against possible after-effects, he is likely to be in bed for some weeks longer, and at present the Civil Surgeon is against moving him to Naini Tal for five or six weeks. Lady Haig is with him in Lucknow. It is very hard on anyone to be ill in Lucknow in September, but particularly trying for him to be confined to bed and isolated at such a critical time in international affairs.

2. Sir Harry did not see the official fortnightly report, of which I attach a copy. There are certain remarks in it in connection with the Khaksar movement and the Punjab Government, in which he might not have concurred.[24] But the draft had been passed by the Premier who had departed to Poona for the conference of Congress Premiers, so there was nothing for it but to send the D.O. as it was.

3. The Premier who had been ill (as mentioned in His Excellency's fortnightly letter of August 9th) went up to Naini Tal on the evening of August 12th and stopped there until Saturday 19th, when he returned unexpectedly to Lucknow, apparently on account of the arrival of Abul Kalam Azad, who had been sent to Lucknow by the Higher Command to make another attempt to settle the Shia-Sunni dispute. The Premier did not benefit much in health from his visit to the hills and was ill most of the time he was there. Today (August 27th) there is a newspaper report that Abul Kalam Azad has persuaded the Shias to drop the public recitation of Tabarra, with various face-saving clauses about the release of prisoners and the dropping of 107 and 144 orders. The Government will also in fact pay the fares of prisoners to their homes on release, although they will not withdraw their order saying that fares are only to be paid to the place of arrest, i.e. Lucknow. I have been told today, however, that this report is incorrect and that the Shia leaders have gone back on an agreement which was practically reached last night. The Premier saw His Excellency for a few minutes in the evening of August 22nd before leaving for Poona next morning. He does not intend to return before about September 10th. But his probable movements and actions in the event of war breaking out were discussed between him and His Excellency, and I understand that if there is war he intends to return at once. The purpose of staying on in Poona after the Premiers' conference is medical treatment and rest. He has distributed his various portfolios among the Ministers here and not left any one of them in charge as Premier. He keeps in touch by telephone and expects to be consulted on any matter of importance. He delayed dealing with the file about the provisional instructions for the control of foreigners in war which were recently received and sent it back without having passed any orders. His general attitude and that of the Ministry appears to be that the consent which they gave some time ago to the entrusting to them of

functions under certain latent sections of the Foreigners Act may be taken as implying their consent to the entrusting of similar functions under emergency legislation until they make a declaration to the contrary. They do not wish to commit themselves but will allow instructions to go out to police officers and magistrates. I understand that the Premier was consulted again today about this on the telephone and his reply was that the orders already passed might be presumed to be still in effect. Their attitude in the event of war breaking out will undoubtedly be dictated to them by the Higher Command.

4. In paragraph 4 of Sir Harry's last fortnightly report, dated August 9th, he stated the position about the Tenancy Bill discussions. The Bill had been referred to a Select Committee of the Legislative Council on July 7th and this Committee was to report by August 10th. The Committee acted throughout as a negotiating committee and did not deal with the Bill clause by clause. The Government finally made an offer of an improvement in the provisions about ejectment in default of payment of rent, which in the opinion of Mudie, the Revenue Secretary and others, represented a very considerable advance and one which the zamindars would have done well to take. There was a difference of opinion in the Select Committee and among the zamindars' advisers of that Committee some of whom wanted further concessions from the Government, on the question of Sir and of acquisition of land by the zamindars. The Government offer was therefore referred on August 9th to a meeting of the opposition members in the Legislative Council who rejected it by a majority. In the Select Committee there were four members who were in favour of accepting the offer and four who felt themselves bound by the decision of the opposition members. The latter moved in the Select Committee that it should ask for an extension of time from the Council. There was an equality of votes on this proposal and lots were drawn with the result that it was rejected. The members of the Select Committee then signed a report, but the four who had wanted an extension of time signed subject to a minute of dissent in which they said they had not had time to consider the Bill clause by clause and that they reserved the right to move amendments to the Bill as there was no time for them to submit a detailed minute of dissent. The report of the Select Committee was laid before the Council on August 10th and consideration postponed until August 21st. In the meantime a lively newspaper controversy took place between the Hon'ble Minister for Revenue, Mr. Kidwai, and Raja Maheshwar Dayal Seth, one of the principal opponents of the Bill and others about the conduct of the landlords' representatives during these negotiations and whether they had shown

themselves as impossible people to deal with, who went on continually increasing their demands without any real intention of ever coming to terms. On the whole, the Minister had the best of the argument, particularly as he was supported as to his facts by most of the moderate members of the Select Committee. When the Legislative Council met on August 21st, it was clear that the Government had a majority and that the Opposition would not be able to get the Bill referred to another Select Committee as had apparently been their intention. The discussion of the Bill was adjourned until August 24th to enable members to table clause by clause amendments, and it is now being discussed from day-to-day. The *bania* members in the Upper House are voting with the Government and the landlords have been so thoroughly split that they cannot agree among themselves which amendments to support. They have discredited themselves, and thrown away a chance of getting a valuable concession by agreement while preserving their unity as a party. They have also lost the opportunity of claiming credit for accepting the Bill, a point which later may be of some importance. There seems every prospect that the Government will be able to carry the Bill through, without substantial amendment[s] other than those inserted in the Select Committee, in about a fortnight's time. It will then have to go back to the Legislative Assembly, of which the session is expected to commence about the last week of September.

5. On August 21st the Legislative Council passed a resolution that no member of the Council should be appointed as an honorary magistrate and that the powers of those who had already been appointed should be immediately withdrawn. It had been alleged that the Government had influenced the votes of certain members of the House by making them honorary magistrates. The Minister for Justice undertook to abide by the verdict of the House, but denied the charge made. He also pointed out that it was in deference to an expressed wish of the House that Government had declared members of the Legislative Council eligible for appointment as honorary magistrates about a year ago when framing the new rules.

6. On August 17th the Hon'ble Mrs. Pandit, Minister for Local Self-Government, was to have visited Cawnpore to perform the opening ceremony of the Lala Kamlapat Memorial new dispensary. She was afterwards attending a garden party. The district authorities informed her by telephone in the morning that they had received information that a Shia demonstration against her was being organised as a protest against the Government's attitude in regard to the Tabarra agitation in Lucknow. They advised her not to come in view of the strained communal and labour

situation at Cawnpore, and the possibility that some incident might prove to be the spark which would produce a major explosion. They did, however, say that if the Minister decided to come, arrangements had been made for her protection. Mrs. Pandit felt herself bound to accept their advice and cancelled her programme. There had been a previous demonstration against her at Bareilly a few days before. She was, however, extremely displeased at having to cancel her visit and her annoyance was probably increased when it was made plain next day that the demonstration would only have been on a small scale. Some 200 Shias had collected to meet her at the Railway bridge. She wrote a strong note to the Premier about the attitude taken by the district authorities. The Premier himself had been feeling indignant at the filthy abuse which the Shias in Lucknow had been publicly indulging in against himself and his family and other members of the Congress Government. He has directed that a strong order should go out to District Magistrates pointing out to them that it is their duty to protect members of the Government against attacks of this kind when they visit their districts; and that the District Magistrates should be prepared to take firm action to deal with demonstrators, and will be protected in doing so.

7. The Minister concerned, Dr. Katju, was unsuccessful in negotiations for settling the lock-out in the New Victoria Mills, Cawnpore. It was reported that a majority of the workers were willing to resume work; and that the Mill committee and the Mazdur Sabha were at logger-heads. The Sabha wrote a conciliatory letter to the Managing Director of the Mills and advised the workers to resume work under the old conditions. Apparently this action was taken because the workers themselves were becoming restless and beginning to apply for reinstatement. A settlement has not been reached up to the time of writing.

8. The districts of the Meerut Division were the only ones in the Province which were complaining of any shortage of rain up to the 15th of August. If the present prolonged break in the rains continues much longer, however, there may be cause for anxiety. The issue of the Provincial loan of two crores has been put off owing to the international situation.

9. The leader of the Khaksars "Allama Mashriqi" Inayatullah Khan arrived in Lucknow two days ago. The movement obviously has dangerous possibilities. The bombastic messages of its leader, however, combined with his constant postponements of action make it hard to know how far to take him seriously. The "public flogging" by his order of a Lucknow leader, held in the backyard of a private house, as the police would not permit it in a public place, came very near to farce. But the punishment

was because the leader had obeyed an order of the District Magistrate; and this is the first time that the Khaksars in Lucknow have encouraged or praised civil disobedience to official authority. The Government look on the movement with much suspicion, but have not so far taken action against it.

Yours sincerely,
J.C. DONALDSON

56

HAIG TO LINLITHGOW[25]
Telegram
MSS.EUR.F 125/18

Personal
No. 259-G

September 3rd, 1939

With reference to your telegram No. 1802, dated 3 September.[26] It is clear that my Ministers are marking time and waiting for policy to be laid down for them by the High Command. Meanwhile although nervous about doing anything which definitely commits them to cooperation they have no objection to ordinary precautionary measures being taken.

Revenue Minister recently noted that this Government is prepared to take all necessary measures to protect life and property in the Province but will not do anything to help the British Government in the prosecution of war against Germany till the question has been settled (between) Government of India and Congress Working Committee. The Premier is in Poona till September 5th primarily for his health and in these circumstances I have not thought it necessary to suggest that he should return earlier. General and press expectation that Ministers will resign almost at once seems daily less pronounced. As regards public the old loyalists are rallying well and sending in offers of services. Suggestion made by some to organise United Provinces Defence Committee to combine all classes in favour of assisting Britain in war. Congress, like Ministry, wait on events. There seems to me to be strong general sympathy for Poland and against German aggression.

57

HAIG TO LINLITHGOW
R/3/1/75

Secret
No. U.P.-296

September 6th, 1939

My dear Lord Linlithgow,

I was not able to write a fortnight ago owing to my unfortunate attack of diphtheria. Donaldson, however, sent Laithwaite some account of affairs in the Province. I have now quite got rid of the diphtheria symptoms, but the doctors insist on keeping me in bed for some time yet as it appears to be necessary physically to go slow after this disease. I fear I shall have to stay in Lucknow for the rest of the month, but I hope I may get up to Naini Tal for a fortnight in October.

2. Now that the infective period is over, I am able to see visitors, and last Monday I saw Kidwai who in the absence of Pant is unofficially functioning as Premier and enjoys the position. In a recent telegram to Your Excellency I reported a rather stiff note about cooperation in the war which he had recorded on a file; but as usual I found him much easier to deal with in conversation than on paper. He raised no difficulties about any of the measures that are required at this time. I mentioned to him the Defence of India Ordinance which had just come out and he made no objection to it. As I explained in my telegram, the Ministers here are marking time and waiting for determination of policy by the Working Committee. I have therefore taken no steps to get Pant back earlier than he had intended. I believe he is likely to arrive here on the 8th. His health is far from satisfactory, but his absence has not proved in any way an embarrassment from the practical point of view.

3. I thought it desirable on Monday to issue a short message to the people of the Province, and I attach a copy.[27] I did this for two reasons. In the first place, the old-fashioned loyal classes were coming forward with very sincere offers of support and help, and with the attitude of the Congress Ministry towards the war so ambiguous I thought that they would appreciate it if the Governor made his position clear. I had to be careful not to say anything that would upset the Ministers and my statement therefore did not amount to much; but I think from this point of view it was worth making. In the second place, I wanted the people of the Province to realise that at this crisis, though I was laid up, I was still functioning.

4. I saw Sir J.P. Srivastava yesterday. I had heard that he was contemplating launching with considerable publicity a United Provinces Defence League to concentrate the loyal activities of the non-Congress elements. It seemed to me that this would be a great embarrassment at the present moment, and I spoke to him about this. I said that I had the greatest appreciation of the loyal feelings and assurances of the non-Congress elements and I hoped that we should be able to take the fullest advantage of them. The ideal, however, seemed to be that the Province should unite in its war effort and should not be split on political lines. I said that much depended on the policy which the Congress might adopt, and that while that was still uncertain it seemed to me a pity that support for the war should be made a political issue. I also pointed out that at the beginning India would be entering the war slowly, and that though I had no doubt there would later be the fullest scope for all the activities and support that the non-Congress elements could give us, at the moment there was probably little of practical importance that such a league could engage itself in. Srivastava appreciated these views, but he said that people of his way of thinking wished to get the public credit for their genuine spirit of loyalty and did not wish to appear to be coming in in support of the war merely as part of a bargain that the Congress might strike. He also said that if the Congress decided to cooperate in the war, people like himself did not wish their efforts to be treated as merely subordinate to those of the Congress. I said I fully appreciated his views and that I hoped that if the Ministry cooperated it would be possible to set up some kind of war organization in this Province in which the non-Congress elements would have the fullest representation and scope for their energy and practical work. He also hinted that the Ministry ought to stop all controversial policies. I said I thought that would be difficult, particularly if he referred to the Tenancy Bill, which is now in its last stages. But I said that I thought there could at any rate be real cooperation on the basis of equality so far as all war activities were concerned. I have heard this morning that Srivastava has decided not to go on for the present with this idea of a United Provinces Defence League.

5. So far as concerns provincial affairs the last fortnight has shown some very satisfactory results. The Tenancy Bill is going through the Upper House rapidly and may well be finished by the middle of the month. The Ministers have got their way, in that they have only conceded the important provisions about ejectment for non-payment of rent, which they had offered to the landlords during the negotiations and which in fact a large section of landlords were prepared to compromise on. They have made no

concession about *sir* rights. The upshot is that the diehard landlords who tried at the last moment to break the compromise have failed.

6. The Sunni-Shia controversy has at last taken a favourable turn. The obstacle to any movement has been the continuance of the Tabarra agitation. Abul Kalam Azad has induced the Shias to suspend this agitation, and I have every hope that it will not be re-started. He dealt direct with the Shia divines, which was undoubtedly wise, for they are the people who have the last word. Previous conversations conducted with politicians always broke down on the opposition of the divines. There will now be conversations between the Sunnis and Shias with a view to reach a friendly settlement. An actual settlement may not be possible for some little time; but this will not matter so much provided that the Tabarra agitation is not re-started, and I do not think it will be.

7. Another very satisfactory development is the collapse of the Khaksar movement in Lucknow. The Khaksar leader with an amazing amount of bombast had attempted to intervene in the Sunni-Shia dispute and had invaded Lucknow with a considerable force with his followers. Their presence was a decided menace to order, and I encouraged the Ministers to take firm action against them. The leader of the movement and several others were arrested and an order was passed that Khaksars from outside the Province should not be allowed to come to Lucknow. The Khaksars were bewildered and dejected at this action. At this stage I thought there was some danger of the Ministers puffed up by success pushing the matter too far and involving themselves in what might prove a long struggle against the Khaksar movement generally. I suggested to them that their objective should be to remove the menace to the peace of Lucknow and not to embark on an attempt to break the Khaksar movement altogether. They accepted these views and on the leader of the Khaksars giving an assurance that he would leave Lucknow and not return for a year and would not send any more of his followers to the United Provinces, he was released and despatched out of the Province together with all the non-United Provinces Khaksars. I think he is entirely discredited and I hope we shall have no more trouble from him.

8. Owing to the international conditions we have been unable to proceed with the flotation of the loan of two crores that we required, and it will now be necessary to review our financial position very carefully and to cut down drastically our capital commitments.

9. I shall be greatly interested to hear the outcome of Your Excellency's conversations with the Congress and other parties.

Yours sincerely,
H.G. HAIG

58

HAIG TO LINLITHGOW
R/3/1/75

Secret *September 11th, 1939*
No. U.P.-299

My dear Lord Linlithgow,

I think I ought to let Your Excellency know about an unfortunate development in regard to the health of my Premier. As I had informed you earlier, he went to Poona about three weeks ago for the conference of Congress Premiers and afterwards stayed on there for the sake of his health. On his way back he went to Bombay and consulted certain well-known doctors. They appear to have taken a very unfavourable view about his health and said that he should go to the hills and do no work for two months. He arrived back in Lucknow two days ago with this verdict and saw doctors here who confirmed it. He has now therefore proceeded to Naini Tal and the present intention is that he should take a complete rest for two months. I had hoped to see him when he returned to Lucknow, but he was confined to bed and was quite unable to get up and come to see me, and we could hardly manage to get our beds laid side by side! I am not very clear what is the matter with him. The earlier diagnosis of the Lucknow doctors was colitis, and it may be nothing more than this. He has persistently neglected it and has been running a temperature now for months. Sooner or later he had to pay the penalty for this, and the time has now come. Some of the doctors I believe suspect T.B., but I do not think there are any assured grounds for such a view. Anyhow I have to face the likelihood that the Premier will be out of action for the next two months.

2. The arrangements for the conduct of business will be the same as they have been during the last three weeks. Kidwai, the Revenue Minister, will be treated as the senior Minister and will in a somewhat indefinite way take the place of the Premier. The Premier's departmental functions have been divided between four of the Ministers. The arrangement has been working satisfactorily during the last three weeks and for normal purposes I do not anticipate any great difficulties. But if we are faced with serious problems affecting the position of the Ministry or possibly some recasting of the Ministry then it will of course be extremely embarrassing to have the Premier out of action. As you know, I have always believed that the only way in which we can put a stop to the present deplorable

communal ill-feeling is by arranging a coalition with the Muslim League, and under the influence of the war and the general impetus to unified action that that is likely to give it may be that these ideas will come up in a practical form. I fear, however, that of all the Ministers Kidwai, a strong Congress Muslim, is likely to be the least favourably disposed to that. Actually I imagine if any question of recasting the Ministry arises, this will in effect be done by persons like Jawaharlal Nehru and Abul Kalam Azad, and that it will not be a matter to be decided by my Ministers themselves. Pant's absence therefore may in fact prove less of an embarrassment than might have been supposed.

3. These are all vague speculations; but I thought Your Excellency would like to know how at the moment the situation presents itself to me. I was greatly interested in your letter of September 8th which I received yesterday, particularly in what you told me about your conversations with Gandhi and various Muslim leaders. I greatly hope that the Working Committee will take a sound line.

Yours sincerely,
H.G. HAIG

P.S. – My Ministers clearly sympathise with the objects of the war, and so, I am convinced, do all moderate Congressmen.

59

HAIG TO LINLITHGOW
R/3/1/75

Secret *September 14th, 1939*
No. U.P.-300

My dear Lord Linlithgow,

In your letter of September 9th, which I was very glad to get, Your Excellency mentioned that you were contemplating inviting both Chhatari and Srivastava to come and see you to discuss the present situation, and you asked me for any other names that occurred to me in the United Provinces of those who might be useful for you to see. The only other person from this Province whom I would suggest it is important for Your Excellency to see is Sir Tej Bahadur Sapru. He is taking a very prominent interest in these developments and is the acknowledged representative of the moderate non-Congress view in the Province. I think that these three between them would present a pretty complete picture of non-Congress opinion in the Province.

Yours sincerely,
H.G. HAIG

60

HAIG TO LINLITHGOW
Telegram
MSS.EUR.F 115/7

No. 263-G *September 17th, 1939*

Your telegram 1950-S, dated September 16.[28] I have no doubt that all my Ministers are genuinely anxious to continue in office and ready if permitted by the higher command to give full cooperation in prosecution of the war. I think in so far as Working Committee's resolution may be interpreted as making this development less probable they are definitely disappointed. But the majority of them seem to believe that a way out will be found. Kidwai speaks optimistically. They certainly do not regard the resolution as closing door on cooperation. There is an idea that through the influence and mediation of Gandhi a satisfactory solution may be found.

2. The attitude of the Ministry to our present problems is satisfactory. Recently they were afraid that some district officers were taking action under the Ordinance against anti-war activities which was upsetting Congressmen at this stage. Instruction was therefore sent to all District Magistrates that they should not take such action without prior reference to the Government. Yesterday I received a paper which showed that a Congress M.L.A. was endeavouring to raise trouble on account of perfectly normal activities of recruiting for the territorial force. I called attention of Kidwai to this in a note. I said I fully appreciated that at this moment the Ministry were anxious that issues, such as active discouragement of recruiting and opposition to the war, should not be brought out unnecessarily into the open, and in pursuit of that policy we had warned District Magistrates to be cautious not to take action without first obtaining the orders of Government. I said that if that policy was to be effective it was essential that equal restraint should be exercised on the other side and that the rank and file of the Congress should not openly encourage anti-war activities or oppose recruitment. Kidwai fully appreciated this point of view and has had an urgent message sent by the Provincial Congress Committee to all subordinate committees to the effect that pending the

next meeting of the A.I.C.C. Congressmen are directed to refrain from delivering speeches on the Congress attitude towards war or acting in a manner which tends to contravene the orders of the British Government in India for the successful prosecution of the war. The situation is not easy, for there are a considerable number of left wing men who are out of control of the Ministry and are trying to work up agitation against the war. But so far as the Ministry can control this difficult intermediate situation they are doing their best.

3. I think the general feeling here including that of many Congressmen is disappointment that the Working Committee have taken a line which presents obvious dangers of leading to non-cooperation, a realisation that a good deal of what is said in the resolution can probably be written off as intended to placate the extremer elements, and a belief that a solution may yet be possible. I should judge that a solution is earnestly desired by the majority of Congress supporters.

61

HAIG TO LINLITHGOW
R/3/1/75

Secret — Camp,
No. U.P.-301 — *September 17th, 1939*

My dear Lord Linlithgow,

I have been turning over in my mind lately the possibilities of having some useful and practical channels into which the very genuine and spontaneous desire of large numbers of people in this Province to assist in the war could profitably be turned. I am sure that this problem has been very much in Your Excellency's mind and in the minds of other Governors, for it seems to me to be one of the most marked problems of the present position. India is at the moment out of the main current of the war, and it is exceedingly difficult to utilise her present very sincere desire to help. If, however, no use is made of the present spirit of the people I fear it may gradually die away and we shall have lost an important moral advantage. Doubtless it would be possible later on when needs develop to rouse feeling again and secure support; but it may not have the same spontaneous quality that it has at present.

2. I realise very fully the difficulties. It is no use enlisting support for activities which are not in fact required. Nevertheless, I think that it is

psychologically wise to develop as early as possible such activities as are likely to be needed later, even though the immediate requirements are not urgent and I think it might be valuable to give an early indication of the directions in which Indian assistance might be required.

3. There would, I think, be a very wide and active response in this Province to any call for recruiting for the army and this would be likely to keep up practical interest in the war. I am well aware of the military view, that the best soldiers are to be found in the Punjab, that there is an ample supply of them in that Province, and that therefore it is on the whole unnecessary to go outside the Punjab for purposes of recruitment. If one admits the correctness of that argument, there is still the question whether we should concentrate purely on military considerations, or whether psychological factors should not be taken into account. I feel myself that for purposes of the attitude of this Province to the war it is a matter of very great importance that we should be given some opportunity greater than we have at present of contributing our quota of soldiers. Without entering into any controversial question of the military value of the material in the United Provinces, we have very long-standing military traditions and connections, the gradual disappearance of which is widely felt in the Province to be a misfortune. As a beginning I would suggest that it might be possible to recruit one or two units in this Province primarily for internal security purposes. It seems probable that, however, the war may develop, we shall gradually be denuded of internal security troops and it might be as well to look ahead and satisfy provincial sentiment in this way.

4. Another call which might meet with a wide response and would certainly appeal to popular feeling is the training of air pilots. I should have supposed, looking at the matter on the broadest lines, that it was important for India to have a considerable trained reserve of pilots, and it might even be possible for India to train pilots for use in Europe. Anyhow, I feel sure it would have an excellent effect if training centres for air pilots could be established early. I have no doubt plans are already being worked out.

5. Another direction in which the United Provinces could certainly help if assistance is required is in the provision of labour corps. I realise that it is not likely that Indian labour corps would be utilised in Europe; but if later a demand should arise for them anywhere, I am sure the United Provinces could be relied upon to provide ample material.

6. Industrially I have no doubt, we shall in due course be called upon to make such contribution as we can. There are of course considerable possibilities in this Province.

7. So far as money contributions are concerned I have just received a letter explaining Your Excellency's intentions regarding the launching of a joint appeal for the Red Cross and St. John Ambulance. I quite agree that the appeal should not be launched until we can have some fairly clear idea of what will be required; but subject to that I think the sooner the appeal is launched the better. I am already receiving occasional contributions, sometimes of a very generous character, for general purposes of the war, and I think at the moment a definite appeal for funds would meet with a good response.

8. I have no doubt that Your Excellency has already considered all these points and that you are formulating your conclusions and plans; but I thought it was only right to give some idea of what I judge to be general popular opinion in this Province and to stress the widespread desire to be of use, and the importance, so far as circumstances permit, of not disappointing that desire.

9. It is of course the case that at the moment the initiation of any activities of this kind would lead to trouble with my Ministers; but the present state of doubt as to their attitude can hardly last very much longer, and it is my view that if the eventual decision of the Congress is to cooperate, my Ministers will be prepared to co-operate genuinely and support all measures of this kind. I think they fully appreciate that it is not possible to adopt an attitude of neutrality towards the war.

Yours sincerely,
H.G. HAIG

62

HAIG TO LINLITHGOW
Telegram
MSS.EUR.F 115/7

No. 264-G *September 18th, 1939*

Continuation my telegram No. 263-G of September 17th. I had a talk today with Katju. His general outlook was much as I have indicated in my telegram. But he stressed the point, possibly influenced by news about Russia, that Indians were seriously concerned about the defence of their country and wished to do everything possible to strengthen it. He remarked that all thinking Indians were gravely disturbed at the defencelessness of this country on modern standards. He was referring mainly to air attack. His own ideas as to what could be done are no doubt crude and unpractical.

But I think it likely that apart from general support for the justice of our cause there is a widespread feeling that safety of India is at stake and that all must help to preserve it. This might make reasonable Congress leaders more ready to come in. It also has some bearing on my letter No. 301, dated September 17th.

63

HAIG TO LINLITHGOW
Telegram
MSS.EUR.F 115/7

Immediate *September 19th, 1939*
No. 265-G

Continuation my telegram 264-G of September 18. I have today seen Mrs. Pandit who has just returned from Allahabad where she and Kidwai have held discussions with Nehru. I judge from what she says that Nehru was mainly responsible for policy of Working Committee resolution, and that majority of Working Committee might otherwise have been content with something more accommodating. He is influenced partly by past commitments and general principles, partly by desire to keep Congress together as long as possible. Anything less uncompromising would have lost support of those inclined to the left. If eventual decision is for co-operation he wants to bring Congress in as united as possible.

2. Nehru seems to desire two incompatible things. He talks of the necessity of getting a declaration that independence is the ultimate gaol, though he must know it is quite impossible to get such a declaration from the British Government. On the other hand it would seem he is anxious that India should play its part in the war. When faced, as he must be soon, with inescapable choice between these two positions Mrs. Pandit suggests he might come down in favour of supporting the war and be content with some fresh statement of dominion status being the gaol, coupled with some practical arrangements for associating those who represent popular opinion with war activities at the centre.

3. At the moment Congress are waiting for a gesture from Simla. The intention of appointing a sub-committee was that they would be able to conduct any conversations with Your Excellency without I understand referring back to the Working Committee. Nehru by himself would probably be able to conduct conversations with authority and it looks as if his word will in fact be decisive. I think he is awaiting an invitation to visit Your Excellency.

4. There is a general feeling that an early decision is urgently required. The present situation in this Province gets rapidly more difficult. I have today seen a report from the C.I.D. which gives a disquieting picture of the rapidly developing organisation and activities of the leftists and revolutionaries of all kinds. A great impetus will be given to these activities by the tour of Bose in this Province which begins I think tomorrow and may last about a week. Mrs. Pandit said that the interest and enthusiasm being worked up particularly among students in favour of Bose was striking and formidable. She realises clearly that if Congress decide to cooperate they will have to tackle the leftists at once and vigorously. But it is dangerous to let this movement gather strength unchecked.

5. Nehru comes to Lucknow tomorrow and proposes to stay for a week so as to be in close touch with Ministers. I think it is realised that at any moment especially during Bose's visit there might be developments which would require important decisions as to action by the Government. This all emphasises the great desirability of earliest possible decision as to attitude of Congress to the war.

64

HAIG TO LINLITHGOW
Telegram
MSS.EUR.F 115/7

Immediate *September 21st, 1939*
No. 266-G

Continuation my telegram No. 265-G dated 19th September. I should be grateful for any indication of policy Your Excellency could give me. Situation in this Province continues to deteriorate and it is dangerous to allow it to go much further. Administratively left wing activities are a growing menace. Politically the large body of right wing Congress who are really in favour of cooperation are muzzled, while the left wing have the field to themselves and are strengthening their position daily. So far as this Province is concerned situation urgently demands earliest possible decision as to whether Congress will or will not cooperate.

65

HAIG TO LINLITHGOW
R/3/1/75

Secret *September 21st, 1939*
No. U.P.-303

My dear Lord Linlithgow,

In my letter No. U.P.-283, dated July 5th, 1939, I said that I proposed to appoint Dible as my third Adviser in place of Gwynne, and Your Excellency in your letter of 15th July accepted this proposal. Since the outbreak of the war I have been reconsidering the position in the light of the conditions that have developed. It is clear that if I have to take over the administration, it will be of the utmost importance to carry with me the large body of opinion which is in sympathy with the policy of the British Empire and is prepared to give active support if it gets a proper lead. I contemplate among other things that it would be desirable to appoint a small War Board, consisting mainly of non-officials, with which one of my Advisers would be associated. In this task of keeping in touch with public opinion and guiding it along right lines I think that Marsh, who is the senior Member of the Board of Revenue, would be very valuable. He has an intimate knowledge of the Indian character and is exceedingly well liked by Indians. I have come to the conclusion that his qualities would be of great value in the conditions that would be likely to confront me. In supersession therefore of the proposal made in my letter of July 5th I should propose to have as my Advisers Marsh, Panna Lall and Sloan. Sloan will handle law and order and also finance.

Yours sincerely,
H.G. HAIG

66

HAIG TO LINLITHGOW
Telegram
MSS.EUR.F 115/7

Immediate *September 23rd, 1939*
No. 268-G

Your telegram 2021-S, dated September 22nd.[29] I agree about formal consultation with Opposition before going into Section 93. From informal conversations I have already had I think there is no chance of their attempting to form an alternative Government. The only possibility that occurs to me is that they might form a Government on an undertaking that after two or three months when they were administratively in the saddle there should be a general election. It is likely enough that at such an election Congress would lose a good deal of ground, but doubtful whether Opposition would secure a majority that would enable them to function.

2. The disadvantage of such a course would be that we should engage ourselves in fierce struggle with Congress and in my view the general position in the Province would be worse than if I took over under Sec. 93 and endeavoured as far as possible to maintain reasonably friendly terms with right wing Congress. Subject to Your Excellency's advice therefore I am not disposed either to suggest such a course to the Opposition leaders or to encourage it if they suggest it. I am fully in agreement with para 3 of your telegram.

67

HAIG TO LINLITHGOW
Telegram
MSS.EUR.F 115/7

Immediate *September 23rd, 1939*
No. 269-G

Your telegram 2020-S, dated September 22nd.[30] I am most grateful for this information. Kidwai yesterday showed me the draft resolution and said it had been taken up in the first instance with the Governor at Bombay.[31] He had said he wanted a week to consider it till the 27th and was understood to be consulting Your Excellency. Our Assembly does not meet till 3rd October. I told Kidwai that a resolution in these terms would be most embarrassing if the Congress intended to reach a settlement. He took the line that resolution meant little. I did not pursue the subject as it seemed clear main decision would be taken on the Bombay reference.

2. Desmond Young had long conversation on 21st with Nehru. Young will be in Simla today and has a note of his interview which he could show Your Excellency. Read with Gandhi's demands I fear outlook for Congress cooperation is gloomy.

3. With regard to provincial situation I am hoping to get Ministers today to agree to give District Magistrates free hand to proceed under Section 108, Criminal Procedure Code against any speaker who instigates violence. This will steady the position if prompt orders are got out.

4. In general I am ready as far as can be foreseen for an emergency.

68

HAIG TO LINLITHGOW
Telegram
MSS.EUR.F 115/7

Immediate *September 24th, 1939*
No. 270-G

Your telegram 2033-S, dated 23rd September.[32] I think committee for purpose of associating public opinion with conduct of war might be of great value even if Congress do not cooperate. My own view would be that while of course constitutionally committee could not be other than advisory its real utility might be in proportion to degree to which in fact it is encouraged to reach conclusions and its conclusions wherever practicable are acted upon. If it is restricted to exchange of information its public standing may be small and its utility limited. One view would be that the aim should be smallest possible body consistent with essential representation of different interests and largest possible authority attached to its recommendations.

2. In regard to suggestion for periodical meetings of Premiers and Princes presided over by Your Excellency I think there would be great advantages and I see no constitutional objection. The meetings would I conceive be in essentials similar to conferences of provincial Ministers that have already been held, but with the additional prestige arising out of Governor-General presiding. I think it is most important that provinces should in this way be kept in close touch with central policy regarding conduct of war and have opportunities of accepting general policies in regard to provincial activities and drawing attention to any difficulties there may be or suggestions provinces may wish to make.

69

HAIG TO LINLITHGOW
Telegram
MSS.EUR.F 115/7

Immediate *September 25th, 1939*
No. 271-G

Your telegram No. 2063-P, dated September 25.[33] I discussed today with Kidwai prospects of a settlement with Congress. I said that if there were no settlement the resulting situation would seem to me not only very unfortunate but even absurd, for they, like us, would be vitally interested in the success of the war and I presumed they would not wish to do anything likely to embarrass its prosecution. It would be against their interests as well as ours. On the other hand if they were not going to oppose the war it was difficult to see why they should quit office or how they can mark their disagreement with us. He said it was precisely on account of such considerations that he was convinced there must be a settlement. He has been in close touch for the last two days with Nehru and he is sure that Nehru feels strongly that India ought to participate in the war. I said the difficulty seemed to lie in the demands that Congress was putting forward, that they seemed to be asking things which the British Government with the best will in the world could not agree to. It could not be expected that His Majesty's Government could make a far-reaching declaration of future policy about India at a moment's notice and in the middle of a war. He said he fully appreciated this and he did not believe that the Congress demands really involved anything of this nature. He was very sanguine that Gandhi when he meets Your Excellency would be able to propose some acceptable solution. He said that the Premiers of Madras and Bombay[34] were in touch with Gandhi and were using their influence for a settlement.

70

HAIG TO LINLITHGOW
R/3/1/75

Secret
No. U.P.-306

September 25th, 1939

My dear Lord Linlithgow,

Our thoughts are mainly centred round the war and the attitude of Congress towards it. I have kept Your Excellency in touch with feeling and developments here and I will only write briefly about other matters. But the general state of the Province arising from greatly increased activities of the Congress left wing and revolutionaries, and secondly the threat of large scale irruptions of Khaksars from the Punjab, are giving cause for anxiety. I have myself been getting on very well[35] and the doctors now say that I may leave for the hills on the 27th instead of the 30th, which was the date they had originally fixed. I shall take advantage of this earlier date. Some of the Ministers are going up to Naini Tal about that time to hold consultations with Pant, who is, I think, getting a little restive at his lack of contact with affairs at this time. I think I shall be as closely in touch with the majority of them there as I should be here, and if a crisis develops, we may have on account of Pant to deal with it in Naini Tal and not in Lucknow.[36] The absence of Pant during these difficult days since the outbreak of war has really not been a disadvantage. Though his attitude would I am sure have been just as definitely in favour of cooperation as the rest of the Ministers, he is always inclined to boggle about decisions or action, and Kidwai has agreed almost without discussion to a number of things about which I am sure we should have had a good deal of trouble with Pant. Kidwai, for instance, agreed immediately to the proposals for increasing the strength of our police.

2. The police have been sending in some rather alarming reports about the activities of the left wing and revolutionaries generally. They are disturbed in particular about the effect of the speeches that are being made and about the possibility of the terrorists embarking before long on a definitely active policy. So far as the speeches are concerned I am hoping to secure the agreement of the Ministers to the issue of instructions to District Magistrates giving them power to proceed under Section 108, Criminal Procedure Code, against all kinds of speeches which incite to violence. Hitherto they have been under the necessity of referring to Government in case the speech was of a type covered by Section 124-A, Indian Penal Code, and were only authorised to act in case of those covered by Section 153-A, Indian Penal Code. This is a matter about which I should certainly have had trouble and much argument with Pant; but though I have not yet got an absolute decision, Kidwai was inclined to agree with little difficulty. On the other hand the Ministers naturally enough are not prepared to agree in this period of suspended judgement to action being taken against speakers who are attacking cooperation in the war or recruitment. For their part, however, they have exercised a very considerable restraint on their own followers. A few days ago we were threatened with a tour by Subhas Chandra Bose in the Province and great preparations were being made. In Lucknow, for instance, loudspeakers were going round everywhere announcing the advent of this great leader. But for some reason which I have not been able to ascertain, the tour seems to have fallen through. This is fortunate, as it would certainly have intensified greatly left wing feeling.

3. The Ministry took prompt action about profiteering. We agreed at once that the most effective step would be that the Central Government should delegate power to us under the Defence of India Ordinance and we got in touch on the telephone with the Government of India. Actually we

found they had already decided to make the delegation and orders were about to issue. We realised the complications that would be involved by attempting to fix prices and decided that it was better to proceed by threatening a drastic use of our powers. This policy was effective, and so far as ordinary commodities are concerned there seem to have been few complaints lately of any attempt to profiteer. Articles imported from Europe present a more difficult problem, for we can do nothing to control the wholesale prices, which in some instances appear to have been raised considerably. But even in the case of drugs the first and quite unreasonable rise in prices has now been appreciably moderated.

4. We have been having a good deal of trouble with the Khaksar movement. I attach a note prepared by the Chief Secretary which gives the main facts about the situation down to the time of the second arrest of the Allama. It was on this note of the Chief Secretary's that we held a Cabinet meeting, the Ministers all coming to my room where I presided from my bed, and decided that it was necessary to prosecute the Allama with a view to getting him a short but adequate sentence of imprisonment. He was in the event sentenced to one month's simple imprisonment which he is now serving in the Lucknow jail. We realised the probability that this would involve an attempted invasion by the Khaksars from other Provinces, and I fear this is now beginning. We are taking such steps as we can to intercept these men as soon as they arrive in the United Provinces, as it is important that they should not reach Lucknow, where conditions are somewhat disturbed. The local trouble in Lucknow though it has been decidedly embarrassing for the last few days will I hope die down before long. The chief disturbing feature is that the Khaksars appear to have got the sympathy of a number of other Muslims. They do not seem to be popular in Muslim provinces, such as the Punjab, but I think Muslim sympathy for them here is part of the desire of the Muslims to find any weapon for attacking the Congress Government. I have written to Craik, Parsons and Graham[37] and asked them if their Governments can do anything to dissuade or restrain the Khaksars from invading the United Provinces. I attach a communiqué which was put out a few days ago by the Government to clear their position. As I mentioned in my letter of September 6th I had warned the Ministers to restrict themselves to removing the menace to the peace of Lucknow and not to embark on an attempt to break the Khaksar movement altogether. In spite of this an order which was perhaps unnecessary was issued, after the Khaksars were removed from Lucknow for the first time, placing restrictions on their movement throughout the United Provinces and this I think was the excuse for the return of the

Allama and his followers. The communiqué makes it clear that the Government have no desire to impose restrictions on the Khaksars in the province except where they are engaged in unlawful activities and the restrictions are being removed now in all districts where the Khaksars are peaceful. The movement is a peculiar one and nobody seems to know quite what is behind it or what its real objects are.

5. We have been more than once in the last fortnight on the brink of a general strike in Cawnpore arising from the trouble in the New Victoria Mills. Some little time ago the workers there struck unjustifiably and the mill was closed down. Recently the management decided to reopen the mill, offering reduced wages. They also took the opportunity to recruit a large number of new hands and get rid of a number of their old workers. These two points have naturally enough been bitterly resented by the Mazdur Sabha. The Sabha offered to submit both points to the arbitration of the Labour Commissioner, but the management of the mill backed up by the Employers' Association appeared to be unwilling to agree. Through the influence of the Ministers a general strike has twice been postponed, and with the return of Sir J.P. Srivastava today to Cawnpore I hope some reasonable settlement may be reached.

6. The Sunni-Shia conversations under the auspices of Abul Kalam Azad are proceeding and I hope there is some chance of a settlement. The Tenancy Bill has now been passed by the Upper House and it only remains for the Lower House to accept certain non-controversial amendments and the legislative procedure will be finished. The Ministry I have no doubt are very anxious to complete this procedure before they go out of office, if it should come to a break.

7. Our financial position gives rise to a good deal of anxiety. We were peculiarly unfortunate in having our loan placed at the bottom of the list by the Reserve Bank and thus failing to have an opportunity of floating it before the war broke out. We required two crores, partly to finance capital expenditure incurred last year and partly for an expensive capital programme this year. Though we have at once closed down all possible capital expenditure, there are still considerable sums of capital which have to be met. In addition our revenue budget is working out very badly, largely owing to extensive remissions of land revenue which have had to be given owing to drought conditions in the west of the province during the *rabi*. The expansion of the police will also mean a good deal of extra expenditure, and though we have at once taken steps to review our budgeted revenue expenditure and to curtail it as far as possible without making major changes in policy, I fear we are likely to be faced with a deficit of at least 50 lakhs

on the revenue budget. It must be remembered that the Ministry took credit for 30 lakhs from the Employments Tax which they clearly will not get. In these circumstances our ways and means position is very difficult and our need for a loan is great. I hope it will be possible for our Finance Secretary[38] before long to proceed to Delhi and explain our difficulties to the Government of India Finance Department.

Yours sincerely,
H.G. HAIG

ENCLOSURE 1 TO NO. 70

NOTE BY PANNA LAL ON THE DEVELOPMENT
OF THE KHAKSAR AGITATION IN THE U.P.

There has been a serious development in the Khaksar agitation which now needs careful consideration and orders by the Government. It will be useful if I give below a brief résumé of the salient facts in order that a complete picture up to date may be before the Government before they take their decision.

2. The Khaksars have been in evidence in this Province for more than a year with branches in many districts with headquarters in Bahraich. They were at first believed to be a body of volunteers for social and religious service. But their military uniform, their marching through the cities in formation carrying a spade soon attracted notice. There were reports from time to time of their growing numbers and influence, but they do not seem to have come in conflict with the authorities or to threaten law and order in any place.

3. The first menace to law and order came in connection with the Shia-Sunni trouble in Lucknow. Inayatullah, the leader of the Khaksars, published in his official papers *Al Islah* of Lahore and *Khaksar* of Calcutta, an account alleging that the Government of the United Provinces was not dealing adequately with the situation and that unless the trouble was ended soon, they would intervene to end it. It was written in both the papers that there are certain leaders among the Shias and among the Sunnis who were responsible for keeping the dispute alive and according to the tenets of the Quran it would be justifiable to have them assassinated. He said that there were three Shia and three Sunni leaders who were mainly responsible and whom he warned. He fixed a date by which the dispute was to be ended, otherwise he would come down in large numbers to Lucknow.

4. On 7th August 1939 Inayatullah sent a telegram to this Government, which reads as follows:

> "Orders 3,000 Khaksars issuing, forcible settlement Lucknow dispute. Ready co-operation Government, provided reasonable conditions acceptable Shias-Sunnis, offered. Please wire intentions."

Government considered it unnecessary to send a reply to a telegram worded as this. Inayatullah sent a reminder on the 9th and again on the 14th. In the latter he said "Khaksars bent on extirpating dispute any cost". But as it was couched in a more proper tone, Government sent a reply on 14th August 1939, in which they said they were anxious for an amicable settlement of the Shia-Sunni controversy, which end would have been achieved had the situation not been complicated by the introduction of the Punjabi element in the dispute. Government said that they would welcome cooperation from any quarter, provided that the methods adopted were peaceful and in accordance with law. Inayatullah was asked if the suggestion that force should be used and Shia and Sunni leaders murdered if necessary had been made in the paper *Al Islah* and if he was responsible for these statements. He sent no answer to this question. But in his paper *Al Islah*, dated 18th August 1939, he came out with a very violent tirade against the United Provinces Government in which after blaming the United Provinces Government for keeping the Shia-Sunni trouble alive, he threatens to destroy the United Provinces Ministry and to shatter it to pieces with the last drop of his blood and take violent action against the leaders of the Shias and the Sunnis. He goes not [?on] to declare the United Provinces Government the enemy of the Muslims and calls upon the Muslims to spend all their energy in fighting the Government which has sent to jail so many Shias. He went on to write that if by starting a fight with the United Provinces Government it would be possible to bring an understanding between Shias and Sunnis it would be a good bargain. He then gave to United Provinces Government time for the last time up to 27th August 1939. Meanwhile he had ordered a large number of Khaksars from the Punjab and a section from Sind called Janbaz (ready to lay down their life) to arrive in Lucknow. The latter were under the command of one Ghulas Mustafa Burguri. The Deputy Commissioner of Lucknow[39] had ordered that spades were not to be carried by the Khaksars and he had also forbidden the proposal to fire 101 crackers in honour of the leader of the Janbaz party. The local leader, Wahid-uddin Haider, obeyed these orders of the Deputy Commissioner and Inayatullah had him publicly flogged for obeying the Deputy Commissioner's orders. This was a direct challenge to the authority of the Government and its officers.

5. About the 25th August 1939 Inayatullah himself arrived in Lucknow and there were many clashes between his men and the local Muslims. He delivered extremely provocative speeches which are under examination. Ahrars raised cries of opposition at these meetings; Inayatullah ordered his men to beat them out.

Two Ahrar newspapers published articles against Inayatullah. The Khaksars beat the newsboy and went to the editor's house and threatened him.

The Khaksars went out enrolling more persons. They came into conflict with certain Muslims and wounded them with their spade; the blood-stained spade was taken in custody by the police.

Inayatullah issued to the press agencies the most offensive statements in which he said things like the following:

> "We do believe in violence. Non-violent people must be stamped out from the face of the world."
>
> "The ultimate aim of the Khaksar movement is to dominate over all spiritually as well as physically."

6. This kind of thing went on the 30th and the 31st. The Tabarra agitation which was the ostensible object of the visit of the Khaksars had ceased. Still Inayatullah did not remove himself and the Khaksars from Lucknow. He sent a list of his demands through the Deputy Commissioner to Government which included items such as these:

> Carrying of *belchas* to be allowed.
> Ahrar newspaper to be prevented from writing against the Khaksars.
> The newsboy to be prosecuted.
> The case under Section 324 against the Khaksars to be withdrawn.
> The Khaksars to be allowed to conduct a route march through the streets of the city.

He was in a most truculent mood. Government ordered his arrest on the morning of 1st September 1939. On 2nd September 1939 he sent messages that he would like to go back if he could be provided with a special train for himself and his Khaksars. Government refused this demand also. On 1st September 1939 the other Khaksars expressed a desire to leave Lucknow, but said that they were penniless. Government bought tickets for them, but at a pre-arranged bugle signal they got down just as the train was to leave and gave a great deal of trouble.

7. On 2nd September 1939 Inayatullah finally signed an undertaking to go back to his province and not to come to United Provinces for a year, nor to send any Khaksar *jathas* here. He was then released, but he gave much trouble. He pulled the communication chord at Malihabad and got down, and then got into another train bound for Lucknow. But on being informed that the police would arrest him, he got down again and went off to Sandila where he waited for another party of the Khaksars from Lucknow to join him. They all travelled without tickets to Delhi.

8. From Delhi Inayatullah started a campaign of abusive vilification of the Government, said that he never signed any undertaking and that it must have been forged by the Government.

9. A very large number of telegrams were sent on the 3rd, 4th and 5th by various persons in the Frontier Province, Punjab, Sind and Bombay, most of them threatening the Ministry and many saying that they were ready to march to United Provinces. The District Magistrates were accordingly warned to prohibit the Khaksars from marching in military formation or from carrying spades and to prohibit the entry of Khaksars from outside into their districts. The Khaksars in Bahraich have, according to the *Leader*, dated 14th September 1939, been holding demonstrations against these orders and have posted handbills saying that Inayatullah gave no undertaking and the Government version was incorrect.

10. On 13th September 1939 the C.I.D., Punjab informed the C.I.D., United Provinces that Inayatullah had started from Lahore for Lucknow with six other persons. Government ordered that if Inayatullah should enter the Lucknow District in violation of the existing orders under Section 144 he should be arrested. At Malihabad he was given the option of returning to his province; he declined to take it. His sole object was apparently to retrieve his lost position by showing to his followers that he had successfully disobeyed the order of the United Provinces Government. He was accordingly arrested and is now in jail pending trial.

11. It is obvious from the above recital that the quarrel has been not of the seeking of the United Provinces Government, but that of Inayatullah. It was he who started the trouble in the United Provinces by threatening to have the Shia and Sunni leaders assassinated. It was he who sent a large body of men from the Frontier and other places. Intercepted letters show that these men were providing themselves with daggers. His stay in Lucknow was prolonged after the ostensible reason for it. It led to clashes and breaches of the peace. He was only willing to depart after imposing humiliating demand which no Government could accept. He ultimately left undertaking not to worry us again, but finding that that lost his prestige

has come back. His sole object is apparently a trial of strength with the Government. The Khaksars have on more than one occasion declared that if there is a conflict between the orders of a Government officer and of a Khaksar officer, they will obey the latter. This is a challenge which no Government can afford to ignore.

ENCLOSURE 2 TO NO. 70

PRESS NOTE ISSUED BY U.P. GOVERNMENT

Khaksars and U.P. Government

The following press note has been issued by the Director of Publicity, United Provinces Government:

"Strenuous efforts are being made by interested persons to represent that the United Provinces Government has for some reason launched upon a campaign to crush the Khaksar movement, and indignation has been expressed in several quarters against this supposed policy of the United Provinces Government of singling out the Khaksar organisation for its attack. Nothing is further from the truth. On the contrary the Khaksars have selected the United Provinces Government as the target of their attack. Khaksar leaders from outside the province intervened with violent threats in the affairs of the province and a number of Khaksars invaded Lucknow and created conditions which threatened the peace of the city.

"It was only as a result of this unprovoked and unreasonable aggression by Khaksars from other provinces that the United Provinces Government took essential steps to maintain the peace of the province and their own authority. So long as this aggressive attitude persists the United Provinces Government will have no hesitation in dealing firmly with its manifestations, and they are determined not to allow the peace of the province to be disturbed by irruptions of Khaksars from outside. But it is not their desire or intention to place any restrictions on the activities of Khaksars belonging to the United Provinces save in such places where they are engaged in or are encouraging any breach of the law or are indulging in activities which threaten the public peace."

71

HAIG TO LINLITHGOW
Telegram
MSS.EUR.F 115/7

Immediate
No. 272-G

September 28th, 1939

Your telegram No. 2092-S, dated 27th September.[40] I am very grateful for information. With reference to para 5 general position stands as stated in para 2 of my letter U.P.-306, dated September 25th. Unfortunately Katju is now taking a hand and has been making trouble about the proposed instructions to District Magistrates there mentioned. Yesterday afternoon before leaving Lucknow I got him to agree to issue of instructions in a modified form but still from my point of view effective. Today I hear on telephone he has gone back on this agreement and has proposed further modification which I could not accept. I am informing him that if he cannot give effect to the agreement we reached yesterday I must press strongly for the original draft, and that if he cannot agree to either conclusion I propose that there should be a Cabinet meeting in Naini Tal tomorrow.

2. My general impression is that the situation has not in fact deteriorated in the last week. I have had no recent reports of increased activity by left wing, though undoubtedly a large number of very undesirable speeches are being made. It has been very fortunate that Bose has not visited the Province.

72

HAIG TO LINLITHGOW
Telegram
MSS.EUR.F 115/7

Immediate
No. 273-G

September 29th, 1939

Continuation my telegram 272-G, dated September 28th. I have seen Kidwai today and have settled with him an acceptable draft which will issue at once. I think this will have the effect of strengthening the hands of District Magistrates, and encouraging them.

2. I questioned Kidwai about the conversations in Lucknow yesterday between Mahadeo Desai,[41] Nehru and Abul Kalam Azad at which he was

present. He told me that Mahadeo Desai reported Gandhi as being very satisfied with his conversation with Your Excellency and definitely hopeful of a settlement. It appeared that they would be content with a declaration of a fairly vague character, and that Gandhi did not anticipate serious difficulty about arrangements for associating a committee representative of public opinion with war policy and activities. I gathered that the general trend of the discussion in Lucknow was strongly in favour of a settlement.

NOTES

1. Lord Linlithgow's letter of 10 June 1939 to Sir Harry Haig is on R/3/1/75.
2. Sir Sikander Hyat Khan was Premier of the Punjab at this date.
3. Lord Linlithgow minuted: 'P.S.V. – I shall be glad to have F[inance] M[ember]'s views as to the sufficiency of the conditions of control by District Officers suggested below.' Sir Jeremy Raisman was Finance Member of the Viceroy's Executive Council at this date.

   On 16 July 1939 Linlithgow wrote to Sir Harry Haig to say that the Government of India were prepared to accept the arrangements for the rural development grant which the Governor had suggested. R/3/1/75.
4. The possible grounds for the Viceroy refusing assent to the U.P. Employments Bill given in paragraph one of his telegram 1139-G of 24 May 1939 were: (1) that even if the tax were legally permissible it was a clear invasion of a sphere of taxation intended to be reserved for the Centre; (2) that they should say without further argument that the tax was a clear invasion of a sphere reserved for the Centre. Ibid.
5. In telegram 1361-G of 5 July 1939 Lord Linlithgow conveyed Lord Zetland's view that, because of congestion in the House of Commons, the introduction of any new and contentious amendments to the Government of India Act would reduce the chances of the amending Bill passing before Parliament was prorogued in the autumn. They must therefore regard that course of action as impracticable.

   In paragraph 3 of the telegram Linlithgow said that his Advisers preferred dealing with the problem by reference to the Federal Court. Zetland preferred the Viceroy invoking his special responsibilities. Linlithgow asked for Haig's views. Ibid.
6. Early in August 1939 Sir Harry Haig reserved the U.P. Employments Tax Bill for the Viceroy's consideration. In his letter of 6 September 1939 Lord Linlithgow informed Sir Harry Haig that Lord Zetland had agreed to add a clause to the forthcoming Bill in the British Parliament which was to amend the Government of India Act. The effect of the new clause would be to make the U.P. Employments Tax legislation ultra vires. The Viceroy intended to ask his acting P.S.V. to write to Mr Donaldson so that the U.P. Ministers would know the situation and the reason why the Viceroy was suspending

consideration of the Bill. This action was delayed (so as not to jeopardise the constitutional negotiations with the Congress High Command) and did not take place before the resignation of the U.P. Ministry. R/3/1/75.

7. Mr P.H.J. Measures was Deputy-Inspector General of Police, Allahabad Range at this date. The Range covered Cawnpore.

   Mr H.C. Mitchell was Superintendent of Police, Cawnpore at this date.

8. Lord Linlithgow minuted: 'P.S.V. – Please tell me what is a Kotwal.' [See Glossary.]
9. Sir George Cunningham was the Governor of the North-West Frontier Province at this date.
10. Sir Henry Craik was the Governor of the Punjab and Sir Sikander Hyat Khan was its Premier at this date.
11. Lord Linlithgow minuted: 'Should love to help him, but it is going to be very difficult.'
12. The Principal of Thomason Engineering College, Roorkee between 1932 and 1939 was Mr H.J. Amoore.
13. Mr J.C. Powell-Price was Director of Public Instruction, U.P. at this date.
14. Mr C.H. Cooke was District Magistrate, Meerut at this date.
15. Copies of the newspaper accounts of Pandit Pant's statements on police firing in Cawnpore and Lucknow are on L/P&J/5/268: ff. 221-5.
16. These extracts are ibid., ff. 226-9.
17. Lord Linlithgow minuted: 'Tell S./S.'
18. Mr N.C. Mehta was Labour Commissioner at this date.
19. Sir Clarmont Skrine was Resident of the Punjab States and Major Robert Burnett was Political Agent, Punjab Hill States at this date.
20. Mr R.F. Mudie was Revenue Secretary at this date.
21. See U.P.P., 1938, No. 77 and its notes.
22. Not included in R/3/1/75.
23. The reply to this letter has not been traced.
24. Paragraph 5 of the U.P. Chief Secretary's Report for the first half of August 1939 (dated 22 August) dealt at some length on the Khaksar situation along the lines of Enclosure 1 to No. 70. The paragraph contained the following passages:

    'The solution has not been rendered easier by the influx of a large number of militant Shias from the Punjab and the Frontier provinces, who are encouraging others and keeping the agitation alive.... The latest combatant to enter this unfortunate arena is Inayatullah Khan.... In his paper, *Al Islah*, he openly declared that the Khaksars would murder the Shia and Sunni leaders unless they came to terms by a certain date.... It is a pity that this paper is published in Lahore with the result that this Government are unable to exercise any control over it.' L/P&J/5/268: ff. 175-6.

25. This telegram was forwarded by Lord Linlithgow to Lord Zetland in telegram 1819-S of 4 September 1939. The text is taken from that telegram.

26. The second world war began on 3 September 1939. The same day (without consulting any political leader) Lord Linlithgow announced that India was at war with Germany. Telegram 1802-S of 3 September evidently asked Provincial Governors for information on the reactions of their Ministries and the public generally to the outbreak of war.
27. A copy of Sir Harry Haig's message is on L/P&J/5/268: f. 72.
28. In his telegram 1950-S of 16 September 1939 Lord Linlithgow asked the Governors of Provinces with Congress Ministries for information and reactions to the lengthy statement which the Congress Working Committee had issued following its meeting at Wardha on 14 September 1939. MSS.EUR.F 125/107.

    With regard to the war crisis in India the Congress Working Committee announced that it had taken no final decision on the matter at that stage. Congress could not 'associate themselves or offer any cooperation in a war which is conducted on imperialist lines and which is meant to consolidate imperialism in India or elsewhere.' The Committee invited the British Government 'to declare in unequivocal terms what their war aims are in regard to democracy and imperialism ... in particular, how these aims are going to apply to India and to be given effect to in the present.'
29. In telegram 2021-S of 22 September 1939 to Provincial Governors, Lord Linlithgow said that, in the event of a break with Congress, he thought it important for Governors to consult the opposition before going into Section 93. It would be of enormous publicity and propaganda value to retain one or two governments in Congress Provinces. In paragraph 3 of the telegram the Viceroy stressed the importance of parting with Congress Ministers on the friendliest terms. Abstention from interference in war activities would be no small contribution on their part. MSS.EUR.F 125/107.
30. In his telegram 2020-S of 22 September 1939, Lord Linlithgow told Provincial Governors that he understood the relevant sub-committee of Congress was to instruct Congress Ministers to move a resolution on the war situation in their Legislative Assemblies. The resolution was to the effect that the Assemblies could not cooperate in the war unless 'principles of democracy are applied to India and her policy is guided by her people'. The British Government was invited to make a clear declaration that they had decided to regard India as an independent nation.

    The Viceroy further reported that Mahatma Gandhi had made a statement that the proposed resolution might be held for a week if the Congress sub-committee agreed. The Viceroy understood that instructions to hold the resolution had been sent to the Provinces concerned.

    In a separate paragraph to Sir Harry Haig only (in answer to No. 64), Linlithgow suggested that the Governor held on and did his best to keep things on the right lines.

    Ibid.

31. Sir Roger Lumley was Governor of Bombay at this date.
32. In telegram 2033-S of 23 September 1939, Lord Linlithgow informed Provincial Governors that he had been considering with Lord Zetland the possibility of creating a broad-based advisory committee on the war. Linlithgow felt it should include representatives of Congress, Congress Nationalists, the Muslim League, Europeans, Anglo-Indians and the Princes.

    Linlithgow also felt there might be advantage in his presiding over a meeting at periodic intervals of the Provincial Premiers and (say) two representatives of the Princes. MSS.EUR.F 125/107.
33. In his telegram 2063-P (in fact dated 24 September) Lord Linlithgow thanked Sir Harry Haig for No. 66. The Viceroy felt it might be quite a good thing if Haig talked quietly and in general terms to his Ministers on the position under Section 93. The Governor might ask them about the possibility of a lasting neutrality on their part and intimate he would do what he could to avoid any abrupt reversal of their policy. He should give the impression that he had been reflecting on a Section 93 situation and was ready for it. Ibid.
34. Mr C. Rajagopalachariar and Mr B.G. Kher were the Premiers of Madras and Bombay respectively at this date.
35. Lord Linlithgow minuted: 'I am so very glad.'
36. Lord Linlithgow minuted: 'Does the G[overnor] think Pant will recover?'
37. Sir Henry Craik was Governor of the Punjab, Lieutenant-Colonel Sir Arthur Parsons was acting Governor of the North-West Frontier Province and Sir Lancelot Graham was Governor of Sind at this date.
38. Mr W. Christie was Finance Secretary, U.P. at this date.
39. Kunwar Jasbir Singh was Deputy Commissioner of Lucknow at this date.
40. In telegram 2092-S of 27 September 1939, Lord Linlithgow gave Provincial Governors an account of his meeting with Mahatma Gandhi on the evening of 26 September. The Viceroy found Gandhi very friendly and thought he was still very anxious to cooperate. But Linlithgow felt some doubt whether the left wing would not be too strong and he was not too optimistic of avoiding a break with Congress.

    Linlithgow did not think that the resolution (summarised in No. 67, note 30) would be pressed as Gandhi had advised him to see Pandit Nehru and Dr Rajendra Prasad which he was doing.

    In a separate paragraph sent only to Sir Harry Haig, Linlithgow said he had impressed strongly on Gandhi their anxieties about the U.P. situation. Gandhi had asked to be given an indication of particular difficulties. Linlithgow was consulting Sir John Ewart (D.I.B.) and asked Haig to let him (Linlithgow) have urgently any point he might have. MSS.EUR.F 125/107.
41. Mr Mahadev Desai was Private Secretary to Mahatma Gandhi at this date.

CHAPTER 4

Documents for 1 October – 31 December 1939

73

HAIG TO LINLITHGOW
R/3/1/75

Secret
No. U.P.-309

October 5th, 1939

My dear Lord Linlithgow,

I was very glad to receive yesterday Your Excellency's letter, dated 2nd October 1939, dealing with the methods by which we can take advantage of the offers of help in connection with the war, and referring in particular to the question of recruitment in the United Provinces. The latter point is so important, and it is so essential in my opinion that the true position should be understood, that I am writing to Your Excellency about it at once without waiting for the report by the Commander-in-Chief which you said you were enclosing, but which is perhaps coming under separate cover. As I shall explain below, I think I am acquainted with the general points that the Commander-in-Chief's report is likely to cover.

2. The day after I arrived at Naini Tal I had a long talk with Brigadier Wakely of the Eastern Command staff who had been asked to see me by the Army Commander[1] who was himself away on tour. Wakely gave me a considerable amount of information in regard to anti-recruiting activities and their effects which had not previously reached me. I was aware that there had been a large number of anti-recruiting speeches, but I had received no information that they were having any practical effect. Moreover, I was not aware that any special recruiting activities, such as the recruitment of two garrison companies, were being pursued in the United Provinces, or that there was as yet any proposal for increasing the number of territorial

battalions in the United Provinces. As soon as I understood the facts I took the matter up at once with the acting Premier, Mr. Kidwai, and I attach a copy of a note which I sent to him on the 2nd October. You will see that I put quite plainly to Mr. Kidwai the probable effects on the policy of the Defence Department of any difficulty in obtaining recruits at the present moment and the importance of stopping these anti-recruitment activities. Two days later, on the 4th October, on getting copies of the reports from Wakely I sent a further note (this was before I had received Your Excellency's letter) in which I suggested that definite action in the way of a serious warning should be taken with those who were reported to be impeding recruitment in the Meerut and Etawah districts.

3. This action of course comes very short of what I should do if my hands were not tied by the present political situation. I should like to explain to Your Excellency my judgement of the existing position. Ever since the war broke out, I have felt myself, as you know, acutely embarrassed by the uncertainty as to whether Congress would or would not cooperate. Once a decision is taken on this point (provided it is not delayed too long) I have felt reasonably confident that the situation could be brought under control fairly quickly. If the Congress decide not to cooperate I would have a free hand and there would be no difficulty in my taking whatever steps are necessary. If the Congress decide to cooperate, I am persuaded from many conversations with my Ministers that the Ministry would be prepared to take all reasonable steps to put a stop to anti-recruitment activities and anti-war activities of every kind. But while the question of whether the Congress will or will not cooperate is hanging in the balance, it is exceedingly difficult to get anything effective done. It is very hard for the Ministry, when they are not sure whether they are to support the war or not, to use the Defence of India Ordinance for the purpose of suppressing the activities of those who belong to the same organisation as themselves. It can of course be argued that so long as they remain responsible for the administration of the Province they are bound to take such steps as are essential both for maintaining order and for giving effect to the policy of the Central Government in such a crucial matter as preparations for war. Those considerations I shall if necessary press definitely upon my Ministers now that I know that this matter of anti-recruitment has become an important practical issue in the Province. Hitherto, however, I have been reluctant to press the Ministers strongly in this matter, partly because I was not aware that these activities were having any practical results, and partly because I have continually been expecting that the main decision as to Congress cooperation will be taken within a very short time. Even

when I wrote my note of the 2nd October to Mr. Kidwai I was under the impression that the decision could not be delayed beyond the 7th October. Now, however, from Your Excellency's telegram No. 2162-S, dated October 4th,[2] it would seem that the decision may still be postponed for a considerable time. This creates a new situation.

4. I hope you will understand from this that no one is more anxious than myself to take what the Commander-in-Chief describes as early and drastic action for the suppression of anti-recruiting propaganda and activities, and that what ties my hands is the delay (which I fully recognise to be inevitable) in reaching a definite decision about Congress cooperation. Once that decision is taken one way or the other, I have no doubt that this anti-recruiting business could be stopped in a very short time. It only needs clear instructions to District Magistrates to use the powers under the Defence of India Ordinance vigorously and a comparatively few prosecutions as a result, and I think we shall hear practically no more of it. But what I should like to impress on Your Excellency and the Commander-in-Chief, is that in my judgement the real feeling of the Province is very definitely in favour of helping in the war and that there should be no difficulty at all in obtaining an ample supply of recruits. If we can once give a lead, make it clear that we need recruits, and not stand inactive and silent as we have to do at present, leaving the field to our opponents, I believe the response would be very great. To give the other side of the picture in contrast to the report of the Recruiting Officer, Delhi I enclose an extract from a letter from the Collector of Aligarh, dated September 28th, which reached me a few days ago. I believe that is a fair indication of the real feeling in the Province.

5. Another point which I should like to make clear is the attitude of my Ministers. I think from what you say in your letter that you are under the impression that my Ministers have little zeal for military service and in fact would themselves, apart from the present situation of suspended judgement, not desire to do anything to help recruitment. My own belief, however, judging by various conversations I have had with the Ministers individually, is that once a decision for cooperation is taken they would be most anxious to encourage recruitment in the United Provinces, and as I say I anticipate no real trouble with my Ministers in dealing with anti-recruitment activities once a decision is taken. Therefore I do not think that the present difficulty really lies with my Ministers but with this indeterminate position in which we all stand at the moment.

6. I do therefore feel very strongly that it would be exceedingly unfair to the Province to penalise it for a purely temporary inability to deal

effectively with anti-recruiting propaganda, an inability for which provincial conditions are really not responsible. Moreover, I believe you will appreciate and sympathise with a view which I hold very strongly, that it would be a grave political blunder to reject the support which the Province as a whole is anxious to give. Our supporters who are very numerous would be bewildered by such a policy, and I do not know how I could explain it to them.

Yours sincerely,
H.G. HAIG

ENCLOSURE 1 TO NO. 73

HAIG TO KIDWAI

October 2nd, 1939

I have had a long talk today on the subject of recruiting for the Indian Army with Brigadier Wakely who is speaking on behalf of the Army Commander who is temporarily absent at Peshawar. I had assumed from the reports that have reached us hitherto that though there have been a very large number of anti-recruiting speeches, they were having little practical effect. It seems clear, however, from certain reports which Brigadier Wakely has shown me and which I will forward to H.M.R. as soon as I have received copies, that in fact these activities are having a very marked effect in decreasing the number of recruits offering themselves in the United Provinces. This result I know is contrary to the policy of the Ministry during the present period of uncertainty.

2. Apart from this practical interference with the normal recruiting activities of the Army in the United Provinces it is clear from my conversation with Brigadier Wakely that this movement to discourage recruiting, which in my view obviously does not represent the real feeling of the majority of the people, is at the moment peculiarly inopportune with reference to the interests of the Province. I have already communicated to His Excellency the Governor-General my view that it is very desirable that new opportunities for recruiting men for the Army should be granted in the United Provinces and that, if possible, certain new units should be formed for the United Provinces. This question I have reason to believe is under consideration, and I think it likely that we may have some additional units for the United Provinces, if it is clear that there will be a good response in the matter of recruiting. A falling off in normal recruiting at the present

moment may well lead the Army authorities to doubt whether they could depend on recruits from the United Provinces and might induce them to recruit from other parts of India units which otherwise might be recruited in the United Provinces.

3. Quite apart from any question of new units referred to above, the Defence Department are endeavouring as part of their normal war scheme to recruit two garrison companies in the United Provinces from retired soldiers; one is to be recruited in Garhwal, the other with Lucknow as its Centre. Brigadier Wakely tells me that the response to the call for recruits for these garrison companies has so far been most disappointing. He thinks that the delay in recruits coming forward in Garhwal may well be due to the difficulties of communication and the great distances, and he does not think there is likely to be any real difficulty about getting the men required from there. He says that from Lucknow the response has been practically nil, and unless conditions can be changed quickly it is likely that the Defence Department will decide to recruit this garrison company from some other part of India.

4. I should be glad if you would consider this position with your colleagues and let me know what action you propose might be taken.

H.G.H.

ENCLOSURE 2 TO NO. 73

HAIG TO PANNA LAL

October 4th, 1939

Chief Secretary.

I attach herewith two reports about anti-recruiting activities received from Brigadier Wakely which I mentioned in my note to H.M.R.

2. With regard to the report of the Recruiting Officer, Delhi, I suggest that the District Magistrate, Meerut, be furnished with a copy of this report at once and asked to enquire into these allegations; and if he is satisfied that they are correct, he should administer a very serious warning to those responsible, that they render themselves liable to punishment under the Defence of India Ordinance.

3. I suggest that the report about anti-recruiting activities in Etawah should also be forwarded to the District Magistrate of Etawah and that he

should be directed to ascertain whether anti-recruiting activities are going on; and if so, to administer a similar warning to those primarily responsible.

H.G. HAIG

REPORT 1

HOGGE TO ARMY HEADQUARTERS, MEERUT DISTRICT

No. Z/2/66

Recruiting Office, Delhi,
25th September, 1939

Subject: Intelligence – Anti-Recruiting Propaganda

I have to report the following cases of Congress anti-recruitment propaganda which came to my notice during the course of a recruiting tour carried out on 22nd September 1939 at village Muradnagar, tahsil Ghaziabad, Mawana, tahsil Mawana, both district Meerut, and Manglaur, tahsil Roorkee, district Saharanpur.

1. At Muradnagar, the attendance was about 30 strong whereas on previous occasions as many as 300 men have turned up for enlistment in the Army. Six weeks ago at Begamabad only six miles away I had large crowds turn up, and had to get in Police to cope with them.

I was not able to get into touch with the Tahsildar or Thanedar of the tahsil so could get no confirmation of the report made by my Paid Recruiter that he had come across many cases of intimidation, i.e. men who were frightened by Congress agents who persuaded them not to turn up before me for enlistment in the Army. Though I could not get any confirmation I am convinced that the statements of the Paid Recruiter are correct in view of my subsequent experience at the two other places.

2. At Mawana the Tahsildar of Mawana, Mushtaq Ahmed Khan, informed me that an individual called Vishnu Shiam Dublish, a small zemindar and cloth merchant, former President of the Meerut district Congress Committee had been very active in carrying out anti-recruitment propaganda. A big meeting, at which over 600 people were said to have been present, was held at Kheri Manyar, five miles away on the 1st and 2nd September at which an individual named Sher Jang was in the Chair, and violent anti-recruitment speeches were made by Vishnu Shiam Dublish and five other speakers. I understand that the Tahsildar had made an official report to his superiors on the above.

From the time of the arrival of our Paid Recruiters and the Paid Recruiters of the Hong Kong and Singapore Artillery in the area advertising our tour, there had been general propaganda against recruitment throughout the tahsil. Paid Recruiters met with obstruction in the following villages:

Pamarpur.

Kheri Manyar.

Bhainsa.

Mubarikpur.

Kaul.

One Paid Recruiter was threatened with violence in Pamarpur and Bhainsa unless he wore a dhoti as opposed to pyjamas.

Another meeting was alleged to have been held in Gesupur in which similar anti-recruitment speeches were made.

3. At Manglaur I had a long talk with Bachan Lall Misra, Tahsildar, and Kishan Singh, Station Officer or Thanedar, about the dearth of recruits, and was informed that very strong anti-recruitment propaganda was being carried out. I also received the same information from two of my Honorary Assistant Recruiting Officers.

An individual named Rameshwar Parshad, village Literheri, tahsil Roorkee, district Saharanpur, alleged to be a paid Congress agent drawing a salary of Rs. 50 per mensem, had made a point of going together with five other men to every village where my Paid Recruiter had been, and persuaded everyone whom my man had chosen as *umed-war* recruits not to turn up. Further a couple of hours before my arrival at Manglaur Rameshwar Parshad had turned up and tried to persuade men not to wait for my arrival nor to enlist in the Army.

Both the Tahsildar and the Station Officer, Mawana, informed me that they had made official reports of the activities of Rameshwar Parshad.

Rao Shafqat Ali Khan, village Salrandee, P.O. Sakranda, district Saharanpur handed me a copy of a pamphlet printed in Urdu and Hindi and published by Shanti Printing Press at Saharanpur which he stated was being freely distributed in all villages. (I was able to obtain one other copy from an individual anxious to get a commission in the Army in India Reserve of Officers.) This pamphlet contains very strong anti-recruitment propaganda. The Tahsildar and Station Officer informed me that this pamphlet had been circulating for the last two or three months, and admitted that its distribution had increased recently, i.e. when the news became known that the Recruiting Officer, Delhi, was coming to collect recruits.

At the request of the Tahsildar and Station Officer at Manglaur, I am proposing to pay another visit to Manglaur on the 9th October 1939, where they have promised to produce recruits for my inspection. They state that they will be able to curtail the activities of Rameshwar Parshad. I am hoping they will be successful, but I am rather doubtful. It is requested that some action may be taken to restrict the activities of such individuals, and to put an end to this anti-recruitment propaganda which is having, and will have, a serious effect on recruiting.

A.H.F. HOGGE
Lieut.-Colonel
Recruiting Officer, Delhi

REPORT 2

CHAUDHRI[3] TO ASSISTANT RECRUITING OFFICER, LUCKNOW

Confidential — Etawah,
No. 418/S.B. — *21st September, 1939*

With reference to your telegram No. 3210, dated 9th September 1939 I may submit that the lists concerned are sent herewith although the number is hopelessly less which is due to two main factors. One is the intensive propaganda of the Congressmen of the district against recruiting or any help to the Government in the matters of war emergency. They are holding day-to-day meetings in the Centres, fairs and other important towns and in the city as well and passed resolutions to that effect. I have personally attended their meetings and have heard them say so. Their leaders say that by the time the local Government orders their arrest which will not be so soon, they will have the mischief done and which will have far-reaching consequences. I cannot say exactly what will be the ultimate end of this all but this much I can say that it has affected our recruitment work at present, for territorials I used to send about 50 men and for a selection there used to be a huge gathering of three to four hundred but this time I could send only about 20 and about 60 or 70 gathered. Besides that this present list is much less as there are many ex-army men here. I am trying to combat the propaganda by going to villages whenever I get time.

Now I have moved all the members of the Board that they should co-operate and send the names of ex-army men who wish to join the Garrison Companies.

Besides this there are other factors also which are working against our interest.

Let us know what steps we are to take in this matter. I had already reported to President about such propaganda.

I have, etc.,
K.K. CHAUDHRI
Lt. Secretary

ENCLOSURE 3 TO NO. 73

EXTRACT FROM LETTER OF NAQVI[4]

September 28th, 1939

Since the outbreak of the war I have received numerous offers of help from the residents of this district. Most of the zamindars, both big and small, have personally called on me and expressed their readiness to help in whatever manner their help is required, while some have also written to me expressing their readiness to help with men and money. I have of course accepted all their offers with gratitude, and have told them that as soon as an opportunity offers itself, I shall request them to render their help. Prominent among those who have written to me are the Nawab Sahib of Chhatari, Kunwar Sultan Singh of Lakhnau, Rao Sahib Sheodhyan Singh of Pisawah, Kunwar Rohini Raman Dhwaj Prasad Singh of Beswan and several others. I was agreeably surprised to receive two letters from Thakur Todar Singh, M.L.A., who, as you know, is a Congressman. In these letters he expressed his readiness to offer his personal services and also to supply recruits. He came to see me yesterday and repeated his offer, and he also said that he would be able to raise a large number of recruits if and when they are required. He asked me why I had not started a recruiting campaign as yet and I told him that when the time comes for recruitment I shall be extremely glad to receive his help. He went on to say that even if the Congress decided not to help Britain, he would render all possible help in his personal and private capacity as many Congressmen had helped the Arya Samajists in the Hyderabad Satyagraha. As you know, Thakur Todar Singh himself went on active service during the last war and also raised over one hundred recruits for field service. Todar Singh's offer gives an indication of the extent to which the people generally are ready to give all possible help.

You will be glad to know that the University as a whole has expressed its readiness to render all possible help. I am sure you have seen the speeches delivered by the Vice-Chancellor and the Pro-Vice-Chancellor recently. I had a talk with Sir Shah Sulaiman, the present Vice-Chancellor, and he told me in confidence that, although as a Judge of the Federal Court it was not possible for him to make any controversial statement, yet he was absolutely certain that the University as a whole was thoroughly loyal and would lend such support as may be required of it. Individual members of the staff have also approached me with offers of help. Captain Haidar Khan, who is the Officer Commanding the U.T.C. in the University, has already written to the Defence Secretary to the Government of India offering his services.

74

HAIG TO LINLITHGOW
R/3/1/75

Secret *October 8th, 1939*
No. U.P.-312

My dear Lord Linlithgow,

I am very grateful for your letter of 2nd October and for your good wishes about my health. I have been in Naini Tal for just over a week, but the weather has not been propitious or seasonable and I find that it is a slow business getting back to quite normal conditions. However, that seems to be the universal experience after this disease. The civil surgeon is anxious that I should stop up here till about the 21st, and I hope to do this unless circumstances call me urgently to Lucknow. You will see from what follows that we have plenty of difficult problems on hand at the moment, but at present I feel that I can keep sufficiently in touch with them by telephone.

2. The Ministers have all returned to Lucknow, where a short meeting of the Assembly was held from the 3rd to 6th October, principally for the purpose of finishing off the Tenancy Bill. The Speaker seized the opportunity to deliver a highly controversial speech about India having been brought into the war without its consent, and about the recent amendment of the Government of India Act having taken away the powers of Provincial Governments. I attach a copy of the speech. Action of this kind makes it difficult to maintain any pretence of impartiality on the part of the Speaker, and I think in the long run will not do him much good. It is to be remembered, however, that before the Congress took office he was the rival of Pant for the post of Premier, and perhaps he has some idea of

reasserting this claim in the future. His health, however, has been very unsatisfactory lately.

3. Pant has remained up here. The civil surgeon tells me that the doctors are still not agreed whether his symptoms indicate tuberculosis or not. The Bombay doctors thought so, but the Lucknow doctors considered there was not sufficient evidence, and this was also the view of the Naini Tal doctors. But I understand that the two doctors who have been in charge of the Bhowali Sanatorium are now rather inclined to believe that it is tuberculosis. The civil surgeon still suspends judgement. I understand that in any case Pant will have to remain almost completely aloof from the details of administration for the next two months. If tuberculosis is finally diagnosed, the civil surgeon tells me that he would have to rest and undergo treatment for six to eight months, which would clearly mean his resignation. I am myself inclined to think that he will not come back to work.

4. I am not yet able to anticipate who might take his place in that event. Kidwai has been functioning as unofficial Premier in a very practical way and I have been well satisfied with his attitude whenever I have discussed problems of difficulty with him. There is the very great advantage that he comes to a conclusion quickly and sticks to it. This is certainly in marked contrast to Pant. He has a great deal of influence in the Party. On the other hand I think there might be a good deal of opposition to a Muslim Premier. Katju would not be a possible choice, as he is not well enough liked by the Party. If any one other than Kidwai has to succeed Pant it would be some one who is not at present in the Ministry.

5. I think it is likely that before long in any case the Ministry will have to be reconstituted. I was talking to Kidwai on the subject only last week. He said that the Ministers were beginning to feel that they needed help and that two or three additional Ministers ought to be appointed.[5] They also felt that if the Ministry were to be expanded it was important to bring in a representative of the Depressed Classes, which is certainly in my opinion desirable. I said that I had always felt that a Ministry of six was not sufficient for the work of this Province, and that I quite agreed that the numbers ought to be increased. But I said that I had hoped that when any question of increasing the number of Ministers arose the opportunity would be taken to effect a coalition with the Muslim League and perhaps bring in two of their representatives. I was rather interested to see how Kidwai as a Congress Muslim would take this suggestion. He took it in fact very well and said that they had often considered the possibility of bringing in Khaliq-uz-Zaman and Muhammad Ismail Khan, the two chief representatives of the Muslim League, and that they thought that they

would fit quite well into the Ministry. He declared that the difficulty was not provincial conditions, but the opposition of Jinnah who was not prepared to allow Muslim Leaguers to take office in Congress provinces unless it were done on an all-India basis. You may remember that when I saw Jawaharlal Nehru and made a similar suggestion to him, he gave me to understand that there would be no particular difficulty in this Province, but that it was a question that had to be handled from the point of view of India as a whole. Recent newspaper telegrams from Delhi suggest that perhaps we are now approaching the point at which this question of coalition between the Congress and the Muslim League in the provinces will be taken up in a practical way. I sincerely hope that it may be, for I am convinced that we shall have no prospect of communal peace until this is done.

6. The official fortnightly report which I enclose is more informative than usual, and what is said about law and order, Khaksars and communal feeling is a fair statement of the position. With regard to law and order I mentioned in some of my recent telegrams that I had got the Ministers to agree to my proposal about giving District Magistrates a freer hand to proceed under Section 108, Criminal Procedure Code. I enclose a copy of the letter which was issued. As I mentioned, Katju had made difficulty about paragraph 4, which was really the crucial passage, and wished to substitute something which I could not accept. But I saw Kidwai when I came up to the hills, and in half an hour we settled the matter to my satisfaction. I hope this letter will lead to more vigorous action by District Magistrates. The Government are also considering, I hope in a more practical way, a number of proposals for prosecution of dangerous individuals under Section 153-A, or 124-A, Indian Penal Code. I think there is no doubt that the attitude of the Ministers is much sounder on these matters than it was before the war broke out. Partly this may be due to the absence of Pant. One recent case was decidedly encouraging. I had repeatedly pressed Pant to take action against the *Kirti Lehar*, the Sikh revolutionary paper which had transferred itself from the Punjab to Meerut. Recently the Commissioner[6] sent up a very bad passage from this paper, with the recommendation that a security of Rs. 2,000 should be demanded. This went to Katju, and without any necessity for me to say a word he agreed to security being demanded. This is a matter of some little importance in itself, and more so I think as indicating a change of attitude on the part of the Ministers. With regard to anti-recruitment activities I have addressed Your Excellency separately at some length. I think it is very probable that Gandhi has given some instructions which have had

their effect on the Ministry, and I am very grateful to Your Excellency for taking up with him these questions of law and order in the United Provinces.

7. The Khaksars have been giving a great deal of trouble during the last fortnight. Their activities in Lucknow have not been on a large scale, though they have more than once shown considerable violence in resisting arrest by the police. But the Lucknow situation is now not giving rise to anxiety. A band of two to three hundred Khaksars, however, about a fortnight ago marched into the Muzaffarnagar district. The authorities had no previous information and the local police that could be gathered at the moment were not in sufficient force to tackle them. Arrangements were made for coordinating police forces in the Meerut division and a sufficient body was collected supported by troops. The local authorities were very apprehensive that these Khaksars, who were in a truculent mood and appeared well organised on military lines, could not be arrested without considerable casualties, and they were quite rightly anxious to avoid this. They therefore entered into conversations with the Khaksars, which in fact prolonged themselves unduly and I think encouraged the Khaksars to feel that the authorities were reluctant to tackle them. However, after a good deal of delay this body of Khaksars which had in the meantime been reinforced and I think numbered about 350, were arrested a day or two ago without resistance. So all is well that ends well. In the meantime, however, other bands of Khaksars had been invading or attempting to invade the Meerut division and it was high time that the Muzaffarnagar contingent was dealt with. A body which attempted to enter the United Provinces from Delhi was stopped on the Hindan bridge, and has dispersed and returned to Delhi. Another body of 500 marched into the province in the direction of Bulandshahr. I have just heard that this split up into two parts; 200 of them seem to have been arrested without difficulty and I hope the remaining 300 will also be secured before long. In these operations we have had the greatest assistance from the military authorities. It is very fortunate that these arrests have been made without firing or casualties, for as the moment [movement] has developed there have been clear signs that Muslim opinion is tending to take up the cause of the Khaksars on communal lines. An adjournment motion was moved in the Assembly by a Muslim Leaguer and there were threats that the Muslim League might support the cause of the Khaksars before long. This is simply political opportunism, the utilisation of a convenient weapon for attacking the Ministry. I have also heard from Craik, with whom I have been keeping in touch, that the Punjab Muslim press have been expressing sympathy with the Khaksars, though the Government have been doing their best to

discourage this, and Sir Sikander Hyat Khan has strongly advised the Khaksars to abandon this movement against the United Provinces. Conversations of some kind are still proceeding at Lucknow, and it is not unlikely that there may be a settlement within the next few days. In the meantime I heard today from the Chief Secretary over the telephone that the Ministers were rather perturbed owing to a telegram from Delhi appearing in the *Pioneer* which suggested that the Government of India looked certainly without disfavour on the Khaksars and were proposing that their military spirit should be utilised by enlisting them as a contingent in the Territorial Force. I told the Chief Secretary to assure the Ministers that I was confident that the Government of India would do nothing whatever to encourage the Khaksars.

8. In addition to the Khaksar trouble in the Meerut division, there has been a serious outbreak of rioting in Meerut city itself. This does not seem to have had any direct connection with the Khaksars, the riot breaking out in the course of a Hindu Mahasabha procession organised in connection with a bye-election that is proceeding. Still the Khaksar proceedings have undoubtedly increased communal tension, and the Muslims were clearly the aggressors in this riot. The position seems to be well in hand now, but it has been a considerable additional embarrassment and has emphasised the necessity of mopping up the Khaksars promptly.

9. The threatened strike at Cawnpore broke out last Monday. I had had some long conversations about the position with Sir J.P. Srivastava, some of the Employers' Association, and my own Ministers shortly before I left Lucknow. The position briefly was that as a result of an unjustified strike by the men of the New Victoria Mills some months ago the mills were closed. Recently the management proposed to reopen. They have, ever since the increase of wages granted as a result of the strike in 1938, maintained that they were unable to run the mills on the new rate of wages which, they say, is higher than is paid in any other mills in Cawnpore. They therefore reduced the wages to what they contend is the general level now paid in Cawnpore, and opened the mills on those terms. They soon secured the necessary labour, partly from their old workers and partly from new men. The Mazdur Sabha said that they could not agree to mill-owners in this way practically fixing their own rate of wages without any inquiry, and also complained that the old workers were not being given a proper opportunity of re-employment. On the latter point it seems that the mills were giving preference to the old workers when they applied for re-employment, but that as many of them were holding back owing to the reduced terms they were now recruiting a large number of new men

who were content to take the wage offered. When I saw Sir J.P. Srivastava I found that the Employers' Association were inclined to take a very stiff attitude on the legal rights of the mills and they declined to agree to any arbitration, urging that the employees of the mills were perfectly satisfied and that the other party to the arbitration was only the Mazdur Sabha, which they contended was not in any way representative of the general body of workers in Cawnpore. They were under the impression moreover that if the Mazdur Sabha declared a strike the workers would not follow them, and they were anxious to deal the Mazdur Sabha what they hoped would be a fatal blow. I put it to Srivastava that it was not sufficient that their case for lowering wages should be a good one (if it was so in fact) but it was also necessary that the public generally should believe that it was a good one, and that I thought it would be a great pity if they spoiled a good case by refusing to submit it to impartial judgement. Finally I was left with the impression that the employers probably would agree to arbitration on the point whether the new wages at the Victoria Mills were on a level with the average wages paid in the Cawnpore Mills and also about the opportunities given for re-employment of the old workers of the mills, but that they objected to the arbitration being entrusted to the Labour Commissioner who was an officer under the Government. They claimed that it should be done by a High Court Judge. I then discussed the matter with Katju and Kidwai and suggested that the best solution would be that there should be arbitration on these points by a High Court Judge. Katju objected to the High Court Judge and was inclined to stick out for the Labour Commissioner; but I said I could see no justification for preferring the Labour Commissioner to a High Court Judge. When I left Lucknow the matter was still hanging in the balance; but a day or two afterwards the Employers' Association agreed to submit to arbitration by a High Court Judge and the Ministry were quite prepared to accept this. At this stage the Mazdur Sabha ran out, having previously agreed to accept arbitration, and said that they could not agree unless in the meantime all the old workers of the Victoria Mills were reinstated. They were, I understand, very unwilling that the case should be put before a High Court Judge. They called a general strike, and contrary to the expectations of the Employers' Association, which are generally wrong on this point, the workers in most of the mills came out. It was rather amusing, however, to find that the workers in the New Victoria Mills, regarding whose conditions the strike was being called, have remained at work. The Ministers were upset at the strike being declared. They had used all the influence they had against it, and when the employers had been got to agree to a reasonable settlement they were very displeased with the Mazdur Sabha for rejecting it. Katju has been over in Cawnpore, and I have heard today by telephone that it is hoped that the strike may be called off within a few days, on the understanding that the New Victoria Mills will find places for about 1,000 of their old workers who had not been re-engaged (a thing which Srivastava had told me in Lucknow, he thought he could manage without much difficulty), leaving out 250 whom the management had always said they would on no account re-employ and with the understanding that when the strike was called off the points in dispute as explained above would be submitted to the arbitration of a High Court Judge. I hope, therefore, that the wheels of industry may be restarted in Cawnpore before long. The Chief Secretary reports to me on the telephone that Katju is now fully persuaded that the Government must take a much firmer line with the Mazdur Sabha than they have in the past, and that he is prepared really to set to work to get some proper organisation of labour in Cawnpore, a course of action which I had vainly pressed on the Ministers nearly two years ago. The Ministers are I think determined that so far as may be within their power there must be an end to these constant interruptions of work in Cawnpore, and that production for war purposes must not be impeded. If this spirit continues, I think we may at last see some possibility of peace in Cawnpore industry. There will still of course remain the sinister influence of Balkrishna Sharma, who is both the head of the local Congress committee and a supporter of the Mazdur Sabha even when its activities are directly contrary to Congress policy. But if the Ministers are in earnest difficulties of this sort can be overcome.

10. I have given above a fairly detailed account of our provincial difficulties, which, though they have needed a great deal of attention, are I think steadily being worked out. Far more important than any of these local matters are the conversations which are progressing at Delhi between Your Excellency and representatives of the various interests and parties with a view to a united effort on the part of India in support of the war. I am grateful to you for keeping me in touch with developments. I very sincerely trust that these efforts will be successful. I am hopeful that if we can really obtain the genuine support of practically all parties in India it should be possible to plan our war effort on a more comprehensive scale than present conditions permit, and that we shall be able to pursue a more active policy towards the war. It would be worth a great deal to have a united country behind us in support of the war.[7]

Yours sincerely,
H.G. HAIG

P.S. – I have just heard in connection with the Bulandshahr Khaksars that it was necessary to fire and that five Khaksars were killed. I have had no details.

ENCLOSURE 1 TO NO. 74

STATEMENT BY TANDON IN U.P. LEGISLATIVE ASSEMBLY ON OCTOBER 3RD, 1939

The Hon'ble the Speaker: There is another important matter to which I have now to make a reference. Since the House met last, very important events have occurred in the world and they have had their effect on the constitution under which we function. Britain is at war with another European power and, our country not having yet an independent constitution and a controlling voice in shaping its own destiny, it is assumed that we are also at war with that power. Without this House or the people's representatives in the Central Assembly having had any say in the matter, we find ourselves subjected to war conditions which we may or may not approve. A far-reaching consequence of the war, so far as this House is concerned, is the violent change introduced by the British Parliament in the Government of India Act by which practically all your powers for governing this province have been taken away and placed in the hands of the Central Executive. Under the provisions recently enacted, the Central Government is authorised to make laws on subjects which were exclusively within your jurisdiction and also to exercise full executive authority in all matters relating to the province – either through officials acting directly under their control or by issuing instructions to our Provincial Executive. That is a matter which, I say, concerns you very deeply.

At the time these provisions were being passed by the House of Commons it was said on behalf of the British Government that these provisions placed the Central Government in India in the same position as the British Government had been placed by the Emergency Powers Act. That analogy rests on the fact that the Emergency Powers Act gives the British Executive large and exceptional powers to override all existing laws and take measures which may be necessary or which may be expedient for securing public safety and carrying on the war efficiently. But fundamentally there is such a wide gulf between the constitution of the British Executive and that of the Central Government of India that the analogy, though it may superficially appear to be applicable, is, even in times of war, valueless. The British Executive, as you all know, consists of elected representatives of the British people and is responsible to them. The Central Executive of India is a body in the shaping of which the Indian people have no hand and which is not responsible to them. In Britain there is one Parliament and there are no Provincial Assemblies with partial powers of control distinct from and excluding the powers of the Central Legislature and the Central Executive. Here in India the Central Legislature has no controlling powers; the Executive, uncontrolled by any democratic institution, governs the country. The Provincial Legislatures were, under the Government of India Act, given partial powers to govern their provinces through elected representatives. And now, under the new provisions, these partial powers also have been withdrawn and are absorbed by the Central Executive in the name of war and the people of India are left to be governed even in small matters by an executive which has nothing in common with them. Surely it is misleading, to say the least, to compare the Emergency Powers Act of Britain with the new provisions of the Government of India Act.

Another important constitutional difference is that while these exceptional powers have been given to the British Executive by an Emergency Act, which by its very nature is temporary and short-lived, the new wide powers in our country have been taken by amending the very constitution which brings the Provincial Assemblies into existence. It may be said that these new provisions can be removed after the war emergency is over, that another Amending Bill can be moved in the British Legislature with that object. But the difference in the methods in which exceptional powers have been taken in Britain and in India cannot escape the attention of a constitutional jurist. It brings into prominence the fact of the very subordinate position which the liberties of the Indian people occupy in the counsels of Britain and the ease and facility with which those liberties can be touched and frustrated, while, whenever there is a question of enlarging them, all imaginable difficulties and obstacles are put forward as grounds for not taking any forward move.

The war is a serious matter. Wars always are. Appeals have been made by high authorities both in Britain and in India for the cooperation of the Indian people. As a matter of fact, the Indian people have not declared that they are at war with any people in the world. The Indian Government, not responsible to the people, have been dragged into the war because of their position in relation to the British Government. But the appeals to the Indian people are based, and rightly so, on grounds of human liberty and democratic principles. At the same time it has been authoritatively said on behalf of the British Government that constitutional questions relating to India and the demands of the Indian people should not be pressed during the war; and even ethical principles have been pressed into service by some British statesmen to persuade the Indian people not to divert the attention of the British authorities but to concentrate on winning the war. By age-long traditions our people are known to be particularly sensitive to appeals to their honour, generosity and humaneness. Appeals of this nature always touch our hearts, even though our own miseries, due to our political subjection, are overwhelming and though such appeals are not new and were repeatedly made during the last war which began in 1914. But it is a very serious matter for the British Government to consider whether it is wise and justifiable, even in the name of war, to keep back fundamental questions affecting the liberties and well-being of such a vast country as ours, when the war itself is being waged to preserve democratic principles in a small country like Poland. That country, naturally, has all our sympathy but that sympathy would have been fuller, the energy to put that sympathy into operation would have been more effective if we ourselves enjoyed the status to secure which for them our assistance is needed.

This House, by a resolution which was discussed at great length, voted on the 2nd October 1937, i.e. soon after it began to function, that the Government of India Act was unsatisfactory and designed to perpetuate the subjugation of the people of India and the House demanded that the Act should be replaced by a constitution for a free India, framed by a Constituent Assembly. If that demand of our House, which was also made by a majority of other Provincial Assemblies, had been met by the British Government in a spirit of sympathy with the principles of democracy, which they said they defended in the last war and which they are out to defend in the present one, our country would beyond doubt have been in a stronger position today to defend itself and to help Britain and other nations fighting in a righteous cause. On behalf of the House I make bold to say that the policy of the British Government in ignoring our resolution has definitely weakened the fighting strength of Britain.

Even the exigency of a war is not good ground for shelving the very important question of India's status. It calls for immediate solution. The war, I say, has made it even more urgent. Statesmen must recognise that to win modern wars it is essential to harness the popular will in their support. And nothing would be more opportune to win the people of India than giving them the initiative and necessary control for carrying on the fight for freedom and democratic principles with enthusiasm and sacrifice, and making them feel that the war in which they are helping safeguards what they value and cherish. These are matters over which each and everyone of you must have thought earnestly and deeply. I have placed them before the House so that honourable members may consider as to what their own part in this crisis is to be.

ENCLOSURE 2 TO NO. 74

PANNA LAL TO ALL DISTRICT MAGISTRATES

L/P&J/5/268: ff. 128-9
Confidential — Police Department, Lucknow,
D.O. No. 211/VIII-1939 — *September 30th, 1939*

My dear Sir,

A number of speeches have come to the notice of Government in which the speakers have definitely preached violence or incited others or people at large to commit acts of violence. It is obvious that such speeches punishable as they may often be under Sections 124-A, 153-A, and other Sections of the Indian Penal Code, are because of their incitements to violence extremely reprehensible, but it seems that, possibly owing to some misapprehension of the legal position, prompt action is not taken by the district authorities to prevent the repetition of such speeches. It is essential for the preservation of public peace and spreading of any possible lawlessness that effective preventive action is taken against all speakers and publications which offend against the law and incite people to violence.

2. In this connexion, I am to invite your attention to Mr. Gwynne's confidential D.O. no. 5092/VIII-1238, dated November 29, 1938 and his subsequent confidential D.O. no. 1118/VIII-179(8), dated May 2, 1939 in which certain suggestions were made for the guidance of District Magistrates. In the latter of these letters, Government said that District Magistrates could take action under Section 107 Criminal Procedure Code and 108 Criminal Procedure Code read with Section 153-A, Indian Penal Code.

3. Prosecutions for the substantive offences of Section 153-A Indian Penal Code, and 124-A Indian Penal Code have always required the previous sanction of the Government. The orders of May 2, 1939 abovementioned, however, extended to District Magistrates the power to initiate security proceedings under Section 108 Criminal Procedure Code with

reference to matter coming under the definition of Section 153-A. Proceedings under Section 108 Criminal Procedure Code for matter falling under Section 124-A Indian Penal Code, however, continued to be subject to the previous permission of the Government.

4. In view of the increase in speeches inciting to violence the Govern-ent direct that District Magistrates may on their own initiative and responsibility take action under Section 108 Criminal Procedure Code in respect of all speeches and publications which contain incitement to commit acts of violence, whether they fall within the definition of Section 153-A Indian Penal Code or Section 124-A Indian Penal Code, without previous reference to Government. They will, however, immediately report their action to Government. If, however, a speech inciting to violence can be dealt with effectively under Section 107, Criminal Procedure Code, Government prefer that that section should be used.

5. The use of Section 107, Criminal Procedure Code, was dealt with in the latter part of the Legal Remembrancer's note dated June 16, 1938, a copy of which was forwarded with Mr. Gwynne's letter of November 29, 1938. Government have further considered the position and are advised that it is not at all necessary that a speech should actually lead to the results desired by the speaker before action can be taken. The language of Section 107, Criminal Procedure Code, is very wide and a person who is likely "to do any wrongful act that may probably occasion a breach of the peace or disturb the public tranquillity" would be liable under that Section. The case *Satindra Nath Gupta* versus *Emperor*, reported in 111 I.C. 1929 on page 397 makes it clear that a person is liable to be dealt with under Section 107, Criminal Procedure Code, not only when he himself is likely to commit a breach of the peace but also where, for any wrongful act on his part, other persons may do things which would probably occasion a breach of the peace or disturb the public tranquillity. An incitement to commit murders or assaults, contained in a speech to an audience, is a wrongful act.

6. It has been represented that action against speakers is difficult in the absence of a verbatim report of the speech made. This may be true in certain cases – e.g., where the interpretation of a particular phrase may depend very largely on the content. Government are advised, however, that it is not essential that a verbatim report should be available. All that is required is reliable evidence, sufficient to satisfy the court, that the gist of a speech is an incitement to violence. Longhand notes, supported by the evidence of reliable persons who heard the speaker, should, in normal circumstances, and in the absence of reliable evidence to the contrary, be sufficient for the purpose.

7. I am also to draw your attention to the provisions of Section 117, Indian Penal Code, which ordinarily is seldom made use of. This Section makes it an offence for a person to abet the commission of an offence by the public generally or by any number or class of persons exceeding ten. "Abetment by instigation" is rather a wide term and Government are advised that it is sufficient under the section to show that the person charged with the offence actively suggested or stimulated others to the act by any means or language, direct or indirect, whether in the form of express solicitation, or of hints, insinuation or encouragement. (Ratan Lal's *Law of Crimes*, 1936 edition, p. 235.) In the case *Nazir Ahmad* versus *Emperor*, reported in XXV A.L.J., p. 149, the accused had suggested that certain tenants who were being mal-treated deserved to be beaten and it was held that he had abetted the offence. In another case reported in A.I.R., 1933 Lahore, p. 660, the speaker incited the audience to murder Englishmen and Government officials and although no consequences followed it was held that Section 117, Indian Penal Code applied. Action under Section 117, Indian Penal Code, would therefore be possible in the case of such a person.

Yours sincerely,
PANNA LALL

75

HAIG TO LINLITHGOW
R/3/1/75

Confidential — Camp,
No. U.P.-313 — *October 11th, 1939*

My dear Lord Linlithgow,

I have today received a file from Lucknow containing a long telegram from Allama Mashraqi, the head of the Khaksar movement at present in jail in Lucknow, addressed to Your Excellency and to a long list of papers. I enclose a copy of this telegram. It is dated the 30th September, was forwarded by the Inspector-General of Prisons[8] with a letter, dated October 5th, and was considered by the Minister on October 6th. The decision on the file was that it was not proper for the Allama to send out such a telegram while undergoing a sentence of imprisonment, and that in accordance with a rule in the Jail Manual prisoners are prohibited from writing letters the subject matter of which extends to politics. Accordingly it was ordered that permission to send the telegram should not be granted. Before the draft issued, however, the case was sent to me. I have sent it back today with a note strongly urging that in the circumstances it would be very unwise for the Government not to allow this telegram to be transmitted to Your Excellency, though I agree that it should not be sent to the Press. I hope that the Government will reconsider their decision and that the telegram will in due course be forwarded to Your Excellency. In the meantime I think you may like to see the telegram.

2. It appears to me that the telegram might possibly afford Your Excellency, if you felt inclined to do so, an opportunity for advising the Allama to withdraw his movement directed against the United Provinces Government. The Government are anxious that this Khaksar attack should cease, and recent developments on the part of the Muslim League suggest that the continuance of this struggle may involve somewhat serious and widespread consequences. The attitude of the Government is that if the Khaksars call off the movement they will withdraw the prohibitions. I do not think the Allama is in a mood to accept such a settlement. He wishes to achieve a victory; but I am hoping that it may be possible before long to reach some reasonable settlement. If there is serious difficulty about reaching a settlement, it might be that Your Excellency's intervention would be of value. The Allama is due for release from jail on the 16th October. I anticipate that conversations of importance will take place immediately after his release.

Yours sincerely,
H.G. HAIG

ENCLOSURE TO NO. 75

INAYATULLAH KHAN TO LINLITHGOW

Telegram

September 30th, 1939

My imprisonment and that of hundreds of prominent Khaksars by United Provinces Government and their intention to crush movement need not detain me further from announcing my attitude towards war. I consider bargaining even with an enemy in trouble mean and unmanly. Muslim character forbids it. Islam prohibits double-dealing. England is now engaged in struggle involving gravest life death consequences and most certainly also future of India. Bania mentality at this crisis unworthy of great people like Mussulmans and we must help England frankly if we want to make her friendship real and sincere. Bitter experience Congress Ministries last three years has taught all ryots to know that the British were much better rulers. Muslims if they want escape annihilation must decide now not being ruled by majority all costs. We must prove to British again that we Mussulmans are actual defenders of India and therefore we above all have natural also inheritary right to control it. Blood and rule have always gone together in all history.

I doubt if Indian National Congress can supply single soldier for defence India anywhere. Any posing therefore by a party that cannot deliver goods is ridiculous and preposterous. Only Khaksars all over India who have rendered selfless practical social service irrespective caste creed nine years can claim playing game of blood this moment. Or again Punjab Premier can give real aid for defence of country. I have thought over the problem and have closely examined all real false or conditional offers. I hereby declare that within three months this announcement I shall be able to place at disposal of His Excellency Viceroy thirty thousand well-drilled best disciplined Khaksar soldiers after nominal training for internal military defence of India, ten thousand for police purposes for maintaining internal peace and another ten thousand of very best quality for help Turkey our ally or if need be through her for fight European soil. Your Excellency has only to test us in order to prove Khaksars fidelity to motherland last drop blood. Request widest publicity this declaration as I am in prison. Dated thirtieth September.

76

DONALDSON TO LAITHWAITE
L/P&J/5/268: FF. 96-107

Confidential
No. 1099/39-G.S.P.

October 13th, 1939

My dear Laithwaite,

H.E. wishes me to send you for the information of H.E. the Governor-General a copy of the report by Sloan, the Commissioner of Meerut, on the firing on the Khaksars at the Bulandshahr Jail on October 8, 1939. The enclosures to the Report are not sent.

Yours sincerely,
J.C. DONALDSON

ENCLOSURE TO NO. 76

REPORT BY SLOAN ON THE FIRING AT BULANDSHAHR JAIL ON OCTOBER 8TH, 1939

Undated

I have not yet received any formal report from the District Magistrate[9] and this report is based on information which I have myself obtained from various sources in Bulandshahr during the last two days. On hearing of the firing at the jail on October 8 I proceeded at once to Bulandshahr arriving there about 2 p.m. I stayed in Bulandshahr till 10 p.m. and returned there again on the morning of October 9 and remained till 6-45 p.m.

2. The leader of the large *jatha* of Khaksars which was encamped at Chola, about 7 miles south-west of Bulandshahr, on October 7 gave an undertaking to the District Magistrate that he and his *jatha* would remain where they were till an emissary who had gone into Delhi for orders returned from Delhi. The emissary returned in the evening about 8 p.m. The District Magistrate sent him in a police lorry to Chola to communicate the orders from Delhi to the *jatha* leader. Soon after the emissary had left, the District Magistrate himself received news that the *jatha* had moved. After he had verified this by a personal visit to Chola, he made all possible arrangements for tracing their movements. Early on the morning of October 8 they were traced to a spot near Khurja. The police force and the cavalry were moved down to Khurja and surrounded the *jatha* about 6-30 a.m. Some negotiations then took place, the outcome of which was that the *jatha* would give themselves up peaceably on the understanding that they would be taken to the Bulandshahr Jail where they would deposit their *belchas* and themselves enter the jail, and thereafter would be taken back to the Delhi province on giving an undertaking that they would not again enter the Bulandshahr district. This arrangement was made with the leader who did not inform his men of it.

3. Arrangements were then made to transport the Khaksars into Bulandshahr by lorry. They were sent off in 15 lorries with an escort of two sub-Inspectors, 2 Under Officers and 20 Constables Armed Police and 2 Under Officers and 20 Constables Civil Police under the command of Sergeant Bacon. One lorry load of police was in front of and one behind the lorries containing the Khaksars. The District Magistrate left before all the Khaksars were loaded into their lorries and taking the Khaksar leader with him went on to the tahsil at Khurja where he waited for the lorries.

Inspector Moti Singh was also sent ahead with one lorry load of police, with orders to pick up some extra police from Mamam bridge on the canal and on reaching Bulandshahr to picket the main road close to the jail in order to prevent a crowd gathering at the foot of the road which leads up from the main road to the jail. Mr. Badan Singh, Superintendent of Police, Aligarh, had been ordered by the Deputy Inspector-General of Police[10] to go from Aligarh taking some of his own men with him to assist the police in Bulandshahr. The District Magistrate states that when he was at the Khurja Tahsil waiting for the lorries, Mr. Badan Singh arrived there from the scene of the arrest and asked that his force of police might be sent back to Aligarh as soon as possible as he was anxious to get back. The District Magistrate states that he told him that his force could not be relieved before the Khaksars were safely lodged in the jail and that he then instructed him to take charge of the advance party of police at the jail and that he and the S.D.O., Khurja would have to take charge of the lorries as they arrived at the jail. The District Magistrate understood that Mr. Badan Singh then went into Bulandshahr taking the S.D.O., Khurja with him in his car. The Khaksars were taken into Bulandshahr without trouble. There were two stops on the way. The first was at Khurja where Sergeant Bacon states that he had instructions to allow the Khaksars to drink. The District Magistrate apparently did not know of these instructions as he stated to me that when he saw the Khaksars getting out of the lorries at Khurja he ordered them back into their lorries and also told a police officer to go along the line of lorries to the S.P. and tell him that he must get them back into lorries and on to the jail. This point is rather important as it suggests that the District Magistrate was under the impression that the Superintendent of Police was in charge of the lorries. A further stop was made at the Walipura Canal bridge without any orders and some of the Khaksars got out to buy fruit but were persuaded to return to their lorries without trouble. The lorries then proceeded to the jail where they arrived without further incident about 9-30 a.m.

4. The courtyard in front of the jail is comparatively small and 15 lorries could not be parked there in an orderly manner without very careful arrangements. The District Magistrate has stated that lorries were parked in the courtyard opposite the main gate in quite good order, but Sergeant Bacon has stated that when he arrived in the last lorry some of the lorries were still standing in the entrance road to the jail while the others were up in the courtyard but not properly parked. It seems to me quite clear that there were no adequate arrangements for parking the lorries and getting

the Khaksars out of them lorry by lorry in an orderly manner. Two Deputy Magistrates, namely, Messrs. Krishan Murari Lal and Amiruddin were present at the jail. Mr. Amiruddin is the S.D.O. Khurja, who along with Mr. Badan Singh had been sent ahead to be in charge of arrangements at the jail. It is not yet clear what Mr. Krishan Murari Lal's duties were. The District Magistrate has stated that when he left his car near the main gate of the jail he walked up to the gate and there arranged with the leader of the Khaksars that his men would proceed into the jail by lorry loads and leave their *belchas* in a room on the right immediately inside the outer gate of the jail. The first batch of prisoners entered the gate, left their *belchas* and proceeded on into the jail without trouble. The leader went into the jail with them and was therefore not present at the main gate when the trouble began. By the time the first batch had entered the jail the second batch had drawn up outside it and most of the remaining Khaksars appear to have by that time got out of their lorries and to have been standing about in the courtyard. When the second batch was asked to enter the main gate they immediately showed resentment and began to bang their *belchas* on the ground in order to break them, saying that they had no use for *belchas* in the jail. Some of them also assumed a threatening attitude and got up on to a *chabutra* adjoining the jail wall immediately outside and on the roadside of the main gate. There they threatened Sergeant Bacon and Krishan Murari Lal saying that they would be killed but they would not enter the jail. The District Magistrate immediately called the leader out of the jail and he placed himself between Sergeant Bacon and his own men, and by this act may well have saved the Sergeant's life. About the same time a considerable number of the Khaksars appear to have surged down the jail entrance road towards the main road brandishing their *belchas*. The District Magistrate is certain that he saw Khaksars on the high ground at the corner where the jail road joins the main road. At this point firing broke out. There is a consensus of evidence that the firing began with a single shot which was immediately followed by heavy firing. Mr. Krishan Murari Lal has stated that he saw some of the Khaksars seize a musket from a jail warder, and he thinks that one of the Khaksars fired this weapon. It is possible that this single shot was from that jail warder's musket. The musket may have been fired either intentionally or accidentally in the course of the struggle. A number of leading Muslims, with whom I had a long talk on the evening of October 8, insisted that this first shot was fired by a Sikh constable from the north side of the jail courtyard, that is the side away from the main road. None of these gentlemen was actually present when the firing took place and their statement therefore is based on hearsay and is open to suspicion for the reason that there is among the Muslims in Bulandshahr very keen feeling against the Sikhs at the present time owing to their proposal to hold a large Sikh conference and procession in Bulandshahr this week. It has also been stated that the first shot was fired by a jail warder either near the main gate or on the far side of the jail from the main gate.

5. There is no doubt whatever that there was firing from three sides, namely, north, west and south. I examined the marks on the jail walls on the evening of October 8, and satisfied myself that shots had been fired from all three directions. According to Sergeant Bacon when he checked the ammunition he found that 69 empties of ball and one of buckshot had been picked up, but there is still some doubt whether the police fired any buckshot. None of the force which was engaged in the arrest of the Khaksars carried buckshot nor did any of the Bulandshahr police who were on duty at the jail. At least two rounds of buckshot and possibly three were fired. I myself found pellet marks on the walls of the jail inside the main gate which faces west, and also on the west wall of the armoury, which is immediately outside the main gate and to the north of it. I am certain these two sets of marks could not have resulted from one shot. Mr. Krishan Murari Lal was also wounded by buckshot when standing on the *chabutra* to the south of the main gate. All the other marks which I saw were ball marks, one at least of which, on the north wall of the armoury had been fired from the north, and the remainder from the west and from the south. One lorry was damaged by bullets as it backed out of the jail entrance road on to the main road and it is stated that another lorry was also hit.

6. Most of the dead and wounded Khaksars were picked up at the foot of the entrance road to the jail and on the ground at the side of that road and close to the main road. This affords the strongest possible evidence that the Khaksars had rushed down the entrance road and were close to the main road when the police opened fire.

7. After the firing stopped order was quickly restored. The injured were first taken into the jail and thereafter the remainder of the Khaksars entered the jail without further trouble.

8. When I arrived about 2 p.m. there was a large crowd of excited Muslims on the main road at the entrance to the jail, but the situation was completely under control. The civil surgeon was then engaged in carrying out post-mortems on the bodies of the dead. Four Khaksars were killed outright and one died shortly after in hospital. 14 were wounded, eight of

whom had serious fractures. One of these has since died. Mr. Krishan Murari Lal, Deputy Collector, who was standing on the *chabutra* to the south of and near the main gate was wounded with buckshot in the left thigh and on the left hand, but not seriously.

9. Immediately after the post-mortem had finished the question of the disposal of the dead bodies arose. The Khaksar leader told me that he could on no account agree to their burial in Bulandshahr and that if that were done it would only mean that more of his men would have to shed their blood. He asked to be allowed to send the bodies back to the Punjab in charge of the relatives of the dead men. I ascertained by telephone from the Chief Commissioner of Delhi[11] that he had no objection to the bodies being taken through Delhi, but that as the men did not belong to Delhi he could not agree to their burial there. I had no time to communicate with the Government of the Punjab. On my responsibility therefore I decided to allow 10 of the relatives of the dead men to take their bodies back to the Punjab by lorry. Before this was finally arranged I was informed that the Khaksars desired to say funeral prayers beside the bodies. Their leader gave me an undertaking that if his men were allowed to come out of the jail courtyard in front of the main gate, he would get them back into the jail without any trouble. I accepted his word. Just before the Khaksars were taken out of the jail for the prayers I was informed that the Muslims who were on the main road at the entrance to the jail also wanted to say funeral prayers and I agreed to the bodies being taken down to the main road and at the entrance of the jail road and to the Muslims saying their prayers with the bodies in front of them. These arrangements were carried through without any hitch and in an orderly fashion. Thereafter the bodies were sent off to Delhi. I allowed 11 Khaksars to accompany them, 10 of whom were to proceed beyond Delhi with the bodies without any undertaking not to return to this province. The eleventh stated that he wished to return from Delhi to jail and I gave him a letter of safe custody. I also sent an express telegram to the Chief Secretary to the Government of the Punjab[12] informing him that I was allowing the bodies to be taken back to the Punjab for burial. The lorry with the dead bodies left about 6-30 and I spent the rest of the evening in listening to what local Muslim leaders had to say about the firing. I returned to Meerut about 11-15 p.m. Before leaving Bulandshahr I made arrangements for the transfer of all the Khaksars from the Bulandshahr to the Meerut Jail the next day, as the accommodation in the Bulandshahr Jail was inadequate. On arrival in Meerut I tried to get an official communiqué through to the Press Association in Delhi. I was unable to make the representative of the Press

Association understand the communiqué and then gave it to the *Statesman* and the *Hindustan Times*. The *Statesman* did not publish it as an official communiqué, but the information contained in the *Statesman* of October 9 was substantially what I had given to them.

10. I returned to Bulandshahr on the morning of October 9. As Government had by that time announced their intention of holding a judicial enquiry into the events of the previous day I did not pursue my own enquiries further, and after visiting the hospital where I saw the injured Khaksars and also Mr. Krishan Murari Lal I spent most of the day in discussions with Muslims and Sikhs in regard to the proposed Sikh Conference on October 14 and 15. I also arranged for the transfer of the injured Khaksars from Bulandshahr to Meerut by ambulance. One of these men was in a serious condition and it was not considered advisable to move him. He has since died. The other 7 are now in the civil hospital in Meerut.

11. It was stated in the press on October 10 on the authority of Dr. Nazar Muhammad, a Khaksar leader in Delhi, that "the arrangement was that the Khaksars would be taken back to Delhi in lorries instead of which they were taken to the district jail in Bulandshahr". That statement implied a definite charge of breach of faith on the part of the District Magistrate and I have contradicted it in a communiqué which has appeared in the press today – after seeing the District Magistrate and the Khaksar leader yesterday. The arrangement was as follows:

(1) The Khaksars would submit to arrest without resistance.

(2) They would be taken to Bulandshahr Jail where they would deposit their *belchas* and enter the jail.

(3) On giving an undertaking not to return to the Bulandshahr district they would be taken to Delhi in lorries.

I saw the Khaksar leader in the Meerut Jail yesterday and in the presence of Major Fowler, who was in command of the squadron of cavalry at the arrest, he agreed that that was the arrangement. I then asked him if the arrangement was known to his men. He replied that it was not, and added that under their system his men were told nothing as their only duty was to obey. This is important as it seems to supply the explanation of the sudden resentment of the Khaksars at the jail. The first batch entered the jail with their leader under perfect discipline. The resentment broke out in the absence of the leader in the jail and when the second batch were asked to enter. The situation had got out of control by the time the leader got outside the jail.

12. As the whole matter is to be the subject of a judicial enquiry, it would be improper for me, on the basis of the incomplete enquiry which I made, to offer any considered opinion as to whether the firing was or was not justified. Nor do I consider it fair at the present stage to express any considered views on the responsibility of the various officers concerned, which must also come under review in the course of the enquiry. But for the confidential information of Government I am placing on record some points which I feel require to be cleared up:

(1) Whether there was a sufficient understanding between the District Magistrate and the Superintendent of Police as to the arrangements at the jail.

(2) Whether the police escort was sufficient and it was wise to leave it to the command of a police sergeant.

(3) Whether the arrangements for parking the lorries and unloading the Khaksars at the jail were adequate.

(4) Whether sufficient use was made of the Khaksar leader in controlling the prisoners on arrival in the jail.

13. I should like to add that the District Magistrate has shown very great activity in his dealings with the Khaksars and that it appears to have been mainly due to his initiative and energy that the Khaksars were located and rounded up early on the morning of October 8 when they were advancing as fast as possible in the hope of reaching the Aligarh district.

14. I attach to this report copies of the communiqués[13] which I have sent to the press.

77

HAIG TO LINLITHGOW
Telegram
MSS.EUR.F 115/7

No. 274-G *October 14th, 1939*

Your letter dated October 11. Conference of Governors' Secretaries. I agree that this would be of value and I should be glad for my Secretary to attend. Question of dates however is of vital importance. I cannot afford to be caught at a disadvantage at the very beginning by my Secretary being absent when it is clear that a crisis is practically upon us. This would be seriously embarrassing to me. I should be grateful for any indication Your Excellency could give me as to earliest date on which crisis might arise.

2. If there is difficulty about assembling all Governors' Secretaries at the same time I would suggest that purpose could be served adequately so far as I am concerned by my Secretary visiting Delhi on some convenient date for two days when some other Secretaries might also be present. It would be of great value that he should be able to convey and discuss with Your Excellency's advisers my views on various points and ascertain their views. But a formal conference of Governors' Secretaries though it would have its advantages does not seem to me essential.

3. I will forward as soon as possible a brief memorandum dealing with the various points raised in Your Excellency's letter and others to which I may wish to draw attention.[14]

78

DONALDSON TO LAITHWAITE
L/P&J/5/268: FF. 94-5

Confidential
No. 1109/39-G.S.P.

Governor's Camp, U.P.,
October 17th, 1939

My dear Laithwaite,

With reference to H.E. Sir Harry Haig's D.O. No. U.P.-309 of October 5, 1939, about anti-recruiting propaganda, he wishes me to send you, for the information of H.E. the Governor-General, an extract from the fortnightly D.O. of the Commissioner, Allahabad Division, for the second half of September, dated October 11, 1939. The Commissioner is Mr. Dible, who has succeeded Mr. Bishop. Mr. Bonarjee is the Collector of Fatehpur. I am also sending a copy to Eastern Command.

Yours sincerely,
J.C. DONALDSON

ENCLOSURE TO NO. 78

EXTRACT FROM DIBLE'S FORTNIGHTLY REPORT
FOR THE SECOND HALF OF SEPTEMBER 1939

October 11th, 1939

Last fortnight Bishop reported a complaint by the Assistant Recruiting Officer from Lucknow that about 40 potential recruits from the Fatehpur district had subsequently declined enrolment as a consequence of anti-recruiting propaganda. Bonarjee has investigated this complaint, and his conclusion is that the recruiting Havildar is to blame for his careless methods in collecting the recruits. He finds no reluctance on the part of cultivators in his district to enlist. On the contrary he is himself receiving applications in court for enrolment.

79

HAIG TO LINLITHGOW
R/3/1/75

Secret
No. U.P.-314

October 18th, 1939

My dear Lord Linlithgow,

I have been, as Your Excellency knows, in some anxiety regarding the rather dangerous conditions that are bound to prevail in the United Provinces during the long period of uncertainty as to whether Congress will or will not cooperate in the war. Soon after the outbreak of war the situation seemed to me to be deteriorating rapidly. I drew attention to this in paragraph 4 of my telegram No. 265-G, dated September 19th, stressed the point that it was dangerous to let the movement gather strength unchecked, and emphasised the great desirability of the earliest possible decision as to the attitude of Congress to the war. I re-emphasised these points in my telegram No. 266-G, dated September 21st. A little later conditions were steadied to the extent that I was able to report in my telegram No. 272-G, dated September 28th, that the situation had not further deteriorated, though a number of very undesirable speeches were being made. I think that probably represents the position today. Gandhi's influence and instructions issued by the Provincial Congress Committee have, I think, had a considerable effect in restraining the more orthodox Congressmen, and even the Left Wing extremists, so far as they are acting under the discipline of their own organisation, seem to me not to wish to press matters too far so long as there is a chance that they will be able to bring in the whole Congress organisation on their side against the war. Nevertheless, there still remains a considerable volume of anti-British and anti-war speeches which must be doing harm. It is too early for me to write with confidence about the effect of the circular giving District Magistrates a free-hand to proceed under Section 108, Criminal Procedure

Code, against any speakers who are instigating violence. (A copy of this circular was enclosed in my letter No. U.P.-312, dated October 9th, 1939.) I think it is bound to have some appreciable effect in restraining the more dangerous speakers. I also directed the Police some weeks ago to report, with a view to obtaining the sanction of Government for prosecution under Section 124-A or Section 153-A, Indian Penal Code, speeches made by the more dangerous revolutionaries. In accordance with these instructions an appreciable number of applications for sanction are now under the consideration of Government, and several of them have recently reached me through Katju. I find his attitude not very satisfactory. He is inclined to grasp at excuses for doing nothing, and I have in several cases made it clear on the files that I am not disposed to agree with him and that in my opinion definite action is very necessary. I am intending to discuss these cases with him when I reach Lucknow.[15] If I find his attitude from my point of view unreasonable, I shall take the matter up with Kidwai. My present intention is to press the Ministers pretty hard over this; but I quite realise that if they are anticipating the probability of their own resignation they may decline at this stage to incur the unpopularity of ordering prosecutions.

2. If I can get some of these prosecutions sanctioned, and if District Magistrates make reasonable use of the power[s] that have been given to them by the circular I have mentioned earlier, I am hoping that this may serve to keep the present situation under control. It is not altogether easy to estimate how things really stand. The Police continue to send in rather alarmist reports. In their last report, dated 12th October, it is said: "The flood of invective against the British continues and this week has seen a very large number of violent and objectionable speeches." They also report that "there is considerable evidence to show that preparations are being made for agitation over the war question in anticipation of a breakdown in the discussions between His Excellency the Viceroy and various leaders", and they say that there is beginning to be talk of no-rent campaigns and civil disobedience. On the other hand the Commissioners' fortnightly reports which have just reached me, while they record a number of objectionable speeches, convey the impression on the whole that there is a lull in open extremist agitation and that the Left Wing as well as the Right are waiting for the outcome of the conversations. I think this is probably a fair estimate of conditions at the moment.

3. The information which Your Excellency has sent me recently[16] suggests that even if the Congress are dissatisfied with the declaration that is to be made, it is likely that there will be no immediate break with

the Congress.[17] I have been trying to picture how the situation is likely to develop in this Province. In the first place, if the Congress, as suggested in paragraph 4 of Your Excellency's telegram No. 2284-S, dated October 15th, while they consider the statement unsatisfactory, endeavour to secure some modifications, we should I imagine still be in the existing position of continuance of negotiations, and conditions in the Province might remain for a further period much as they are at present.

4. The Congress might, however, merely reject the statement made on behalf of His Majesty's Government as inadequate and unsatisfactory and leave the resulting situation in the Provinces to work itself out. In other words, they would let the Ministries carry on until the position became impossible. There has been talk from time to time to the effect that Congress Ministries would not resign, but would wait to be dismissed by the Governors. There would, in my view, be no question of dismissing my Ministers. If I came to the conclusion that it was impossible to retain them, there would I think be no difficulty in forcing their resignation by insisting under my special powers on certain action being taken in which they could not acquiesce.

5. If the situation is to develop on these lines, I think it might be advisable, looking merely at the conditions of this Province, for me to take the initiative very quickly. The Ministers, I think, would be anxious to remain in office as long as possible partly with the idea that assent might be given to the Tenancy Bill, partly in order to complete other schemes. It would, in any case, take a considerable time to give assent to the Tenancy Bill, which I shall not do without a fairly full reference to Your Excellency; but I should certainly not propose to grant assent while the question of the Ministers remaining in office was still hanging in the balance.[18] But while the Ministers may be anxious for various reasons to stay in office as long as possible, I am disposed to think it would be dangerous for me to allow such a situation to continue for long. If there is going to be trouble it is in my opinion necessary to take far more drastic action than the measures which, as I have explained above, are now being taken. The longer that action is postponed, the more difficult the eventual situation is likely to be. The Left Wing are undoubtedly working hard and making their preparations. A considerable volume of anti-British and anti-war speeches goes unchecked. The knowledge that Government are hesitating, and that the ample powers they possess under the Ordinance are not being used is unsettling. This state of uncertainty may well have an unsettling effect on the services, and it is discouraging to those who want to support us. All

these factors will be greatly intensified when it appears that the Congress are not really prepared to cooperate in the war, and that therefore a break is inevitable. The present hesitation is widely recognised as being that of the Ministers. In the circumstances, however, which I am considering, the hesitation would clearly be that of the Governor, and this would produce a very damaging impression. I quite appreciate that it is necessary to subordinate provincial requirements to all-India policy; but if in fact it becomes clear that a break is inevitable, it looks as if I may have to ask Your Excellency's concurrence to my forcing a break pretty soon.

6. The third possibility is that the Congress would not only declare themselves dissatisfied with the declaration of His Majesty's Government, but would proceed to call out the Provincial Ministries simultaneously.[19] This would be a straightforward situation. I understand, however, that you do not think it is a likely development.

Yours sincerely,
H.G. HAIG

80

HAIG TO LINLITHGOW
L/P&J/5/268: FF. 83-6

Secret *October 18th, 1939*
No. U.P.-316

My dear Lord Linlithgow,

I am enclosing a copy of a letter I have written to Craik about the Khaksar movement, as I think Your Excellency ought to know both the nature of the activities of the Khaksars, and the difficult problem arising from the fact that we are really defending ourselves against a movement which uses the Punjab and Delhi as its bases.

Yours sincerely,
H.G. HAIG

ENCLOSURE TO NO. 80

HAIG TO CRAIK

No. U.P.-315 *October 18th, 1939*

My dear Craik,

I have been interested to read para. 6 of your D.O. letter No. 188-F.L. dated 13th October to H.E. the Viceroy, regarding the Khaksars.[20] I was afraid that the firing at Bulandshahr was bound to cause a good deal of excitement in the Punjab, and the whole incident was exceedingly unfortunate. With reference to the despatch of the bodies of the five men killed at Bulandshahr, I feel that we owe you some apology. I cannot do better than send you an extract from the report of the Commissioner (Sloan), which will show the circumstances in which he decided that the bodies should not be buried at Bulandshahr but should be sent to their homes.[21] I am sorry that he did not succeed in consulting your Government before action was taken.

2. With regard to the general attitude of the Punjab Government, we have been grateful for the instructions which were issued to District Officers to discourage the irruption of Khaksars. The fact remains, however, that the Khaksars continued to invade the United Provinces in considerable numbers and in very menacing formed bodies, and that, as I understand it, to a large extent they were carrying on their operations from a base or bases in the Punjab immediately adjoining the U.P. border across the Jumna. These large *jathas* arrived in the Meerut Division usually without any notice and caused us the gravest anxiety. I was greatly encouraged when I heard from you that your Premier had on the 30th September seen some of the leading Khaksars in Lahore and that they had promised that the Khaksars at Jagadhri and Delhi should be ordered to return and that no further *jathas* should be sent from the Punjab. Unfortunately, no effect seems to have been given to these assurances. Four days after the conversation with your Premier, the situation in the Meerut Division was reaching its most dangerous point. On the 4th October a large *jatha*, originally estimated at 500, but probably only about 300, crossed the Jumna from Delhi province into the U.P. and made for Bulandshahr. This was the body of men which after its arrest was taken to Bulandshahr Jail where the firing occurred on the 8th October. If the Khaksar leaders had carried out their undertaking to your Premier this *jatha* would never have invaded the U.P.

3. This Khaksar movement, with its military formations and its formidable weapons, masquerading as merely a civil resistance movement, presents a new problem in India, as far as I am aware. If they offer violent resistance, the only safe weapons to use against them are fire-arms, and yet the use of fire-arms is bound to give rise to an outburst of feeling. In view of those considerations the local authorities actually held their hands with regard to the first *jatha* which invaded the Muzaffarnagar district for something like a fortnight, though they had an ample force of police and troops to overpower resistance. But the local officers judged that an attempt to arrest these men would result in heavy casualties.

4. An equally serious problem is presented by the fact that a movement of this kind can be organised securely from bases in a neighbouring province. I fully recognize the political and practical difficulties which limit the action your Government might find itself able to take. I am still not without hope that by methods of publicity, which my Ministers have hitherto neglected, we may be able to force on the Allama a cessation of his operations. He will not listen to the persuasions of Jinnah. But if the movement continues unabated, I think we may have to ask your Government whether they will cooperate with us by definite action. It might cripple the movement, if we could seize their funds. It is a curious thing that the Khaksars belonging to the U.P. are giving practically no trouble, and remain quiet.

5. I am sending a copy of this letter to His Excellency the Viceroy, as it raises important issues of all India politics.

Yours sincerely,
H.G. HAIG

81

HAIG TO LINLITHGOW
Telegram
MSS.EUR.F 115/7

No. 276-G *October 19th, 1939*

Reference para 4 your telegram No. 2284-S dated October 15th.[22]

Today I saw Kidwai who has come to Naini Tal and questioned him about the effect of Your Excellency's statement. I usually find him frank and I think he was frank with me today. He has hitherto always been optimistic about a settlement; but today he said that the statement would be entirely unsatisfactory to the Congress, and he regarded it as inevitable that they would reject it.

2. He stressed in particular the form of the statement which he thought was very discouraging, with its references to the past. He said that if the substance of the statement could have been put in a different way, with emphasis on the future, it might not have been unacceptable: if it had been said, for instance, that H.M.G. hoped that it would be possible for India to get Dominion Status at an early date after the war and that for that purpose they would at that time hold consultations and see whether a Constitution could be devised with agreement of the various interests and communities. He suggested that the only faint possibility of avoiding a break was if the emphasis could be turned round in that direction in the course of a debate in the Commons.

3. He told me he thought the Muslim League would also find the statement unsatisfactory as not holding out sufficient hope for advance in the future. I gathered that Jinnah has now really become anxious for an understanding with the Congress, and he seemed to suggest that the Muslim League might unite with the Congress in expressing dissatisfaction at the statement.

4. With regard to the future he said the Ministry would have to await instructions, but he seemed to contemplate an early resignation and spoke of the possibility of the Congress ordering all Ministries to resign. I told him that as he knew I was disturbed about conditions in the Province and that if the Ministry resigned, I should find it necessary to take vigorous action against the left wing revolutionaries. At the same time I said I hoped that I should not be brought into any conflict with the right wing of the Congress, and that they would not take an active anti-war attitude. He seemed to appreciate the necessity for action against the left wing, and gave me the distinct impression that the right wing would not be at all anxious to be drawn into conflict with us and would not wish to oppose war activities. He spoke indeed with some apprehension about the possibilities of India being attacked by Russia and clearly had in mind the danger of internal disturbances when external danger might be threatening.

5. You will have seen the statement issued from Lucknow by Nehru and Abul Kalam Azad.[23] I shall reach Lucknow on the morning of the 21st and will telegraph further impressions from there. But I should judge that Kidwai's attitude about the unacceptability of the statement is representative of Congress opinion.

82

DONALDSON TO LAITHWAITE
L/P&J/8/592: FF. 118-26

Secret
No. 1115/39-G.S.P.

Governor's Camp, U.P.,
October 19th, 1939

My dear Laithwaite,

With reference to para 3 of H.E. Sir Harry Haig's telegram No. G-274, dated October 14, 1939 to H.E. the Governor-General, I am directed to forward three copies of the memorandum which he promised to send.[24]

Yours sincerely,
J.C. DONALDSON

ENCLOSURE TO NO. 82

MEMORANDUM BY HAIG

Secret

October 19th, 1939

1. *General Policy and Tactics in the Province*

In the present circumstances of the Province if the Governor assumes control under Section 93 it will be essential to hit the extremists hard at once without waiting for further action on their part. They have already got a very considerable start. Whatever policy the right wing may adopt, we can count on immediate and determined opposition from the extremists, and we must try to paralyse them at once and prevent them from becoming the instigators of widespread opposition. The types of men I have in mind are:

(*a*) known terrorist leaders;
(*b*) communist leaders;
(*c*) irreconcilable left wingers, such as Bishambhar Dayal Tripathi, M.L.A., perhaps half dozen other M.L.As., and certain others such as Parmanand.

My present intention is to pick up some 50 of these at once under Rule 129 of the D.I. Rules, and subsequently proceed against them either on specific charges, for which in many cases material is available, or else by restrictive orders. This action, I should hope, would not only go a considerable way to paralysing the extremists for the time being, but would be a great encouragement to Government officers, who would feel that they could depend on a vigorous policy.

There will remain a large number of local firebrands, particularly the violent speakers. I propose to let District Officers have a free hand in prosecuting these under Rule 38 and 34 (6) of the Defence of India Rules. The object will be to institute such prosecutions as may be necessary for maintaining order in the district and a peaceful atmosphere, and putting a stop to racial or class incitements, and also to check anti-recruitment activities and other actions which will impede the prosecution of the war. At the same time District Officers will be instructed to use these powers with discrimination and not to proceed in a mechanic way against persons who are not really dangerous, and above all, not to proceed against Congressmen as such at the outset. We must endeavour as far as possible to retain the sympathy of the right wing Congressman. We must make every allowance for their position and not take advantage of speeches and actions to which they may be driven to some extent against their wish.

This action against extremists will provoke a certain amount of feeling, but we must put out a strong statement of our case against them and appeal to the reason of the moderate elements in support of its necessity. The removal of the leaders and prompt and judicious use of the D.I. Act should keep the rank and file in check.

A main difficulty which we must expect is that of demonstrations organised by right wing leaders. If allowed unchecked they rouse popular feeling and excitement. If prevented they bring us to the position we wish to avoid of having to deal with mass movements. There is no easy way out of these difficulties, and there is considerable danger that we may gradually drift by this channel into direct conflict with the right wing. We must certainly expect some trouble at the outset, but it may perhaps die down from lack of interest later if we can handle it on the right lines, and after allowing some steam to be blown off.

2. *Powers*

In my opinion the powers given by the Defence of India Rules and the ordinary law would be sufficient to meet the initial strain of a Section 93 situation. If matters came later on to widespread civil disobedience, it might be necessary to increase them, but at that stage there would probably not be the same disadvantage in enacting further powers. I agree that at the moment we should avoid bringing in the draft Revolutionary Movements Act and that it is unnecessary to do so.

In this Province the U.P. Special Powers Act 1932 is fortunately still in force and that Act gives ample powers to deal with a no-rent campaign. H.E. the Governor-General has already suggested one useful additional power which could be provided by a rule under the Defence of India Act, that of compelling newspapers to publish news and communiqués in a desired form. I agree that such an additional rule is desirable.

It seems desirable to consider to what extent the Central Government proposes to delegate any of its powers under the Defence of India Rules to Provincial Governments or District Magistrates.

If later on it should come to a mass civil disobedience movement, difficulty is likely to be experienced in the speedy trial of cases, unless some provision can be made for summary courts such as could be constituted under Ordinance X of 1932 and were provided for in the draft Revolutionary Movements Act. These would not be necessary at the outset, but the possibility of their being required later on should, I think, be considered now and the necessary plans be made in advance.

3. *War Board*

I am hoping to constitute a war board which would concern itself with all activities connected with the war. It would be a large body consisting mainly of non-officials, with a few necessary officials. The work would be done by a small executive committee with an official secretary. I contemplate that the non-official members of this executive could be utilised to a large extent as a kind of non-official shadow Cabinet. District war boards under the main war board [would] be set up for each district under the chairmanship of the District Officer. In this way I should hope to arouse interest in the objects of the war and activities in its support and to keep close touch with our non-official supporters throughout the Province.

The institution of District war boards should help to mobilise supporters and we shall need from the Centre the fullest information about the part which India is expected to play in the war and the opportunities for service which are open to those who wish to help us. In fact opportunities for service must be created in order to use and keep warm the very genuine enthusiasm which has appeared in many quarters but may easily fade away if not given some encouragement. A big positive drive in favour of the war must be started and nourished by material advantages in the shape of employments and rewards. We must have an active constructive policy to oppose to that of the Congress which will catch the imagination.

4. *Publicity*

The importance of propaganda cannot be over-emphasised. We have a strong case, but during this period of negotiation little or nothing has been done to get it to the masses, though observers agree that Indian sympathies are definitely on the side of the allies in their struggle against German aggression. The problem must be tackled with the greatest energy from the outset. Sir J.P. Srivastava has promised me his assistance and advice in organising this branch. He has given it much study and there is probably no one in the Province who has a better grasp of the essential requirements or more practical experience of political propaganda work.[25] We are fortunate in that of the five English dailies which mainly circulate in the Province, three, the *Pioneer*, *Leader*, and *Statesman*, are on our side and can be trusted to state our case adequately as against the *National Herald* and *Hindustan Times*. The Urdu and Hindi Press is mainly against us. It will have to be dealt with partly by the purchase of space and support directly or indirectly, and partly by control through the Press Act and the D.I. Rules. The vernacular Press is an extremely powerful influence on public opinion. There are few villages now to which a vernacular newspaper of some kind does not penetrate fairly regularly and the villager is far better informed and takes a far greater interest in political matters than he used to do. The success or failure of our propaganda machinery will depend greatly on the extent to which it can employ the medium of the Vernacular Press for its own material and check the poisonous streams of abuse of Britain and the British Government with which a majority of the papers are now filled. I propose to appoint a senior British Officer at once as Director of Public Information, with Indian assistants and to make him responsible for both propaganda and Press control. It will take a little time, however, to get the Press side of the propaganda work going effectively. In the meantime the old district publicity organisations, used in the civil disobedience movement, must be revived in every district. I hope it will be possible to combine these organisations with the District war boards, which I contemplate setting up. These district publicity organisations must be used for the widest distribution of leaflets stating our case, and must also arrange as much verbal explanation of it by means of public meetings, itinerant lecturers and so forth as can be managed. The initial propaganda explaining the British Government's declaration, the reasons for the suspension of the Constitution, and the future policy of the Governor in regard to such matters as the Tenancy Legislation, and warnings against anti-recruitment speeches and other offences against the Defence of India Rules, must be taken up in this way as it is the way which can be most quickly developed. More subtle methods can be employed later but at the outset we must get the main facts of the situation out into the villages as quickly as possible and these are the most rapid methods.

5. *Staff*

Owing to the recall of officers from leave we are for the present well up to strength. I would not, therefore, press for the return of any officers from the Government of India immediately. Our present strength is, however, a maximum and as time goes on and it is reduced by casualties, leave in India and unforeseen demands, we shall feel the need of reinforcement. There are many individual officers with the Government of India who might be particularly useful and far more so than officers lent direct from other Provinces without knowledge of our system and the local language and customs. If by any misfortune we had really heavy casualties, some of the younger men who have recently gone to the Political Department might prove the most useful type of temporary reinforcement.

6. *Attitude of Government Servants*

I do not anticipate that Government servants generally will have any reluctance in doing their duty against the extremist element. Their loyalty as regards the war is beyond question, and I consider that there is no sympathy among them for the extremists and revolutionaries and that they look on these not only as troublesome pests but as dangerous and unscrupulous enemies both to their service prospects and to themselves personally if given any opportunity to injure them. If it came to action against prominent right wing leaders and men whose personal character inspires respect, there might occasionally be some hesitation, but I think that in the great majority of cases officials will do their duty fearlessly. This probability can be strengthened by good leadership and if they feel that we really mean business and intend that there shall be firm government until the war is won. The present regime has not won the confidence of any grade of the services, but has done much to cause them uneasiness. General official opinion would, I think, be quite favourable to a respite by a return to the old conditions with the chance that it might be prolonged.

7. *Jail Accommodation*

The elasticity of the jail accommodation of the Province has recently had a severe test when room had to be found for over 10,000 Shia prisoners from the Tabarra agitation in addition to the ordinary population. The Jail Department proved equal to the strain, and, with this experience behind it, should be able to cope with numbers up to the extent of those imprisoned in the last civil disobedience movement. We hope, however, that the numbers will be very much less. The military authorities gave us valuable assistance in the case of the Shia prisoners by allowing us to use barracks at Sitapur and at Benares which were not in use at the time by them. I understand from the G.O.C.-in-C., Eastern Command that similar assistance will be forthcoming should it be required in future.

8. *Deportation of Prominent Leaders*

This would undoubtedly intensify resentment and should in my opinion certainly be avoided at the outset. If later on the situation greatly deteriorated and it became obvious that the break was irrevocable and that we were in for a prolonged and widespread conflict, deportation might then be advisable and necessary; but unless such a situation arises, I do not think that we should contemplate using them.

H.G. HAIG
Governor, United Provinces

83

DONALDSON TO LAITHWAITE
L/P&J/8/592: FF. 114-17

Secret *October 21st, 1939*
No. 1118/39-G.S.P.

My dear Laithwaite,

In continuance of my secret D.O. No. 1115/39-G.S.P. of October 19th, and with reference to the second para. of H.E. the Viceroy's telegram No. 2335-G of October 19th,[26] I am desired to send you the enclosed note, which may be treated as a further addendum to the Memorandum sent on October 19th.

Yours sincerely,
J.C. DONALDSON

ENCLOSURE TO NO. 83

NOTE BY HAIG

October 21st, 1939

My general views on the questions raised in His Excellency the Governor-General's telegram No. 2335-G, dated 19th October, 1939, are as follows:

(1) (*a*) If we are engaged against the Congress as a whole,[27] it is important, as far as possible, to avoid being forced to imprison or otherwise deal with very large numbers. The wise policy is to restrict our action, as far as we can, to leaders, including in that term the fairly numerous local men in a district who have some influence and powers of mischief. I should certainly endeavour to maintain the policy of not having indiscriminate prosecutions and impressing on District Magistrates that prosecutions are intended as a means to an end, that end being the preservation of peaceful and orderly conditions in the district.

(*b*) With regard to those against whom action is taken, I consider that the normal rule should be to prosecute all who can be prosecuted on a definite charge. I look upon Rule 26 as a reserve power, normally to be used only against those whom we cannot get on a specific charge. It is far easier to deal with men in prison than if they are merely interned in a village or otherwise restricted. We can enforce the latter orders in the case of a limited number of persons, but if large numbers of such restrictive orders are issued, it would be difficult to enforce them adequately. And it must be remembered that while treatment by restrictive order is actually lenient, it is open to attack as being taken without legal proof and therefore arbitrary.

(*c*) If it is necessary, however, to deal with persons of standing such as Ministers it might be advisable, in order to spare them the indignity of ordinary imprisonment, to serve them with restrictive orders. This course would, however, be of no advantage unless it was known that the persons concerned would abide by the orders. Otherwise they would disobey the orders and would then have to be imprisoned for disobedience.

(2) The use of the Criminal Law Amendment Act depends on how formidable the movement is that we are up against. So far as the Congress organisation is concerned, I should be reluctant to use the Criminal Law Amendment Act until it became quite clear that they were using all their resources against us. It might, however, at a very early stage, and even if the Congress does not come in actively against us, be necessary to use the Criminal Law Amendment Act against such bodies as the H.S.R.A., Youth League, Kisan Sabha, etc.

(3) There are varying degrees in which the Congress as a whole might come in against us, and I should hope that it might be some time before they would, if they do, openly declare a policy of civil disobedience. During this intermediate period I think we should be well advised to pursue as lenient a policy as possible towards the right wing, as it is clear that they would not have their heart in an open struggle against Government. There is always a chance, even though a remote one, that they might not be forced or drift into this situation; and in any case I feel that there would be less bitterness and consequently less conviction about their action if we did nothing to provoke it. My general inclination therefore would be to postpone drastic action against the right wing Congress as long as is reasonably possible, even though that might involve the sacrifice of certain initial advantages. I contemplate taking vigorous action from the very beginning against the dangerous left wing of the Congress.

2. With reference to the powers of issuing orders under Rule 26 of the Defence of India Rules I am not quite clear whether a Provincial Government is authorised to pass an order of externment from the Province. I should not of course want to pass an order of externment except in the case of persons who do not belong to the U.P.; but in their case it might be very valuable to have the power of externing them from the Province.

H.G. HAIG
Governor, United Provinces

84

HAIG TO LINLITHGOW
Telegram
MSS.EUR.F 115/7

No. 277-G *October 22nd, 1939*

In continuation of my telegram No. G-276, dated October 19, on return to Lucknow yesterday I saw Sampurnanand and Kidwai, the only Ministers now here. Sampurnanand is in a very depressed mood. He seemed to regard a break as inevitable, and said that when the Ministries resigned he did not see how the Congress could remain inactive. They would be forced to launch a movement of opposition. He admitted that such a movement, embarrassing to British and encouraging to Germans, would in its effect be contrary to the general attitude of the Congress towards the war, and that if it tended to affect the results it would be contrary to the interests of India. Nor did he expect that it would succeed in making the British

Government change their attitude towards constitutional reform. He said, however, that the principles and past commitments of Congress made it inevitable for them to embark on this struggle which was in the nature of a forlorn hope.

2. Kidwai seemed to think there was still some faint hope of a compromise if Gandhi saw Your Excellency. He still thought that if the Ministries resigned the Congress as a whole might for a time adopt an attitude of neutrality; but recognised that circumstances were likely to be too strong and that even if the situation started like this, before long the Congress would be drawn into active opposition.

3. There is no doubt that ministerial circles would greatly regret a breach and that they would embark on a struggle with reluctance. They realise that they are faced with a dilemma, and would certainly do all they can to encourage any move of conciliation.

4. Views of other parties and interests are, I should judge, pretty accurately reflected in the press. I have no firsthand information about Muslim League policy, but Ministers are still in friendly contact with Jinnah over Khaksar question.

85

HAIG TO LINLITHGOW
Telegram
MSS.EUR.F 115/7

Immediate *October 23rd, 1939*
No. 278-G

Your telegram 2361-G, dated October 21.[28] With regard to adequacy of police forces we have been trying since outbreak of war to recruit 300 more ex-servicemen who would be immediately useful. But the response has been most disappointing, and I do not think we can look any more to this source. We shall therefore have to recruit new material. When a break comes I shall probably authorise immediate recruitment of 1,000 men. The Inspector-General tells me that he hopes by putting them through a special course of three months' training to make them available after that period. He assures me that he anticipates no difficulty in recruiting and that we shall have an ample supply of excellent recruits from the province.

2. Arrangements to protect public buildings, important industrial plants and strategic railways and certain vital points on non-strategic railways have already been concerted carefully with military authorities and brought

into operation. If it is proposed to have extensive protection of non-strategic railways this might impose demands on our resources which we should be unable to meet.

3. In my memorandum dated October 19, 1939 I have explained arrangements contemplated for publicity. There has been a very general complaint of lack of central publicity in connection with war, and I am very glad to know this is being taken up. It is an essential part of our provincial publicity campaign. Admittedly India is not doing much in connection with the war; but there is a strong feeling that the public ought to know much more of what is being done both on the military and industrial sides.

86

HAIG TO LINLITHGOW
Telegram
MSS.EUR.F 115/7

Immediate *October 23rd, 1939*
No. 279-G

I discussed this evening with Kidwai question of resignation of Ministry. He said their instructions were to tender their resignations not later than 31st October unless there was some important practical work to be completed, in which case they might remain in office for a few days longer. They would also be prepared to meet my convenience by remaining in office for a day or two after resignations were tendered in order to enable me to complete my preparations. He suggested that they might tender their resignations on the 31st. I said that while I greatly appreciated the consideration they were showing I felt that it placed both the Ministers and myself in a false position if the Ministry remained in office for any length of time after it had been irrevocably announced that they were going to resign. It really meant that any business involving a possible difference of opinion between us was paralysed. Nor was there any particular question that required to be finished off. Kidwai fully agreed with these views and said that they would be prepared to tender their resignations on any date that might be convenient to me. I suggested that as they were passing their resolution on the 26th it might be convenient if the resignations were tendered on the 28th. He said he was quite agreeable to this programme. I told him however that before expressing a final view I would consult Your Excellency.

2. I am assuming that nothing can now happen which will prevent the resignation of the Ministry. On that assumption I feel strongly that delay will be inexpedient. Our subversive forces will from now onwards intensify preparations and I am anxious not to wait unnecessarily before taking action. I should be grateful if you would let me know whether there is any objection to my Ministers tendering resignations on the 28th.

87

HAIG TO LINLITHGOW
R/3/1/75

Personal
No. U.P.-319

Camp,
October 27th, 1939

My dear Lord Linlithgow,

I am writing to repeat what I said yesterday that the discussions I was able to have with Your Excellency regarding the general situation and particular problems that confront us will be of great value to me, and in particular I was glad to get your advice on certain matters, such as the Tenancy Bill. It was also a great pleasure to me to have the opportunity of meeting Your Excellency again, and being able to say my goodbyes to you and Lady Linlithgow in person.

2. I saw Chaudhri Khaliq-uz-Zaman this morning. He fully realised the objections to the Muslim League attempting to form a Government and has no desire to undertake the task; but he is getting confirmation from Jinnah. He raised the question of non-official Advisers. I explained to him the reasons why I was not disposed in the first instance to have non-official Advisers. He quitc appreciated the force of these reasons. I then explained to him my idea of a War Board and he welcomed this with marked enthusiasm and said it would provide an excellent opportunity for the cooperation of the Muslim League without the difficulties that would attach to more formal association with the Government.

Yours sincerely,
HARRY HAIG

88

HAIG TO LINLITHGOW
Telegram
MSS.EUR.F 115/7

No. 282-G *October 30th, 1939*

Ministry tendered their resignation this evening.[29] I explained to Premier that apart from necessity of considering alternative arrangements I thought it undesirable to accept their resignation finally as long as discussions were proceeding between Your Excellency and Congress. We both agreed that resignation when accepted should be final, and that it was very undesirable to have resignation accepted and then the Ministry taking office again after a few days. Premier is therefore agreeable to Ministry remaining until situation clears itself. I should be grateful to know when that may be expected.

2. In communiqué I am merely stating that before accepting resignation I must consider alternative arrangements to be made.

89

HAIG TO LINLITHGOW
Telegram
MSS.EUR.F 115/7

Immediate
No. 283-G *October 31st, 1939*

I saw today Khaliq-uz-Zaman, leader of Muslim League party, and asked him whether he was in position to form a Government. I arranged that he would return tomorrow and give me the answer which will of course be negative.

2. He suggested to me that the outcome of the conversations in Delhi, if they were successful, might be, apart from decisions about Centre, agreement to form coalition Ministries in provinces, and he suggested it might be easier to form such a Ministry in this Province if resignation of existing Ministers had been accepted and I had taken charge. The idea is that in such a situation it would be easier to drop some of the existing Ministers whom it would be difficult to fit in. On the other hand I have already in my possession resignation of my Ministers, and it would I think be possible, without going through the stage of my assuming charge, to

treat the resulting situation as one of the formation of a completely new Ministry in consequence of the resignation of the existing one.

3. I am not at all anxious on administrative grounds to take charge of the Province myself while still practically bound by the situation as indicated in your telegram No. 2430-S, dated October 28,[30] not to take any vigorous action.

90

HAIG TO LINLITHGOW
Telegram
MSS.EUR.F 115/7

No. 285-G *November 1st, 1939*

Your telegram 2462-S, dated October 31.[31] Legislative Council already stands prorogued. I have today prorogued Assembly.

91

HAIG TO LINLITHGOW
R/3/1/75

Confidential *November 1st, 1939*
No. U.P.-321

My dear Lord Linlithgow,

The Tenancy Bill was submitted for my assent shortly before the Ministry resigned. A copy is attached to this letter,[32] and advance copies have already been sent to your Secretary (Public), and to the India Office.

2. The Bill is of great importance. It has occupied the time of the Legislature from the end of April 1938 to October 4th, 1939 and has formed almost throughout its discussion the subject of acute controversy between the Ministerial party and the landlord interests. At various stages there have been proposals for compromise, but these have always broken down in consequence of the disunity of the landlords, the resistance of some sections of the landlords sterilising the willingness of other sections to compromise. Nevertheless, some important concessions have been obtained by the landlords in the course of the discussions, and in particular the Bill would not have gone through the Upper House in its final stages as it did with comparatively little discussion and opposition had it not

been that the Government made a concession in regard to the procedure for ejectment for non-payment of arrears of rent, which was felt by the landlords generally to be not unreasonable and which an appreciable section of them were prepared to accept as a settlement of the Bill as a whole. The main outlines of the Bill have been made known widely in the villages by Congress workers, and I believe that they are generally understood. It is also now well known in the villages that the Bill has been passed.

3. I am advised that the Bill contains nothing which would render its reservation necessary under Section 107. Procedure in Rent and Revenue courts comes in the Provincial Legislative List (Item 2) and that covers almost all the provisions of this Bill about which at first sight there was any room for doubt in this respect. I am also advised that there is nothing in the Bill which would render its reservation necessary under Article XVII of the Instrument of Instructions, provided that I do not feel any doubt whether the Bill does or does not offend against the purposes of Section 299. In view of the importance of the Bill and of certain claims made by the Taluqdars, to which I shall refer later, I feel it necessary to consult Your Excellency and inform you of the facts before taking action, although, as you will see, I am clear in my own mind what my action should be.

4. A note is attached[33] which shows the principal changes made in the Tenancy Law of the Province by this Bill. The important changes which the Bill makes in the existing law to the detriment of the landlords are as follows:

(*a*) The Tenancy Law in Agra has hitherto been more favourable to the tenant than the law in Oudh. For example, a large proportion of tenants in the Agra Province already have hereditary rights. The remainder have a life tenancy, but the heir of a deceased tenant may retain the holding at the same rent for five years after the death of his predecessor. A life tenancy of this kind is called a "statutory tenancy". In Oudh, speaking broadly, there were no hereditary tenancies. Since the amendment of the Oudh Rent Act, 1886, in 1921 practically all tenancies in Oudh have been statutory tenancies of the type mentioned. The new Act (Section 29) [makes] statutory tenants in Oudh hereditary tenants. The estimated numbers of tenants who will benefit are approximately:

Agra – No figure available	... ...	68,00,000 acres.
Oudh – 1¾ million tenants	... ...	78,00,000 acres.

The minority Ministry which was predominantly zamindar in sympathy had practically agreed to the grant of hereditary rights to a similar extent.

The actual difference in value to a landholder between a hereditary and a statutory tenancy is uncertain and depends on fortuitous circumstances. Under the old Act it was possible for the landlord to sell occupancy (hereditary) rights to his statutory tenants for cash. Several indebted Court of Wards Estates tried to do this, but there was not a great demand and tenants in general were not willing to pay a large price for the conversion. One or two years' purchase of the rent was about the usual offer.

(*b*) *Sir.* "Sir" may be explained as land which has been cultivated by the zamindar himself for a period of time and is deemed to have acquired the character of his permanent cultivation, which it retains even when he does not actually cultivate it. When it is let, the tenants are tenants at will, and there is no restriction on the amount of their rent other than agreement between them and the landlord, and the force of competition. If a landlord's property is sold, whether by private treaty or by a court for debt, he retains the right of cultivating the land which was his "Sir" at a favourable rate of rent. The land revenue assessment on "Sir" land is lighter than on ordinary tenancy land.

The declared motive of the Government in the provisions of the Bill dealing with "Sir" is to give some protection to the tenants of "Sir" who, as I have stated, are at present tenants at will. Landlords contend that the position of such tenants is comparable to that of sub-tenants of hereditary tenants, who also have no protection. They further state that they find it necessary to give out their "Sir" land to estate servants to cultivate as part of their remuneration and that unless they can give land they cannot get servants.

When the Oudh Rent Act, 1886, was amended in 1921 and when the present Agra Tenancy Act was passed in 1926, one of the concessions which was allowed to the landlords in order to induce them to accept other provisions in the Bill was that certain other land which they had in their cultivation was allowed to acquire the permanent character of "Sir". The area in Oudh was 3,70,000 acres out of a present total of 7,20,000 acres "Sir" and in Agra was 16,00,000 acres out of 49,10,000 acres "Sir".

One of the provisions of the present Bill to which the landlords most strongly object is clause 6 (*a*) according to which in the case of the larger landholders (paying land revenue of Rs. 250 per annum or over), they will lose their "Sir" rights in land owned by them which became "Sir" as a result of the legislation I have mentioned in 1921 and 1926. The area affected is estimated at 5,60,000 acres in Agra and 1,20,000 in Oudh – total 6,80,000 acres of which 1,80,000 acres is let to tenants.

It may perhaps be pointed out here, with reference to all the "Sir" provisions, that they mainly affect the landlords whose "Sir" is at present let. Where a landholder is still cultivating "Sir" which is affected by the provisions of the Act, it may lose its character of "Sir", but he continues to cultivate it and is not much the worse, unless he subsequently lets it to a tenant. If he is sold up, he will retain "expropriatory rights" in it if he has been cultivating it, just as he would if it had remained "Sir". On the other hand, if the land is at present let and under the provisions of the new Act now loses its character of "Sir", the tenants who are at present in occupation become hereditary tenants, instead of tenants at will and the landholder cannot get rid of them. 24.2 per cent. of the "Sir" area in Agra is let and 39 per cent in Oudh. The total let is 11,91,000 acres.

Clause 16 also affects only those zamindars who pay Rs. 250 per annum land revenue and over. It applies in the case of such landlords to all "Sir" and not merely to land which became their "Sir" under the legislation of 1921 and 1926. It only applies, however, to such a landlord if he has over 50 acres of "Sir". If at the present time he has "Sir" rights in more than 50 acres, but is cultivating all the land himself, he is not affected, and will not be until he wishes to let some of the land to a tenant. But if some of the land is let, then the tenants of any portion up to the area by which the "Sir" exceeds 50 acres will immediately become hereditary tenants. The underlying idea of this clause is apparently that a landholder should not require more than 50 acres in his own cultivation and farming, or at any rate should not be given the special privileges applicable to land cultivated by the owner himself for a larger area than 50 acres. He may cultivate more, but he gets no special privileges. It is estimated that not more than 1,00,000 acres will be affected.

There is no doubt that a number of landholders, particularly some of the big estates in Oudh, possess a large quantity of "Sir" land, which they never cultivate themselves, but let to tenants at rack rents. On the other hand the "Sir" question has little practical importance for a considerable number of landlords, particularly in Agra, and their concern is more in regard to the principle, which they consider to be confiscatory.

It is not possible to state accurately the amount of "Sir" which will be affected by Clauses 6 (*a*) and 16. The estimate is 6,80,000 acres under Clause 6 (*a*) and 1,00,000 under Clause 16. There are no separate statistics of the amount of "Sir" owned by landholders paying over Rs. 250 per annum land revenue. Clause 20 confers a further benefit on tenants of "Sir" at the expense of the landholder: every person who is now a tenant or may in future be admitted as a tenant of "Sir" gets a five-year lease of the "Sir" instead of being a tenant at will. 11,91,000 acres are now sublet.

Some 2½ to 3 lakhs of "Sir" tenants will benefit under this Clause.

(c) *Ejectment for arrears of rent.* The following are new provisions limiting or affecting the landlord's right of ejectment:

(*i*) Section 158. If a tenant is ejected for arrears of rent from the whole or any portion of his holding, all arrears, whether decreed or not, in respect of such holding which cannot be adjusted against anything payable to him as compensation for improvements, crops or trees, shall be deemed to have been paid.

(*ii*) Where a decree for arrears of rent against a tenant is not satisfied within one year from the date of the decree, the tenant may be ejected from a portion of the holding, the annual rent of which does not exceed one-sixth of the decretal amount: (Section 168). The Section also gives the tenant a certain period of grace during the ejectment proceedings. It is thought that in practice this Section will be little used.

(*iii*) A landholder may sue for an arrear of rent under the provisions of Section 148 *et seq.* and obtain a decree. He may also at a certain season of the year, apply to have a notice issued to a tenant demanding the payment of an undecreed arrear of rent (which may not exceed the annual rent of the holding) and stating that in default of payment the tenant will be ejected. Provided the amount claimed is found to be due, the tenant will be ejected if he does not pay the arrear in the period ending on "the 31st of May next following the expiry of a period of one year from the date of the passing of the order of payment" (Section 165). He will also be ejected if he does not pay his current rent punctually during this period (Section 165). This is a point of great value to the landlord. It may take a landholder about two years to get a tenant ejected under this procedure, who fails to pay the amount claimed in the notice. But the procedure has been accepted by the majority of landlords as not unreasonable.

(*iv*) Section 256. A court in execution of a decree for arrears of rent may put the whole or a part of a tenant's holding to sale. The amount realised is paid in satisfaction of the decree. Certain classes of persons are given a right of pre-emption, at the highest bid. The effect of this Clause is that a landlord may be given a tenant in the selection of whom he had no voice. The procedure has, I understand, been in vogue in Bengal and Bihar for some time, but it is novel in this Province, and disliked by many of the landlords.

(*v*) Section 256 (*a*). A court executing a decree for arrears of rent may, as an alternative to selling the whole or part of a holding, lease it for a period to some person who pays up the decreed amount and undertakes to pay the current rent during the period of his lease.

5. These are the main provisions of the Bill which can be regarded as diminishing the landlords' rights. There are a number of smaller provisions dealing with tenants' houses, trees, reinstatement of ejected tenants and so forth, which also affect the landlord's full enjoyment of his property. If, however, the main items which I have mentioned are considered to be justified on grounds of public policy, then the smaller concessions which are granted to the tenants must be held to be similarly justified.

The method of realising rent by distraint of crops has been completely abolished. The provisions in the present Acts by which a landlord could, under certain circumstances, acquire land held by occupancy or statutory tenants for his own use for farming or building, have been very greatly curtailed (Section 54).

6. The landlords contend that the provisions regarding "Sir" are confiscatory. They certainly introduce very considerable restrictions on the landlords' existing rights in "Sir" land. It is necessary to make it clear, however, that when it is said that the landlord is deprived of certain "Sir" land, he is not deprived of his ownership in the land, but only of certain rights which attach to "Sir" land. The landlords' rights in "Sir" land constitute practically a denial of rights to tenants; they include the power of ejectment at will and no restriction on rack-renting. While therefore it is admitted that under clause 6 (*a*) certain lands which were under the Acts of 1921 and 1926 declared as "Sir" are now removed altogether from that category, and while under Clause 16 the amount of existing "Sir" which can be retained as "Sir" is drastically reduced in the case of landlords paying over Rs. 250 land revenue, the change amounts only to a denial or restriction of certain rights of landlords, which in present conditions may be held to be unreasonable. The provisions regarding ejectment have formed the subject of very prolonged consideration, and broadly speaking in my judgement they provide sufficient means to the landlord to secure the due payment of rent. As stated above a considerable section of the landlords are prepared to accept these provisions.

7. Clause 81 which provides that scattered trees situated in the holding of a tenant which at present belong to the landlord shall vest in the tenant, is in its nature confiscatory. Any attempt, however, to have this Clause modified would inevitably lead to widespread disputes in the villages and possibly to extensive cutting of the trees by the tenants. The matter is not one of major importance to the landlords, and though in principle it is wrong, in practice it will probably tend to eliminate from the villages an existing source of friction.

8. It has been argued by the landlords that it is very unreasonable that

they should not be allowed to take from tenants to use for their own purposes more than the small areas of land held by tenants which they will be entitled to acquire under Clause 54-A, of the Bill. Actually, however, the much wider provisions contained in the existing Agra Tenancy Act and Oudh Rent Act have been used very little by the landlords. In the year 1937-38 the total amount of land acquired by landlords for their own purposes, subject to the existing restrictions which make it necessary for them to satisfy the Collector that the purpose is a genuine one, amounted only to 154 acres in the Province of Agra and 62 acres in the Province of Oudh.

9. The Oudh Taluqdars have raised the special contention that they hold their estates under *sanads* granted by the Chief Commissioner of Oudh under the authority of the Viceroy. Copies of two forms of these *sanads* are attached.[34] The terms of the *sanads* were incorporated in and qualified by the Oudh Estates Act 1869. Their contention is that by these *sanads* the British Government promised to maintain them as proprietors of their estates and conferred on them the full proprietary right, title and possession of their estates. They maintain that any subsequent legislation dealing with the relations of landlords and tenants and by which rights have been conferred on tenants, has only been passed after obtaining the consent of the representative body of Taluqdars, the British Indian Association of Oudh. They maintain that this was done when the Oudh Rent Act of 1886 was passed and when it was amended in 1921. They say that originally it was definitely held that tenants in Oudh had no right of occupancy. The present Bill, they allege, infringes and diminishes their rights in their property. In particular it prevents them from resuming and getting possession of their land for the purpose of farming it themselves or using as they please.

In my opinion, this contention cannot be upheld. It is to my mind extremely doubtful whether the terms of the *sanads* and of the accompanying declarations did exclude the right of Government to provide by law for fair treatment of their tenants by the Taluqdars. Even if this was the intention at the time the grants were made, it can hardly be held to be binding upon the Legislature created by the Government of India Act, 1935. It is evident that the framers of that Act contemplated that the Legislatures created by it might propose legislation which would alter the character of the Permanent Settlement of Bengal, a much more specific and binding obligation contracted by the British Government than these Taluqdari grants. The real question is whether the provisions of this Bill are so definitely unjust and unfair to the landlords as a class that the interests of that class should be safeguarded in opposition to the interests of the larger class composed of their tenants and to the wish of the electorate as a whole as expressed by the majority of its representatives. In my view the competence of the Legislature in this matter is not restricted by anything outside the Government of India Act. It is understood that the Taluqdars intend to challenge the validity of the Bill on this ground in a court of law. That, however, does not appear to me to be any cause for withholding my assent. In this connection I enclose a copy of a memorial which the Taluqdars presented to me on October 25th and a summary of my reply.[35]

10. The general conclusion of the matter in my opinion is that this Bill though it makes extensive modifications in the existing rights of the landlords, cannot be regarded in the words of paragraph 5 of the Secretary of State's letter to Your Excellency, dated September 28th, 1939, as "grossly discriminatory or having regard to all the attendant circumstances otherwise morally indefensible". On the contrary the general provisions of the Bill are salutary and as a whole the improvement in the rights of the tenants is in my opinion fully due. There are certain provisions which I would have preferred to see omitted; but I am clear that they are not of sufficient importance either in practice or in principle to justify withholding my assent to the Bill or referring it back to the Legislature for further consideration. I therefore propose, if Your Excellency has no objection, to grant assent to the Bill.

11. It has been necessary to consider the possibility of the Ministry resigning, and the Governor administering the Province under the provisions of Section 93 of the Government of India Act. I have considered very carefully whether in these circumstances it would be justifiable to take a different line to that which in my opinion is clearly marked out in the event of the Ministers remaining in office. It might be argued that there is no obligation on the Governor to give assent without modification to legislation passed by a Ministry which has resigned office, and that it would not be unreasonable to make certain modifications in the Bill by means of an amending Act passed by my own authority which would remove some of the objections most strongly stressed by the landlords. I am convinced, however, that such a course would not be wise. If the Ministers resign it is on general principles desirable that there should not be any abrupt reversals of policy, and any changes made in this Bill would be open to serious attack on the ground of interference with policy so recently approved by both Houses of the Legislature. Moreover, from the practical point of view if any change is made in this Bill on the authority of the Governor, it will provide the Congress with opportunity for widespread misrepresentation and agitation in the villages. If assent is given to

the Bill as passed by the Legislature any disappointment that may be felt in the villages in regard to its provisions will fall on the head of the Congress itself; but if any change is made by the Governor all defects in the Bill are likely to be laid to his charge.

12. If the Bill receives assent as passed there is a reasonable chance that no serious agitation will be started in the villages. If, however, agitation is started by bodies such as the Kisan Sabha, then the Governor will be in the strongest possible position for dealing with that agitation firmly on the ground that all reasonable grievances have been removed by the Bill passed by the Congress Government itself. I attach great importance to this point and consider that leaving the Bill unmodified will greatly strengthen my hands in dealing with Kisan Sabha agitation. A further point is that any modifications made by the Governor under Section 93 (4) of the Government of India Act will have effect only for two years after the Section 93 situation ceases.

13. I am aware that the grant of assent to the Bill, particularly if I have assumed powers to myself under Section 93, will be a cause of considerable disappointment to the landlords who will feel that they have not received from the Governor the support they might have expected. In a Section 93 situation the support of the landlords will be of considerable importance to the Governor, and at first at any rate this may on account of such disappointment be less vigorous than it would otherwise have been. But I am convinced that it would be both wrong and unwise in this matter to compromise the principle in order to try and obtain a temporary tactical advantage. I believe that it is in the interests both of the landlords and of the Governor that the Bill should now become law as it stands, and I believe that after a time the landlords themselves will come to recognise that fact.

14. I wish to emphasise a point which I recently mentioned to Your Excellency, that it is a matter of primary importance that a decision should be taken regarding the grant of assent to this Bill at the earliest possible moment. If the matter remains in doubt for any appreciable time in a Section 93 situation opportunity will be given to start agitation in the villages on the ground that assent is being delayed and that the Governor intends to deprive the villagers of the rights given them by this legislation; and it might be difficult to overtake that agitation. I would therefore be very grateful if I could have approval to the course which I propose at a very early date.[36]

Yours sincerely,
H.G. HAIG

92

HAIG TO LINLITHGOW
Telegram
MSS.EUR.F 115/7

Immediate *November 2nd, 1939*
No. 286-G

Your telegram 2495-S, dated November 1.[37] I agree in circumstances explained that it is not wise unduly to delay application of Section 93. Present situation involves me in embarrassments. I propose therefore to accept resignation of Ministers on morning November 3rd and I request sanction to issue of proclamation under Section 93 immediately thereafter.[38]

2. I fully appreciate in present circumstances desirability of confining consequent action to minimum possible. I have abandoned idea of taking action under Rule 129 against terrorists or communists. I shall issue orders in regard to prosecution of individuals whose cases are now pending before Government, and in regard to future speeches shall give District Magistrates free hand to prosecute local firebrands under Defence of India Rules. I shall also give them a free hand against anti-recruiting activities. I propose also to organise at once in districts constructive activities in favour of war. I do not think any of these steps could reasonably be attacked as going beyond the requirements of the situation even though discussions at Delhi may still be proceeding.

93

HAIG TO LINLITHGOW
R/3/1/75

Secret *November 8th, 1939*
No. U.P.-325

My dear Lord Linlithgow,

I did not send you a letter a fortnight ago, as just at that time I was paying you a visit at Delhi and was able to discuss all our main problems. The situation has in fact worked out rather differently to what I had been anticipating at that time in the event of a break. The change has been effected very quietly and smoothly, with no attempt so far on the part of the Right Wing of the Congress to do anything that could embarrass us, and with no indication that has yet reached me of any intensification of

Left Wing or terrorist activities. Consequently I have not only found no difficulty in following the general policy of going slow, but that policy is at the moment clearly the right one for the Province. Immediately on taking charge under Section 93, I discussed with my Advisers the issue of a letter to all District Magistrates, and on the 4th November, the day after I had taken over charge, a letter was issued, a copy of which I enclose. You will see that the action authorised goes not quite as far as I had indicated in paragraph 2 of my telegram No. 286-G., dated November 2nd. In discussion with my Advisers we were all agreed that it was desirable as far as possible to use the ordinary law against speeches rather than the Defence of India Rules. The District Magistrates have been given full authority to proceed against dangerous speakers under Sections 107 and 108 of the Criminal Procedure Code, while they will have to apply for sanction under the ordinary law for prosecution under Sections 124-A and 153-A of the Indian Penal Code. It is not my intention at present that the Defence of India Rules should be used in respect of speeches that can be dealt with under the ordinary law. Its use will be confined for the moment to anti-recruiting activities. If the instructions we have given do not go far enough to meet the situation in any particular district, we shall soon hear of it and wider powers can be given; but at present I think what I have done will be sufficient. A certain number of the more dangerous men regarding whom applications for sanction to prosecute under the Penal Code were pending before the late Government will be dealt with now, but with action being taken under the ordinary law I do not think there should be much occasion for criticism.

2. I said good-bye to Pant when he came to tender the resignation of the Ministry on the 30th October. He was returning at once to Naini Tal. Nothing could have been more friendly than his attitude, and he said that whatever happened he hoped he would have an opportunity of seeing me once more and saying good-bye before I left India. The next few days were a period of some difficulty. There were certain proposals made by Ministers which I clearly could not accept, as I should have had to reverse them on assuming charge myself. Consequently I held them up. On the other hand, there was a certain tendency in one or two cases to rush through decisions without my having been consulted at all. The Khaksar problem was also a great embarrassment. It was clearly desirable to show considerable forbearance in Lucknow. At the same time the Ministers did not like this, as the Khaksars, though openly declaring their willingness to stop the agitation if I took charge, still maintained their intransigent attitude as against the Ministers. I telegraphed to you on November 2nd that the

situation involved embarrassments and that I proposed to accept the resignation of the Ministers next morning. After sending that telegram I had a letter from Kidwai complaining in rather petulant terms about the difficulties of the situation, particularly in connection with the Khaksars, and saying that the Ministers felt their position and authority were being jeopardised and questioned. I discussed the position with him that evening and made it clear that while I recognised their difficulties, the situation from my point of view also was far from easy, and I told him that I hoped to let him have a definite answer the next morning. On the 3rd November, having heard from Your Excellency, I wrote to Kidwai saying that I had decided regretfully to accept the resignation of the Ministers, and they came formally for the acceptance of their resignations at 12-30 that morning. They were a small party, as Pant was in Naini Tal and Mrs. Pandit in bed with fever. We parted with mutual expressions of regard, and they seemed quite pleased to sit for a photograph which I had arranged. That same evening I broadcast a statement,[39] a copy of which I enclose, which was also communicated to the press.

3. Conversations for a settlement of the Khaksar question were already very far advanced when I took over charge, and I felt it was important to conclude these without any delay. The persons who were speaking on behalf of the Allama were Mian Ahmad Shah, who has always taken a reasonable line, and curiously enough, Sir Ziauddin Ahmed, who claims to occupy a position of some authority on behalf of the Khaksars. Mian Ahmad Shah showed a written authority from the Allama to conclude a settlement, and an agreement was reached and signed on the evening of November 4th. I attach a copy of the agreement. The main point was that the Khaksars stopped their hostile activities against the United Provinces Government and we withdrew our restrictive orders and released the Khaksars who were in jail either convicted or awaiting trial. With regard to the question of compensation I agreed to what Dr. Katju had already communicated some time ago to Jinnah as one of the Government terms. I do not think in fact it is likely to involve the payment of any compensation. We also agreed to pay the fares of the men back to their homes. I should have preferred to omit both these terms, but it was clear that if we wanted an immediate settlement we would have to accept something on these lines and I felt it was better to settle at once than to run the risk of long discussions with a possibly doubtful issue. A curious stipulation made by the Khaksars was that they did not want a communiqué put out and we agreed to this subject to our right of correcting any mis-statements. Actually Mian Ahmad Shah issued some kind of a statement next day. But so far it appears that little attention is being paid to the matter, and it looks as if we

may get the Khaksar situation liquidated without any appreciable public discussion, which would be a great advantage. There is no doubt that they themselves were in a chastened mood and had felt the strain of the struggle. From my point of view it was extremely desirable not to be involved in the prolongation of a quarrel which had at various times roused a good deal of general Muslim feeling.

4. A small Sunni-Shia riot broke out on the last day the Ministry were in office and it unfortunately involved some deaths. But it did not lead to any serious consequences. I fear the Sunni-Shia question is very far from settled. It may be that a further effort will now be made under my auspices to get it settled; but I am not proposing to take any initiative in this matter unless I am approached and am satisfied that there is a reasonable chance of a settlement.

5. I have sent my Adviser who deals with Labour over to Cawnpore to discuss the situation there with the millowners and the Mazdur Sabha. There are still a good many loose ends to be tied up, and in particular there is the commitment to hold an inquiry by a High Court Judge, which in fact I think neither side really wants to see carried out.

6. I have unfortunately had something of a setback physically since I saw you in Delhi. The doctors describe the symptoms as post-diphtheritic neuritis and say I ought to keep as quiet as possible – an admirable counsel which it is not very practicable to carry out. However, I am cancelling an Investiture which I was to hold on the 16th and which is always a considerable physical strain. It is unfortunate that I have a great many farewell functions to go through during this last month, but I hope in another fortnight or so I may be practically all right.

Yours sincerely,
H.G. HAIG

ENCLOSURE 1 TO NO. 93

MUDIE TO ALL DISTRICT MAGISTRATES

Secret and Personal
D.O. No. 2755-C.X.

Lucknow,
November 4th, 1939

Dear Sir,

I am desired to convey to you His Excellency the Governor's instructions as to policy now that he has assumed the charge of the Province under Section 93 of the Government of India Act, and particularly as to the use of the Defence of India Ordinance and Rules. The Defence of India Ordinance will very shortly be replaced by the Defence of India Act, which has been passed by the Central Legislature but not yet been brought into force. The Act differs very little from the Ordinance and the Rules made under the Ordinance will continue to be valid under the Act.

2. The situation at the moment is by no means clear. Conversations between His Excellency the Viceroy and the Congress leaders have not been broken off, and it is still possible that a satisfactory settlement may be reached and that a Ministry may before long be constituted again. At the same time, while His Excellency remains in charge of the Province, it is not his intention to allow order to be threatened or war activities to be impeded. Your policy should therefore be directed to the attainment of certain definite objectives. These are:

(*a*) The preservation of law and order and a peaceful atmosphere in your district, and in particular putting a stop to racial, class or communal incitements.

(*b*) The prevention of any acts such as anti-recruiting activities which will impede the prosecution of the war.

In carrying out this policy you should, as far as possible, make use of the ordinary law. As regards speeches which are objectionable with reference to (*a*), you should, unless the case is of sufficient importance to justify action under Section 124-A, or 153-A, Indian Penal Code, make full use of your powers under the preventive sections of the Criminal Procedure Code. To enable you to do so, the restrictions imposed by Chief Secretary's confidential demi-official letter of September 30th, 1939, are hereby removed and you may take action under Section 108 Criminal Procedure Code, without reference to higher authority. You should not use your powers under the Defence of India Rules except to prevent anti-war activities, which do not come within the ordinary law. But it is essential that vigorous action be taken to put a stop to these activities, particularly when they are directed to prevent or restrict recruiting. You should not, however, use your powers under these rules in respect of anything done before the date of the Proclamation. If you consider that the situation in your district justifies a wider use of powers under the Defence of India Rules than is laid down in this letter, you should refer the matter to Government through your Commissioner. In the case of an M.L.A. or M.L.C. or of a person of more than local prominence, action should not be taken without reference to Government through your Commissioner.

3. While you are expected to exercise your powers vigorously and without hesitation, it is equally important that action should not be

indiscriminate. It should not be taken in a mechanical way against persons who are not really dangerous. Allowance must be made for the difficulties of Right Wing Congressmen and no attempt should be made to take advantage of speeches and actions to which they may be driven to some extent against their wish. The situation in this respect may change later if it becomes clear that the Right Wing of Congress are taking an active part in opposing the war or embarrassing the Government. But for the present it must be assumed that that is not their intention, and your action should be directed only against those who may be reasonably classed as revolutionaries or who are engaged in specific and deliberate activities in conflict with the purposes stated at the beginning of paragraph 2 above.

4. The powers of preventive arrest which are given by Rule 129 of the Defence of India Rules are at present only to be exercised on the direct orders of the Government. District Officers and Police Officers must not make use of powers under this rule unless with the previous sanction of the Government.

5. An Officer is being appointed as Director of Public Information to deal with all matters connected with the Press and propaganda. His name will be announced shortly. Any information about newspapers and other publications should be addressed to him. The importance of propaganda need hardly be emphasised. So far, little or no attempt has been made to get the case of the Allies against Germany and the case for India's participation in the war put properly before the villagers. It will now be possible to do this, and every effort should be made to do it effectively and to rouse interest in India's own war effort. For this purpose, a district publicity organization will have to be created at the earliest possible moment. You will get detailed instructions about this from the Director of Public Information. In the meantime, you will make what preparations you think will be useful. The intention is to form in each district a District War Board, which will function under the control of a Central War Board. The District War Board will work under the chairmanship of the District Officer and it is intended that the most prominent non-officials who are prepared to give their active support to the war should be members of it, and that the Board will be the focus in each district for every kind of war activity and publicity.

6. The Indian Press (Emergency Powers) Act of 1931 continues in force, and the provisions of that Act about taking security from printing presses and from publishers of newspapers will be available if needed. At present it is desirable to go slowly in this matter and avoid precipitate action.

7. You are asked to devote particular attention to the preservation of

discipline in jails used to detain persons convicted for political offences and to seeing that such persons are kept under proper conditions in regard to accommodation and sanitation. In this connection, your attention is drawn to paragraph 952 of the Manual of Government Orders.

8. Until further instructions, will you please forward in duplicate to your Commissioner each Monday a brief report of your proceedings and the state of public feeling in your district?

9. I am to ask you for an acknowledgement of this letter.

Yours sincerely,
R.F. MUDIE

ENCLOSURE 2 TO NO. 93

AGREEMENT BETWEEN AHMAD SHAH AND MUDIE

November 4th, 1939

It is agreed that:

(1) Mian Ahmad Shah, acting under the authority conveyed by Allama Inayatullah Khan in his writing, dated 12th September 1939 and 25th October 1939, will order all Khaksars deputed from outside the Province to leave it.

(2) Government will cancel all bans at present imposed on Khaksars, it being understood that Khaksars will obey all orders now in force or to be made in future, which are necessary for the maintenance of law and order.

(3) All Khaksars at present in custody, whether convicted or under trial, will be released and Government will provide them with sufficient money to enable them with the money which they themselves possess to reach their homes.

(4) The Khaksars will not interest themselves further in the Shia-Sunni dispute.

(5) Government are prepared to consider any specific case where a claim may be made on the ground of any unauthorised or unjustified action on the part of a public servant.

(6) Government will issue no communiqué in the matter, it being understood that should Government action be misrepresented in the paper *Al Islah*, Government retain the right, should they consider it necessary, to do so.

MIAN AHMAD SHAH
R.F. MUDIE

94

HAIG TO LINLITHGOW
R/3/1/75

Secret *November 21st, 1939*
No. U.P.-326

My dear Lord Linlithgow,

Since I last wrote to you on November 8th, the general situation in the Province has remained practically unchanged. The curious lull continues, and on the surface it would seem that the great mass of the people have taken the disappearance of the Congress Ministry with indifference or with relief. This, however, takes no account of the ability of the Congress organization to stir up trouble and rouse feeling. One might say that [the] ocean lies at the moment calm and with hardly a ripple; but the same ocean would present a very different appearance under the influence of a strong gale. There seems no doubt that just at present the ordinary Congress workers are doing nothing, and in a perplexing situation, are waiting for instructions. The official fortnightly letter gives a fair summary of the reports we have been receiving from the districts which record this general condition of tranquillity. At the same time it would be a mistake to suppose that the Left Wing have in any way changed their views or intentions. I should judge that they are reluctant to embark on any serious activities so long as they hope to be able by waiting to bring the Right Wing in with them. But sooner or later, with or without the Right Wing, I think they are bound to start their campaign.

2. I was greatly interested in what Your Excellency told me of the situation from your point of view. I am writing from Allahabad where the Working Committee is now conferring. I think there is a general recognition of the fact that no further move at present can be expected from your side. On the other hand in view of the very rigid attitude that the Congress has publicly adopted, I do not see what genuine approach Gandhi could make to Your Excellency, though he might well try manoeuvre. It looks to me as if the situation is heading steadily for civil disobedience, though Gandhi with his usual technique requires a period of more or less open preparation. The only thing as it seems to me that might prevent this development is a Hindu-Muslim agreement, but I cannot say that I regard that as likely. Here again, however, I think the Congress will manoeuvre so as to try to put the Muslims in the wrong, and may make some offer which would not go far enough.

3. In the circumstances described above District Officers have found it necessary to take very little action on their own responsibility. I have sanctioned a few prosecutions which I regarded as important, all of them cases which had come up before the Ministry and on which they had postponed taking a decision. The most important is the prosecution of Bishambhar Dayal Tripathi, M.L.A. of the Unao district. He is the Secretary of the Forward Bloc in this Province and for months past has been a great embarrassment to my late Ministry. He has not only been making a series of bad speeches, but he had worked up tenant feeling to a very considerable extent in the district and the position was regarded as having its dangers. He had been openly defying the Government to prosecute him, and it seemed to me important that in his case there should be no delay in making it clear that I intended to maintain order. His arrest which was effected about a week ago created very little excitement and has not been much commented on in the local Congress paper. I think we arrested him just at the right time, for after orders had issued, I heard that he was starting on another of his whirlwind tours of speech making round the district. Another person who has been arrested in respect of a bad speech made a little time ago is Manmatha Nath Gupta, one of the ex-Kakori prisoners, a man who has for a long time past been writing and speaking in an unrestrained and violent manner. It will be a good thing to have him out of the way.

4. Nothing more has been heard of the Khaksars since I last wrote. With their departure to their homes we have been left in peace, and so far as this Province is concerned I hope that interest in the Khaksars will rapidly disappear. Indeed, it might almost be said to have disappeared already. There is of course the possibility that they may press their claim for compensation in respect of the Bulandshahr firing. In that connection we have now received the report of Hunter, the Judge who made the enquiry. I cannot say I think it is a good report. The earlier part discusses the Khaksar movement and Government policy without any attempt having been made to ascertain the facts, on which conclusions could be based; while the latter part, though it is satisfactory from the point of view that everybody seems to be exonerated, is not very convincing in some of its judgements. The main points that emerge are that the Khaksars' behaviour was most menacing, that they snatched away the guns from three jail warders and tried to use them, and that a large body of them ran down the road brandishing their *belchas* in a very formidable manner. It was, however, an unpremeditated and short-lived outbreak. On the other hand, the discipline of the police clearly broke and firing was opened independently and without orders. The reasons for this appear to be partly that the police

dispositions in the neighbourhood of the jail were unsatisfactory, and partly that the police consisted of a somewhat heterogeneous collection of men brought in from several districts. The firing lasted less than two minutes. There are many points which will require careful examination by the Inspector-General of Police in regard to the police, by the Government in regard to general policy, and by the lawyers as to certain legal points that have been raised. We all agree that it would be most undesirable to publish the report, and my present intention is to do nothing to call attention to it and in the meantime to pursue at our leisure the various matters which clearly require attention. The less we say about it publicly, the better. On Hunter's findings I do not think there is any case for giving compensation to the Khaksars.

5. In my last letter I had mentioned that I sent Panna Lall, my Adviser who deals with industrial problems, over to Cawnpore to discuss the situation there with the millowners and the Mazdur Sabha. He had some important conversations. It seems clear that neither side want the suggested arbitration of a High Court Judge. The matter which is immediately giving cause for some discontent is that a considerable number of old employees of the New Victoria Mills are still unemployed. We have made it clear to the millowners and Sir Jwala Prasad Srivastava that we attach special importance to those men being re-employed as soon as possible, and Sir Jwala Prasad has promised that he will do all he can to expedite this. If this problem can be got out of the way, I do not think there is any other matter which is likely to cause trouble just now, unless there is a deliberate attempt by the Communists to bring about a strike as part of a revolutionary movement. Indeed, Cawnpore labour is at the moment quiet, and it is doubtful whether they could be moved except on an economic issue. It is, however, necessary to look ahead, and under my instructions Panna Lall is taking up actively the question of reorganizing the Mazdur Sabha, so that it may receive recognition by the millowners – a policy which the millowners themselves are now definitely anxious to support – and also the question of giving effect to a number of uncontentious recommendations made by the enquiry committee some 18 months ago on which action does not seem to have been taken. The most important matter is the improvement of housing, and everyone is agreed that this should be taken up. The present affords an excellent opportunity for taking a real initiative in these Cawnpore labour problems.

6. I have had several conversations last week in connection with my idea of forming a War Board for the Province. My general plan is to have a fairly large body of about 100 or 150, who would really do nothing

except most occasionally, and have an Executive Committee of about 20 non-officials plus my Advisers and the new Secretary in our Publicity Department who would meet with more frequency – I hope not less than once a month – and try and get our war activities organised and developed. There would also be a District War Board in each district working in conjunction with this organisation. The general idea has been well received. Sapru told me he would be glad to join the Executive Committee and he thought that Chintamani would too. Chhatari and Srivastava have also agreed. But a difficulty has arisen with the Muslim League which has made me hold my hand for the moment. When I saw Chaudhri Khaliq-uz-Zaman who is the provincial leader of the Muslim League at the time of the resignation of the Ministry, I discussed this idea with him and he showed himself very definitely in favour of it. When, however, I saw him again last Friday and asked him whether he and another person to represent the League would join the Executive Committee, he said he could take no action without consulting Jinnah. He explained to me the reason, which I will mention later, on account of which Jinnah might prefer that the Muslim League should keep out of this. At the same time he said that he would have no objection to Muslims who were members of the Muslim League joining the Executive Committee, provided that they were not regarded as directly representing the Muslim League. For instance, he said there would be no difficulty about Chhatari or Jehangirabad or Muhammad Yusuf joining the Board. Khaliq has referred the matter to Jinnah and I am now awaiting his answer. The reason he gave me for a possible reluctance on the part of the Muslim League to join the War Board was this. He said that if Congress decided on civil disobedience the Muslim League did not want either to leave the resulting struggle to be fought out between the British and the Congress, or to take part in it merely as supporters of the British. They did not wish on the one hand to be charged with being "toadies", nor on the other hand did they look with any equanimity on the prospect of a struggle by the British alone against the Congress, at the end of which the British, if successful, might well say that they had no obligation to the Muslims who had not supported them; while on the other hand there was a possibility that the British might make terms with the Congress which would be very damaging to the Muslims. His conclusion was that the Muslims must fight this matter out themselves with the Congress. He did not wish it to develop into a struggle between the British and the Congress, and he was perfectly confident that if it became a fight between the Muslims and the Congress it would be over in a short time. He clearly contemplated Hindu-Muslim riots, and if this is in fact the policy of the Muslim League, Gandhi's apprehensions of the result of declaring civil disobedience are more than justified. I told Khaliq that such a policy would cause very serious embarrassment to my administration; but he said that he asked for no favour and was quite prepared to see the law enforced impartially against both sides. It was against this background that the doubt arose whether the Muslim League would be prepared at this stage to cooperate publicly with the British. While he assured me that they had every sympathy with us in the prosecution of the war, they appear to be exceedingly anxious to maintain their own independence of action. I saw Chhatari two days ago. He was somewhat nervous about the attitude that the Muslim League might take, and I am inclined to think that if the League decline to be represented on the War Board, it may be necessary to drop the idea of a central non-official organisation, and to work things officially from the Centre with non-official district War Boards.

7. Sapru when I saw him had evidently not yet fully recovered from his serious operation and I thought he was a little lacking in vigour. While approving of the idea of a War Board, he at the same time seemed a little apprehensive in case it involved conflict with the Congress. I said that it seemed to me that this was a time when those who did believe in the war should come out and support their opinions openly. He agreed, but still, I thought, without great enthusiasm. I think really there is a great deal of truth in what you said in your last letter that none of the critics would stand up to the Congress if it came to a show down. Certainly there are a great many people who are more ready to criticise than to fight. Many of the landlords and the old-fashioned loyalists would I believe fight, but I fear the Liberals on the whole would prefer talking.

8. Speaking of the landlords I have recently sent you a telegram in connection with the legal difficulty about giving assent to the Tenancy Bill in consequence of the terms of the Proclamation under Section 93. In this I have emphasised the point that in my judgement assent ought to be given quickly. It will not be a pleasant thing for me to have to do, but I am fully prepared to do it, as I am convinced it is in the interests of the Province and really ultimately in the interests of the landlords themselves. I think this represents a very general feeling among my most experienced officers. As I told you, my three Advisers are unanimous on the point and I found yesterday that the Commissioner of Lucknow[40] and Nethersole whom I have brought in to do our publicity work also had exactly the same views. The Commissioner of Allahabad[41] to whom I have been speaking today is also emphatic on this point. Obstruction or amendment of the Tenancy Bill is the one thing that will give the extremists a chance to rouse the Province.

9. One of the last acts done by Dr. Katju before going out of office was to pass orders about the minimum price for sugar cane. It is an exceedingly complicated subject. He wrote a long note in a great hurry and ordered the Secretary on the ground that time was short to issue the orders at once. The Secretary, a man in whom I have little confidence, issued the orders and then sent the file to me. There was nothing to be done at the time, and indeed the factors were so complicated that it was difficult for me to reach any early conclusion as to whether Katju's orders were right or wrong, though on the face of it the price seems to have been fixed too high. I could not resist the suspicion that this was done in order to give the tenants a parting bribe. The sugar industrial interests have been bombarding me with representations ever since and they are going to lay their case before Marsh, my Adviser. Katju went somewhat beyond the recommendations of a committee representing both the factories and the growers and it might be possible to get back to those conclusions. The rates are fixed I think every fortnight with reference to the current prices of sugar. Another complicating factor is the existence of red rot on a large scale in the eastern districts, and this will undoubtedly affect the quality of the cane.[42]

10. My physical symptoms have unfortunately not improved.[43] However, the doctors tell me that in myself I am going on steadily and that there is nothing to worry about. I came over to Allahabad yesterday for a week for my farewell visit and have a full programme to get through.

Yours sincerely,
H.G. HAIG

95

HAIG TO LINLITHGOW
R/3/1/75

Secret
No. U.P.-327

December 4th, 1939

My dear Lord Linlithgow,

Many thanks for your long and interesting letter, dated December 1st 1939, and for its very illuminating analysis of the present situation.[44] I will endeavour in accordance with your request to give my own impressions; but I am sure you will realise that my attention recently has been concentrated more on our provincial problems than on the very difficult all-India issues that confront Your Excellency, and that I am writing under considerable pressure of time on the eve of my departure. I hope therefore you will make allowance for these two factors.

2. With regard to our provincial situation, I have already mentioned the remarkable lull that has existed ever since the Ministry resigned. That is of course in the main due to the fact that the Congress Right Wing have taken no action, as they are still groping for a policy, and the Left Wing have kept quiet, as they do not wish to embark on any serious movement without the support of the Congress organisation behind them. But I think there is more to it than that. One is inclined to assume that because we have a Legislature overwhelmingly Congress, the feelings of the masses correspond. Actually I have been receiving information for many months past that in the villages generally the first enthusiasm of the Congress victory has died down and that Congress influence is very much less than it used to be. This is partly due to disappointment at many unfulfilled promises, partly to the realisation that local Congress workers, though they may be useful, require, like the minor functionaries of the administration, payment for their services and are very often unable in the end to deliver the goods. It would be a mistake to suppose that the masses are naturally enthusiastic supporters of the Congress. A year before the general election the Province gave every sign of being peaceful and contented, Congress influence appeared generally negligible and Congress activities small. I do not think this was an illusion. It was only in the few months immediately preceding the general election that feeling was worked up by an intense Congress campaign and reckless promises of what the Congress would do if they came into power. Having secured their majority by these means the Congress had no difficulty in rivetting their authority on the Province. The masses think in terms of "raj", and it was quite clear that Congress "raj" had come. They accepted this at first with great hope and enthusiasm, but latterly without any great interest. Now that Congress "raj" has suddenly disappeared, they accept with more or less equal indifference the Governor's "raj". I do not underestimate the power of Congress to rouse the masses when there is any subject which can really appeal to them. But left to themselves, the masses are indifferent to Congress aims and are only stirred by what appears to them to be a possible improvement of their own conditions.

3. We have been accustomed for some time to rate the influence of the Left Wing of the Congress in this Province very high. In the party organisation the Left Wing influence has been strong, and the obvious reluctance of the Right Wing to take any action against them or to restrain their activities even when illegal had created an impression that they were

more powerful than perhaps they really are. I am now inclined to the view that if the Left Wing were hit pretty hard they would not be found to have as much resisting power as one might have supposed a little time ago, and I think perhaps they recognise this and that is why they are reluctant to embark on a movement unsupported by the Right Wing.

4. The Congress as a whole seem to me to have got into a very difficult and weak position. They have taken the occasion of a war, to which they cannot really declare themselves opposed, to demand certain political concessions. That may have been perfectly sound tactics up to a certain point, provided they would be content with such concessions as might reasonably be expected and did not push matters to an actual fight with the British Government. In the early stages I thought in fact that that was their policy. But whether by accident or deliberately they have now passed away from that position and seem to me to be making most unreasonable demands just at the time when they have voluntarily surrendered one of the chief elements of their power. By ordering the resignation of the Ministries they have, as it seems to me, lost a great deal of their hold on the people. That is certainly the interpretation I put on the position in this Province. If the resignations were to be followed at an early date by a civil disobedience movement, the action would have been intelligible. But for reasons which I will mention in a moment they are I believe most reluctant to embark on civil disobedience. At the same time if after throwing away their position of authority in virtue of the Ministries they remain quiet and do not start any big popular movement, it seems to me inevitable that they will steadily lose influence and position, and it will be very difficult for them to reconcile themselves to that.

5. The reasons why I think the Congress are very reluctant to embark on civil disobedience are:

(*a*) They have no issue which is really likely to rouse the masses at this moment, and the masses are not likely to support them without some such issue; in other words they are not on good ground in launching a civil disobedience movement at present.

(*b*) If they do launch such a movement, the violent Left Wing elements are almost certain to gain control of it. This will both bring the movement into discredit and weaken the position of the Right Wing.

(*c*) A movement of this kind is almost bound to result in serious communal rioting and to show the world in an unmistakable manner how bitter are the feelings between Hindus and Muslims. Moreover, the Hindus are not likely to get the better of such rioting and their whole position may be shaken by it.

6. I think it is important to realise what a very weak and difficult position the Congress are in. They are of course talking very bravely, and they still hope that they will be able by means of propaganda to talk His Majesty's Government into making concessions which would establish them in a position of great strength. But words seem to me at the moment the principal weapon in their armoury.

7. The Muslim League attitude is of crucial importance. It is beginning to look as if the only escape the Congress may have from an exceedingly weak position is if they can secure the support of the Muslims, which could only be obtained at a pretty high price. The Muslims naturally look on this matter entirely from the point of view of their own interests: will it be better for them on the whole to support the British or to make terms with the Congress? That position was put to me quite frankly in a recent conversation by Chaudhri Khaliq-uz-Zaman, the leader of the Muslim League in this Province. He said that if Jinnah thinks, as a result of his communications with Your Excellency, that when it comes to devising a new constitution after the war, they can depend on firm protection from the British, then they will reject the Congress overtures. If on the other hand they think that the British will not in fact give them safeguards that they would consider adequate, they will probably make such terms as they can with the Congress. I myself, however, doubt whether the Congress would really be prepared to make the very big concessions on which the Muslims would probably insist as their minimum, and whether the Muslims would trust the Congress to keep faith. Assuming that there is no agreement between the Muslim League and the Congress, the attitude of the Muslim League seems to me to make anything like mass civil disobedience a most dangerous step for the Congress to take. As I have mentioned in an earlier letter, Khaliq declares that in that event the Muslims would come out on their own and would fight the Congress, and certainly I have little doubt that the Muslims would not remain more or less neutral spectators of a conflict between the British and the Congress.

8. This brings me to the crucial question, namely, what kind of constitution is contemplated after the war. The attitude of the Congress I should have supposed was not so much a demand that Parliament should recognise them as the one real organisation to be reckoned with in the country, as that Parliament should agree to a type of constitution which would in effect entrench them permanently in power. The type of constitution which will have that effect is one based on extreme democratic principles. The Congress are thus in the matter of propaganda which is meant to influence British or world opinion on very good ground. The

British Government perhaps tend to think mainly in terms of maintaining certain elements of control and maintaining certain interests. I am not sure that it would not be wiser to face a very considerable surrender of power if we could devise a constitution which would not leave India entirely at the mercy of the Hindus, and as the inevitable result of an extreme democratic system, at the mercy of the most extreme Hindus. I feel myself that the worst feature of the present constitution is the franchise. That was forced upon us by the somewhat theoretical democratic ideas of the British Parliament in face of the protests, I believe, of every Local Government. Now after the experience we have had it is widely recognised that with a franchise even on the present scale the Congress, and increasingly the extremist Congress elements, are bound to rule the country. The Congress realising this are now pressing for adult franchise. This I take to be the root of the obvious fears of democracy expressed by the Muslims. I do not for a moment suggest that we can have a system either of autocracy or bureaucracy; but I do think that in any revision of the constitution we should see whether we cannot do something to modify the very serious dangers in a country like this of an extreme form of democracy.

9. I have not had time to look up the various pronouncements that have been made with regard to the future policy of His Majesty's Government. They have been made piecemeal, and I am not sure that they have left on the public mind a very clear impression. It might at some future time be desirable to state more positively what is intended, and to express our policy as something that the Government really believe in and wish to carry out rather than something dragged reluctantly out of them by Congress demands. But broadly speaking it seems to me that we have gone as far as we reasonably can, and that it would be extremely damaging both to the future of India and to our present position to go further at the moment, for it would be regarded as a capitulation to Congress threats. I would therefore say that we must broadly speaking stand fast on the existing position and face the consequences. Gandhi seems to me to be pursuing his normal tactics. He makes very far-reaching public demands and then says he is prepared to negotiate about them. By making the extreme demands he encourages his extremists. By expressing a desire to negotiate he seeks to conciliate reasonable opinion in India and elsewhere. Any further concessions that he can get by these methods are interpreted as due to the fear of his extreme threats and greatly strengthen his position. But in fact, as I have suggested above, it is probably the Congress and not the British who are really in a weak position at the moment, and I would say that we should face a break rather than make any further substantial concessions.

10. If a break were to come, I do not myself think that the war effort of India would be greatly impeded. At present in fact India's war effort is comparatively negligible. I do not underestimate the moral value of appearing to have India's whole-hearted support in the war; but from the practical point of view I do not think the Congress in any event are going to do much for us. I think in the light of the Provincial conditions which I have sketched in the beginning of this letter, we could face a break without undue apprehension. I am confident that a Congress civil disobedience movement would not succeed, and its failure would gravely weaken the Congress. It might lead to a very serious split in their ranks which might on a broad view be not without its advantages. We must not in such an event rely merely on repression. We must have an active, reasonable and constructive policy, and we must produce the impression that we really believe in that policy and want to see it carried through. I personally would be prepared to go far, but not under the compulsion of Congress. For many years I have regarded our position and policy in India as that of fighting a rear-guard action. We are deliberately surrendering our power and we ought to do it with a good will; but we must not let the rear-guard action turn into a rout. There are times when we have to stand and fight, even though at the end of it we continue to retire; and I think we may perhaps before long reach such a stage.

Yours sincerely,
H.G. HAIG

96

HALLETT TO LINLITHGOW
R/3/1/75

[Unnumbered] Government House, Lucknow,
December 5th, 1939

My dear Lord Linlithgow,

We have arrived at our destination and are both glad to be free from journeys and to be able to settle down. My visit to Delhi was both invaluable and enjoyable, and I am most grateful to Your Excellency for giving me the opportunity of becoming acquainted with the position and of discussing the numerous and difficult problems which confront us. It has been a great encouragement to me on the eve of taking over charge of this Province.

Haig, I am glad to find, seems better and says he has made a good deal of improvement during the last few days. A complete rest now should ensure a complete recovery.

With our most grateful thanks for a visit which both my wife and I greatly enjoyed.

Yours very sincerely,
MAURICE HALLETT

97

HAIG TO LINLITHGOW
Telegram
R/3/1/75

Immediate
No. 296-G

December 6th, 1939

Your telegram No. 2773-G of December 5th.[45] After discussion with Hallett I have decided to give assent to Tenancy Bill today.

2. With regard to danger of creation of a large class of unprotected sub-tenants I see no reason why this Bill should lead to such results. The restrictions on sub-letting remain practically the same as they have been for many years in the case of the very large class of occupancy tenants in Agra. What might in my judgement lead to creation of such class would be if hereditary rights were made transferable. This, however, is a principle which has been rigidly excluded from the Bill. The result is that the tenants in chief are, and in my judgement are likely to remain, for greater part genuine cultivators and will have little desire to sub-let on a large scale. So far as Sir land is concerned the existing sub-tenants are being converted to a large extent into tenants in chief.

3. I do not think a declaration as suggested in paragraph 2 of your telegram would be appropriate for that is not a danger which is generally anticipated as shown by prolonged discussions on Bill. Moreover it seems to me that a declaration by a Governor could not possibly bind governments in future, and it is dangerous to make a commitment of this kind which it might prove impossible in future to implement. I think that public opinion in the United Provinces is fully alive to the dangers which Secretary of State mentions.

4. With regard to greater protection of interests of sub-tenants this may well come at a later stage and there is nothing in the Bill to prevent it.

98

HAIG TO LINLITHGOW
R/3/1/75

Secret *December 6th, 1939*
No. U.P.-328

My dear Lord Linlithgow,

I am writing a hasty line on the point of departure which I am afraid must serve as my last fortnightly report. I have, however, written to Your Excellency at considerable length a few days ago about the general political situation, and our official fortnightly letter gives a full and accurate account of the ordinary provincial administrative problems.

2. The Province remains as before, very quiet, and the change over from the Congress administration has been effected so far without the least difficulty. Recently when I was away from Lucknow a stupid and unfortunately worded press statement was put out, in which it was said that I had accepted the charge of the Province as a trust for the Congress Ministry. The matter did not attract my attention at first; but when I made enquiries I found that it had been put out by the Director of Public Information, apparently with good intentions, but without the essential control that was necessary in the issue of such a statement. Any communiqué of this sort should of course have been seen by me. It was I am afraid a failure in arrangements owing to our new Publicity Secretary being a new man. I hoped that it would not attract much attention but finding that it was still being quoted when I returned to Lucknow I got the correspondent of the *Statesman* to mention it in one of his statements that it had been put out without my authority and did not represent my views which were contained in the statement I made when I accepted the resignation of my Ministers. I do not think it will have created much misunderstanding in the Province.[46]

3. You will have seen all about the Congress flag incident at the Allahabad University and my refusal to preside at the Convocation and to deliver the Convocation address. The policy had already been fully discussed with you two years ago when a similar incident seemed likely to arise, and I think my action was inevitable. Actually both Gandhi and Nehru, besides other Congress leaders, advised the students to pull the flag down by 1 p.m. and thus enable me to preside; but they were not prepared to listen to reason. I do not think they have done themselves any good. All reasonable

opinion in Allahabad was against them. The *Leader* backed up my position completely, and the Vice-Chancellor[47] has since written me a letter which he begged should be published, though I was rather reluctant to keep the issue open, because he said he felt he was regarded as having treated me with some lack of consideration.

4. I am afraid I have to leave the Shia-Sunni controversy as a difficult legacy to Hallett. While I was at Allahabad, I had a very friendly letter from Abul Kalam Azad, who had been for some time past trying to reach an agreement. He said that he regretted he had been unable to get an agreement between the parties, and had the Congress Ministry remained in office, he would have made recommendations to them for action which they would have been expected to carry out. In the new circumstances he felt that it might not be suitable for him to send his recommendations to me, and he mentioned as two alternatives that he should publish them, or that he should do nothing about it. After reflection, I replied thanking him for his courtesy and consideration and for his efforts to reach an agreed settlement, and saying that on the whole I felt in the changed circumstances it would not be altogether proper for him to send me his recommendations and that as between the other two courses I felt it difficult to advise him, but had no objection to either. I do not know what he will do. Actually the recommendation that he was apparently proposing to make is not one that I think could be accepted.

5. I am leaving the War Board for Hallett to decide about. Personally I think now it had better stand over, and that I believe is Hallett's view also. Today questions of price control have suddenly become urgent, but that is a matter which I shall have to leave to Hallett to deal with.

Yours sincerely,
H.G. HAIG

99

HAIG TO LINLITHGOW
MSS.EUR.F 125/107

Secret
No. U.P.-329

Camp,
December 6th, 1939

My dear Lord Linlithgow,

Your letter of November 29th asking for details of instances of the effectiveness of the safeguards is by no means easy to answer as far as this Province is concerned. The late Ministry contained two Muslim Ministers out of six, and one of these was the Minister who, apart from the Premier, took the keenest interest in postings and personal cases and had the greatest influence in such matters. There was no member of the Scheduled Castes in the Ministry, a fact which was sometimes made a ground of complaint, but two of the thirteen Parliamentary Secretaries belonged to the Scheduled Castes. One of these was attached to the Education Minister and the other to the Minister for Development. To a large extent, the intentions of the Ministry both in regard to the Depressed Classes and to the Muslim minority were of the best. The consequence was that in cases in which the question of treatment of these classes came up, they were nearly always willing to take a hint if I suggested that their proposals were unfair to these minorities, or liable to be misrepresented as being unfair. They made considerable efforts to increase the recruitment from the Scheduled Castes into the public services, and I cannot recall any case in which we had a difference of opinion about special treatment of these classes. As regards the Muslims, the Ministry started off with generous intentions; and in the matter of appointments I think that they always acted with commendable fairness. Latterly it had seemed to me that owing to the persistent hostility of the Muslim League which they greatly resented (and the Muslim Ministers most of all) they were disposed to take unduly severe administrative measures against certain Muslims, and I should probably have had to take up some of these cases with them, had they remained in office. But this was really an example of retaliating on their political opponents rather than unfair treatment of a community. No case occurred in which I actually used my special powers or power of individual judgement for the protection of the minority communities.

2. On the other hand, in matters affecting law and order and the Public Services, there were frequent and prolonged differences of opinion. The only case in which this reached the stage of my having to issue orders which my Ministers had refused to issue, was that of the prosecution of Pandit Parmanand for a violent anti-British speech in November 1937. As Your Excellency will remember, this almost led to the resignation of the Ministry. The prosecution was finally withdrawn on the conviction of Parmanand in the Delhi Province, but a warning against a repetition of the offence was given to him by the Ministry.[48] In February 1938 the Ministry resigned on the ground that acting on the instructions from Your Excellency under Section 126 (5) of the Government of India Act, I declined to accept their advice to release certain terrorist prisoners. Apart from these two major instances, there were numerous occasions, chiefly in connection with reports of violent speeches and proposals from local officers for prosecution, or with proposed proscriptions of seditious literature, etc., in

which I dissented from the advice given by my Ministers and argued the cases with them. In some instances they modified their views and accepted mine in whole or part. In others, they maintained their position and I was unable to consider the question at issue as of such importance as to constitute a grave menace to the peace or tranquillity of the Province. Similarly in regard to the services, there were numerous cases in which our opinions differed, and I pressed my point of view with greater or less success. In the case of the Employments Tax Bill I warned my Ministers at the time of its introduction that I considered it highly probable that the Bill, if passed, would attract my special responsibility for the protection of the services. In considering proposals for the abolition of special pay, I gave a similar warning. The Ministry did not eventually proceed with these proposals. A question of the application of new scales of pay for the Provincial services to existing members of those services when promoted to posts outside the time-scale was pending for months. The Ministry eventually agreed to maintain the existing practice for a period of five years after which it was to be reconsidered.

3. I was able to block a proposal for the creation of District Advisory Councils which were intended to absorb a good many of the powers of District Officers. Criticism of proposals for the separation of executive and judicial functions produced some satisfactory modifications in the original scheme, but the modified scheme was still pending when the Ministry resigned and I think that the Ministers themselves had entirely lost their enthusiasm for it and would have been prepared to drop it quietly if their followers would allow this. In the case of their proposal for the abolition of Commissioners Your Excellency will remember that I forwarded their proposals for communication to the Secretary of State with a despatch in which I expressed my own dissent.

I did indicate my view that Government appeared to be sending an unduly large number of cases against Muslim police officers to the Anti-Corruption department, and I interfered in a certain number of these cases with benefit. I also gave a certain amount of advice about the handling of the Lucknow Shia-Sunni dispute and of the Khaksar movement directed to saving them from any imputation of communal bias.

4. In short, the safeguard powers, in matters to which they applied, have remained in the background, their existence known to both sides; but not mentioned in the discussions, on which, nevertheless, they had a useful influence.

Yours sincerely,
H.G. HAIG

100

HAIG TO LINLITHGOW
R/3/1/75

[Unnumbered] Camp,
December 6th, 1939

My dear Lord Linlithgow,

I have just received your very kind letter of the 5th December[49] and want to send one word in reply. We have certainly been through difficult times in this Province, and no one in my position would have escaped criticism. On the other hand I think the Province has, in spite of a certain amount of alarmist rumours, kept on the whole an even keel, or as even as might have been expected, and I feel that it is all to the good that we got through two and a half years of very novel conditions without a breakdown. I have been very grateful to Your Excellency for your advice and support throughout these difficult times, when we were dealing with such a variety of problems.

I have now very nearly thrown off the neuritis symptoms, and I am confident that in a week or two I shall be quite fit again.

Many thanks from my wife and myself for all your good wishes, and we wish to thank you and Lady Linlithgow for many kindnesses.

Yours sincerely,
HARRY HAIG

101

HAIG TO LINLITHGOW
Telegram
R/3/1/75

[Unnumbered] *December 6th, 1939*

I am most grateful to Your Excellency for your very kind telegram of farewell.[50] In these difficult times your counsel and support have been a sure guide through novel and anxious problems. My wife and I thank Your Excellencies for your many kindnesses.

102

HALLETT TO LINLITHGOW
Telegram
MSS.EUR.F 125/107

Immediate *December 16th, 1939*
No. 298-G

Your telegram No. 160-S.C. of December 13th.[51]

Paragraph No. 2 (*a*). Government of Bihar published on March 11th very detailed reply to Pirpur report, but here though no reply was published directly, Premier gave pamphlet marked Confidential to Press Consultative Committee on January 11th referring to report. I am sending copy by post. The pamphlet was on the whole an effective reply to report.

Paragraph No. 2 (*b*). Premier in statement of policy in Legislature on August 2nd referred to Congress declaration of fundamental rights made at Karachi session which guaranteed freedom to all and said that he would follow that policy and adopt sympathetic attitude to minorities; but apart from this there was not either in statement or discussion thereon any detailed reference to minorities, still less to any instructions from Patel.

Paragraph No. 2 (*c*). This as far as my recollection goes is wholly untrue. You will recollect my trouble in Bihar over question of aborigines who are also minority community. Prime Minister[52] there never asked for my intervention and would have resented it.

Paragraph No. 2 (*d*). This is also untrue and while I was in Bihar Prime Minister did not invite my attention to Jinnah's charges. It is true, however, that I considered these charges unwarranted and did not conceal my view to Muslims and Ministers. I am consulting Haig but I am pretty certain that he will confirm my reply. My letter to Prime Minister of Bihar, No. 221-G.B., dated February 2nd, copy forwarded to you with my letter, dated February 16th, No. 260-G.B.,[53] may be of interest in this connection.

103

HALLETT TO LINLITHGOW
Telegram
R/3/1/75

Important *December 18th, 1939*
No. 299-G

In continuation of my telegram No. 298-G of December 16th. Haig writes as follows: "I have no recollection of anything even remotely resembling the communications alleged to have been made in (*c*) and (*d*). I cannot even remember any definite conversation with Premier about these charges at all. We may in the course of (gr. corrupt) [?conversation] some time have touched on them, but if we did, I should probably have said that I did not consider there was any substance in the charges themselves. Several times, however, I impressed on Premier the seriousness of the communal situation and my view that it could only be mended by a coalition."

104

HALLETT TO LINLITHGOW
Telegram
MSS.EUR.F 125/107

No. 300-G *December 23rd, 1939*

Your telegram No. 217-S.C., dated December 19th.[54] I have consulted my advisers who suggest Sir Maharaj Singh who would represent Indian Christians and Sikhs. He has wide circle of friends in (the) two Provinces and is vigorous exponent of views of provincial services. I hardly know him personally and formed a rather unfavourable opinion of him by reason of his policy as President of the anti-corruption committee, but my opinion based on a single instance is not of much value. His record is well known and Clay and Williamson[55] could give further information to Secretary of State if necessary. Possibly he does not satisfy conditions suggested but I know of no one else.

NOTES

1. General Sir Douglas Baird was G.O.C.-in-C., Eastern Command at this date.
2. In telegram 2162-S of 4 October 1939 Lord Linlithgow reported to Provincial Governors details of a long discussion he had had the previous day with Dr Rajendra Prasad and Pandit Nehru. No very marked progress was made as the Indian leaders reiterated their claims for (a) a full and unambiguous declaration by the British Government (including a reference to the absolute freedom of India after the war and the right of the Indian people to elect their form of government through a Constituent Assembly) and (b) some immediate practical application of the principle involved by way of sharing power at the Centre.

   The Viceroy was not over-optimistic as to the prospects of reaching a settlement. He would see Mr Jinnah and might also see Mahatma Gandhi again. Linlihgow felt that Rajendra Prasad was reasonably open-minded but Nehru left the impression of having made up his mind in advance. MSS.EUR.F 125/107.

3. Lieutenant K.K. Chaudhri was Secretary, District Soldiers Board, Etawah.
4. Only this extract is printed in R/3/1/75. Mr A.T. Naqvi was Collector of Aligarh at this date.
5. Lord Linlithgow minuted: 'Doesn't sound like early resignation!'
6. Mr T. Sloan was Commissioner of the Meerut Division at this date.
7. Lord Linlithgow minuted with reference to the Enclosure: 'The rarest treasure of Tandon's eloquence is omitted. It was that he must insist on the privilege of the Chair, and decline to allow comment upon his observations!'
8. Lieutenant-Colonel H.M. Salamat Ullah was Inspector-General of Prisons, U.P. at this date.
9. Mr Sucha Singh was District Magistrate, Bulandshahr at this date.
10. Mr H.A. Inglis was Deputy Inspector-General, Agra Range at this date. The Range included Bulandshahr.
11. Sir Evan Jenkins was Chief Commissioner of Delhi at this date.
12. Mr J. Penny was Chief Secretary to the Government of the Punjab at this date.
13. Not printed.
14. In telegram 275-G of 17 October 1939 Sir Harry Haig told Lord Linlithgow that he was arranging for his Secretary to attend the meeting of Governors' Secretaries in Delhi on 30 October if circumstances permitted. MSS.EUR.F 115/7.
15. Lord Linlithgow minuted: 'He can do whatever he feels necessary now.'
16. In telegram 2284-S of 15 October 1939, Lord Linlithgow sent Provincial Governors details of his Statement 'India and the War' which was to be issued in New Delhi on 17 October 1939 (Cmd. 6121). The Viceroy felt that even if Congress considered the Statement as entirely unsatisfactory, he would be rather surprised if there was an immediate break. Linlithgow asked Governors for a telegraphic report of reactions in their Provinces. MSS.EUR.F 125/107.

    In his Statement Lord Linlithgow announced that he was authorised by the British Government to say that at the end of the war they would be very willing to enter into consultation with representatives of the several communities, parties and interests in India, and with the Indian Princes, with a view to securing their aid and cooperation in the framing of such constitutional modifications as might seem desirable. Lord Linlithgow also announced the immediate establishment of a consultative group, representative of all major political parties in British India, and of the Indian Princes, which would have as its object the association of public opinion in India with the conduct of the war and questions relating to war activities.
17. Lord Linlithgow minuted: 'I think now that I was probably wrong.'
18. Lord Linlithgow minuted: 'S./S.'

19. Lord Linlithgow minuted: 'This event will now show.'
20. See Lionel Carter (ed.), *Punjab Politics, 1936-1939: The Start of Provincial Autonomy. Governors' Fortnightly Reports and Other Key Documents* (New Delhi: Manohar, 2004), No. 111.
21. This extract consisted of the first six sentences of paragraph 9 of Enclosure to No. 76 together with the sentence 'I also sent an express telegram to the Chief Secretary to the Government of the Punjab informing him that I was allowing the bodies to be taken back to the Punjab for burial.'
22. See note 16 above.
23. In a statement issued on 18 October 1939, Pandit Nehru and Maulana Azad said that they had read the Viceroy's Statement with deep regret. There was no mention in it of independence, freedom, democracy or self-determination. There was no attempt to justify dragging India into the war. The objects appeared to be the preservation and maintenance of the British imperial and financial structure in India and abroad.
24. On the copy of Sir Harry Haig's Memorandum on MSS.EUR.F 125/107 Lord Linlithgow minuted: 'P.S.V. – A spirited and encouraging document. There is nothing like a touch of typhoid to pull a man together!'
25. In a further letter on 20 October 1939 (U.P.-317), Sir Harry Haig wrote that it had occurred to him that Lord Linlithgow might wish to appoint Sir J.P. Srivastava to the Viceroy's Consultative Committee. Haig would not wish to stand in the way of this and Srivastava would still be able to offer him valuable help in the U.P. Ibid.
26. Lord Linlithgow's telegram 2335-G of 19 October 1939 related to the meeting the Viceroy was holding with Provincial Governors' Secretaries on 30 October. Linlithgow asked the Secretaries to be in possession of Governors' views on how they should deal with anti-war agitation in which Congress as a whole was taking an active part. In particular: (1) should breaches of the Defence of India Rules be invariably followed by prosecutions and prison sentences or should they use powers to intern or place restrictions on war agitators; (2) should they use the Indian Criminal Law Amendment Act, 1908 to declare certain organisations (e.g. Provincial Congress committees) as illegal organisations; (3) whether a lightning war by government, using drastic action from the start, was likely to be successful. L/P&J/8/592: f. 168.
27. On 22 October 1939, at its meeting at Wardha, the Congress Working Committee gave its reaction to the Viceroy's Statement on 'India and the War'. (See note 16 above.) The Working Committee felt the Statement was 'wholly unsatisfactory and calculated to arouse resentment. . . . The Committee cannot possibly give any support to Great Britain, for it would amount to an endorsement of the imperialistic policy which the Congress has always sought to end.' The Working Committee called on Congress provincial governments to tender their resignations. At the same time it warned all Congressmen against civil disobedience and political strikes.

28. In telegram 2361-G of 21 October 1939 to Provincial Governors, Lord Linlithgow asked for information on two points in connection with the Conference of Governors' Secretaries: (a) the adequacy of police forces; and (b) arrangements to guard against sabotage. Linlithgow stressed the importance of Governors reviewing the adequacy of their publicity staff to cope with a Section 93 situation. MSS.EUR.F 125/107.
29. See Appendix 2.
30. In telegram 2430-S of 28 October 1939, Lord Linlithgow drew the attention of Provincial Governors to the line taken by the British Government in the House of Commons the previous day. Emphasis had been laid on its anxiety to keep the door open, remove misunderstandings and to secure India's co-operation in the war subject to the essential preliminary agreement between the parties.

    The Viceroy proposed to see Mr Jinnah and Mahatma Gandhi together to ascertain whether there was any possibility of reconciling differences. If there was such a possibility, it might be possible to consider some further modification of the type of arrangement proposed for the Centre.

    Linlithgow suggested to the Governors of Congress Provinces that, in these circumstances, they might take up to three or four days to accept any resignations tendered by Ministers. Without intermitting preparations for a break, Governors should proceed quietly and avoid prejudicing the atmosphere. MSS.EUR.F 125/107.
31. In telegram 2462-S of 31 October 1939, Lord Linlithgow warned Governors of Congress Provinces to ensure that the houses of their legislatures were prorogued before Section 93 was proclaimed. Congress were proposing that the officers of the legislative chambers (including Speakers) should not resign at this time. Governors would lose their powers to summon or prorogue the houses once Section 93 was in force. Ibid.
32. Not printed.
33. Not included in R/3/1/75.
34. Not printed.
35. Not printed.
36. In telegram 294-G of 16 November 1939 to Lord Linlithgow, Sir Harry Haig said he had now discussed the Tenancy Bill with his three Advisers who were unanimous that he should give his assent to the Bill, without amendment, at an early date. Haig hoped it would be possible to allow this without delay. R/3/1/75.
37. In telegram 2495-S of 1 November 1939, Lord Linlithgow reported to Provincial Governors the outcome of his meeting that day with Mahatma Gandhi, Mr Jinnah and Dr Rajendra Prasad. The Viceroy had stressed that an essential pre-condition to progress was an agreement between the communities in the Provinces. If they could reach an agreement, he had in mind a small expansion of his Executive Council to include persons from

the political parties. The Viceroy left it to the leaders to decide if they wished to see him again.

Linlithgow reported that Gandhi showed no desire to go slow on the acceptance of Ministerial resignations. The Viceroy advised Governors of Congress Provinces that they should not delay too long in accepting the resignations. However it would be wise, if possible, to avoid coercive and punitive measures while discussions between the leaders were proceeding.

In telegram 2552-S of 4 November 1939 to Provincial Governors, Linlithgow said Congress had replied the previous night to his offer of discussions. Congress reaffirmed it was unable to accept the Statement on 'India and the War' as supplemented. Gandhi in a final interview that day had pleaded strongly for an understanding attitude towards speeches, etc., by ex-Ministers and other Congress leaders and towards Congress activities. He expressed great anxiety to avoid civil disobedience. He hoped that with proper management and a desire to avoid trouble on both sides, this could be achieved. MSS.EUR.F 125/107.

38. The United Provinces was governed under Section 93 of the Government of India Act, 1935 from 3 November 1939.
39. Not printed. A copy of Sir Harry Haig's statement is on L/P&J/5/268: ff. 73-4.
40. The reference here may be to Mr G.M. Harper.
41. Mr W.C. Dible was Commissioner of the Allahabad Division at this date.
42. Lord Linlithgow minuted: 'All this seems a bit inconclusive.'
43. Lord Linlithgow minuted: 'I am so sorry.'
44. Lord Linlithgow's letter of 1 December 1939 to Sir Harry Haig is on MSS.EUR.F 115/2B.
45. In telegram 2773-G of 5 December 1939, Lord Linlithgow told Sir Harry Haig that he had consulted Lord Zetland over the question of assent to the U.P. Tenancy Bill. Zetland was concerned that it would give rise to a class of tenants who would sub-let under conditions which would create disabilities comparable to those which the Bill was intended to remove.

    If Haig felt that the benefits of the new legislation would at present go mainly to the cultivating tenants, then Zetland agreed to assent being granted. However the Secretary of State suggested that Haig should issue a declaration 'that obligation will rest upon the Government of the United Provinces, however, constituted at some future time to prevent exploitation of actual cultivators by non-cultivating tenants who enjoy the benefits of this measure.' R/3/1/75.
46. In telegram 297-G of 12 December 1939, Sir Maurice Hallett told Lord Linlithgow that he was proposing to put out a statement on 14 December making it clear that the D.P.I's. statement had not been authorised by the Governor. Hallett's statement continued:

    'Under Section 93 the responsibility for the government of the Province rests with the Governor who is himself responsible for the discharge of his duties to the Governor-General [and] the Secretary of State.' R/3/1/75.

47. The Vice-Chancellor of Allahabad University was Dr Amaranatha Jha at this date.
48. See U.P.P., 1936-37, Appendix 17.
49. Appendix 5.
50. This telegram read: 'My best good wishes to you both for your journey home and for the future. I well know the burden and the importance of the great office which you have held and I am deeply grateful to you for all your help and cooperation while we worked together during so critical a period in India's destinies. Viceroy.' MSS.EUR.F 115/2B: f. 339.
51. Lord Linlithgow's telegram 160-S.C. of 13 December 1939 was sent to the Governors of Provinces which had had Congress Ministries. It followed a statement made by Sardar Patel on the conduct of the Congress Ministries towards minorities which itself followed a statement made by Mr Jinnah on 6 December in which he had strongly criticised the Ministries for their treatment of Muslims and called on all Indian Muslims to observe Friday, 22 December as a day of deliverance and thanksgiving that the Congress governments had at last ceased to function.

    Linlithgow asked the Governors for information on the following points emerging from Patel's statement: '(a) that a report was published by the respective Provincial Governments on Pirpur allegations which showed that the charges were entirely unfounded; '(b) that an instruction was given by Patel when Congress Ministries took office to Ministries scrupulously to respect the rights of minorities; '(c) that every Premier at Patel's instance had invited his Governor unhesitatingly to intervene in matters affecting the interests of minorities whenever the Governor felt that action of Ministry was not correct; '(d) that when Jinnah "recently made charges I [Patel] again instructed every Premier to invite his Governor's attention to them as they also affected him and I was informed that Governors considered charges as unwarranted."' MSS.EUR.F 125/107. For the Pirpur Report see No. 39, note 48.
52. Mr Sri Krishna Sinha was the Premier of Bihar at that date.
53. Sir Maurice Hallett's letter (with enclosure) of 16 February 1939 to Lord Linlithgow is on R/3/1/19.
54. Telegram 217-S.C. of 19 December 1939 was sent by Lord Linlithgow to all Provincial Governors. Lord Zetland had asked the Viceroy for suggestions as to whom might succeed Sardar Mohan Singh whose term on the India Council was expiring the following April. Zetland was inclined to have a representative of a minority rather than someone who might merely be regarded as a second Hindu. Zetland was disposed to give a turn to a minority other than the Sikhs. MSS.EUR.F 125/107.
55. Sir Joseph Clay and Sir Horace Williamson were Advisers to Lord Zetland at this date.

Appendices

APPENDIX 1

HAIG TO PANT
MSS.EUR.F 115/4

Personal and Confidential *March 23rd, 1939*

Dear Govind Ballabh Pant,

I think our discussion this morning regarding the newspaper *Sipahi* published at Meerut left us perhaps with some misunderstandings, and I am writing to you with a view to clearing up, if possible, certain considerations on which I am inclined to think we cannot have clearly understood each other's point of view. Our conversation on this important matter had unfortunately to be a brief one owing to the necessity of your attending the Assembly, and in consequence I think the arguments on both sides were compressed, which does not tend to proper elucidation of a problem.

2. I start with the assumption that the statement in the Chief Secretary's note is generally correct, that "thc object of the paper seems definitely to be to promote disaffection among Indian troops and to encourage a feeling amongst them that they should not assist Great Britain in any future war". I am aware that you wish to be further satisfied on this point and are making inquiries with that object; but unless the review given to us by the C.I.D. is misleading, it seems to me difficult to draw any conclusion other than that drawn by the Chief Secretary.

3. Now an attempt to promote disaffection amongst Indian troops would, if it were successful, gravely affect public order in the Province, and the maintenance of public order is the responsibility of the Provincial Government. I made the point that recent events showed how closely the preservation of public order in the Province depended on the ultimate

support of the Army, but anything that affects the loyalty and obedience of the Army will not only have the negative effect of reducing the efficiency of what is our ultimate security for peace and tranquillity in the Province, but might even have the positive effect of creating disorder. The Provincial Government is therefore as it seems to me very vitally interested in preventing attempts to promote disaffection in the Army.

4. Not only is the Provincial Government vitally interested in this matter, but it is the only authority which is in a position to control such attacks on the loyalty of troops which originate in its own territories. If the Provincial Government does not take action under the legal powers which it alone can exercise, no one else can do so. We cannot therefore remain indifferent to activities of this kind proceeding to our knowledge within our Provincial boundaries.

5. So far I feel I shall have your agreement. This morning I had some doubt whether you did accept this position, but on reflection I feel sure that I must have misunderstood your views owing to the fact that we were discussing at the same time both the question of principle and the question of the precise action that might be necessary to deal with such a situation.

6. If the position I have described above is accepted, it is of course a matter for discussion as to what particular action is likely to be most effective and what are the objections to taking such action. On that point there are no doubt differences of opinion which are based on a difference of outlook, and though I have my own views as to the action which it is desirable to take, I quite recognise that this is a matter which we shall have to discuss together when the facts are clearer. But it will greatly facilitate discussion if we are in agreement about the fundamentals which I have put down in paras. 3 and 4 above.[1]

Yours sincerely,
[H.G. HAIG]

APPENDIX 2

PANT TO HAIG
MSS.EUR.F 115/7

Lucknow,
October 30th, 1939

Dear Sir Harry Haig,

You are no doubt aware that the statement[2] issued by H.E. the Viceroy in response to the request made by the Working Committee of the Indian

National Congress asking for a clear exposition of Britain's war aims in general and particularly in relation to India, has been almost universally held in this country to be disappointing and unsatisfactory. The pronouncements subsequently made by responsible Ministers of His Majesty on this subject have not allayed this feeling of dissatisfaction. It was confidently expected that the present war, which, it is professed, is being waged to preserve freedom for small and weaker nations in Europe would also mean the attainment of similar freedom and independence by India. It was recognized that the framing of a constitution for a free India could perhaps not be conveniently undertaken during the preoccupations of the war, but it was felt that consistently with this principle substantial transference of power in the administration of the internal and external affairs of the country could be made forthwith. If India is expected to help in the conduct of the war it can only do so on the basis of willing and voluntary cooperation and on terms of absolute equality. I regret to say that in the Viceroy's statement and the other pronouncements to which I have referred there is no clear recognition of this claim and nothing to inspire confidence. On the other hand undue stress has been laid on sectional differences and they have been made a plea for delaying India's freedom. My colleagues and I myself therefore feel that it is impossible for us to cooperate with the British Government in the management of affairs, and particularly in the conduct of the war in so far as the task may devolve upon Provincial Governments, in the absence of a satisfactory settlement of this essential problem. The Provincial Legislative Assembly also has passed this afternoon by an overwhelming majority a resolution expressing the same opinion, a copy of which I enclose. I beg therefore to tender hereby the resignation of my colleagues and myself, who are Members of the Council of Ministers in the United Provinces.

I take this opportunity to express our thanks to you for the courtesy and guidance which we have received from you in the discharge of the duties pertaining to our office.[3]

Yours sincerely,
GOVIND BALLABH PANT

ENCLOSURE TO APPENDIX 2

RESOLUTION PASSED BY U.P.
LEGISLATIVE ASSEMBLY

October 30th, 1939

This Assembly regrets that the British Government have made India a participant in the war between Great Britain and Germany without the consent of the people of India and have further in complete disregard of Indian opinion passed laws and adopted measures curtailing the powers and activities of the Provincial Governments. This Assembly recommends to the Government to convey to the Government of India and through them to the British Government that in consonance with the avowed aims of the present war, it is essential in order to secure the cooperation of the Indian people that the principles of democracy with effective safeguards for the Muslims and other minorities be applied to India and her policy be guided by her people; and that India should be regarded as an independent nation entitled to frame her own constitution and further that suitable action should be taken in so far as it is possible in the immediate present to give effect to that principle in regard to present governance of India. This Assembly regrets that the situation in India has not been rightly understood by His Majesty's Government when authorizing the statement that has been made on their behalf in regard to India, and in view of this failure of the British Government to meet India's demand this Assembly is of opinion that the Government cannot associate itself with British policy.

APPENDIX 3

HAIG TO PANT
MSS.EUR.F 115/7

November 4th, 1939

Dear Pandit Govind Ballabh Pant,

You will have heard direct from Donaldson yesterday morning that I had decided to accept the resignation of the Council of Ministers which you tendered to me on the 30th October. When we discussed the matter on that occasion we both recognised that the indeterminate situation after the Ministers had tendered their resignations and before they had been accepted was likely to involve embarrassments both for Ministers and myself. At the same time we both felt that it would be a mistake to terminate the relations between Hon'ble Ministers and the Governor if there was any prospect of an early settlement of the general discussion between His Excellency the Viceroy and the Congress leaders. While I have by no means abandoned hope that the discussions may lead to a settlement, it seemed to me evident that such a settlement must take a little time. Meanwhile, practical conditions in the Province, of which the Khaksar problem is an example, pointed strongly to a termination of our indefinite situation here. This was felt equally by the Hon'ble Ministers and by myself and accordingly with great regret I accepted their resignations yesterday.

I am particularly sorry that on this formal termination of our relations I was not able to say goodbye to you in person and to tell you how greatly I have appreciated working with you in conditions which were bound from time to time to be difficult. I have the highest regard for you personally, and it has been a matter of the greatest regret to me that during these last months I have been deprived of active consultation with you. I sincerely hope that now that you are relieved of the burden of responsibility your health will improve and that the rest will do you good. If it is in any way possible I should very much like to see you and say goodbye before I leave the Province on the 6th December.

Yours very sincerely,
[H.G. HAIG]

APPENDIX 4

PANT TO HAIG
MSS.EUR.F 115/7

Naini Tal,
November 14th, 1939

Dear Sir Harry Haig,

Please accept my cordial thanks for your letter of 4th inst. I highly value the generous sentiments you have expressed about me and shall cherish them with gratitude.

I fully appreciate the reasons which impelled you to accept the resignation of the Council of Ministers on the 3rd November. Uncertainty is always embarrassing and prolongation of the period of suspense tends to create needless complications. The situation was becoming progressively difficult for all concerned and my colleagues received your decision with a genuine feeling of relief. The differences between the Congress and the British Government have not yet been resolved, and none can safely anticipate the future course of events. In the circumstances nothing would have been gained by any further delay in the matter.

I share your regret over my unavoidable absence from the final leave taking function on the 3rd. I hope that it will be possible for me to bid you goodbye personally before you lay down the reins of office. I should feel greatly disappointed if I am unable to do so. You will be retiring after a strenuous life of more than thirty years, having devoted the best of your time, talents and energy to the conscientious discharge of multifarious duties and responsibilities attached to the high offices filled by you. I wish you the joyful peace of a well earned and active rest for many a happy year. I feel sad to think that this wish will not be realised so long as the devastating tragedy which has enveloped and afflicted this world lasts. Let us hope that this catastrophe will soon come to an end and the new era of reason and everlasting peace and voluntary federation of free peoples of the world will dawn on this tormented earth.

I am improving and hope to regain my normal health in the next few weeks.

Trust this finds you and Lady Haig in the best of health.

Yours sincerely,
G.B. PANT

APPENDIX 5

LINLITHGOW TO HAIG
MSS.EUR.F 115/2B: FF. 336-7

Secret and Personal

The Viceroy's House, New Delhi,
December 5th, 1939

My dear Haig,

I am most grateful to you for your secret letter No. U.P.-327 of 4th December,[4] and for the very valuable analysis of the situation which it contains. I will send a copy of it to Zetland, for I am sure it is important that he should know your view.

2. I am very sorry to think that this should be the last letter which I shall receive from you as Governor of the United Provinces, and I would like to take the opportunity to thank you for all the help that you have given me in that most heavy and responsible post. There can be few, if any, provinces

in India that present a more consistent succession of difficult problems of one sort or another, and I fully realise the weight which it had fallen to you to carry over a period of such critical importance. I could only wish that you had been spared in addition to the strain of that heavy charge, the burden of the strain of your recent illness particularly trying as it coincided with so critical a period in the constitutional field. I hope that you will have an early and complete recovery, and I send my best thanks to you, and my best good wishes to Lady Haig and to yourself for your journey home and for many happy years.

Yours sincerely,
LINLITHGOW

APPENDIX 6

DONALDSON TO CHRISTIE[5]
R/3/1/76

Secret
No. 11/40-G.S.P.

Camp,
January 5th, 1940

My dear Christie,

In reply to your D.O. No. 23-G.G.(C.) of January 2nd, 1940,[6] I am desired to say that His Excellency Sir Harry Haig considered the question of leaving notes before he went and decided that, as the Ministry had resigned and it was uncertain that the same Ministers would ever return to office if and when a fresh Congress Ministry was formed, it was not necessary for him to send notes on the late Ministers in his then state of health, as there was a heavy rush of other business. He did, however, approve certain notes which I had drafted on the Hon'ble Speaker, Deputy Speaker, and the Hon'ble President and Deputy President. These notes are in continuation of the notes previously sent[7] and should be read in conjunction with them. These persons are still in office, and I enclose copies of those notes as approved by His Excellency Sir Harry Haig. They may be taken as effective up to December 31st, 1939.

Yours sincerely,
J.C. DONALDSON

ENCLOSURE 1 TO APPENDIX 6

SPEAKER, UNITED PROVINCES LEGISLATIVE ASSEMBLY – THE HON'BLE SHRI PURUSHOTTAMDAS TANDON

January 1st to December 1st 1939

3. The Speaker fell ill with Angina Pectoris in March 1939 and was absent from the Assembly during the budget debates and the important meetings in April. He went away for treatment to Puri, and only returned in July 1939. He is apparently much better. His position remained as it was. He is believed not to be popular with the Ministry. He tends to assert his position as Speaker. He did not attend the Simla Conference of Presidents and Speakers this summer owing to the state of his health. He took opportunities to advertise himself by long speeches of a controversial nature to the House on the Government of India (Amendment) Act and on the war resolution. He still aspires to the Premiership. He is polite in manners but cross-grained and pugnacious in business dealings. Has recently made some strongly partisan speeches at public political meetings, particularly attacking the Muslim League.

ENCLOSURE 2 TO APPENDIX 6

DEPUTY SPEAKER, UNITED PROVINCES LEGISLATIVE ASSEMBLY – MR ABDUL HAKEEM

January 1st to December 1st 1939

2. While the Speaker was ill and on leave, Mr. Abdul Hakeem has presided during the budget session and the important meetings over the Tenancy Bill quietly and effectively, with assistance from members of the panel of Chairmen. Has increased his reputation.

ENCLOSURE 3 TO APPENDIX 6

PRESIDENT, UNITED PROVINCES LEGISLATIVE COUNCIL – THE HON'BLE DR. SIR SITA RAM

January 1st to December 1st 1939

Sir Sita Ram continued to be dissatisfied with his treatment by the late Government and a pessimist about the future. It was alleged that he used his influence in the Upper House to have the Employments Tax Bill there referred to a Select Committee against the wishes of the Government. However the Select Committee disappointed expectation and let the Bill through unchanged, and so eventually did the Upper House. The allegation may not be true; but apart from it he has not attracted attention.

ENCLOSURE 4 TO APPENDIX 6

DEPUTY PRESIDENT, UNITED PROVINCES LEGISLATIVE COUNCIL – BEGUM AIZAZ RASUL

January 1st to December 1st 1939

Was a successful Deputy President. She also took a prominent part as one of the representatives chosen from the landlord party in the Legislative Council to carry on negotiations with the Government about the passage of the Tenancy Bill. None of the chief landlord leaders has a seat in the Council. The representatives were therefore agents, not plenipotentiaries, and were closely directed by the real leaders. Of the representatives the Begum seems to have been the most intelligent and broad-minded and to have taken the leading part. The negotiations were unsuccessful, but the failure was due to the leaders rejecting a pretty good offer in the hope, which proved quite mistaken, that they could hold up the opposition majority together and secure better terms or hold up the Bill. The Begum was in favour of taking the terms, and events proved her wisdom.

NOTES

1. There is no reply from Pandit Pant on the file.
2. See No. 79, note 16.
3. A copy of Pandit Pant's letter and its Enclosure was sent to Mr Laithwaite by Mr Donaldson under cover of his letter 1144/39-G.S.P of 31 October 1939. R/3/1/75.
4. No. 95.
5. Mr W.H.J. Christie was Deputy Private Secretary to the Viceroy at this date.
6. Mr Christie's letter of 2 January 1940 to Mr Donaldson has not been traced. It evidently asked for reports on the U.P. Ministers covering 1939.
7. See No. 2.

Index

Certain terms, such as Hindus, Muslims and United Provinces, occur in almost every document and have therefore not been indexed. For the same reason there are no index entries for Lord Linlithgow as Viceroy nor for Sir Harry Haig and Sir Maurice Hallett while they served as Governor of the United Provinces. Footnotes are indexed under the document to which they are attached. References to documents in the Appendices are preceded by the letter 'A'.

The index entries refer to document numbers